International Law and Muslim States

This book analyses the general interaction of international law and Islamic law in the Muslim world today. It interrogates factors that often form the root of the tension between the two legal regimes. Literalist interpretations of Islamic law and the modern international law's disposition that does not give due consideration to differences among cultures and civilizations are some of these factors.

This work examines the Saudi Arabia textualist approach to the interpretation of the two primary sources of law in Islam, the *Qur'an* and *Sunnah*, and argues that a liberal approach of interpretation has become *sine qua non* especially now that myriad issues are confronting the Muslim world generally and Saudi Arabia in particular.

This book provides a timely examination of the issue of modern Saudi Arabia, Islamic legal order *vis-à-vis* the contemporary concept of international law and international relations in specific areas such as international human rights law and trans-national economic matters. As such it will be of interest to academics and researchers working in Islamic law, international and comparative law, human rights law, and law and religion.

Dawood Adesola Hamzah is a Teaching Fellow at the School of Oriental and African Studies, University of London, UK, and a lecturer at the University of Ilorin, Nigeria.

I0894907

Islamic Law in Context

Series Editor: Javaid Rehman, Brunel University, UK

The Islamic Law in Context series addresses key contemporary issues and theoretical debates related to the Sharia and Islamic law. The series focuses on research into the theory and practice of the law, and draws attention to the ways in which the law is operational within modern State practices. The volumes in this series are written for an international academic audience and are sensitive to the diversity of contexts in which Islamic law is taught and researched across various jurisdictions as well as to the ways it is perceived and applied within general international law.

Woman's Identity and Rethinking the Hadith
Nimat Hafez Barazangi

Changing God's Law
The dynamics of Middle Eastern family law
Edited by Nadjma Yassari

Applied Family Law in Islamic Courts
Shari'a courts in Gaza
Nahda Shehada

Islamic Law and International Commercial Arbitration
Maria Bhatti

For more information about this series, please visit: www.routledge.com/Islamic-Law-in-Context/book-series/ISLAMLAWCXT

International Law and Muslim States

Saudi Arabia in Context

Dawood Adesola Hamzah

Routledge
Taylor & Francis Group
LONDON AND NEW YORK

First published 2022
by Routledge
2 Park Square, Milton Park, Abingdon, Oxon OX14 4RN

and by Routledge
605 Third Avenue, New York, NY 10158

Routledge is an imprint of the Taylor & Francis Group, an informa business

© 2022 Dawood Adesola Hamzah

The right of Dawood Adesola Hamzah to be identified as author of this work has been asserted by him in accordance with sections 77 and 78 of the Copyright, Designs and Patents Act 1988.

All rights reserved. No part of this book may be reprinted or reproduced or utilised in any form or by any electronic, mechanical, or other means, now known or hereafter invented, including photocopying and recording, or in any information storage or retrieval system, without permission in writing from the publishers.

Trademark notice: Product or corporate names may be trademarks or registered trademarks, and are used only for identification and explanation without intent to infringe.

British Library Cataloguing-in-Publication Data
A catalogue record for this book is available from the British Library

Library of Congress Cataloging-in-Publication Data
Names: Hamzah, Dawood Adesola, author.
Title: International law and Muslim states : Saudi Arabia in context / Dawood Adesola Hamzah.
Other titles: Islamic law in context.
Description: Abingdon, Oxon ; New York, NY : Routledge, 2021. | Series: Islamic law in context | Includes bibliographical references and index.
Identifiers: LCCN 2021007142 (print) | LCCN 2021007143 (ebook) | ISBN 9780367679187 (hardback) | ISBN 9780367679194 (paperback) | ISBN 9781003133384 (ebook)
Subjects: LCSH: International law—Saudi Arabia. | International and municipal law—Saudi Arabia. | Conflict of laws—Saudi Arabia. | Islamic law—Saudi Arabia. | International and municipal law—Islamic countries. | International law (Islamic law)
Classification: LCC KMT2325 .H36 2021 (print) | LCC KMT2325 (ebook) | DDC 341.09538—dc23
LC record available at https://lccn.loc.gov/2021007142
LC ebook record available at https://lccn.loc.gov/2021007143

ISBN: 978-0-367-67918-7 (hbk)
ISBN: 978-0-367-67919-4 (pbk)
ISBN: 978-1-003-13338-4 (ebk)

Typeset in Galliard
by codeMantra

Contents

Preface

This book was originally submitted to the School of Oriental and African Studies, University of London as a doctoral dissertation in international law and Islamic law. It is an attempt to explore a world of legal, cultural, and civilizational diversities. Over the years there have been persistent calls for collaboration and a desire for mutual understanding without having to sacrifice the identity of different cultures and civilizations.

Modern International law evolved at the end of World War II, especially under the patronage of the United Nations (UN) and the influence of the historical de-colonization process of the second half of the twentieth century.[1] The most authoritative normative framework of this regime is the UN Charter of 1945. Globalization has seemingly driven this international norm to a new phase introducing new frameworks of intercontinental legal and social systems that are different from the traditional model that emerged from the European nation-states. For example, the universal application and jurisdiction in international human rights law and transnational economic, financial, and trade rules and regulations transcend the Westphalian conception and vision of sovereignty.[2]

Muslims constitute the world's second largest religious group estimated at 1.8 billion people, making up about 24.1% of the world population.[3] They constitute the majority population in 44 states[4] and hold tenaciously to the *Shari'ah* – a value system they consider sacrosanct and applicable to every aspect of their daily life irrespective of geographical location in a world of "complex

1 An-Na'im, A.A., and Odeh, L.A., 'Islam and International Law: Toward A Positive Mutual Engagement to Realize Shared Ideals', *Proceedings of the Annual Meeting (American Society of International Law)*, Vol. 93 (2004), pp. 159–168, at p. 161.

2 Ibid.

3 Michael, L., and Hackett, C., 'Why Muslims Are the World's Fastest-Growing Religious Group', *Pew Research Center* (2017), www.pewresearch.org/fact-tank/2017/04/06/why-muslims-are-the-worlds-fastest-growing-religious-group/ (accessed 08 February 2021).

4 An-Na'im, A.A., supra at p. 161.

interdependence"[5] and "internationalization of production".[6] Saudi Arabia as an example adopts the *Shari'ah* as State Law and the Hanbali School known for its literalist approach, as officially adopted interpretation of the law.

Muslims, like any other communal entities in the world, incline towards adopting their own ways of being themselves, as a basic ideal of self-determination under international law.[7] Therefore, the reality of the interlink between Islam, Muslims, and international law is no longer in question. But the question remains in the definition of this interlink. Is it cooperative or confrontational?

To address this question, this book offers a theoretical and historical synthesis of the concept of sovereignty, and general nature of international law, focusing particularly on the traditional and evolving perceptions of its relationship with domestic law in theory and practice. It examines the theory of sovereignty and the principle of non-intervention under modern international law in relation to the domestic law-making of modern nation-states contextualizing Saudi Arabia a leading modern Islamic state.

This book examines the theoretical framework and development of Islamic law by analyzing its history and nature as a system of law consisting of sources, methods, and principles. It also examines its practical evolution and application as a formal legal system in Saudi Arabia with a view to establish that Islamic law is capable of evolution and adaptation to changes particularly in a Muslim-majority state.

This book explores the history, theory, and practice of *Siyar* (the Islamic Law of Nations) *vis-à-vis* the interplay of international law and Islamic Law in Saudi Arabian foreign policy. It also investigates how Saudi Arabia domesticates international treaties against the background of theory and practice of classical *Siyar*. It attempts to establish the relevance of the Islamic perspective of territorial statehood and nation-state with a view to contextualize the Saudi Arabia as a modern nation-state maintaining relations with non-Muslim states.

This book examines international human rights law and institutions from the perspectives of Islamic laws against the background of Saudi Arabian's state practice. This is underscored by the Saudi Basic Law which makes the *Qur'an* and the *Sunnah* the dual *Grundnorm* of its law.

Saudi Arabia's participations in international human rights forums are also critically examined with a view to understanding the extent of how it maintains a balance between two legal regimes –human rights and Islamic laws.

This book further examines the trans-national economic and trade laws with focus on International Monetary Fund (IMF) and the World Trade Organisation (WTO). The membership of Saudi Arabia in these two organizations raises questions around the issue of *riba* (usury) in banking and finance and *gharar*

5 Shaw, M., *Theory of the Global State, Globality as Unfinished Revolution*, Cambridge: Cambridge University Press (2002), p. 84.

6 Cox, R.W., *Production, Power and World Order: Social Forces in the Making of History*, New York: Columbia University Press (1987), pp. 253–265.

7 An-Na'im, A.A., supra at p. 163.

(speculation in the insurance business) that are prohibited under Islamic law. It brings into focus the Saudi Arabian *Ulama'* and jurists' position on these issues vis-à-vis membership of the Kingdom in the two international institutions. Similarly, the intellectual property is also a subject of debate among modern Muslim scholars and jurists that is interrogated against the membership of Saudi Arabia in the WTO.

The practice of international arbitration was a framework that evolved to allow parties from different legal cultures to consensually resolve their disputes generally without a strict adherence to the formalities of their respective legal and court systems. *Tahkim* (arbitration), on the other hand, existed in the pre-Islamic era, but the advent of Islam transformed it to a better means of attaining alternative justice. Integral to the conflict over oil demand and supply, numerous trade disputes involving issues have found themselves regulated by different legal systems. This book attempts to interrogate how arbitral rules and regulations of the classical Hanbali Islamic jurisprudence and Euro-centric modern international arbitration laws interact in the Saudi Arabia legal system. What exactly have Saudi Arabia's 1983 and 2012 Arbitration Laws that were enacted under the shadow of the New York Convention and the UNCITRAL Model Law established – collaboration or confrontation between different legal regimes?

I remain forever thankful to Allah for His guidance and countless favours. I express my profound appreciation to my family, particularly my wife Zilfah Oyepeju Hamzah for her patient and understanding. I also thank friends, and colleagues as well as anonymous men and women of goodwill who gave me their support in turning this book into a collective effort. Due to lack of space, I may not list names. However, I wish to register my thanks to Professor James Piscatori, Deputy Director at the Australian National University Centre for Arab and Islamic Studies; Professor Javaid Rehman, Brunel Law School, College of Business, Arts and Social Sciences, Brunel University, London; Professor Kasim N. Sheikh, Head of the Law School, University of Huddersfield; and Professor Mashood A. Baderin, Faculty of Law and Social Sciences, School of Oriental and African Studies, University of London for their remarkable support.

Dawood Adesola Hamzah
London
10 February 2021

Foreword

James Piscatori

A study of international law and Saudi Arabia is doubly challenging. The interaction between Islam and the West has been subjected to misrepresentations and caricatures, not least the presupposition that Muslim states are unable or unwilling to accept the diplomatic and legal norms of the prevailing Westphalian international order. The spectre of jihads and hostage-taking looms large in the popular, if not sometimes also the policy, imagination. But Saudi Arabia is also often seen through the prism of paradox: religious asceticism but modernisation, supposed guardian of the Holy Places of Islam but closely allied with the United States, historically ambivalent towards outsiders but a member of the G20. Even as it undergoes social and economic, though not political, transformations as outlined in its Vision 2030, it remains enigmatic to many observers, even notorious to some.

Dawood Hamzah penetrates these double presuppositions and, with conceptual facility and impressive empirical substantiation, he illuminates how a Muslim state such as the Kingdom can be at home with international norms and conventions. In the process, he shows that Saudi Arabia has not abandoned Islamic law, but also not understood it as a straitjacket; its legal framework has proven adaptable in line with the pragmatic demands of international coexistence.

There is an overlapping of norms and, perhaps more significantly, of interests between Muslim states and other states. The emergence of a mostly ordered international economic system and the near universal participation in international organizations are indicative of this. But the idea that Islamic norms and values inevitably clash with those of the prevailing system is entrenched and based on the inter-related, faulty assumptions that cultural zones are monolithic, frozen in time, and impervious to outside influences. The reality is inevitably less neat than such formulations would lead us to believe. Indeed, political elites have generated rules of co-operation and engagement that allow a system of interaction to evolve. In effect, a diplomatic culture has emerged whereby governments, regardless of the underlying cultural differences of their societies, regularly communicate with each, conclude agreements, and address points of conflict and disagreement mostly without resort to force.

The Muslim world is no exception. "Islam" is often presented as a uniform force, operating everywhere in the same way, exercising similar pulls on identity and affiliation. Muslims invoke textual authority to substantiate their arguments, but their identities and practices are also shaped by a number of other considerations such as nationalism, economics, and social position. Islam is an aggregation of beliefs and practices that is in part informed not only by doctrine, but also by a variety of contingent contexts. Consistent with a view which argues that traditions are constructed, the content of Islamic traditions is largely reworked over time, even though the form may stay roughly constant. For example, on one pious reading, Islamic law is thought to be the immutable word of God and further legislation impossible. Yet, in fact, Muslims have steadily expanded and transformed the law in light of changing conditions, and permissive, if also vague, principles have been utilised to overcome the apparent contradiction between the reality of legal innovation and the concept of a revealed and conclusive law. This has been apparent even in Saudi Arabia, which has become a kind of testing case on the assumption that it occupies the conservative endpoint of a Muslim state spectrum. For at least a half century, if not before, it has relied on concepts like the "public interest" (*maslaha*), "sovereign discretion" (*siyasa shar'iyya*), and "legal eclecticism" (*takhayyur*) to validate legal innovations.

This process of re-inventing and formalising tradition is apparent in Muslim states' acceptance of international law. A familiar view, building on the concept of *jihad* and the Islamic juridical bifurcation of the world into *dar al-Islam*, the realm of peace, and *dar al-harb*, the realm of war, holds that Muslims reject an international order that is based on the sovereign equality of states and committed to the peaceful resolution of disputes. Yet, members of the Saudi political and religious establishments, supportive of a *status quo*-oriented foreign policy, have consistently argued that *jihad* is not an instinctive call to arms, and, among other attempts at international mediation, the Kingdom famously put forward in 2002 the perhaps still-relevant Arab Peace Initiative in the Arab-Israeli conflict. In the absence of direct Islamic guidance, the Saudis have relied heavily on predominantly occidental treaties, diplomatic notes, court cases, and Western scholars to elucidate general acceptance of the rules-based system, such as the law of the sea and international finance. More fundamentally, Saudi and other Muslim elites have found no difficulty in observing the principle of *pacta sunt servanda*, noting its analogue in the Islamic legal precept that contracts, honestly concluded, must be upheld. The Muslim state record in meeting treaty obligations appears no worse than that of other states.

Dr Hamzah takes the analysis further and makes two signal contributions. First, he skilfully explains why international law has been readily accepted. While pressure and normative congruence may play a part, it is principally a cost-benefit analysis, illuminating the practical advantages of adherence, that is compelling. Radical Islamists like al-Qa'ida and the Islamic State of Iraq and al-Sham (ISIS) reject the international *status quo*, seeing states like Saudi Arabia as part of the problem, but Muslim state elites have adapted to the structure of order in international relations. Resentful as these elites may sometimes be at Western power, they understand the advantages to be derived from the conventional system.

In short, they find redress for their grievances, and legitimisation of their right to rule, through participation in the system.

Second, Dr Hamzah insightfully and provocatively argues that international law has not only been accepted but also incorporated in the domestic legal system of Saudi Arabia, in the process of helping to reshape it. Rather than a foreign spectre "out there", international law becomes domesticated and even transformative – the latter, a point of view that would neither be shared by many traditional religious scholars nor openly conceded by the political elite whose legitimacy depends in great part on defending the traditional religious order.

Yet, in the pages to follow, Dr Hamzah lucidly demonstrates that the Saudis have adhered to international conventions that might have been thought to pose a problem under conservative interpretations of Islamic law. Despite the predominant Hanbali jurisprudence, intellectual property rights have been enthusiastically endorsed, for example. Scriptural sources, customary practice, and the broad purposes of the law (*maqasid al-shari'a*) are invoked to endorse modern copyright, patent, and trademark rules. More problematic in theory has been Saudi participation in the International Monetary Fund, which it joined in 1957, and especially acceptance of the Special Drawing Rights. At contention is sensitivity over *riba*, the interpretation of which is subject to disagreement. The Saudi consensus has been that usury or excessive interest is forbidden, but the advantages of membership have clearly outweighed theological disputation. A more permissive interpretation of the law which, in effect, finds that the public good is served by membership in the international organisation has held sway. Even more impactful has been the incorporation into domestic law of World Trade Organisation rules, to which it has subscribed since 2005. To ease entry into the world body, the Saudis had adapted their legislation to allow foreign ownership of businesses and property, and the Saudi Minister of Commerce had given assurances that *shari'a* courts were flexible enough to handle disputes over trade and foreign investment. But, given the complexities of commercial transactions, the Saudi position on international arbitration has evolved and reflects a productive bridging of domestic and international law. Arbitration has a long history in Islamic law and history, and its value in facilitating modern commercial agreements is clearly understood. Saudi Arabia's acceptance of the New York Convention on the Recognition and Enforcement of Foreign Arbitral Awards thus seemed unproblematic, except when arbitral awards involved *riba*. But the Convention also allows exceptions to obligation on the basis of a state's "public policy", interpreted in the Saudi case as respect for, if not deference to, Islamic law.

Dr Hamzah also skilfully takes the analysis into the more contentious realm of human rights law. As with other issues, Muslim thinking on human rights spans a wide spectrum and is subject to considerable interpretation and political posturing. Yet, it is indisputable that, as the example of women's rights indicates, culturally bound values, such as those of the family, have widespread resonance in the Muslim world. It is not surprising, therefore, that the Saudis, like others, have objected to some aspects of the expanding human rights regime, especially in the areas of gender equality, social rights, and religious freedom. Yet, however much they may have disagreed with particular provisions, such as the right to change religion, many Muslim states not only fully participated in international fora, but also subtly reformulated their notions of human rights in the dominant international idiom. Pakistan, the Shah's Iran, and Egypt, for example, moved in various ways to accord women greater personal status and civic rights, and even conservative Saudi Arabia has adopted the discursive framework of human rights, thereby creating a future standard by which to judge the legitimacy of the regime. It has moved a long way from 1948 when it argued that the Universal Declaration of Human Rights was not needed as the Islamic legal system was complete and sufficient.

Indeed, the Saudis have begun to establish domestic oversight bodies such as the Human rights Commission and to codify and revise judicial mechanisms and procedures. Though scarcely powerful or always independent, they are nonetheless indicative of at least a passive acceptance that the Kingdom benefits from deferring, even minimally, to evolving international standards. The nuanced argument put forward here is that, rather than a radical divergence between Western and Islamic views of human rights or an outright convergence of practice, there is an evolving but still-grounded accommodation of sorts: neither endorsement nor rejection *tout court*, but, as the author incisively puts it, "international law consciousness" within a Saudi framework. Where some professed to see in a re-assertive Islam a revolt against the West, a *modus vivendi* should have been apparent.

Like others, however, Saudi Arabia's international legal credentials do not assure good international citizenship. As this volume shows, it has been slow to comply with reporting and other requirements, such as established by the Convention Against Torture to which it adhered in 1997, and it has not accorded the civil and political rights that international conventions prescribe as integral to the modern state. Arrests, maltreatment, judicial executions, and extra-judicial murder of dissidents and critics have been widely condemned. Amnesty International and other non-governmental as well as governmental organisations routinely criticise the Saudis for violations of human rights, and, with the Saudi intervention in the Yemeni war since 2015, of the laws of war and humanitarian law. Concerned with violations in that conflict, the British government spent £2.4 million from 2016 to 2020 in the hope of helping Saudi Arabia "comply with international law" (*The Guardian*, 13 January 2021).

The irony of Britain as moral tutor apart, its historical failings, and especially those of the United States in Vietnam, Afghanistan, Iraq, and elsewhere in upholding legal obligations have been well documented. But, unlike Saudi Arabia and other Muslim states, their ability to accept the very idea of international law has not been questioned. What this volume so expertly does is pierce the entrenched misapprehension that international law is a Western system of order, which, if adhered to at all by Muslims, is accepted either insincerely or at the cost of abandoning principle. Dawood Hamzah, with his confident command of international and Islamic law and astute appreciation for historical trends, offers a less simplistic and more persuasive interpretation: neither has the Islamic legacy precluded the Muslim world's permeability to international law nor has the Islamic framework remained unaffected in the process. As the Saudi case shows, internal legal and institutional changes have been stimulated in line with more liberal Islamic interpretations encouraged by international best practice. Theological controversies and inconsistent observance are bound to continue. But the masterful achievement of this work is both to rise above culturally coded assumptions about the universality of international law *and* to alert us to its potential for encouraging domestic change as well as international order.

Abstract

Individual sovereign states are the basic building blocks of the international legal system. Traditionally, states were presumed to be sovereign in the sense that they were legislatively independent and entered treaty relations that promoted their interests as defined by themselves. This was the basic traditional vision of international law as a non-interventionist system in the domestic law-making of individual nation-states. But the legal regime of contemporary international law has grown beyond this vision, whereby the absolute sovereignty of modern nation-states has steadily diminished and the concept of sovereignty called into question, especially in relation to domestic law-making by states. Today, international law impacts on domestic laws either directly or indirectly, and states must, while embarking on domestic law-making, be conscious of probable violations of international rules on issues that are basically domestic and under their sovereign control. This impact of international law in the domestic legal sphere of states raises significant questions on the application of Islamic law as domestic law of a modern Muslim-majority state like Saudi Arabia.

Traditionally, the Shari'ah as the general value system that stands as a source of Islamic law is considered as divine in nature and thereby immutable. It is therefore often claimed that Islamic law cannot accommodate the encroachment of contemporary international law in the domestic law-making of modern Muslim-majority states. Nevertheless, many modern Muslim-majority states remain part of the international legal order, while they continue to adopt domestic laws that are underpinned by Islamic law. How have they been able to sustain their domestic law-making based on Islamic law within the ambit of the encroachment of modern international law as identified above?

In that context, this study examines the international law and Muslim states from the perspectives of Saudi Arabia, which is a modern Muslim-majority state that has clearly declared Islamic Shari'ah as the basis of its domestic laws and governance.[1] This study is important considering not only the constraints but also the benefits associated with the interaction between international law and the domestic laws of modern Muslim-majority states generally and how that relationship could be accurately interpreted.

1 See Art. 1, Saudi Basic Law of Governance (1992).

The main argument of this study is that modern international law, which is conceivably underpinned by Western and specifically Eurocentric values, has, despite the traditional concept of sovereignty, steadily encroached upon the domestic legislation of modern nation-states generally, and in particular, Saudi Arabia, a Muslim majority state that strictly adheres to Islamic law as the basis of its domestic legislation. It is argued that while international pressure may be a factor, the inherent benefits of modern international law also play a significant role in influencing Saudi Arabia to maintain necessary equilibrium between its classical and conservative interpretation of Islamic law and relevant rules of modern international law.

Abbreviations

AAA	American Arbitration Association
ADR	Alternative Dispute Resolution
AI	Amnesty International
ARAMCO	Arab American Oil Company
CA	Court of Appeal
CADE	Convention Against Discrimination in Education
CAT	Convention Against Torture and other Cruel, Inhuman or Degrading Treatment or Punishment
CCPR	Covenant on Civil and Political Rights
CEDAW	Convention on the Elimination of All Forms of Discrimination Against Women
CERD	Convention on Elimination of Racial Discrimination
CESCR	Covenant on Economic, Social and Cultural Rights
CRC	Convention on the Rights of the Child
ECHR	European Convention of Human Rights
ECOSOC	Economic and Social Council
GATT	General Agreement on Tariffs and Trade
GCIV	Fourth Geneva Convention
GDP	Gross Domestic Product
IACAC	Inter-American Commercial Arbitration Commission
ICC	International Criminal Court
ICC	International Chamber of Commerce
ICCPR	International Covenant on Civil and Political Rights
ICERD	International Convention on the Elimination of All Forms of Racial Discrimination
ICESCR	International Covenant on Economic, Social and Cultural Rights
ICJ	International Court of Justice
ICJ	International Commission of Jurists
ICSID	International Centre for Settlement of Investment Disputes
IDB	Islamic Development Bank
ILO	International Labour Organization
ILC	International Law Commission

IMF	International Monetary Fund
INGOs	International non-Governmental Organizations
ISESCO	Islamic Educational, Scientific and Cultural Organization
LCIA	London Court of International Arbitration
NHRC	National Human Rights Commission
NYC	New York Convention
OIC	Organization of Islamic Cooperation
OP-CAT	Optional Protocol to the Convention against Torture
PBUH	Peace Be Upon Him
SAMA	Saudi Arabian Monetary Agency
SC	Security Council
SC	Slavery Convention
SDR	Special Drawing Right
SJC	Supreme Judicial Council
STIPSS	Slave Trade and Institutions and Practices Similar to Slavery
TRIPS	Trade Related Aspects of Intellectual Property Rights
UN	United Nations
UNCHR	United Nations Commission on Human Rights
UNCITRAL	United Nations Commission on International Trade
UNESCO	United Nations Educational, Scientific and Cultural Organization
UNGA	United Nations General Assembly
VCLT	Vienna Convention on the Law of Treaties
WIPO	World Intellectual Property Organization
WTO	World Trade Organisation

Glossary of legal terminology

Ab initio From the Beginning
Ad hoc For present purposes or impromptu
Consensus ad idem Meeting of the minds, mutual agreement, and, mutual assent
De novo From the beginning, afresh, anew, and, beginning again
Ex cathedra With the full authority of office especially that of the Pope, implying infallibility as defined in Roman Catholic Doctrine
Incommunicado A Situation in which communication with outside world is impossible
Inter alia Among other things
Inter partes Legal procedures between the parties involved
Jus in Bello Law that regulates the conduct of armed conflicts
Magna Carta The great charter of the liberties of England
Modus operandi Method of operation
Nullum crimen sine lege "No crime without Law" is a moral principle in criminal law and international criminal law that a person cannot or should not face criminal punishment except for an act that was criminalized by law before he/she performed the act.
Numeraire Basic standard by which value is computed, which is one of the functions of money, to serve as a unit of account: to measure the worth of different goods and services relative to one another
Pacta Sunt Servanda "Agreements Must be Kept" (Legal Principle Adopted at Vienna Convention on the Law of Treaties Signed in 1969
Per se In Itself
Rebus sic Stantibus Tacit condition attached to all treaties to the effect that they will no longer be binding as soon as the state of facts and conditions upon which they were based changes to a substantial degree
Response – "responsum" That part of rabbinic literature concerned with written rulings in answer to questions
Stare decisis A precedent or authority established from previous legal case that is either binding on or persuasive for a court or other tribunal when deciding subsequent cases with similar issues or facts
Superanus Greatness

Glossary of Islamic legal terminology

'Adl Justice
Ahadith Sayings of Prophet Muhammad
Ahkam Rulings
Ahl al-dhimat Non-Muslim Citizens of an Islamic State
Ahl al-Hadith Classical Literalists
Ahl-ra'y Rationalists /Modernists
Ahkam 'itiqadiyah Doctrinal Rules
Ahkam khulqiyah Ethical Rules
Ahkam Al-Mu'amalaat Rules of Human Activities/Conducts
Al-Ahkam Al-Ahawal Al-Shakhasiyah Private (family) Law
Al-Ahkam Al-Iqtisadiyah Wa Al-maliyah Economic and Fiscal Rules
Al-Ahkam Al-Janaiyah Criminal and Penal Law
Al-Ahkam Al-Madaniyah Municipal Law
Ahkam Al-Murafa'at Procedural Law
Al-Ahkam Al-Dusturiyah Constitutional Law
Al-Ahkam Al-Daoliyah International Law
Al Mabahith Al Amma Intelligence Services (Saudi Arabia)
Aman Pledge
Amir King or Rulers
Ansarites Medinah Helpers of Islamic Cause
Asabiyah Tribal Kin feeling
Ayat Verses of the *Qur'an*
Batil Void
Bay'a Pledge of Allegiance
Bid'ah Innovation
Da'if Weak
Dar al-harb Abode of War
Dar al-hudna Land of non-Believers Under a Truce
Dār al-Islām Abode of Peace
Diwan al-Mazalim Board of Grievances (Saudi Arabian)
Fai'da Benefit or a Reasonable Rate of Interest
Falasifa Philosophers
Fasid Voidable

Fatawa Judicial Decisions and Learned Opinions
Fiqh Islamic Jurisprudence
Fulus Money other than Gold and Silver
Gharar Excessive Speculation
Hasan Agreeable
Hay'ah al-Muraqabah al-Qadha'iyyah Commission on Judicial Supervision
Hikmah Wisdom
Hijaz Arabian Peninsula
Hijra Islamic Calendar or Migration
Hirabah Banditry
Hudud Punishments fixed for Crimes as fornication (zina) (extramarital sex), Consumption of Alcohol or other intoxicants, and Apostasy
Ijma Consensus
Ijtihad Struggle or Exercising Judgment in Legal Matter
Ikhtilaf Differences
'Ilm al-rijāl Science of Narration – "Knowledge of Men"
Imam Leader
Isnad Chain of Transmission
istidlal Inference
Istihisan Juristic Discretion
Al-Istinbat Deduction
Al-*Istiqra' al-tam* Complete Induction
Al-istiqra' al-naqis Incomplete Induction
Jahiliya Pre-Islamic era
Jihad Striving in the Cause of Islam or Good Deeds
Jizya Poll Tax
Ka'bah A cuboid Structure at the centre of Islam's most sacred mosque, Al-Masjid al-Haram, in Makkah, Saudi Arabia
Kafalah Sponsorship
Khalifa or Caliph A title used for Islamic rulers who are considered politico-religious leaders of the Islamic community of believers, and who rule in accordance with Islamic law. A state ruled by a caliph is a caliphate.
Kharäj Land Tax
Madhab School of Thought in Islamic Jurisprudence
Mu'amalat Human Worldly Dealings
Muhajirun Emigrants from Makkah
Al-Mahakim al-Mustajilah Expeditious Courts (Saudi Arabia)
Al-Mahakim Ash-shariayyah Shari'ah Courts (Saudi Arabia)
Al-Majlis al-'Ala li al-Qadha' High Council of Judiciary (Saudi Arabia)
Mutawatir First category of Hadith with successive chains of transmission conveyed by narrators so numerous that it is not conceivable that they have agreed upon an untruth thus being accepted as unquestionable in its veracity. The number of narrators may be unspecified.
Maqasid al-Shari'ah Overall Goals of the Shari'ah
Maqbul Accepted

Mardud Rejected
Mashhur Widespread
Al-Maslahah al-Mursalah Public Interest
Maysir Gambling
Mujtahid/Mujtahidun Qualified Person/s to Exercise Ijtihad
Mukallaf A Legally Responsible Person
Mustahab Recommended
Mutawatir Recurrent
Nuss Text
Nuqud Money
Qat'i Certain
Qat'i al-Dalalah Certain in Proof
Qatl Murder
Qisas Equal "retaliation" or revenge. In the case of murder, it means the right of a murder victim's nearest relative to, if the court approves, take the life of the killer
Qiyas Analogical reasoning
Qur'an Holy Book of Islam and first primary source of Islamic law
Ra'y A personal opinion in adapting Islamic law
Riba Usury/interest
Sahih Authentic
Shari'ah The moral code and religious law of Islam
Shoura Consultation
Sulh Peaceful Settlement
Sunnah Denotes the practices of the Prophet Muhammad that he taught and practically instituted as a teacher of the Sharīʻah and the best exemplar. Technically it denotes second source of Islamic law
Sura Chapter of the *Qur'an*
Ta'zir Punishment, usually corporal, that can be administered at the discretion of the judge as opposed to the hudud
Tahkim Arbitration
Tanzima Legislative enactment
al-Tanzimat al-Assasiah The Basic Regulation (Saudi Arabia)
Thiqāt The reliability
Ulum *al-hadith* The science of Hadith
Umma Muslim Community
Urf Custom
Usul al-Fiqh Usul al-Fiqh Principles of Jurisprudence – the study of the origins, sources, and principles upon which Islamic jurisprudence (or Fiqh) is based
Usulists Jurists or experts in Islamic Jurisprudence
Ulema Scholars
'Urf Custom

Table of cases

Abdu Qadir v. Suhan The High Court of Makkah: Case No. 53, vol. 46 (1375 A.H., 1956 A.D.)

Alabama Claims Arbitration United States of America v Great Britain, Moore (1872), 1 Int. Arb. 495 at 656

Bagazi v. 'Awwad on behalf of *Musira* The High Court of Makkah: Case No. 83, vol. 1 (1380 A.H., -1960 A.D.)

Haardt v. Binzagr, (1986), No. CIV.A.H-83-5846, 1986 WL 14836, at *1 (S.D. Tex. Dec. 19, 1986)

Le Parmentier v. La Societe Miss France, XXX Y.B. Comm Arb. (2004)

Libyan American Oil Company (LIAMCO) v. Libyan Arab Republic (1977), 20 I.L.M. (1981)

L'Industrie Du Papier, 508 F.2d 969,975 (2d Cir. 1974)

Mahdi b. Salih v. The State

Nura bint Salih al-ʿUmairi and Husn bint Muslih'Imairi v. Abdul-Qadir al-Kiraidimi High Court of Makkah: Case No. 258 vol. 7

Oriental Commercial and Shipping Company, Ltd. v. Rosseel, N.V. (1985), 609 F. Supp. 75 (S.D.N.Y. 1985)

Parsons & Whittemore Overseas Co., Inc. v. Societe Generale De L'Industrie Du Papier, 508 F.2d 969,975 (2d Cir. 1974)

Parsons & Wh. Ov. Co., Inc. v. Societe G. Ee l. Du P. (R.) (1974), Nos. 174 and 637, Docket 74-1642 and 74-1676

Petroleum Development (Trucial Coast) Ltd. v. Sheikh of Abu Dhabi (1951) 18 I.L.R. 144

Rhone Mediterranee Compagnia v. Lauro, 712 F.2d 50, 53 (3d Cir. 1983)

Ruler of Qatar v. International Marine Oil Co. Ltd (1953), 20 ILR

Saudi Arabia v. Arab American Oil Co. (ARAMCO) (1963), 27 ILR 117

Scherk v. Alberto-Culver Company (1974) 417 U.S. 506

Wahat Al-Buraim (Buraimi Oasis Case, (1954) HMSO Cmd 9272, cited in Kelly, J.B., 'The Buraimi Oasis Dispute', *International Affairs,* 32/3 (July 1956), pp. 318–324

Walkinshaw v. Diniz (2000), 2 All E.R. (Comm.) 237 (Q.B.)

Zalikha and Barnaw - High Court of Makkah, vol. 1, No. 105, 1963

Table of treaties and declarations

Treaties

American Convention on Human Rights 'Pact of San Jose, Costa Rica' (1969)
Arab Charter on Human Rights (2004)
Convention Against Discrimination in Education (December 14, 1960)
Convention Against Torture and Other Cruel, Inhuman or Degrading Treatment of Punishment (1984)
Convention on the Elimination of all Forms of Racial Discrimination (1966)
Convention on the Inter-Governmental Maritime Consultative Organization (7 December, 1959)
Convention on the Prevention and Punishment of The Crime of Genocide (1948)
Convention on the Rights of Persons with Disabilities (2006)
Convention on the Rights of the Child (1989)
Council of Europe Convention on Action Against Trafficking in Human Beings (16/05/2005)
Covenant on the Rights of the Child in Islam (2005)
European Convention for the Protection of Human Rights and Fundamental Freedoms (1950)
Havana Convention on Treaties (1928)
International Convention for Facilitating the Circulation of Films of an Educational Character (1933)
International Covenant on Civil and Political Rights (1966)
International Covenant on Economic, Social and Cultural Rights (1966)
New York Convention (1958)
Supplementary Convention on the Abolition of Slavery, the Slave Trade, and Institutions and Practices Similar to Slavery, September 7, 1956
The Protocol to Prevent, Suppress and Punish Trafficking in Persons, especially Women and Children (15 November, 2000)
The United Nations Charter (26 June, 1945)
Treaty of Versailles (1919)
UN Convention on the Consent to Marriage, Minimum Age for Marriage and Registration of Marriage (7 November, 1962)
Vienna Convention on the Law of Treaties (1969)

Declarations

Cairo Declaration on Human Rights in Islam (1990)
Declaration on the Rights and Care of the Child in Islam (1994)
Universal Declaration of Human Rights (1948)
Universal Declaration on Cultural Diversity (2 November, 2001)
Vienna Declaration and Programme of Action of 1993

Table of statutes and fatwas

Statutes

Fatwas

Fatwa No.18453 signed by Sheikh Abdul-Azeez ibn Baaz (late), Abdul-Azeez Aali-Shaikh, and Saalih al-Fauzaan and Bakr Abu Zaid

Fatwa of Sheikh Ibn Baz, Abdulaziz, Vol. 3, Ruling on Female Driving of a Car – Part No. 3 pp. 351–353

Fatwas of Ibn Uthaymeen, Mohammad, Ruling on Female Driving of a Car in Al-Juraysi, Khalid (ed,) *Fatwa Ulama al-Balad al-Haram,* 1st print (no publisher) (1999)

Islamic Fiqh Academy Resolution No. 43(5/5) – Incorporeal Rights (Fifth Session of the Council of the Islamic Fiqh Academy 1st–6th Jumada Al-Oula 1409H (10th–15th December 1988 in the Kuwait – City (State of Kuwait)

1 Introduction

1.1 Introductory remarks

Despite the traditional theoretical debate about whether international law is really law,[1] there is no doubt that international law is today an established system that regulates the relationship and practices not only between states but also between states and other entities such as international organizations and even individuals. Malcolm Evans has rightly observed that the scope of international law today is immense.[2] Consequently, it is practically impossible today for states not only to ignore the importance of international law generally, but also to be weary of the effect it has on their domestic laws.

Certainly, international law and its institutions have the potential, through cooperation between states, of performing beneficial functions in a world in which peace has for so long been preserved by a balance of violence.[3] Thus, the concept of sovereign equality of nation-states with the international objective "to save succeeding generations from the scourge of war" and "to reaffirm faith in fundamental human rights"[4] underscored the emergence of international rules and norms and, of course, the creation of the United Nations (UN) in 1945. It was a roadmap towards a "new world order" in which international political and legal cooperation was to serve as an important means to achieve world peace and security by the "international community". Modern developments of international law have been classified into distinct critical "phases" aptly described by Javaid Rehman as "milestones", namely, the Treaty of Westphalia, the Congress

1 See e.g. Kleinfeld, J., 'Sceptical Internationalism: A Study of Whether International Law Is Law', *Fordham Law Review*, Vol. 78, No. 2 (2010), pp. 2451–2530.

2 Evans, M., *International Law* (7th edn), Cambridge: Cambridge University Press (2014), p. 31.

3 Header, H., in Foreword to Goronwy, J.J., *The United Nations and the Domestic Jurisdiction of States, Interpretations and Applications of the Non-Intervention Principle*, Cardiff: University of Wales Press (1979), p. vii.

4 Heiberg, M., *Subduing Sovereignty: Sovereignty and the Right to Intervene*, Guildford and Kings Lynn: Biddle Ltd. (1994), p. 9.

of Vienna, the creation of the League of Nations, the founding of the United Nations, and the collapse of the Berlin Wall.[5]

Although the term "international community" has been a recurring phrase in legal texts and UN Resolutions and invoked in international forums, its membership and values as well as the nature of its authority remain debatable.[6] However, it can be distinguished from other social or political entities by two peculiarities. One is a characteristic of requiring interaction among its diverse membership of nation-states, and second is a degree of interdependence that makes its diverse members to be aware of common interests that bind them together.[7] More than that thereof however, a community of this nature also relies on shared norms and values and their interaction.[8] It is in relation to this need for shared norms and values between members of the "international community" that the "Muslim World" and the application of Islamic law becomes relevant with regard to the realization of international political and legal cooperation as a means to achieve world peace.

The UN is an international organization whose authority depends essentially upon the measure of national sovereignty which its member nation-states are prepared to forego in order to provide it with the necessary jurisdiction to effectuate details of its international roadmap.[9] Under modern international law, state sovereignty is essentially a secular conception and entails the recognition of the claim by a state to exercise supreme authority, including domestic legislation, over a clearly defined territory.[10] Individual states are the basic building blocks of the international system.[11] States are sovereign in the sense that they are jurisdictionally independent and can enact domestic laws as well as enter into treaties that promote their domestic and international interests as they themselves define them.[12]

This notion of state sovereignty which is understood to be a reciprocal agreement among national governments giving independent states the right to pursue policies within their own territory free from external interference dates back to

5 Rehman, J., *Islamic State Practices, International Law and the Threat from Terrorism – A Critique of the 'Clash of Civilizations' in the New World Order*, Oxford and Portland, OR: Hart Publishing (2005), p. 7. For in-depth analysis of the history of International law see for example, Koskenniemi, M., *The Gentle Civilizer of Nations: The Rise and Fall of International Law 1870–1960*, Cambridge: Cambridge University Press (2002). See also Fassbender, B. et al., (eds) *The Oxford Handbook of the History of International Law*, Oxford: Oxford University Press (2012).

6 Zaum, D., *The Sovereignty Paradox, The Norms and Politics of International State-Building*, Oxford: Oxford University Press (2007), p. 8.

7 Ibid at p. 9.

8 Ibid.

9 Goronwy, J.J., supra note no. 3 at p. 14.

10 Zaum, D., supra, note no. 6 at p. 3.

11 Krasner, S.D., *Sovereignty: Organized Hypocrisy*, Princeton, NJ: Princeton University Press (1999), p. 1.

12 Ibid.

the Peace of Westphalia of 1648.[13] In other words, it is a package of norms[14] with a corollary of "non-intervention".[15] However, international law realists[16] such as Stephen Krasner argue that the concept of sovereignty is simply a "paradox"[17] and "organized hypocrisy",[18] considering a variety of events in the contemporary world including the apparent direct and/or indirect encroachment of international norms on domestic norms and practices of States. For example, in relation to the impact of international law on domestic legislation of modern nation-states particularly Muslim-majority states, it has been alleged that since the 1980s, Muslim countries have started replacing their laws with extreme and barbarous '*sharia*'.[19] Such critical comments against the application of the *Shari'ah* in modern Muslim-majority states are often apparently motivated by international human rights considerations. Yet, it has also been claimed in the context of state sovereignty that "each country has different national characteristics [and that] there are varying perceptions and practices with regard to human rights...".[20] This could apparently create legislative contradictions with respect to the interaction between international law and Islamic law in modern Muslim-majority states. This research aims at interrogating that problem through an examination of the impact of international law on the application of Islamic law in Saudi Arabia.

1.2 Background to the study

The architects of the UN Charter at Francisco in 1945 came out with a piece of "legislation" indicating the powers which the member-states would be required to delegate to this international organization.[21] This was carefully designed to ensure that it would not intervene in matters which were to remain under the control or within the domestic jurisdiction of the member-states.[22] Modern international law appears to have gone beyond the dimension that was initially

13 Ibid.

14 Crawford, J., *The Creation of States in International Law*, Oxford: Clarendon Press (1979); Hillgruber, C., 'The Admission of New States to the International Community', *European Journal of International Law*, Vol. 9, No. 3 (1998); Roth, B.R., *Governmental Illegitimacy in International Law*, Oxford: Oxford University Press (1999); Zaum, D., supra note no. 6.

15 Ibid.

16 For the different realist perspectives of international Law see e.g. Krasner, S., 'Realist Views of International Law', *Proceedings of the Annual Meeting (ASIL)*, Vol. 96 (2002), pp. 265–268.

17 See generally Krasner, S.D., *Problematic Sovereignty, Contested Rules and Political Possibilities*, New York: Columbia University Press (2001).

18 Krasner, S.D., supra note no. 11 at p. 24.

19 Otto, J.M., *Sharia Incorporated, A Comparative Overview of the Legal Systems of Twelve Muslim Countries in Past and Present*, Leiden: The Leiden University Press (2010), p. 11; see also generally, Marshall, P. et al., Radical Islam's Rules: *The Worldwide Spread of Extreme Sharia's Law*, Lanharm, Maryland: Rowman & Littlefield Publishers (2005).

20 Tian Jin, 'Complexities of Human Rights in Today's World', *Beijing Review*, Vol. 33 (May 28–June 3, 1990), pp. 10–12; as quoted by Heiberg, M., supra note no. 4 at p. 62.

21 Goronwy, J.J., supra note no. 3 at p. 14.

22 Ibid at p. 18.

envisioned. The present widened scope of modern international law as well as its overwhelming trans-national impact has resulted in direct and/or indirect intrusions into matters and issues that were hitherto basic national and domestic affairs of individual states, which has led to anxieties in some states.[23] Hathaway observes that international law now reaches not just interactions between states but states' behaviour within their own borders as well.[24] Thus, it can be argued that sovereignty of modern nation-states has apparently further diminished, and the entire notion of the concept has come under critical question.

Within this theoretical overview, this study intends to examine the impact that international rules have exacted on the Muslim States from the perspective of Saudi Arabia as a notable Muslim-majority state that applies Islamic law as part of State law. This impact will be examined against the background of the classical notion of Islamic law generally, but particularly the conservative literalist *Hanbali* School of Islamic law. This School of Islamic law is officially applicable in Saudi Arabia. It is known for its traditional rigid approach which gives no room for radical change or liberal interpretation of law especially from the perspective of modernist jurists.[25] How have the domestic legislations of Saudi Arabia, underpinned by its literalist interpretation of Islamic law, responded to contemporary international norms relating to issues such as international human rights law, international economic and trade law, and international commercial arbitration, all of which are critical aspects of modern international law?

This study is underpinned by two main theoretical arguments. First is that the concept of state sovereignty is no longer sacrosanct, particularly in respect of the legislative sovereignty of states. International law has today intruded significantly into legislative matters that are purely domestic and essentially concerns modern nation-states. As a result, modern nation-states and particularly Muslim-majority states, whose domestic laws are underpinned by the *sharia,* are generally curtailed in their domestic legislative agendas as their domestic laws are susceptible to the influences and monitoring of international norms. What accounts for this development forms an important point of focus in this study. An important argument advanced in this book is that while the legislative process under the Islamic legal system is underpinned by divine sources, its development and application are essentially human and do respond to necessary changes in human society from time to time. As Hashim Kamali has rightly observed, any attempt to insist on limiting the law to the traditional and classical approach of the essentialists' notion of the law will be counterproductive[26] for modern times.

23 See e.g. Charlesworth, H. et al., 'Deep Anxieties: Australia and the International Legal Order', *Sydney Law Review, 25* (2003) 423–464 at 424.

24 Hathaway, O.A., 'International Delegation and Domestic Sovereignty', *Law and Contemporary Problems,* 71 (2008), pp. 115–149 at 115.

25 Amanat, A., and Griffel, F., *Islamic Law in the Contemporary Context,* Stanford University Press (2007), p. 184

26 Kamali, M.H., *Principles of Islamic Jurisprudence,* The Islamic Text Society, Cambridge (2003), p. 259.

1.3 Objectives

It is normally construed that sovereignty as a concept has three inter-related core elements, namely, international legal sovereignty, Westphalian-cum-Vattelian sovereignty, and domestic sovereignty.[27] International legal sovereignty amounts to juridically independent territorial entities with attached rights and privileges recognized by international organizations. These rights and privileges include the ability to enter into agreement in form of treaties with other states and entities, as well as diplomatic immunity for their representatives and access (if and when needed) to the resources of international financial institutions.[28] It is also basic in Westphalian-cum-Vattelian sovereignty[29] that each state has the right to determine its own authority structures, which signifies that states should refrain from intervening in each other's internal affairs.[30] Domestic sovereignty is in reference to authority structures within states and the competence of these structures to effectively administer and regulate behaviour.[31]

The UN was established in 1945 following the Second World War and was legally brought into existence by virtue of the UN Charter. The aim was to prevent another such conflict and to promote international peace and cooperation among nation-states. It was a replacement for the earlier League of Nations founded in 1920 as a result of the Paris Peace Conference that ended the First World War but which failed on many fronts including not preventing a Second World War.[32] With regard to the membership of the nation-states in the UN, its Charter was formulated to indicate the powers which the UN member-states would be required to delegate to this international body with a view to ensure that it would not be empowered to intervene in matters which were to remain under the control or within the domestic jurisdiction of the member-states.[33] The implication of this legislative outline is that sovereignty of the member-states is subject to the provisions of the Charter.[34] The Charter itself contains express provisions to the effect that the "Organization is based on the principle of the sovereign equality of all its members"[35] and that "nothing contained in the ...

27 Krasner, S.D., 'The Case For Shared Sovereignty', *Journal of Democracy*, Vol. 16, No. 1 (2005), pp. 69–83 particularly pp. 70–71.

28 Ibid.

29 See Krasner, S.D., supra note no. 11 at p. 3 where he describes this as an aberration of intellectual history, saying that as the principle of non-intervention is traditionally associated with the Peace of Westphalia, which ended the Thirty Years' War in 1648, the doctrine did not actually receive explicit articulation until a century later. He added that many of the specific provisions of the Peace of Westphalia, notably those related to religious toleration, violated what came later to be called "Westphalian" sovereignty.

30 Krasner, S.D., supra note no. 27.

31 Ibid.

32 Tomuschat, C., *The United Nations at Age Fifty: A Legal Perspective*, Leiden: Martinus Nijhoff LOL Publishers (1995), p. 77.

33 Goronwy, J.J., supra note no. 3 at p. 14.

34 Ibid at p. 18.

35 Article 2(1) of the Charter of the United Nations.

Charter shall authorize the United Nations to intervene in matters which are essentially within the domestic jurisdiction of any state..."[36]

Against the background of the legislative norm in these provisions, the conventional rules of sovereignty and *de facto* autonomy for sovereign entities are however not absolute.[37] In practical terms and in view of international realities, new rules can be defined for new situations, based on the political power and interests of the most powerful nations.[38] Consequently, this has given rise to a debate as to the true nature of the concept of sovereignty under modern international law.[39] Thus, the notion that states are, based on the concept of sovereignty, immune from the intrusion of international law, particularly with respect to their domestic legislative authority, is a contentious and debatable issue that will be fully addressed in Chapter 2 of this book.

Relatedly, there has been a long debate in Islamic legal theory as to whether Islamic law accommodates secular principles, such as those of international law, despite its foundation on divine sources believed to be immutable. On the one hand, the classical Islamic literalists were rigid.[40] Robert Gleave has observed that "nearly all classical Muslim writers of Islamic jurisprudence were literalists in that they privileged the literal meaning: they not only believed in its existence but also accorded it a sort of primacy in the interpretation process".[41] They hold that there is no room for the *Shari'ah* to change or to be understood differently by different generations of Muslims,[42] suggesting that international law, with its secular underpinnings, should have no impact on it even in modern times. On the other hand, are the modern liberal pragmatists who, within the context of Islamic legal theory (*usul al-fiqh*), favour Islamic legal reform and not bound strictly by the traditional thinking but argue for the evolution of Islamic law in response to the changes in time and place.[43] They are sometimes seen as being too liberal and pro-Western in relation to modern challenges, whereby they tend to totally subdue Islamic law to modern international norms. Therefore, there is a need for a continued attempt at finding a balance between these two main perceptions of Islamic law, to achieve, despite the complexity and diversity of Islamic societies, a common acceptable understanding that would assist Muslim-majority states, such as Saudi Arabia, in facing and dealing with the reality of the encroachment of international law upon their domestic laws.

36 Article 2(7) ibid.

37 Krasner, S.D., *Problematic Sovereignty, Contested Rules and Political Possibilities*, New York: Colombia University Press (2002), p. 323.

38 Ibid.

39 Ibid at p. 24.

40 Weiss, B.G., *The Spirit of Islamic Law*, Athens, Georgia: University of Georgian Press (2006), p. 38.

41 Gleave, R., *Islam and Literalism – Literal Meaning and Interpretation in Islamic Legal Theory*, Edinburgh: Edinburgh University Press (2012), p. 2.

42 Amanat, A., and Griffel, F., supra note no. 25 at p. 7.

43 See e.g. Hallaq, W., *A History of Islamic Legal Theories*, Cambridge: Cambridge University Press (2005), pp. 207–254.

The desirability of finding a balance in that regard is based on the unavoidable need for interaction between international law and domestic legal systems and thus with Islamic law.

This study is aimed at engaging with the above issues and contributing to knowledge on this important subject. Although focused on Saudi Arabia, the research will serve as an important contribution to the larger debate on the relationship between Islamic law and international law in the modern world. While there has been vast diverse general literature on that larger debate in the past ten years or more,[44] there has been very few literatures focusing specifically on Saudi Arabia on the subject, despite the country's historical importance. It is the cradle of Islam and a principal and vital Muslim-majority state in the modern world.[45]

The main hypothesis of this study is that modern international law is conceivably underpinned by western and specifically Eurocentric values. It has, despite its traditional concept of sovereignty and non-intervention norms, steadily encroached upon the domestic legislation of modern nation-states generally. This encroachment is particularly apparent on the legal system of Saudi Arabia, a Muslim-majority state that strictly adheres to Islamic law as the basis of its domestic legislation. It is argued that two factors might have been responsible for this encroachment. International pressure is the first. The inherent benefits of modern international law might have also played a significant role. These two factors have influenced Saudi Arabia to maintain necessary equilibrium between its classical and literalist interpretation of Islamic law and relevant rules of modern international law. Challenges posed by the modern human advancement and development must have been the fundamental driving forces.

Some salient hypothesis intended to interrogate in this study include: Is the concept of domestic sovereignty of states still sacrosanct in view of the direct and/or indirect encroachment of international rules on domestic legislations today? In what ways has, modern international law impacted on the application of Islamic law? How has Saudi Arabia maintained a balance between its domestic law with its intrinsic *Hanbali* classical and literalist interpretation of Islamic law and secular international law especially in the domains of international human rights and international economic, commercial, and trade matters? Conversely, has Islamic law also impacted in any way on any area of applicable rules of international law in Muslim-majority states such as Saudi Arabia?

44 For example, Khadduri, M., *War and Peace in the Law of Islam*, Clark, New Jersey: The Lawbook Exchange, Ltd. (2010); Frick, M.L., and Miller, A.T., *Islam and International Law*, Brill (2013); Baderin, M.A., *International Law and Islamic Law*, Farnham: Ashgate Publishing (2008); Baderin, M.A., *International Human Rights and Islamic Law*, Oxford: Oxford University Press (2003); Rehman, J., supra note no. 5; Khan, M.A., *Human Rights in the Muslim World: Fundamentalism, Constitutionalism and International Politics*, Durham, NC: Carolina Academic Press (2003); Baderin, M.A., 'The Evolution of Islamic Law of Nations and the Modern International Order: Universal Peace through Mutuality and Cooperation', *The American Journal of Islamic Social Sciences*, Vol. 17 (2000).

45 Vogel, F.E., 'Shari'a in the Politics of Saudi Arabia', *The Review of Faith and International Affairs*, Vol. 10, No.4 (2012), pp. 18–27 at 18.

1.4 Theoretical perspectives

Theoretically, the basic norms of sovereignty and equality of nation-states serve as the constitutional basis upon which modern international law is founded.[46] Sovereignty is an expression of supremacy of the governmental institutions of a state and the supremacy of the state as a legal entity at international level.[47] Sovereignty as a concept, is a set of practices that are historically contingent – a mix of both international and intra-national processes, including self-determination, international law, and ideas about natural right.[48] The principal inferences or consequences of sovereignty and equality of states include jurisdiction which is exclusively under the control and authority of the state concerned, and permanent population living within that jurisdiction.[49] Corollaries of sovereignty include an obligation of non-intervention in the area of exclusive jurisdiction of other states; and, the dependence of obligations arising from customary law and treaties on the consent of the obligor state.[50] The interaction of international law and domestic law often demonstrates the struggle between state sovereignty and the international legal order.[51] In the course of this interaction, international law intrudes[52] into certain issues which are basically domestic leading to a violation of the basic rules of non-intervention.[53] In the effort to explain the tension between these two systems of law, reference is usually made to the so-called monist or dualist theories of international law.[54] This will be examined in Chapter 2 of this book.

The relationship between states is cardinal especially now that life among people across borders, and in terms of advanced information and communication technology, has assumed complex dimensions. Apart from political and economic factors, the legal aspect of that relationship is often determined by two legal regimes. The first one comes from nation-state constitutions together with other local statutory laws. The second comes from rules that develop from

46 Shaw, M.N., *International Law* (6th edn), Cambridge: Cambridge University Press (2008), p. 487.

47 Ibid, quoting Jennings, R.Y., and Watts, A.D., *Oppenheim's International Law* (9th edn), London: Longman (1992), Introduction and Part 1, p. xxxvi.

48 Howland, D., and White, L., *The State of Sovereignty, Territories, Law and Population*, Bloomington: Indiana University Press (2009), p. 1.

49 Brownlie, I., *Principle of Public International Law* (7th edn), Oxford: Oxford University Press (2008), p. 289.

50 Ibid.

51 Dixon, M.; McCorquaodale, R.; Williams, S., supra note no. 127 at p. 101.

52 See generally Bradley, A., and Goldsmith, J.L., 'Customary International Law as Federal Common Law: A Critique of the Modern Position', *The Harvard Law Review Association*, Vol. 110, No. 4 (1997), pp. 815–876. See for example, Fowler, M.R., and Bunck, J.M., *Law, Power, and the Sovereign State: The Evolution and Application of the Concept of Sovereignty*, University Park: The Pennsylvania State University Press (1995); Maritain, J., 'The Concept of Sovereignty', *The American Political Science Review*, Vol. 44, No. 2 (1950).

53 Ibid.

54 Ibid. See also Borchard, E., 'The Relationship between International Law', *Virginia Law Review*, Vol. 27, No. 2 (1940), p. 137.

basic principles of modern international law. While modern international law envisions to establish a secular based family of nations with diverse cultural and legal norms, Islamic law on the other hand, envisions an independent socio-legal system based on divine revelations.[55] As both systems operate through the instrumentality of law, one would certainly impact on the other. The degree of this impact is contentious, but recognizable especially when evaluated on legislative developments of a modern nation-state like Saudi Arabia – a traditionally conservative Muslim-majority state.

Saudi Arabia, as a sovereign state, wields a significant influence in an overlapping series of global, regional, and Islamic arenas. It eclipses and bestrides the Arabian Peninsula and is considered as the unnamed "international capital" of the "Muslim World", which is of global spread. It was one of the 51 founding member nation-states of the UN. Thus, it plays prominent roles in several international, regional, and Pan-Islamic organizations. Shortly after the discovery of oil in commercial quantities in 1938, Saudi Arabia evolved from a basic agricultural society into a regional and global economic power with modern sophistications. In world security, its impact in the Gulf and the wider Middle East is also significant as all that constitute some of the most crucial dilemma in global affairs generally today.[56] This fame has given it a niche of global attention particularly academic analysis of a country that has now come face to face with a world that is moving rapidly towards a presumably universal legal order. International law, it is argued, has impacted the legislative development of this country in different areas. But Saudi Arabia claims strong adherence to its culture and Islamic law. Observers note that it is a country that is swinging (as a pendulum) within the range of old culture and tradition on one hand, and dynamics of modernization on the other hand.[57] It has thus attempted to cope with the encroachment of international norms on its Islamic traditional values through creative accommodation without secularization.[58] From the perspective of Islamic law the scope of such accommodation can be well debated and contextualized within the broad principles of Islamic legal theory (*usūl al-fiqh*).[59]

55 Khadduri, M., 'Islamic Law', in Larson, A., Jenks, C.W. and others (eds), *Sovereignty within the Law*, England: Stevens & Sons Limited (1965), pp. 172–174. See also Moschtaghi, R., 'The Relation between International Law, Islamic Law and Constitutional Law of the Islamic Republic of Iran – Multilayer System of Conflict?', *Max Planck Yearbook of United Nations*, Vol. 13 (2001), pp. 375–420 at pp. 394–395.

56 Niblock, T, *Saudi Arabia – Power, Legitimacy and Survival*, London and New York: Routledge, Taylor and Francis Group (2006), pp. 1–2.

57 Hashimilion, *A Modernization Paradox: Saudi Arabia's Divided Society*, Arabia Today, posted: 04 May 2011, http://arabia2day.com/reports/a-modernization-paradox-saudi-arabias-divided-society/ (accessed 19 October 2012).

58 Long, D.E., *Culture and Customs of Saudi Arabia*, Santa Barbra, California: Greenwood Press (2005), p. 30.

59 See generally, Abu-Sulayman, A.H., *Towards an Islamic Theory of International Relations: New Directions for Methodology and Thought*, Ontario, Canada: International Graphics (1993); Hashimilion, supra note no. 57.

The arguments in this book with respect to Islamic law will be buttressed by reference to relevant aspects of Islamic legal theory.

1.5 Methodology

As a systematic analysis of the methods applied to a field of study, methodology typically, encompasses concepts such as paradigm, theoretical model, phases, and quantitative or qualitative techniques.[60] In this research, a multidisciplinary approach is adopted using international law and Islamic jurisprudence as the basis of proposition with a view to interrogate and draw logical conclusions from their respective legal philosophies, political and international relations theories. For example, the scope and limits of sovereignty has always been an important question at the heart of the philosophy of international law.[61] Thus the engagement with the concept of sovereignty under international law and its scope in relation to the legislative sovereignty of states is not only an issue of international legal philosophy but also of political theory and international relations. Conversely, the engagement with how Islamic law, as part of state law in Saudi Arabia, interacts with international law within the framework of modern nation-states and the scope of their international obligations, will require engaging with issues relating to Islamic legal theory (*usul al-fiqh*), Islamic political theory (*siyasah shar'iyyah*), and international relations (*al-siyar*).[62] Specific points of discussion will cover relevant principles of international law, rules of international economic relations; international commercial arbitration and human rights on the one hand, and relevant principles of Islamic law relating to these issues on the other. Saudi Arabia and its domestic legislations are particularly used to illustrate the influence and significance of the contemporary international norms on domestic laws.

In view of this theoretical approach, there is need for a methodological means and sources that are consistent with the fundamental basis of argument stated above with a view to providing a broad overview of the subject of this research. In this regard, a comparative analytical approach is used as a general framework to identify possible areas of complementarity between international law and Islamic law on the different issues examined. For example, it is argued that international law does not necessarily have to be divorced from religion (bearing in mind the basis of Saudi Arabia's law), for both have, as their common end, the unification and betterment of humanity.[63] Thus, an attempt will be made through this

60 See generally Irny, S.I., and Rose, A.A., 'Designing a Strategic Information Systems Planning Methodology for Malaysian Institutes of Higher Learning (isp- ipta)', *Issues in Information System*, Vol. VI, No. 1 (2005), p. 2.

61 See e.g. Besson, S., and Tasioulas, J. (eds) *The Philosophy of International Law*, Oxford: Oxford University Press (2010), particularly Section VI.

62 See e.g. AbuSulayman, A.H., *Towards an Islamic Theory of International Relations: New Directions for Islamic Methodology and Thought* (2nd revised edn), Herdon, VA: IIIT (1993).

63 Ghunaimi, M.T., *The Muslim Conception of International Law and the Western Approach*, The Hague: Martins Nijhoff (1968), pp. 30, 90, and 34.

comparative analysis to balance the domineering tendency of one over the other. To this end, Saudi Arabia's value system based on the Islamic *Shari'ah* and its strict interpretation of this value will be examined against the backdrop of the irresistible forces of modernism propelled by internationalization.

In legal study great care must be taken in analysing facts with a view to avoid any faulty argument that may produce negative inferences or invalid conclusions.[64] Therefore, the method of analysis adopted in this study is inductive and deductive reasoning, which are compatible to both international law and Islamic law. Induction and deduction are two methods of reasoning for establishing facts of knowledge.[65] On the one hand inductive reasoning seeks to establish or increase the probability of its conclusion. In an inductive argument, the premises are intended only to be so strong that, if they were true, then it would be *unlikely* that the conclusion is false.[66] On the other hand deductive reasoning links premises with conclusions. If all premises are true, the terms are clear, and the rules of deductive logic are followed, then the conclusion reached is necessarily true.[67] These explain the criticality of both inductive and deductive reasoning in legal argument and methodology particularly when constructing an analogy for arriving at a conclusion.

Both inductive and deductive reasoning are particularly pertinent to the study of Islamic jurisprudence. Induction here is known as *al-istiqra'* which has been generally defined as "testing the issue's particulars to reach a semi-certain conclusion".[68] There are two types of *al-Istiqra'*, namely, *al-Istiqra' al-tam and al-istiqra' al-naqis. al-Istiqra' al-tam* is the perfect and complete induction which goes to test all the particulars of an issue. Despite that this type of induction is considered a certain proof among all the four schools of Islamic jurisprudence, it is difficult to realize due to basic requirements set out for its attainment. *Al-istiqra' al-naqis* which is the second type is known as partial induction which puts to test most of the particulars of an issue and which leads to an uncertain (*zani*) conclusion. It is commonly applied in exercising *Qiyas* which is the analogical reasoning which belongs to the group of secondary sources or methods of law in Islamic jurisprudence.[69] Muslim jurists lay down certain criteria before *al-istiqra' al-naqis* can be applicable to an issue of *Qiyas*. Those criteria go to minimize the degree of its uncertainty.[70]

64 Ronald J.W. et al., *The 12 Secrets of Persuasive Argument*, Chicago, IL: American Bar Association (2009), p. 1.

65 See generally Copi, I.M. et al., *Essentials of Logic* (2nd edn), Upper Saddle River, NJ: Pearson Education, Inc. (2007).

66 Halperm, D.F., *Thought and Knowledge: An Introduction to Critical Thinking* (4th edn), Hillsdale, NJ: Lawrence Erlbaum Associates Inc. (2002), pp. 231–235.

67 Sternberg, R.J., *Cognitive Psychology*, Belmont, CA: Wadsworth (2009). p. 578.

68 Mahmood, O., *Al-Qamous al-Mubeen fi Istilahat al-Usuliyeen*, Riyadh: Dar al-Zahim (2002), p. 51.

69 Ibid at p. 52.

70 Kamali, M.H., *Principles of Islamic Jurisprudence*, Cambridge: The Islamic Text Society (2011), p. 265.

Al-Istinbat is the deductive reasoning in Islamic jurisprudence. Technically, it means extracting a rule, reason or meaning from the basic sources.[71] Application of *al-istinbat* must be based on the meaning of the text that might hide from ordinary understanding otherwise it would render such *al-istinbat* exercise baseless and illogical.[72] While applying the principle of *al-istinbat,* a distinction must be drawn between the general and the specific rules of the *Shari'ah*; the apparent and the hidden, reason (*illah*) or wisdom (*hikmah*) and the differences (*ikhtilaf*) arising from this exercise among jurists.[73] In the light of the above, it is submitted that both inductive and deductive reasoning are relevant and compatible to the study of both international law and Islamic law, and thus, relevant to this work.[74]

1.6 Selection of Saudi Arabia as country of focus

Saudi Arabia is selected as the country of focus in this research for some reasons. Historically, it is the cradle of Islam and continues to be home to the two holy cities, Makkah and Medina. Constitutionally, the first article of the Basic Ordinance (1992) of this country states that the Holy *Qur'an* and the *Sunnah* (traditions) of the Prophet Muhammad are its constitution and that Islamic *Shari'ah* is the basis of its legal system.[75] It is greatly influenced by the *Hanbali* School of Islamic jurisprudence, which is known to be an embodiment of textualism (to the exclusion of rationality). This raises curiosity about how a modern Muslim-majority state following a literalist interpretation of Islamic law coupled with its economic fortunes has managed to deal with the encroachment of liberal international norms into its domestic legislation. The country thus provides a very suitable and valid case study for assessing the general interaction between international law and Islamic law in the Muslim world today.

1.7 Literature review

Some scholarly works have been produced about the effect of international law in Saudi Arabia. Most of these works originate from academic scholars and PhD researchers. However, it is observed that most of the discussions pay little

71 Mahmood, O., supra note 68 at p. 52.

72 Hassan, K., *Mu'jam Usul Al-Fiqh* (1st print), Ajman, UAE: Al-Raudah (1998), pp. 34–35.

73 Al-Khari, M., *Usul al-Fiqh* (1st edn), Cairo: Daru Al-Hadith (2001), pp. 5–19; see also Hallaq, W.B., 'Consideration on the Function and Character of Sunni Legal Theory', *Journal of the American Oriental Society*, Vol. 104, No. 4 (1984), pp. 679–689; Shehaby, N., 'Illah and Qiyas in Early Islamic Legal Theory', *Journal of the American Oriental Society*, Vol. 102, No. 1 (1982), pp. 27–46.

74 The use of both inductive and deductive reasoning is reflected particularly in the discussions of the substantive issues in Chapters 5–7 and the conclusions drawn there.

75 Eijk, E.V., 'Sharia and National Law in Saudi Arabia', in Otto, J.M. (ed), *Shariah Incorporated, A Comparative Overview of the Legal Systems of Twelve Muslim Countries in Past and Present*, Leiden: The Leiden University Press Series on Law (2010), p. 139.

attention to the consequential specific impacts arising from the interaction between the applicable Islamic law of this country and modern international law. An examination of some of the issues raised in some of the existing literature attests to the encroachment of modern international law into the domestic affairs of modern nation-states and demonstrates the ostensible impact it bears on the domestic legislation of a country like Saudi Arabia which has provoked an intensive debate. To serve as necessary background for this research a brief review of some of the relevant existing literature is provided below *The Relationship between Saudi Arabia Domestic Law and International Law: A Study of the Oil Agreement with Foreign Companies* is a 1970 dissertation by Mohammed Madani for the degree of Doctor of Juridical Science of the George Washington University.

The author discusses oil concessions under International law and Saudi Arabian national law. Having examined the relevant principles of international law relating to the subject matter, he notes that the Saudi Arabian government adopted the Calvo clause[76] in its post-war-agreement, arguing that the reason behind the adoption was to protect the country from unnecessary interference by the concessionaire's government. He pays specific attention to Article 49(b) of the clause.[77] He further argues that the legal principles to be used in determining the parties' rights and duties must be derived from a few sources, namely, national law, international law, and Islamic law, which according to him have a role in determining rights and duties under the Saudi Arabia oil concession agreements. He observes that in resolving legal problems arising from oil concession agreement, resort may be had to conciliation or arbitration while in some instances, submission to jurisdiction of Saudi Arabian courts.[78]

76 Calvo Clause is a provision in an agreement between a private individual and a foreign country which states that:

> the aliens are not entitled to rights and privileges not accorded to nationals, and that, therefore, they may seek redress for grievances only before local authorities. Under this Clause, a claimant waives the right to apply to his or her government or to another forum for protection if a claim is denied by local authorities. It is a legal clause originated from a concept propounded by Carlos Calvo, the famous Argentine jurist. It is based on three propositions that: 1) equality, sovereignty and independence are paramount rights of the States, 2) States, being equal, sovereign and independent, have the right to expect non-interference from other States, and, 3) aliens have to abide by the local law of the State wherein they reside without invoking diplomatic protection of their governments in the prosecution of claims arising out of contracts, insurrection, civil war or mob violence.

See Carlos, C., *Le Droit International Theorque et Pratique* (5th edn), Paris (1896), Vol, sec. 256, pp. 231–232 as quoted in Garcia-Mora, M., 'The Calvo Clause in Latin American Constitutions and International Law', *Marguette Law Review*, Vol. 33, No. 4 (1950), pp. 205–206.

77 Madani, M.O., *The Relationship between Saudi Arabian Domestic Law and International Law: A Study of the Oil Agreements with Foreign Companies* (A Dissertation submitted to the Faculty of Law School of the George Washington University in Partial Fulfilment of the Requirements for the Degree of Doctor of Juridical Science) (1970), p. 68.

78 Ibid at p. 71.

In concluding this study, the author observes *inter alia*, that, Saudi Arabia though, has been able to resolve most disputes arising from concession agreements through negotiation and conciliation, the differences arising from these disputes are sometimes sharp and irreconcilable. In those circumstances, the parties may have to resort to arbitration which unfortunately has not been optimally utilized since the Onassis case[79] due to the absence of an appropriate forum to hear such disputes.[80]

The Legislative Process and the Development of Saudi Arabia is another instructive literature in this regard. It is also a PhD dissertation by Hamad Sadun Al-Hamad submitted to the University of Southern California in 1973. Al-Hamad examines the development of the traditional Saudi Arabian legal system against the background of the dramatic development witnessed in the Kingdom. He began by looking into the development of legal and judiciary system especially during the unification era in Saudi Arabia. He cites the Board of Grievances and its modern regulations as good examples. According to him, the establishment of *Diwan Al-Mazalim* or the Board of Grievances in 1954 was an important indication of the development and complexity in the governmental apparatus both politically and administratively.[81]

The Council of Commerce and its modern code which contained 630 articles covering issues related to naval and land commerce is a good example of modern legal development in the Kingdom. According to Al-Hamad, its contents have similarity to the Ottoman law of commerce as well as to those of other Arab and Western countries. It is a mixture of Islamic law and modern Western legislation[82] Despite Al-Hamad's argument that establishing an entirely new legal system based upon a foreign model would threaten the entire existing Islamic-Arabian culture and value system and weakening legitimacy of its sovereignty,[83] he could not deny the apparent impact of international norms on the legal processes in the Kingdom.[84]

Fouad Al-Farsy's book titled: *Modern and Tradition – The Saudi Equation*,[85] is an extension of an earlier work of the author.[86] The present book focuses on general development of the country from different perspectives. It is divided into 20 chapters, covering issues such as the geography and history of the Saudi Arabia. It also discusses, Islamic tenets, the judicial, political, social, economic, agricultural, educational, health care development systems as well as government structure and development plans. It also examines Saudi Arabia's foreign

79 (1958) ILR 27, pp. 117–229.

80 Ibid at p. 228.

81 Al-Hamad, H.S., *The Legislative Process and the Development of Saudi Arabia*, Los Angeles, California: Faculty of the Graduate School, University of Southern California (1973), p. 114.

82 Ibid at p. 164.

83 Ibid at p. 183.

84 Ibid at pp. 114–178.

85 Al-Farsy, F., *Modern and Tradition – The Saudi Equation*, London and New York: Kegan Paul International (1990).

86 The original work is titled: *Saudi Arabia: A Case Study in Development*, Ibid p. xi.

relations particularly its relations with Western Europe, United States of America, and the Communist Bloc.

Chapter 3 of this book examines Islam as a subject of history and foundation of Saudi Arabia sovereignty,[87] while Chapter 4 briefly examines the Saudi Arabia judiciary with an illustrative sketch of courts' hierarchies.[88] Chapter 5 examines the political system saying that the Holy *Qur'an* is the Constitution of the Kingdom with the King as the Head of Government and the Council of Ministers (*Majlis Al Wuzara*) as well as the Regional Governments. Chapter 15 of this book discusses in some details the Kingdom of Saudi Arabia's relations with the Arab world, Western Europe, the United States of America, and the Communist Bloc; the establishment of the Gulf Co-operation Council (GCC);[89] and relations with other Arab countries especially at the platform of the Arab League.[90] It discusses the formation of the Arabian American Oil Company (ARAMCO), originally known as Caltex.[91]

The present study is different from Fouad Al-Farsy's work in that it is essentially on how the modern International Law impacts on the application of the Islamic Law in Saudi Arabia. Al-Farsy's work focuses on general development of the country with focus on different perspectives of such development.

Javaid Rehman in his book titled: *Islamic Practices, International Law and the Threat from Terrorism – A Critique of the 'Clash of Civilizations'* in the New World Order,[92] focuses on aspects of Islamic law and Islamic international law otherwise known as *Siyar* relating to the subject of international terrorism and violations of human rights. The author attempts to ameliorate the prevalent and erroneous beliefs that have linked the Islamic legal norms and values to terrorism with reference to Saudi Arabia on some of key issues.[93]

The author interrogates the relationship between Islamic law, States practices, and the phenomenon of International terrorism. Towards achieving the objectives of the book, he did an in-depth analysis of the sources of Islamic law against the background of some specific legal issues including Jihad, religious freedom, and minority rights within the Shari'ah and Siyar. The author carries out an extensive review of the remarkable contributions of Islamic States in the development of international law, including norms on the prohibition of terrorism. This was done with a view to correct the aged-long attitude of underplaying the dynamism of Islamic law and its contributions in this area of study. To buttress his argument, he asserts the contributions of the Islamic law on fundamental issues within classical and modern Islamic State practices such as diplomatic

87 Ibid at pp. 24–33.
88 Ibid at pp. 34–38.
89 Ibid at pp. 274–276.
90 Ibid at pp. 276–281.
91 Ibid at p. 287.
92 Rehman, J., supra note no. 5.
93 Ibid at pp.58, 67, 140, 160,188

immunities, prohibitions on hostage-taking, aerial and maritime terrorism, and the financing of terrorism.

The book which is divided into eight chapters covers issues including the sources of *Shari'ah* and the ethos of "Islamic" Identity; the *Shari'ah* and *Siyar* in the development of the Law of Nations; conceptualising terrorism in the international legal order, hostage-taking in international law and terrorism against "Internationally protected persons"; aerial and maritime terrorism; financing of international terrorism; OIC and the approaches towards international terrorism; and, concluding observations.[94] The author contextualizes Saudi Arabia in the debate and argues that there is no connection between the *Shari'ah*'s principles and modern day terrorism.[95]

The author notes that Saudi Arabia and other Islamic States are endowed with vast coastline. That perhaps explains their compelling interest in having legal frameworks to regulate maritime and sea affairs. They have aversion for the acts of piracy and maritime terrorism which was evident in their unanimous condemnation of the seizure of *Achille Lauro* by a disparate group of the Palestinian Liberation Organization (PLO).[96] During the 57th Session of the International Maritime Organisation Council in June 1986, Egypt, alongside Austria and Italy proposed drafting of a specific convention to deal with the phenomenon of maritime terrorism.[97] Saudi Arabia advanced a radical proposal to call for expanding the scope of liability of individuals and governments involved in the maritime terrorism. Though its proposals were not adopted for its likely to ignite controversy and criminal liability of the States, it shows its aversion for terrorism and especially maritime terrorism.

In his concluding observations, the author notes that critics view Islam as an aggressive, authoritarian religion which sanctions violence and terrorism. Thus, its value systems are often regarded as violating internationally recognized human rights.[98] This might be due to the undemocratic and authoritarian regimes of many contemporary Islamic States which, in his words, "perpetuate their existence through fear, violence and terrorism".[99]

Like the present study, it, in a sense, goes to affirm the general impact of international law on Islamic law but, from different perspectives. It is specific on the menace of terrorism – a phenomenon that has constituted a serious challenge to the entire international community including the Muslim World.

The Muslim Conception of International Law and the Western Approach[100] by Mohammd Talaat al-Ghunaimi is an exposition of the traditional doctrines

94 Chapters 1–8.
95 Rehman, J., supra note no. 5 at p. 59.
96 Ibid at p. 159.
97 IMO Doc C57/25, 1 October 1985 as quoted by Rehman, J., supra note no. 5 at p. 159.
98 Rehman, J., supra note no. 5 at p. 221.
99 Ibid.
100 Al-Ghunaimi, M.T., *The Muslim Conception of International Law and the Western Approach*, Leiden: Martinus Nijhoff/The Hague (1968).

of Islamic law regarding international relations. In its introduction the author notes that the expression "Muslim International Law" may raise the curiosity of Western thought as some of the European authorities and writers on the subject of international law disregard the very existence of this subject, citing Henry Wheaton, Charles G. Fenwick, and Oppenheim as typical examples.[101] He holds that this might be due to two factors, namely, the remarkable deficiency in the contribution of modern writers to the interpretation of Muslim international law and of course, the inherent rigidity of the classical notion of Islamic law which had foreclosed the right of *Ijtihad*. This, according to him has prompted a belief that radical differences exist between Muslim international law and the modern law of nations.[102] He delves into historical reasons why Islam is adaptable to new development and what would be the objectives of Muslim international law considering its theological background.[103] As part of historical background to the development of this subject, the writer, for example, examines what he calls

> The Arab "Jus Gentium" saying that 'the Romans noticed that certain legal principles had been common to all nations – irrespective of any mutual relations – which they identified as "*jus naturale*" since it should have originated from the rational notion of justice and injustice innate in men.[104]

He examines the historical development;[105] sources and methods of interpretation;[106] subjects and domain of Muslim international law;[107] Muslim classical conception of international law which covers the subjects of *Jihad* and its characteristics, prisoners of war; *dar al-Islam* and *dar al-harb*, treaties and their precarious characters, the legal status of *dhimmis*, among others.

The present study is different from al-Ghunaimi's work for a couple of reasons. First, substantively al-Ghunaimi simply focuses on the theory of international relations from the perspective of the classical Islamic law and tries to establish that through the concept of *ijtihad* the principles of classical Islamic international law can evolve and be adaptable to new developments in modern international relations. The present work builds on that argument and takes it further by specifically examining and interrogating the practices of a Muslim-majority state in three main subject areas of modern international law. Secondly, the time-lag between al-Ghunaimi's work and the present work is over 50 years and significant international developments within that period have impacted in different ways on the theories and practices of Islamic law in different parts of the Muslim world justifying a fresh examination of the subject.

101 Ibid at p. 1.
102 Ibid.
103 Ibid at pp. 2–3.
104 Ibid at p. 14 and footnote no. 3.
105 Ibid at pp. 28–31.
106 Ibid at pp. 106–118.
107 Ibid at pp. 123–128.

The Islamic Theory of International Relations: Its Relevance, Past, and Present,[108] is another work on international relations also from the perspective of the traditional concept of *Siyar*. This work attempts to contextualize the classical theory of *Siyar* within the framework of modern international law. From the classical notion of international relations under *Siyar*, the author shifts attention to the attitudes of modern Muslim policymakers towards international relations in the contemporary time.[109] He suggests a review of the classical theories of *Siyar*. He emphasizes the need to depart from a traditional legalistic approach by Muslim states and adopting an ideological framework free from space-time limitations and building on a systematic empirical approach which he suggests in Chapter 3 of his work.[110]

The present work differs from Abu-Sulayman as his work focuses on the theory of international relations from the classical notion of *Siyar*. Conversely, the present work focuses on modern international law and its impact on the application of Islamic law in a modern Muslim-majority state, even though relevant principles, and aspects of *Siyar* are examined within the context of Islamic law. While Abu-Sulayman explores the possibility of *Siyar* evolving in meeting contemporary challenges, he, unlike this work, does not focus on any Muslim-majority state. He merely cites some Muslim countries as examples but, in generic terms.

Abu-Sulayman's work is also mostly theoretical with some analytical exploration of the basic principles of *Siyar*, unlike this work which examines the state practices of Saudi Arabia on some relevant topical issues. The lapse of time between this work and that of Abu-Sulayman is about 47 years during which there have been significant legal developments in many Muslim countries in international law and relations. Muslim nations have, for example, practically abandoned the classical notion of dividing the world into abodes of Islam and war as well as the concept of *dhimmis*.[111] This is exemplified by present Saudi Arabian foreign policy and relations, which are ostensibly dictated mainly by economic, political and security interests as will be analyzed in the relevant chapters of this book.

Islam and the International Legal Order: The Case of Saudi Arabia[112] is another PhD dissertation submitted to the University of Virginia in in 1976 by

108 Abu-Sulayman, A.H.A., *The Islamic Theory of International Relations: Its Relevance, Past, and Present* (A Dissertation in International Relations Presented to the Faculty of the Graduate School of Arts and Sciences of the University of Pennsylvania in Partial Fulfillment of the Requirements for the Degree of Doctor of Philosophy) (1973).

109 See, Abu-Sulayman, A.H.A., *Towards an Islamic Theory of International Relations: New Directions for Methodology and Thought* (after series of editorial revision of the original Thesis cited above), IIIT (Islamization of Knowledge Series (1) (1993), p. 57.

110 Ibid pp. 197–204.

111 Kroff, B.S.A., 'An Introduction to the History of International Law', *AJIL*, Vol. 18, No. 2 (1924), p. 247.

112 Piscatori, J.P., *Islam and the International Legal Order: The Case of Saudi Arabia*, Woodrow Wilson Department of Government and Foreign Affairs, Charlottesville, Virginia: University of Virginia (1976).

James Paul Piscatori. The subject of this work can be said to be in close semblance to the present study. Piscatori questions the validity of the search for an enforcement mechanism for international law and suggests that attention should be shifted from obedience to observance, from external to the internal sanction. He contends that culture is a significant variable, and thus, the Islamic culture of Saudi Arabia is not inherently an obstacle to acceding to the Euro-centric nature of international law.

Piscatori focuses attention on Saudi Arabia's attitude towards the background assumption of international law and reveals that the totality of its attitudes differs only in intensity of belief. He specifically explores these attitudes on several concrete subjects including the law of the sea, human rights, and treatment of aliens in the Kingdom. He concludes that Saudi Arabia is favourably disposed to international law and does in fact adheres to many modern rules of international law. He also argues that Islam is not intrinsically antithetical to the prevailing international legal order even though obstacles do exist in this regard.

The present study and Piscatori's study differ in several significant respects. In the first instance, Piscatori's perspective of the international legal order is essentially on an enforcement mechanism with a suggestion for a shift from obedience to observance. He argues in that regard that the reality of the international environment suggests that international law cannot really be enforced, and that the enforcement model is the legacy of misdirected Austinianism whereby law is viewed as essentially an authoritative command. He then makes a case for persuasive observance of international law instead, using Islamic law in Saudi Arabia as case studies. In contrast, this present study focuses specifically on the impact of international law on the application of Islamic law in Saudi Arabia and interrogates the extent of the direct and indirect encroachment of international norms into substantive domestic legislation in Saudi Arabia and how it has reacted to that.

Secondly, Piscatori focuses on culture as a significant variable to argue that the Islamic culture of Saudi Arabia is not inherently a barrier to the acceptance of international law. Conversely, this study examines the issue from the perspective of Islamic law and legal theory, rather than culture *per se*. It acknowledges, in the context of the strict textualism of the *Hanbali* School of Islamic jurisprudence officially applicable in Saudi Arabia, that classical *Hanbali* jurisprudence can be in conflict with some norms of modern international law, but explores how Saudi Arabia has been able to negotiate through such conflicts.

Also while Piscatori examines specific positions of Saudi Arabia on a number of issues of international law, namely, the law of the sea, treatment of aliens, and human rights, this study on the other hand, examines international law as relating to trans-national economic policies on issues such as "bank interests" in membership of IMF, intellectual property rights law, and international commercial arbitration. Piscatori's observations (in 1976) in respect of human rights appear to have been overtaken by a few legislative developments in Saudi Arabia. There has been a gap of about 44 years. With the gap of about four decades between Piscatori's work and this present study, there would certainly have been significant developments and changes in the impact of international human rights norms on Saudi Arabia's domestic laws, which needs researching into as undertaken in this present study.

In the class of scholarly journal articles, Mashood Baderin's "A Comparative Analysis of the Right to a Fair Trial and Due Process under International Human Right Law and Saudi Arabia Domestic Law" is relevant.[113] Here the author undertakes a comparative analysis of the right to a fair trial and due process under international human rights law, Islamic law, and Saudi Arabian domestic law. He argues that the importance of identifying the existence and scope of this right within the framework of domestic law of every state cannot be overemphasized. This, according to him, is to ensure the protection of other human rights generally. He notes that the significance of the right of a fair trial and due process underscores the protection, liberty, and security of individuals to ensure equity and fair play in the administration of criminal justice by the state. Therefore, it is a basic civil right that embodies important principles of the rule of law.[114]

Baderin observes that Saudi Arabia is one of the states that has constantly been criticized in different human rights reports for the violation of the right to a fair trial and due process, especially in its criminal justice system. He notes that however, most of the reports have mainly focused on exposing general practical violations of this right in relation to international human rights instruments without much attention paid to the legal question of whether there are relevant domestic provisions for its guarantee that can be relied upon by litigants under the Saudi Arabia legal system. He argues that this is essential for legal certainty and for purposes of domestic litigation when those rights are violated by the state or its organs.[115]

Against the backdrop of the three levels of criminal trial and rights attached to each, namely, pre-trial rights, in-trial rights, and post-trial right, he explored the scope of right of a fair trial and due process under various international human rights instruments.

Analyzing the scope of Right to a Fair Trial and Due Process under Islamic Law, he notes that this subject is covered mostly by the methods rather than by the sources of the Islamic Law *per se*. He then delves into historical details of *Fiqh* as formulated by the Islamic Jurists on the subject.

Baderin examines the Saudi Arabia Legal System against the background of protecting human rights generally and the right of fair trial and due process particularly. He observes that though, the Saudi Arabia Basic Law contains a list of only a few clear rights, and not all possible rights available under the *Shari'ah*, nevertheless, it makes a definite statement on the obligation of the state

113 Baderin, M.A., 'A Comparative Analysis of the Right to a Fair Trial and Due Process under International Human Right Law and Saudi Arabia Domestic Law', *The International Journal of Human Rights*, Vol. 10, No. 3 (2006), pp. 241–284.

114 Ibid at p. 241.

115 Ibid at p. 242.

to protect certain rights of individuals, including some elements of the right to a fair trial and due process.[116] He notes that prior to the enactment of the Saudi Basic Law, there was no specific and identifiable legal provision for the right to a fair trial and due process. However, in the year 2000, the state, through its Ministry of Foreign Affairs, issued a document titled: *Protection of Human Rights in Criminal Procedure and in the Organization of the Judicial System* (PHR Document 2000). This law, according to him, was a "description of criminal and judicial procedure in the Kingdom of Saudi Arabia and provisions for the protection of human right during the three stages of criminal proceedings".[117]

He came to conclusion that the right to a fair trial and due process under international human rights law is also recognized under Islamic law and neither the Saudi Basic Law nor the Saudi PHR Document 2000 contradicts this fact. He opines that the three levels of this right, namely, pre-trial rights, in-trial rights, and post-trial rights as guaranteed under international human rights law are apparently available under different Saudi Arabian domestic legislations. Whether or not these are enforced in practice is another question.[118]

Similarly, of relevance is Raed Alhargan's article on "The Impact of the UN Human Rights System and Human Rights International Non-Governmental Organizations (INGOs) on the Saudi Government with Special Reference to the Spiral Model".[119] The author assesses the impact of the UN human rights system and human rights NGOs in Saudi Arabia applying the spiral model with a view to clarify the impacts of trans-national human rights networks on states. It assesses the usefulness of the model's five phases as an explanation of the changes in the Saudi government's human rights practices from 1990 to early 2011. He thus investigates women's rights arguing that human rights INGOs supported with advocacies resulting from, particularly, the UN human rights treaty-based bodies will lead to more concessions and adaptations to new norms by Saudi Arabia.[120]

1.8 Structure of book

To establish the arguments advanced herein, this book is divided into eight chapters. Chapter 1 presents a general introduction of the research. Chapter 2 examines some basic principles of modern international law, particularly the concepts of sovereignty, legislative sovereignty, and non-intervention in relation to the interaction of international law with domestic law in theory and practice. Chapter 3 examines the basic principles of Islamic law as well as the history and concept

116 Ibid at p. 247.

117 Ibid.

118 Ibid at p. 274.

119 Alhargan, R. A., 'The impact of the UN human rights system and human rights INGOs on the Saudi Government with special reference to the spiral model', *The International Journal of Human Rights*, Vol. 16, No. 4 (2012), pp. 598–623.

120 Ibid at p. 598.

of *Ijtihad* and the emergence of School of Islamic jurisprudence particularly the *Hanbali* which is the officially adopted School in Saudi Arabia. It also examines the concept of *Maqasid al-Shari'ah*. It thus contextualizes these basic principles within the framework of legislative developments in Saudi Arabia with a view to lay the foundation for exploring how it balances between the divine and the temporal and between conservatism and moderation in its application of Islamic law.

Chapter 4 examines Saudi Arabia between theory and practice of international law in the context of *Siyar* (Islamic International Law) against the background of its foreign policy and incorporation of international treaties into its domestic legal system taken into account the classical and contemporary nature of the Islamic concept of territorial statehood and nation-state. It attempts to put this theoretical analysis to test by examining views and opinions of stakeholders on international law in the contemporary Saudi Arabia. Chapter 5 examines Saudi Arabia's involvement in the international human rights systems against the background of its membership of the United Nations (UN), its membership of the Human Rights Council, and its ratification of some international human rights treaties. How, despite its declared strict adherence to Islamic law, it is responding to international human rights principles and fulfilling its international obligations in that regard. It also interrogates its refusal to ratify some international human rights instruments and ratifying others with reservation as well as the present human rights development in the Kingdom. Chapter 6 then follows with an examination of how Saudi Arabia's involvement in international economic relations has impacted on its strict adherence to conservative interpretations of the *Shari'ah*, particularly with respect to the question of *Ribā* (interest) when it comes to its membership of international organization such as the International Monetary Fund (IMF) and the World Trade Organization (WTO). This is to determine the extent of encroachment of the rules of international economic law into and their impact on Saudi Arabian local legislations in that area. Chapter 7 examines international commercial arbitration within the theoretical frameworks of international law and Islamic jurisprudence and applicable international commercial arbitration rules in Saudi Arabia against its ratification of international conventions such as the New York Convention Riyadh Convention on international commercial arbitration.

Chapter 8 draws conclusions from the study and makes some recommendations in respect of the interaction between international law and Islamic law in Saudi Arabia, particularly in the specific areas covered by the research.

Bibliography

Books

Abu-Sulayman, A.H.A., *The Islamic Theory of International Relations: Its Relevance, Past, and Present*, a Dissertation in International Relations Presented to the Faculty of the Graduate School of Arts and Sciences of the University of Pennsylvania in Partial Fulfilment of the Requirements for the Degree of Doctor of Philosophy, (1973).

Abu-Sulayman, A.H., *Towards an Islamic Theory of International Relations: New Directions for Islamic Methodology and Thought* (2nd revised edn), Virginia: IIIT (1993).

Al-Farsy, F., *Modern and Tradition – The Saudi Equation*, London and New York: Kegan Paul International (1990).

Al-Ghunaimi, M.T., *The Muslim Conception of International Law and the Western Approach*, The Hague: Martinus Nijhoff (1968).

Al-Hamad, H.S., The Legislative Process and the Development of Saudi Arabia, Faculty of the Graduate School, Los Angeles, California: University of Southern California (1973).

Al-Khari, M., *Usul al-Fiqh* (1st edn) Cairo: Daru Al-Hadith (2001).

Amanat, A., and Griffel, F., *Islamic Law in the Contemporary Context*, Redwood City, California: Stanford University Press (2007).

Baderin, M.A., *International Human Rights and Islamic Law*, Oxford: Oxford University Press (2003).

Besson, S., and Tasioulas, J. (eds) *The Philosophy of International Law*, Oxford: Oxford University Press (2010).

Brownlie, I., *Principle of Public International Law* (7th edn), Oxford: Oxford University Press (2008).

Carlos, C., *Le Droit International Theorque et Pratique* (5th edn), Paris: Rarebooksclub.com (1896).

Copi, I.M., et al., *Essentials of Logic* (2nd edn), Upper Saddle River, NJ: Pearson Education, Inc. (2007).

Crawford, J., *The Creation of States in International Law*, Oxford: Clarendon Press (1979).

Eijk, E.V., 'Sharia and National Law in Saudi Arabia', edited by Otto, J.M., *Shariah Incorporated, A Comparative Overview of the Legal Systems of Twelve Muslim Countries in Past and Present*, Leiden: The Leiden University Press Series on Law (2010), pp. 139–180.

Evans, M., *International Law* (7th edn), Cambridge: Cambridge University Press (2014).

Fassbender, B., et al. (ed) *The Oxford Handbook of the History of International Law*, Oxford: Oxford University Press (2012).

Fowler, M.R., and Bunck, J.M., *Law, Power, and the Sovereign State: The Evolution and Application of the Concept of Sovereignty*, Pennsylvania: The Pennsylvania State University Press (1995).

Frick, M.L., and Miller, A.T., *Islam and International Law*, Brill (2013); Baderin, M.A., *International Law and Islamic Law*, Leiden: Ashgate (2008).

Ghunaimi, M.T., *The Muslim Conception of International Law and the Western Approach*, The Hague: Martins Nijhoff (1968), pp. 30, 90, and 34.

Gleave, R., *Islam and Literalism – Literal Meaning and Interpretation in Islamic Legal Theory*, Edinburgh: Edinburgh University Press (2012).

Goronwy, J.J., *The United Nations and the Domestic Jurisdiction of State, Interpretations and Applications of the Non-Intervention Principle*, Cardiff: Cardiff University of Wales Press and Welsh Centre for International Affairs (1979).

Hallaq, W., *A History of Islamic Legal Theories*, Cambridge: Cambridge University Press (2005).

Halperm, D.F., *Thought and Knowledge: An Introduction to Critical Thinking* (4th edn), US: Lawrence Erlbaum Associates Inc. (2002).

Hashimilion, *A Modernization Paradox: Saudi Arabia's Divided Society, Arabia Today*, posted: 04 May, 2011, http://arabia2day.com/reports/a-modernization-paradox-saudi-arabias-divided-society/ (accessed 19 December 2012).

Hassan, K., *Mu'jam Usul Al-Fiqh*, (1st print), Ajman: Al-Raudah (1998).

Header, H., in Foreword to Goronwy, J.J., *The United Nations and the Domestic Jurisdiction of States, Interpretations and Applications of the Non-Intervention Principle*, Cardiff: Cardiff University of Wales Press (1979).

Heiberg, M., *Subduing Sovereignty: Sovereignty and the Right to Intervene*, Guildford and Kings Lynn: Biddle Ltd. (1994).

Howland, D., and White, L., *The State of Sovereignty, Territories, Law and Population*, Bloomington: Indiana University Press (2009).

Kamali, M.H., *Principles of Islamic Jurisprudence*, Cambridge: The Islamic Text Society (2003).

Kamali, M.H., *Principles of Islamic Jurisprudence*, The Islamic Text Society (2011).

Khadduri, M., 'Islamic Law', edited by Larson, A. and Jenks, C.W. and others, *Sovereignty within the Law*, England: Stevens & Sons Limited (1965).

Khadduri, M., *War and Peace in the Law of Islam*, Clark, New Jersey: The Lawbook Exchange, Ltd. (2010).

Khan, M.A., *Human Rights in the Muslim World: Fundamentalism, Constitutionalism and International Politics*, Durham, NC: Carolina Academic Press (2003).

Koskenniemi, M., *The Gentle Civilizer of Nations: The Rise and Fall of International Law 1870–1960*, Cambridge: Cambridge University Press (2002).

Krasner, S.D., *Problematic Sovereignty, Contested Rules and Political Possibilities*, New York: Columbia University Press (2001).

Krasner, S.D., *Problematic Sovereignty, Contested Rules and Political Possibilities*, New York: Colombia University Press (2002).

Krasner, S.D., *Sovereignty: Organized Hypocrisy*, Princeton, NJ: Princeton University Press, (1999).

Long, D.E., *Culture and Customs of Saudi Arabia*, Santa Barbra: Greenwood Press (2005).

Madani, M.O., *The Relationship between Saudi Arabian Domestic Law and International Law: A Study of the Oil Agreements with Foreign Companies*, (A Dissertation submitted to the Faculty of Law School of the George Washington University in Partial Fulfilment of the Requirements for the Degree of Doctor of Juridical Science, (1970).

Mahmood, O., *Al-Qamous al-Mubeen fi Istilahat al-Usuliyeen*, Riyadh: Dar al-Zahim (2002).

Marshall, P., et al., *Radical Islam's Rules: The Worldwide Spread of Extreme Sharia's Law*, Lanharm, Maryland: Rowman & Littlefield Publishers (2005).

Niblock, T., *Saudi Arabia – Power, Legitimacy and Survival*, London and New York: Rutledge, Taylor and Francis Group (2006).

Otto, J.M., *Sharia Incorporated, A Comparative Overview of the Legal Systems of Twelve Muslim Countries in Past and Present*, Leiden: The Leiden University Press (2010).

Piscatori, J.P., *Islam and the International Legal Order: The Case of Saudi Arabia*, Woodrow Wilson Department of Government and Foreign Affairs, Charlottesville, Virginia: University of Virginia (1976).

Rehman, J., *Islamic State Practices, International Law and the Threat from Terrorism – A Critique of the 'Clash of Civilizations' in the New World Order*, Oxford and Portland, OR: Hart Publishing (2005).

Ronald J.W., et al., *The 12 Secrets of Persuasive Argument*, USA: American Bar Association (2009), p. 1.

Roth, B.R., *Governmental Illegitimacy in International Law*, Oxford: Oxford University Press (1999).

Shaw, M.N., *International Law* (6th edn), Cambridge: Cambridge University Press (2008).

Sternberg, R.J., *Cognitive Psychology*, Belmont, CA: Wadsworth (2009).

Tomuschat, C., *The United Nations at Age Fifty: A Legal Perspective*, Leiden: Martinus Nijhoff LOL Publishers (1995).

Weiss, B.G., *The Spirit of Islamic Law*, Athens, Georgia: University of Georgian Press (2006).

Zaum, D., *The Sovereignty Paradox, The Norms and Politics of International State-Building*, Oxford: Oxford University Press (2007).

Journals

Baderin, M.A., 'A Comparative Analysis of the Right to a Fair Trial and Due Process under International Human Right Law and Saudi Arabia Domestic Law', *The International Journal of Human Rights*, Vol. 10, No. 3 (2006), pp. 241–284.

Baderin, M.A., 'The Evolution of Islamic Law of Nations and the Modern International Order: Universal Peace through Mutuality and Cooperation', *The American Journal of Islamic Social Sciences*, Vol. 17 (2000).

Borchard E., 'The Relationship between International Law', *Virginia Law Review*, Vol. 27, No. 2 (1940).

Bradley, A., and Goldsmith, J.L., 'Customary International Law as Federal Common Law: A Critique of the Modern Position', *The Harvard Law Review Association*, Vol. 110, No. 4 (1997).

Charlesworth, H., et al, 'Deep Anxieties: Australia and the International Legal Order', *Sydney Law Review*, Vol. 25 (2003).

Garcia-Mora, M., 'The Calvo Clause in Latin American Constitutions and International Law', *Marguette Law Review*, Vol. 33, No. 4 (1950).

Hallaq, W.B., 'Consideration on the Function and Character of Sunni Legal Theory', *Journal of the American Oriental Society*, Vol. 104, No. 4 (1984).

Hillgruber, C., 'The Admission of New States to the International Community', *European Journal of International Law*, Vol. 9, No. 3 (1998).

Irny, S.I., and Rose, A.A., 'Designing a Strategic Information Systems Planning Methodology for Malaysian Institutes of Higher Learning (isp- ipta)', *Issues in Information System*, Vol. VI, No. 1 (2005).

Kleinfeld, J., 'Sceptical Internationalism: A Study of Whether International Law is Law,' *Fordham Law Review*, Vol. 78, No. 2 (2010).

Krasner, S., 'Realist Views of International Law', *Proceedings of the Annual Meeting (ASIL)*, Vol. 96 (2002).

Krasner, S.D., 'The Case for Shared Sovereignty', *Journal of Democracy*, Vol. 16, No. 1, (2005).

Kroff, B.S.A., 'An Introduction to the History of International Law', *AJIL*, Vol. 18, No. 2 (1924).

Maritain, J., 'The Concept of Sovereignty', *The American Political Science Review*, Vol. 44, No. 2 (1950).

Moschtaghi, R., 'The Relation between International Law, Islamic Law and Constitutional Law of the Islamic Republic of Iran – Multilayer System of Conflict?', *Max Planck Yearbook of United Nations*, Vol. 13 (2001).

Shehaby, N., 'Illah and Qiyas in Early Islamic Legal Theory', *Journal of the American Oriental Society*, Vol. 102, No. 1 (1982).

Tian Jin, 'Complexities of Human Rights in Today's World', *Beijing Review*, Vol. 33 (May 28–June 3, 1990).
Vogel, F.E., 'Shari'a in the Politics of Saudi Arabia', *The Review of Faith and International Affairs*, Vol. 10, No.4 (2012).

Statutes, regulations, reports, and resolutions

Article 2(1) of the Charter of the United Nations.
IMO Doc C57/25, 1 October 1985.

2 Interaction of international law and domestic law

Between theory and practice

2.1 Introductory remark

Theoretically, sovereignty is an expression of supremacy of the governmental institutions of a state and the supremacy of the state as a legal entity at international level.[1] As a concept, the principal inferences or consequences of state sovereignty includes a state's exclusive control over its jurisdiction and populations within that jurisdiction as well as exclusive legislative and enforcement powers within its jurisdiction.[2] It has been argued in that regard that state sovereignty and international law are two paradoxes.[3] This is because while the fundamental principle of state sovereignty is that a state ought to be able to govern itself, free from outside interference, the bedrock of international law is the idea that external rule ought to be able to check and limit state behaviour and powers.[4] This apparently suggests that neither sovereignty nor international law could reign absolutely without one conquering or subjugating the other.[5]

Practically, individual sovereign states are the basic building blocks of the international system,[6] and in line with the principle of non-intervention, modern nation-states are considered sovereign in the sense that they are legislatively independent and can only enter into international agreements that promote their interests as they themselves define them without external intervention.[7] Thus, the principle of non-intervention was specifically enshrined in the United Nations (UN) Charter to the effect that "nothing contained in the present Charter shall authorize the United Nations to intervene in matters which are

1 Besson, S., 'Sovereignty, International Law and Democracy', *European Journal of International Law*, Vol. 22, No. 2 (2011), p. 373 at p. 376.

2 See generally Brownlie, I., *Principle of Public International Law* (7th edn), Oxford: Oxford University Press (2008), p. 289; and Howland, D., and White, L., *The State of Sovereignty, Territories, Law and Population*, Bloomington: Indiana University Press (2009).

3 Janis, M.W., *International Law* (5th edn), The Netherland: Wolters Kluwer, Law & Business (2008), p. 165.

4 Ibid.

5 Ibid.

6 Krasner, S.D., *Sovereignty: Organized Hypocrisy*, Princeton, NJ: Princeton University Press (1999), p. 1.

7 Ibid.

essentially within the domestic jurisdiction of any state".[8] However, the regime of contemporary international law has practically grown beyond that basic traditional conception. Today international law and domestic law have become much more "entangled" with one another.[9] For example, the legislative sovereignty of modern nation-states has steadily diminished in the sense that international law and norms have a strong impeding influence on domestic legislations of individual states to the effect that states are constantly conscious of the need for their domestic legislations to be in conformity with international law.

No modern nation-state is today truly legislatively sovereign in the absolute sense, to the extent that when engaging in domestic law-making, every state is conscious of the need not to violate international rules on issues that are inherently domestic and under the control of states. Hathaway has noted in that regard that "[i]nternational law's strength and reach have grown significantly over the last half-century" and that it "now reaches not just interactions between states but states' behaviour within their own borders as well" covering almost every aspect of domestic law.[10] Considering this practical reality in modern international relations, it is submitted, preliminarily, that the theory of sovereign non-intervention guaranteed under Article 2(7) of the UN Charter is no longer strictly sacrosanct, particularly in respect of the legislative sovereignty of states.[11] International law now does constantly intervene, albeit often indirectly, in the domestic legislation of states.

In pursuing the above propositions, this chapter is aimed at laying the foundation for the main thesis of this book in respect of the impact of international law on the Muslim States especially from the perspective of Saudi Arabia. It will first discuss the concept of sovereignty, history, and general nature of international law, focusing particularly on the traditional and evolving perceptions of its relationship with domestic law in theory and practice. It will then examine the theory of sovereignty and non-intervention principle under modern international law in relation to domestic law-making.

2.2 Concept of state sovereignty: historical and evolutional perspectives

"Sovereignty" is derived from the Latin word *superanus*; meaning greatness, supremacy, etc.[12]; or it is originally derived from the French term '*souverain*';

8 Article 2(7) of UN Charter.

9 Nolkaemper, A., and Hey, E., 'The Relationship between International Law and National Law', *International Law FORUM du Droit International*, Vol. 3, No. 1 (2001), pp. 9–11.

10 Hathaway, O.A., 'International Delegation and Domestic Sovereignty', *Law and Contemporary Problems*, Vol. 71, No. 151 (2008), pp. 115–149 at 115. See also Charlesworth, H. et al., 'Deep Anxieties: Australia and the International Legal Order', *Sydney Law Review*, Vol. 25 (2003), pp. 423–464 at 424.

11 Nagan, W.P., and Hammer, C., 'The Changing Character of Sovereignty in International Law and International Relations', *Colombia Journal of Transnational Law*, Vol. 43, No. 1 (2004), p. 1.

12 Bedi, S., *The Development of Human Rights Law by the Judges of the International Court Justice (Studies in International Law)*, Oxford: Hart Publishing (2007), p. 44; Ray, B.N., *Political Theory: Interrogations and Interventions*, New Delhi: Authors Press (2006), p. 177.

meaning a supreme rule not accountable to anyone, except perhaps to God.[13] Towards the end of the dynastic and imperial struggles of the Middle Ages, monarchical authorities in early modern Europe developed the concept of sovereignty,[14] aimed at consolidating their grip on power and to oppose and invalidate the feudal claims by the elites and aristocrats as well as religious pontificating authority of the papacy.[15] George Kennan observed that:

> ... this concept of sovereignty, the supremacy of a single ruler, was often conceived to have universal significance – to be applicable, that is, to all of the known civilized world. The particular rule in question laid claim to be superior to any other ruler in authority. His supremacy was expected to be acknowledged by anyone else who had any authority over people anywhere.[16]

With the passage of time civilization blossomed, human development crystallized, international communities expanded in reach and ranks, diversity, and complexity, and eventually merged into a single international society.[17] Consequently, the import and significance of "sovereignty" became uncertain and variable in its conceptualized notion.[18] By the emergence of modern nation-states, reference was made to sovereignty to denote not just domestic authority within a state, but, on the relative independence of individual states.[19] At local level, sovereignty denoted supremacy over all other potential authorities within the boundaries of a state, while, in foreign affairs, it denoted concentrated power sufficient to secure independence from other states.[20] Sovereignty, therefore, became a concept to connote the independence of a state interacting in a system of states rather than the potential supremacy of one state over other rivals.[21] With this, coupled with the emphasis on independence, came the idea of reciprocity.[22]

13 Duchacek, I.D., *Nations and Men: International Politics Today*, New York: Bolt Rinehart and Winston (1966), p. 47; Fowler, M.R., and Bunck, J.M., *Law, Power, and Sovereign State: The Evolution and Application of the Concept of Sovereignty*, Pennsylvanian: Penn State Press (2010), p. 4.

14 Fowler, M.R., and Bunck, J.M., ibid.

15 Wright, Q., *The Existing Legal Situation as It Relates to the Conflict in the Far East*, New York: Institute of Pacific Relations (1939), p. 18; Fowler, M.R., and Bunck, J.M., supra note no. 13 at p. 5.

16 Kannan, G.F., *Around the Cragged Hill: A Personal and Political Philosophy*, New York: W.W. Norton (1993), p. 87; Fowler, M.R., and Bunck, J.M., supra note no. 13 at p. 5 at its footnote no. 23.

17 Watson gives an extensive historical account of this process in his Watston, A., *The Evolution of International Society*, London: Rutledge (1992); Fowler, M.R., and Bunck, J.M., supra note no. 13 at p. 5 and footnote no. 24.

18 Fowler, M.R., and Bunck, J.M., supra note no. 13 at p. 5.

19 Ibid.

20 Hinsley, F.H., *Sovereignty* (2nd edn), New York: Basic Books (1986), pp. 107, 122–132; Fowler, M.R., and Bunck, J.M., supra note no. 13.

21 Fowler, M.R., and Bunck, J.M., supra note no. 13 at p. 5.

22 Ibid.

2.2.1 Classical perception of sovereignty

Traditionally, sovereignty theoretically signified absolute authority,[23] overlordship or complete suzerainty.[24] It is the supreme power of the state; and as Bluntschli simply puts it, it is, "every authority which gives a final decision".[25] Burgess said that: "it is an original, absolute, unlimited, universal power over the individual subject and over all associations of subjects".[26] Thus, sovereignty has the theoretical characteristics of being, universal, absolute, permanent, indivisible,[27] and inalienable.[28]

The theory of sovereignty was first advanced in Aristotle's *Politics*, and the classic body of Roman law. In his treatise, Aristotle postulated that there is recognition of the fact that there must be a supreme power existing in the State, and that this power may be in the hand of one, or a few, or of many.[29] The Romans' idea of sovereignty is elucidated in the expression that "The will of the Prince has the force of law, since the people have transferred to him all their right and power".[30] The newly discovered works of Aristotle in the thirteenth century revealed that it was the struggle between Church and State that gave rise to the theory of sovereignty.[31]

Jean Bodin (C. 1530–1967), the renowned French thinker and political scientist, in his *La Republique* published in 1576 AD was said to be the earliest jurist who embarked on a systematic study of the nature of sovereignty.[32] But it does not mean that the concept did not exist before Bodin.[33] Bodin defined "sovereignty" as the supreme power of the state over its citizens and subjects and unrestrained by law.[34] He postulated that it is a perpetual, humanly unlimited,

23 Hinsley, F.A., *Sovereignty* (2nd edn), Cambridge: CUP Archive (1986), p. 1.

24 Paul, W.W., *Sovereignty, a Study of Contemporary Political Notion*, Oxforshire: Routledge (2010), p. 4.

25 Bluntschli, J.K., *The Theory of the State* (translated from German 6th edn, by Ritchie Matheson, and Lodge), Ontario: Batoche Books (2000), p. 463.

26 Burgess, J.W., 'Political Science and Comparative Constitutional Law', *Boston*, Vol. 1 (1890), p. 52.

27 Ibid at pp. 52–56; al-Jurf, T., *Nazariyyat al-Daulah wa Al-Usus al-'Ammah lil Tanzim al-Siyasi*, Cairo: al-Hayah al-Misriyah al-Ammah lil-Kitab (1964), pp. 143–145.

28 Ghali, P.P., and 'Isa, M.K., *Mabadi' al-Ulum al-Siyasiyyah* (1st edn), Cairo: Maktabat al-Angelo al-Mesriah (1962), p. 203.

29 Charles, E.M., *History of the Theory of Sovereignty since Rousseau*, Kitchener: Batoche Books (2001), p. 5.

30 Ibid at p. 6.

31 Ibid.

32 Merriam, E., *History of the Theory of Sovereignty since Rousseau*, New York: Columbia University Studies in the Social Sciences (1900), p. 13.

33 Ibid.

34 Dunning, A., 'Jean Bodin on Sovereignty', *Political Science Quarterly*, Vol. 11, No. 1 (1896), pp. 82–104 at p. 91; Durga, K.S., *Political Science* (2nd edn), New Delhi: New Age International Publishers (2004), p. 64; also Hoveyda, A., and Ranajay, K., *Political Theory*, London: Dorling Kindersley (2012), p. 143.

and unconditional right to make, interpret, and execute law.[35] According to him, the existence of such a right is necessary for any well-ordered state.[36] In the opinion of Grotius, sovereignty is the supreme political power in him whose acts are not subject to any other and whose will cannot be overridden.[37] Burges defines sovereignty as "original, absolute, unlimited power" over the individual subject and over all associations of subjects.

The Dutch Jurist Hugo Grotius usually referred to as the "father of modern International Law"[38] further developed the concept after Bodin. Grotius' outstanding contribution in this regard was in his introduction of the idea that legal thought and legal reasoning, which implicated rationality, could be deployed in a way that brought reason to the conduct of sovereigns among themselves.[39] In his intellectual effort to integrate the independence and autonomy of the sovereign state, the challenges of developing orderly relations between states in period of war and peace, he explored a great deal of evolvement of international law through the imperatives of sovereign power and authority and the constraint suggested by reason and expressed in the form of international law.[40]

Some later Western jurists who also contributed their ideas to the theory of sovereignty include, John Locke, Jean-Jacque Rousseau, John Austin, James Bryce, Harold Laski, etc.[41] For example, Austin held that a determinate human superior, who is not in a habit of obedience to a person of like manner, receives obedience from the bulk of a given society or community, that determinate person is sovereign in that society, and the society is a political and independent entity.[42] Bryce and Laski and other modern jurists contend that the attributes of sovereignty are: "permanence, all comprehensiveness, individuality, exclusiveness and absoluteness".[43] They also argue that it is the power of the state to make and enforce the law with all the coercive power it cares to employ.[44]

The classical notions of sovereignty as discussed above had however been highly modified in contemporary theory and practice, particularly by the intervention of international law.

35 Hoveyda, A., and Ranajay, K., ibid.

36 Ibid.

37 Durga, K.S., supra note no. 34 at p. 64.

38 Steinberg, P.E., *The Social Construction of the Ocean*, Cambridge: University of Cambridge Press (2001), p. 31.

39 Grotius, H., *On the Land of War and Peace* (*De iure Belli Ac Pacis*), Stephen C.N., ed (2012) Prologue Section, p. 28.

40 Nagan, W.P., and Haddad, A.M., 'Sovereignty in Theory and Practice', *San Diego International Law Journal*, Vol. 13 (2011–2012), pp. 429, 445.

41 Ibid.

42 See e.g. Austin, J., 1832, *The Province of Jurisprudence Determined* (edited by W. Rumble), Cambridge: Cambridge University Press (1995).

43 Garner, J.W., *Political Science and Government*, American Book Co. (1928), p. 170; Laski, H.J., *A Grammar of Politics*, New Haven: Yale University Press (1925), p. 52.

44 Sharma, U., and Sharma, S.K., *Principles and Theory of Political Science*, London: Atlantic (2007), pp. 143–145.

2.2.2 Contemporary perception of sovereignty

Despite its historical trajectory, world leaders and diplomats had assessed the value and relevance of the traditional notions of sovereignty. They raised question whether the notion is still having bearing in the contemporary world.[45] For example, in 1992, the then UN secretary-general, Boutros Boutros-Ghali noted in his report to the Security Council that: "respect for [the state's] fundamental sovereignty and integrity [is] crucial to any common international progress. The time of absolute and exclusive sovereignty, however, has passed; its theory was never matched by reality".[46] Almost a decade after this report, and due to failures of the UN to meet apparent needs for action and intervention in Bosnia, Somalia, Rwanda, and Kosovo, the new UN Secretary-general, Kofi Annan noted in his 1999 annual report to the General Assembly that: "[o]ur post-war institutions were built for an inter-***national*** world, but we now live in a ***global*** world". He then subjected the traditional notions of sovereignty to a critical appraisal, noting that:

> A global era requires global engagement... If States bent on criminal behaviour know that frontiers are not the absolute defence; if they know that the Security Council will take action to halt crimes against humanity, then they will not embark on such a course of action in expectation of sovereign impunity.[47]

Nagan and Hammer have identified at least 13 different overlapping meanings of the term "sovereignty" in the contemporary perception.[48] According to them, the word sovereignty infiltrates the language of law and politics,[49] and it critically affects the language of practical diplomacy in international law.[50] They argue that in the operation of international law, sovereignty is a key because

45 Jackson, J.H., 'Sovereignty – Modern: A New Approach to Out-Dated Concept', *American Journal of International Law*, Vol. 97 (2003), pp. 782–802, 787.

46 An Agenda for Peace – Preventive Diplomacy, Peace-making, and Peace-keeping, Report of the Secretary-general, UN Doc. A/47/277-S/24111, para. 17 (1992), UN Sales No. E.95.1.15 (1995).

47 Kofi A. Annan, Secretary-General's Speech to the 54th Session of the General Assembly, UN Doc. SG/SM/7136 (1999).

48 Nagan, W.P., and Hammer, C., 'The Changing Character of Sovereignty in International Law and International Relations', *Colombia Journal of Transnational Law*, Vol. 43, No. 1 (2004), p. 143. These 13 different meanings include: Sovereign as a personalized monarch (real or ritualized); sovereign as absolute, unlimited control or power; sovereignty as political authority; sovereignty as self-determined, national independence; sovereignty as governance and constitutional order; sovereignty as a criterion of jurisprudential validation of all law (Grundnorm, rule of recognition, sovereign); sovereignty as the juridical personality of sovereign equality; sovereignty as international recognition; sovereignty as a formal unit of a legal system; sovereignty as legal immunities; sovereignty as jurisdictional competence to make and/or apply law; and sovereignty as basic governance competences (constitutive process), see pp. 143–145.

49 Ibid.

50 *See* Bull, H., *The Anarchical Society: A Study of Order in World Politics*, New York: Columbia University Press (2002), p. 122.

international law is "a body of rules which binds states and other agents in world politics in their relations with one another and is considered to have the status of law".[51] It also exerts significant impact on international relations.[52]

2.2.3 Islamic perspective of sovereignty

The Islamic perspective of sovereignty precludes the two sovereignties known in the Middle Ages (i.e. the Roman Emperor and the Pope). It also differs from the meaning given to it by the later modern absolute and non-responsible single sovereign presented by Bodin (1530–1596), Hugo Grotius (1583–1645), Hobbes (1588–1679), or Austin (1613–1669) whose positions were influenced and dictated by special circumstances which swept Europe in the sixteenth century.[53] Similarly, it is different from the Western principles of international law as espoused in the historic Treaty of Westphalia.[54]

In Islam, the notions of *Ummah* and the law (the *Shari'ah*) regarding sovereignty are significant. The first emphasizes the community of Muslims as a whole, while the latter emphasizes the exclusive legislative rights of God as the Lawmaker. Thus, in Islam there is no division between religion and politics and so governance is based upon the dictates of the *Qur'an* and the *Sunnah* – the primary sources of law.[55] Thus, Bernard Lewis argues that the Islamic State was in principle a theocracy not in the Western sense of a state ruled by the Church and the clergy but in the more literal sense of a polity ruled by God.[56] However, it is observed that Bernard's position appears to portray Islamic polity as a despotic state as God is hardly the sort of ruler Who could be held responsible or Who would need to consult with any of His subjects. Thus, Rachid al-Ghannouchi argues that sovereignty in Islam means *rule of law* (*hukm al-qanun*), "government by the people".[57]

Therefore, sovereignty in Islam is characterized by the divine commands as stipulated in the *Qur'an* and represents the embodiment of law and constitution of the nation and the state.[58] These are expressly stated in several *Qur'anic* verses.[59] It follows that the Prophet of Islam himself was not above the law of

51 Nagan, W.P., and Hammer, C., supra note no. 48.

52 Ibid, quoting Fowler, M.R., and Bunck, J.M., supra note no. 13 at 11–32.

53 Khatab, S., and Gary, D.B., *Democracy in Islam*, Oxfordshire: Routledge (2007), p. 12.

54 Saikal, A, 'Westphalian and Islamic Concepts of Sovereignty in the Middle East', in Jacobsen, T. et al. (eds), *Re-Envisioning Sovereignty: The End of Westphalia?* Aldershot: Ashgate Publishing Ltd (2008), pp. 73–81.

55 Ibid.

56 Bernard, L., 'Islam and Liberal Democracy', *Atlantic Monthly*, Vol. 27, No. 2 (1993), pp. 89–98.

57 Ghannouch, R., *Muqarabat fi al-'Ilmaniyyah wa al-Mujtama' al-Madani* [Approaches to secularism and civil society], London: al-Markaz al-Magharibi lil-Buhuth wa al-Tarjamah (1999), p. 155.

58 Khatab, S., and Gary, D.B., supra note no. 53 at p. 14.

59 See *Qur'an* 23:68, 84, 88.

God. He was directed to declare that: *Say: I am but a man like yourselves. It is revealed to me that your God is One God'.*[60] *'We send not a messenger, but to be obeyed, in accordance with the will of God.*[61]

2.2.4 Sovereignty under international law

The concept of sovereignty becomes an enigma against the background of controlling power of international law.[62] In other words, the imposition of obligations or conferment of rights on the state by international law might not connote doing all that to a being that is not human, but a kind of superhuman entity.[63] International law obligates and authorizes the state to behave in a certain way by obligating and authorizing human beings in their capacity as organs of the state to behave in this way.[64] The fulfilment of obligations imposed, and exercising the rights conferred by international law on the part of individuals as organs of the state, means only that such behaviour is referred to the personified legal order that determines the individuals who have to fulfil these obligations and exercise the rights emerging from the rules of international law.[65] The basic rule under international law is that a sovereign state formally recognized assumes a status of legal personality internationally, which confers rights and duties on the state.

Sovereign states may not appreciate full implications of a binding obligation especially when entering into a treaty that entails delegating authority to a supranational body.[66] The implication can range from simple differences in outcome on particular issues, to authority over decision making on an issue-area to more fundamental encroachments on state sovereignty.[67] Such agreements may, for example, restrict the power of states to regulate their borders (like for instance, requiring them to allow goods, capital, or people to pass freely) and to implement important domestic policies (as when, for instance, free trade intrudes and diminish the value of labour, safety, or environmental rules), thus, resulting in the encroachment of other aspects of sovereignty.[68]

This assumes greater dimension when states accede to external authority to exercise jurisdiction and take decisions over critical and sensitive domestic issues. There are a number of treaties (both bilateral and multilateral) that may expressly or by necessary implications open doors for international actors (who are neither elected nor otherwise subject to domestic scrutiny) into engaging in procedures

60 *Qur'an* 18:110.

61 *Qur'an* 18:57.

62 Stankiewicz, W.J., *In Defence of Sovereignty*, New York: Oxford University Press (1969), p. 115.

63 Ibid.

64 Ibid.

65 Ibid.

66 Charlotte, K., and Diehl, P.F., *International Law, Classic and Contemporary Readings* (2nd edn), Boulder, CO and London: Lynne Rienner Publishers (2003), p. 63.

67 Ibid.

68 Ibid.

leading to taking decision on a number of domestic critical and sensitive issues. These arrangements may limit the ability of states to govern whole classes of issues – such as social subsidies or industrial policy – or require states to change domestic laws or governance structures.[69]

Where international agreements impact negatively on the relations between a state and its citizens or territory, the veracity of the traditional (Westphalian) sovereignty comes into question. Where, for example, rules of international human rights restrict authority of a state from determining domestic policies of its citizens. The ostensible presumption is that the "Westphalia sovereignty" is an international order marked by "sovereign, equal, territorial states in which non-intervention into the internal affairs of another state is the rule".[70] However, it has been noted that "Westphalia" is afflicted with what Falk describes as "an inevitable degree of incoherence by combining the territorial/juridical logic of equality with the geopolitical/hegemonic logic of inequality".[71]

Different stakeholders in world affairs including rival states, world "superpowers", and local elites and mafias frequently, and sometimes with impunity, violate and circumvent sovereignty and equality when and where it serves their interests to do so.[72] The phenomenal colonialism and neo-colonialism with their consequences had undermined and rubbished the "Westphalia dreams" by rendering the established borders to mere geographical theory.[73] That explains why, as Kayaoglu puts it "its Eurocentrism and anachronisms..." and "a myth or narrative that does more to obfuscate the realities of international relations than it does to elucidate them".[74] The United States of America's refusal to be a signatory to the Rome Statute of the International Criminal Court (ICC) is a good explanation. The US's refusal to be signatory to this international statute is not unconnected with its concern that the ICC might claim jurisdiction over US soldiers participating in international peacekeeping activities or other foreign endeavours,[75] which will essentially conflict with the US's domestic obligation to protect members of its armed forces who are sent on international missions.

Similarly, when a state becomes a signatory to international agreements such as the Law of the Sea Convention, the tendency is to restrict itself from exercising sovereign authority over a variety of territorial rights. This convention redefines national territory such as delineating jurisdiction over a territorial

69 Ibid.

70 Schmidt, S., 'To Order the Minds of Scholars: The Discourse of the Peace of Westphalia in International Relations Literature', *International Studies Quarterly*, Vol. 55, No. 3 (2011), pp. 601–623 at p. 602.

71 Falk, R., 'Revisiting Westphalia, Discovering Post-Westphalia', *The Journal of Ethics*, Vol. 6, No. 4 (2002), pp. 311–352 at p. 312.

72 Krasner, S.D., supra note no. 6.

73 Keene, E., *Beyond the Anarchical Society: Grotius, Order, and the Anarchical Society*, Cambridge: Cambridge University Press (2002).

74 Kayaoglu, T., 'Westphalian Eurocentrism in International Relations Theory', *International Studies Review*, Vol. 12, No. 2 (2010), pp. 193–217.

75 Ibid.

sea, exclusive economic zone, and the continental shelf. It limits the capacity of states to restrict its use by establishing, for instance, rights of innocent passage.[76] Although a state is capable of withdrawal from such convention, such withdrawal has far-reaching effects.[77]

All states within the international community have, through adoption of the UN Charter, today delegated some of their sovereign powers to organs of the UN. The implication of this is that sovereignty of nation-states is restricted by and subjected to the provisions of the UN Charter. In other words, they have freedom and possess sovereignty within the prescribed limitations of the Charter.[78] And by extension, they have undertaken upon themselves, in good faith, to observe the rules of membership of the Organization. However, the residue of the so-called sovereign powers still remains with them.[79] To preserve this residue of sovereign power of the states, the drafters of the UN Charter included a provision to ensure that the UN would not be empowered to intervene in matters which were to remain under the control or within the domestic authority of the member nation-states.[80] Thus, the principle of non-intervention was given special recognition and expressed under the provisions of Article 2(7) of the UN Charter.[81]

2.3 A historical appraisal of international law

Although Western culture and political organization were the foundation of modern international law, its basic concept was discernible in political relationship thousands of years ago.[82] One of the first pieces of evidence of international law is a solemn treaty signed around 2100 BC between the rulers of Lagash and Umma (small city States in Mesopotamia) which defined boundaries between them.[83] In the middle ages, Church power and control were prevalent in Europe as the entire continent was holding to Christianity, and the ecclesiastical law applied to all, notwithstanding tribal or regional affiliations.[84] This period was characterized by struggles between the religious authorities and the rulers of the Holy Roman Empire, which were eventually resolved in favour of the

76 Ibid.
77 Ibid.
78 Goronwy, J.J., *The United Nations and the Domestic Jurisdiction of States, Interpretations and Applications of Non-Intervention Principle*, Cardiff: Welsh Centre for International Affairs (1979), p. 18.
79 Goodrich and Hambro, *Charter of the United Nations, Commentary and Documents*, Boston, MA: World Peace Foundation (1946), p. 64.
80 Goronwy, J.J., supra note no. 78.
81 Codification Division Publications, 'Charter of the United Nations', *Repertory of Practice of United Nations Organs*, https://legal.un.org/repertory/art2_7.shtml (accessed 30 July 2020).
82 Shaw, M.N., *International Law* (6th edn), Cambridge: Cambridge University Press (2008), p. 13.
83 Alina, K., *Public International Law* (4th edn), London: Routledge (2010), p. 8.
84 Nussbaum, A., *A Concise History of the law of Nations*, London: Macmillan (1954), pp. 17–23.

Papacy. However, the triumph of the Church over secularism was relatively short.[85] It is noted that at that point in time, the authority of the Holy Roman Empire and the supranational character of canon law were in vogue, particularly the influence of the Church on the rules governing warfare and the binding nature of agreements.[86] Despite that, commercial and maritime law developed expeditiously. It is also noted that English law established the *Law Merchant*, a code of rules covering foreign traders, and this was declared to be of universal application.[87]

Following the rise of the modern state and the emancipation of international relations, the concept of sovereignty was analyzed systematically in 1576 by Jean Bodin in his *Six de la Republique*.[88] He based his analysis on his perception of the politics of Europe rather than on a theoretical discussion, focusing on the necessity for a sovereign power within the state that would make the law.[89] He argued that while such a sovereign could not be bound by the laws he himself made, he was subject to the laws of God and of nature.[90] The early scholars of international law were, thus, deeply involved with the ideas of natural law and, thus, used them as the basis of their philosophies. Shaw notes that "included within that complex of natural law principles from which they constructed their theories was the significant merging of Christian and natural law ideas that occurred in the philosophy of St. Thomas Aquinas".[91] Aquinas maintained that natural law formed part of the law of God and was the participation by rational creatures in the eternal law. It is complimentary part of the eternal law which had been divinely revealed. The reason, Aquinas argued, was that it is the essence of man and thus must be involved in the ordering of life according to the divine will.[92]

The new approach to modern international law can be traced back to the Spanish philosophers of that country's Golden Age – the leading figure of this school was Francisco Victoria, Professor of Theology (1480–1546).[93] Francisco was a Spanish Renaissance Roman Catholic jurist, philosopher, and theologian known to be the founder of the School of Salamanca.[94] Due to his religious background he is noted for his contribution to the theory of just war (*jus bellum iustum*) a concept also known as a tradition of military

85 Shaw, M.N., supra note no. 82 at p. 19.

86 Nussbaum, A., supra note no. 84 at pp. 17–18.

87 Holdsworth, G., *A History of English Law*, vol. 5, London: Methuen And Co. Ltd. (1924), pp. 60–63, as quoted by Shaw, M.N., supra note no. 82 at p. 19.

88 Shaw, M.N., supra note no. 82 at p. 21.

89 Ibid.

90 Meron, T., 'The Authority to Make Treaties in the Late Middle Ages', *AJIL*, Vol. 89 (1995), p. 1.

91 Shaw, M.N., supra note no. 82 at p. 22; also Nussbaum, A., supra note no. 84 at pp. 79–93.

92 Ibid.

93 Nussbaum, A., supra note no. 84 at pp. 79–93.

94 See e.g. Woods, T.E. (Jr.), *How the Catholic Church Built Western Civilization*, Washington, DC: Regnery Publishing (2005).

ethics.[95] His contribution to international law is significant. However, there is controversy whether he could be described as the father of international law along others such as Aberico Gentili and Hugo Grotious.[96] Suarez (1548–1617) was also a scholar and Professor of Theology. He postulated that the obligatory character of international law was based upon natural law, while its substance derived from the natural law rule of carrying out agreements entered into.[97] However, Hugo Grotius (1583–1645), a Dutch scholar and theologian, was the one who finally excised theology from international law. He conceived of a comprehensive system of international law and his work became the popular text on the subject.[98] He reiterated the theological distinction between a just war and an unjust war. This was a notion that was soon to disappear from treatises on international law, but which in some sense underpins modern approach to aggression, self-defence, and liberation.[99]

The 1648 Peace of Treaty of Westphalia to the 1815 Congress of Vienna marked a new beginning in the history of international law. It is considered as the period of formation of "classical" international law. It is noted that international law in its modern version begins with the break-up of the feudal State system and the formation of society into free nation-states, which is commonly traced back to the period leading up to the 1648 Peace Treaty of Westphalia and which brought the Thirty Years War in Europe to an end.[100] It will be recalled that this was a war that took place in Central Europe and lasted for a period between 1618 and 1648. About 8 million people were killed and 20% of them were German citizens.[101] It was known to be one of the most destructive war encounters in the anal of human history.[102] Initially, it was underscored by religious sentiment and was restricted to the Protestant and Catholic states within the enclave of the Holy Roman Empire. Later, it spread across the Europe involving the then great powers. It became less about religion and more of political rivalry which was a carry-over of conflict between France and Habsburg in their struggle for continental political pre-eminence coupled with Habsburg attempt to rebuild the imperial authority in Germany.[103]

95 Charles, G., and Michael, Q., *"Ill: The Structure of the Tradition"- Just War: The Just War Tradition: Ethics in Modern Warfare*, London: Bloomsbury Publishing PLC (26 September 2007), pp. 11–15.

96 Anthony, P., 'Victoria: Political Writings', in Kant, I. et al. (eds), *The History of Political Thought*, Cambridge: Cambridge University Press (1991), p. xvi.

97 Ibid at pp. 84–91 and also pp. 92–93.

98 Shaw, M.N., supra note no. 82 at p. 24.

99 Ibid.

100 Alina, K., supra note no. 83 at p. 11.

101 Micheal, C., *Warfare and Armed Conflicts: A Statistical Encyclopedia of Casualty and Other Figures, 1492–2015*, North Carolina: McFarland (2017), p. 40.

102 Wilson, Peter H., *Europe's Tragedy: A New History of the Thirty Years War*, London: Penguin (2010), p. 787.

103 See generally Roberts, J.M., *The Penguin History of the World* (6th revised edn), Westad, Odd Arne. London: Penguin (2014).

The main aim of the 1815 Congress of Vienna was to establish a new balance of powers of political forces in Europe which would ensure lasting peace and maintain the *status quo* in Europe by repressing political revolution. Thus, from the 1815 Congress of Vienna to WW1, international law was based on a number of principles, namely, sovereignty, balance of power, legitimacy (in the sense of restoration of "legitimate" governments to power and prevention of political revolutions), and equality between nations.[104]

It is interesting to note that at around the same time when international law was developing in Europe, the early Muslim jurist were also writing on a similar concept of transnational law and relations called *Siyar*. Abu Hanifa al-Nu'man ibn Thabit (d. 150/767) was the first Muslim jurist to compile treatise on *Siyar*.[105] Details of this will be discussed in Chapter 4 of this book.

2.3.1 Nature of international law

A critical examination of various definitions of modern international law shows that all elements that make up many of those definitions are controversial.[106] The controversy stems from several issues. First, whether international law may properly be described as law in a strict jurisprudential sense; whether its rules extend to bodies and persons other than the State; whether there exists an international community; and whether there is a source of international law other than the consent of sovereign States.[107] Basically, the international legal order might not comply with most of the Austinian definition of law[108] (which stipulates that "the law is command issued y the un-commanded commander – the sovereign; such commands are backed by threats of sanctions; and, a sovereign is one who is habitually obeyed"). Therefore, the strength of international legal order might be subjected to enquiry from the point of its compliance with other prerequisites widely accepted to be essential to any legal system.[109] These prerequisites include the possession of a sufficient degree of uniformity, generality, and precision; the effective regulation of matters vitally affecting the life of the community as distinguished from matters of minor and formal importance; and, above all, its conformity with a general sense of right and

104 Alina, K., supra note no. 83 at p. 11.

105 Abu al-Wafa al-Afghani, *Introduction to Abu Yusuf, al-Radd 'ala Siyar al-Awza'i* (edited and translated by M.A. Ghazi) Pakistan: IIU (n.d.), p. 1 as quoted by Labeeb, A.B., *International Treaties (Mu'ahadat) in Islam: Theory and Practice in the Light of Siyar (Islamic International Law)*, Montreal: Institute of Islamic Studies, McGill University (2003), p. 27.

106 Lauterpacht, H., *International Laws* (edited by E. Lauterpacht), Cambridge: Cambridge University Press (1970), p. 9.

107 Ibid.

108 See generally Austin, J., *Province of Jurisprudence Determined*, London: John Murray, Albemarle Street (1832); Austin, J., *Lectures on Jurisprudence or the Philosophy of Positive Law* (3rd edn, revised and edited by Robert Campbell), London: John Murray, Albemarle Street (1869), pp. 81–88.

109 Lauterpacht, H., supra note no. 106 at p. 12.

justice.[110] Consequently, international law has, on the one hand, been derided or disregarded as law properly so-called by many of the world's foremost jurists and legal commentators.[111] They have questioned, first, the existence of *any* set of rules governing inter-state relations; second, its entitlement to be called "law"; and, third, its effectiveness in controlling states and other international actors in "real life" situations.[112]

On the other hand, another group of jurists have advanced arguments to prove the reality of international law. According to them, the most potent and persuasive argument for the existence of international law as a *system of law* is that members of the international community recognize that there exists a body of rules binding upon them as law.[113] States believe that international law exists. This acceptance of the reality of international law by the very entities to which it is addressed exposes the weakness of those who argue that international law does not exist.[114] Lauterpacht has thus provided an appropriate "descriptive working definition" of international law as

> the body of rules of conduct, enforceable by external sanction, which confers rights and impose obligations primarily, though not exclusively, upon sovereign States and which owe their validity both to the consent of States as expressed in custom and treaties and to the fact of the existence of an international community of States and individuals.[115]

While international law has never been wholly dependent on a system of institutionalized enforcement, the absence of a "police force" or compulsory court of general competence does not mean that international law is ineffective.[116] Secondly, there is no doubt that a very important practical reason for the effectiveness of international law is that it is based on the consent of states, their common self-interest, and necessity.[117] Contemporary international society is more interdependent and highly sophisticated than ever and the volume of inter-state activity continues to be on the high side.[118] International law is therefore needed to regulate activities within and beyond borders in order to ensure a stable and orderly international

110 Ibid.

111 Dixon, M., *Textbook on International Law* (6th edn), Oxford: Oxford University Press (2007), p. 1.

112 Shaw, M.N., *International Law* (4th edn), Cambridge: Cambridge University Press (1997), p. 5; Hart, H.L.A., *The Concept of Law (Claredon Law Series)* (2nd edn), Gloucestershire: Claredon Press (1997), p. 217.

113 Peter, M.A., *Modern Introduction to International Law* (7th revised version), London and New York: Routledge (1997), p. 7 (online).

114 Dixon, M., supra note no. 111.

115 Lauterpacht, H., supra note no. 108.

116 See generally, Kirgis, F.L., 'Enforcing International Law', *ASIL*, Vol. 1, No. 1 (1996). http://www.asil.org/insight1.cfm

117 Lauterpacht, H., supra note no. 108.

118 Ibid.

society.[119] Like any domestic or national legal system, international law cannot be said to be free of defects. That explains why it has historically achieved track records of successes and at the same time, dissatisfactory points of failures.[120]

Essentially, modern international law is a product of Euro-Christian civilization and was for many centuries a European law of nations.[121] Its foundation as it is understood today lies firmly in the development of Western culture and political organization.[122] At the emergence of notions of sovereignty and independent nation-state in Europe, it was felt that there should be an acceptable method in conducting inter-state relations that conformed to accepted "universal" standards of behaviour, and apparently international law satisfied that feeling.[123] It all began in the sixteenth and seventeenth centuries in Europe even though communities of states regulated by law had previously existed there and elsewhere.[124] Learning from subsequent world history, nation-states that formed Europe at that time, introduced a body of rules to regulate the diplomatic, commercial, military, and other relations of their society and that provides the basis for what was referred to as "law of nations" and later known as "international law".[125]

At that nascent stage, international law was about states only, but now other entities have become active participants in its operational ramifications.[126] For example, by virtue of an advisory opinion of the International Court of Justice (ICJ) in 1949, international organizations such as the United Nations and its specialized agencies were accorded status of international legal personality[127](and later non-governmental organizations by virtue of Article 71 of the UN), which has significant impact on the practices of states today.

2.3.2 International law and the question of legitimacy

The existence and operation of international law are essentially dependent on the degree of legitimacy it enjoys particularly among individual sovereign states that are the basic building blocks of its legal system. The question then is what is legitimacy? It is defined as

> a property of a rule or rule-making institution which itself exerts a pull towards compliance on those addressed normatively because those addressed

119 Ibid.

120 Ibid.

121 Jennings, R., and Watts, A. (eds), *Oppenheim's International Law*, vol. 1 (9th edn), London: Longman (1992), pp. 87–91.

122 Shaw, M.N., supra note no. 82 at p. 13.

123 Ibid.

124 Harris, D.J., *Cases and Materials on International Law* (6th edn), London: Sweet & Maxwell (2004), p. 12.

125 Harris noted that the term "international law" would appear to have been invented later by Bentham (1748–1832). See foot-note no. 42, ibid at p. 12.

126 Dugard, J., *International Law, A South African Perspective* (3rd edn), Claremont: Jute & Co. (2010), p. 1.

127 Ibid.

> believe that the rule or institution has come into being and operates in accordance with generally accepted principles of right process.[128]

The fundamental condition for the sustainability of law are the existence of a political community, and the recognition by its members of settled rules binding upon them in that capacity; international law seems on the whole to satisfy these conditions in relation to states.[129]

Legitimacy, argues Shaw, will depend upon four specific properties, namely, determinacy (or readily ascertainable normative content or "transparency"); symbolic validation (or authority approval); coherence (or consistency or general application); and adherence (or falling within an organized hierarchy of rules).[130] These four attributes go to confirm that there exist objectively verifiable yardsticks which help in ascertaining why rules of international law are complied with by states and, thus, why international norms are effectively operative.[131] However, the concept of legitimacy is often called to question, considering the "emerging right to individuality"[132] with the context of a "global identity crisis" in which the growth of supranational institutions and the collapse of a range of states combine to undermine traditional certainties of world order.[133]

Having said that, international law is law in the sense that it has relevance to daily lives of people.[134] For example, it enables international telephone calls to be made, overseas mail to be delivered, and travel by air, sea, and land to occur relatively easily.[135] Doubt of enforcement of law is rarely the sole criterion to measure compliance; rather the behaviour of states and people often is modified depending on the substance of the law, as well as its aspirational and inspirational aspects.[136] The nature and legitimacy of international law as analyzed above have significant impact on its relationship with domestic law as examined below.

2.3.4 Relationship between international and domestic laws

The structure of the domestic polity of nation-states normally consists of a law-making body, an executive or law enforcement body, and a compulsory

128 Ibid at p. 62. See also Franck, T.M., *The Power of Legitimacy among Nations*, Oxford: Oxford University Press (1990), p. 24.

129 Harris, D.J., supra note no. 124 at p. 3 and its footnote no. 5. See also Sir Frederick Pollock, *First Book of Jurisprudence for Students of the Common Law*, Philadelphia: The University of Pennsylvania (1897), p. 28.

130 Shaw, M.N., supra note no. 82 at p. 62.

131 Ibid.

132 Franck, T.M., *The Empowered Self*, Oxford: Oxford University Press (1999), p. 1; Shaw, M.N., footnote no. 64, ibid at p. 62.

133 Shaw, M.N., supra note no. 82 at p. 62.

134 Dixon, M. et al., *Cases and Materials on International Law* (5th edn), Oxford: Oxford University Press (2011), p. 1.

135 Ibid.

136 Ibid.

system of courts as essential features of its legal system.[137] Lack of these established institutions is a critical deficiency inherent in international law and a critical point of difference between it and municipal laws of nation-states. The UN, which can be described today as the leading institution in enacting rules binding upon all states under international law, lacks a central legislative body *per se*.[138] The concept of legislation is unfamiliar in international law.[139] If legislation implies a normative act promulgated unilaterally by an authorized organ and containing general abstract and directly binding legal norms,[140] there is nobody or no process in international law entrusted with the power to habitually enact legislation. Instead, law-making in the international system is multi-sourced and multi-layered, while its content and binding force varies.[141] The General Assembly is empowered to adopt recommendations which of course, are not binding upon member states.[142] Under Article 25 of UN Charter, the Security Council is empowered to take decision binding on all member states, but action of this kind is determined by the Security Council as, for example, in matters that constitute threat to international peace and security. Despite that, the Security Council is encumbered from making such decisions by the veto power vested in each of the five permanent member states.[143] Similarly, treaties and international custom re-enacting agreements between sovereign states are rules that are not imposed from above by any central law-making body.[144]

In executing its decisions, the UN is not a world government and thus, it lacks the power to direct states to comply with the law; and it lacks a permanent police force to punish violators of the law.[145] While it is true that the UN is able to raise forces to police certain situations, the fact remains that there is no permanent force at its disposal for restoring peace and order instantly.[146] Similarly, while international courts, such as the International Court of Justice (ICJ), exist under the ambit of international law, unlike the judiciary under sovereign states, these international courts have adjudicating powers only over those states that have consented to their jurisdiction.[147]

137 Dugard, J., supra note no. 126 at p. 2.

138 Ibid at p. 3.

139 Nicholas, T. *Security Council Legislation, Article 2(7) of the UN Charter and the Principle of Subsidiarity*, Adam Smith Research Foundation Working Papers Series 2011:05, (2011), p. 3.

140 See Brunee, J., *International Legislation*, Max Planck Encyclopaedia of Public International Law at: www.mpepil.com.

141 See generally Boyle, A., and Chinkin, C., *The Making of International Law*, Oxford: Oxford University Press (2007).

142 Ibid.

143 Szasz, P., 'The Security Council Starts Legislating', *American Journal of International Law (AJIL)*, Vol. 96 (2002), p. 901; Dugard, J., supra note no. 126.

144 Dugard, J., supra note no. 126.

145 Ibid.

146 Ibid.

147 Ibid.

The interplay between international law and domestic law often manifests the struggle between state sovereignty and the international legal order.[148] Gerry Simpson sees in the interplay between equality and inequality, between great power and outlaw status, "the essence of international law since at least 1815".[149] The basic focus of international law is primarily in seeking to organize international society in accordance with the general interests of the international community. The doctrine of state sovereignty can be advanced as an argument to protect a state against the intervention of international law into its national legal system.[150] As international law began to intrude[151] into certain issues which are basically domestic in outlook, there has been a constriction and diminution in the areas of law which can be governed exclusively by the municipal law of a state.[152]

In the effort to explain the tension between these two systems of law, reference is usually made to the so-called monist or dualist theories of international law.[153] The dualist theory views domestic law and international law respectively as separate and distinct entities, each with its own power to settle the effect any external rule of law might have within it.[154] They differ, in the first instance, in terms of their sources – sources of domestic law are customs grown from within the boundaries of the state concerned and statutes enacted by the local legislature, while the sources of international law are customs grown up among states and law-making treaties concluded by them.[155] Secondly, the two legal systems differ in terms of the relations they regulate. While domestic law regulates relations between individuals under the authority of a state and the relations between the state and the individual, international law regulates relations between independent sovereign states.[156] Thirdly, the two are different in terms of the substance of their legal provisions. Whereas domestic law is a law of a sovereign over individuals subjected to its authority, the international legal order is not above, but between, sovereign states, and is therefore a weaker law.[157]

All these imply on one hand that, international law is generally not thought to be able to make itself effective in a domestic legal order depending on the

148 Dixon, M. et al., supra note no. 136 at p. 101.

149 Simpson, G., *Great Powers and Outlaw States, Unequal Sovereigns in the International Legal Order*, Cambridge: University of Cambridge (2004), p. vii.

150 Ibid.

151 See generally Bradley, A., and Goldsmith, J.L., 'Customary International Law as Federal Common Law: A Critique of the Modern Position', *The Harvard Law Review Association*, Vol. 110, No. 4 (1997), pp. 815–876.

152 Ibid.

153 Ibid. See also Borchard E., 'The Relationship between International Law', *Virginia Law Review*, Vol. 27, No. 2 (1940), p. 137.

154 Janis, M.W., supra note no. 3 at p. 165.

155 Dixon, M. et al., supra note no. 136 at p. 101.

156 Ibid.

157 Ibid; see also Chellaney, B., 'International Law only for Weaker States?' *The Hindu*, www.thehindu.com/opinion/lead/international-law-only-for-weaker-states/article5479314.ece (accessed 25 April 2015).

constitutional provisions of a particular domestic legal system itself.[158] Domestic law on the other hand, is thought incapable of imposing itself on the international legal order as a state may not rely on its own domestic law as a ground for repudiating for example, an international legal obligation.[159]

Conversely, the monist theory views international law and municipal law as component parts of a single "universal legal order" in which international law has a certain supremacy.[160] Monists reject the dualists notion that the subject of the two systems of law are essentially different, arguing that apart from there being a single universal legal order, it is ultimately the conduct of the individuals that is regulated by law, the only difference being that in the international sphere, the consequences of such conduct are attributed to the state.[161] They argue further that in both legal realms, law is essentially a command binding upon the subjects of the law independently of their will.[162] They assert that the two legal systems must be regarded as manifestations of a single conception of law.[163]

It must be stated that, international and municipal law as systems cannot really come into conflict.[164] What may likely occur is, strictly speaking, as Harris puts it: "conflict of obligations, or an inability for the State on the domestic plane to act in the manner required by international law".[165] He further explains that international law does not necessarily purport to govern the content of national law in the national field. It simply stipulates that certain things are not valid according to its rules, and that if a State in the application of its domestic law acts contrary to those rules in these respects, it will commit a breach of its international obligations.[166] It must be noted however that this "fear" of committing a breach of international obligations often compels states to be wary of international law when enacting or applying their domestic laws.

The notion of international and domestic legal systems of both the dualists and monists were considered while drafting the UN's Article 13 of the Draft Declaration on Rights and Duties of States 1949, which provides that:

> Every state has the duty to carry out in good faith its obligations arising from treaties and other sources of international law, and it may not invoke provisions in its constitution or its laws as an excuse for failure to perform this duty.[167]

158 Janis, M.W., supra note no. 3.
159 Ibid.
160 Kelsen, H., *Principles of International Law* (2nd edn), Van Dyke Ave: Tucker (1966), pp. 553–588; Janis, M.W., ibid at p. 88.
161 Dixon, M. et al., supra note no. 136 at p. 102.
162 Ibid.
163 Ibid.
164 Harris, D.J., supra note no. 124 at p. 68.
165 Ibid and italics are mine.
166 Harris, D.J., supra note no. 124 at p. 68.
167 Draft Declaration on Rights and Duties of States with Commentaries (1949), https://legal.un.org/ilc/texts/instruments/nglish/commentaries/2_1_1949.pdf (accessed 30 July 2020).

Several judicial and arbitral decisions had been taken on the provisions of this Article 13. For instance, in *Alabama Claims Arbitration*[168] the Arbitral Tribunal rejected the argument that because its constitutional law provisions did not confer on it the power to interfere with the private construction and sailing of the ships concerned, Great Britain had not violated its obligations as a neutral state in the United States Civil War by allowing the construction and sailing to occur; saying that Britain cannot justify itself for a failure in due diligence on the plea of insufficiency of the legal means of action which it possessed.[169] It is noted that many courts or tribunals do not expressly apply monist or dualist theory. In the above case, the ICJ held, that "a piece of national law cannot be regarded as an excuse for the breach of obligations given by international law". The court said that: "…the government of Her Britannic Majesty cannot justify itself for a failure in due diligence on the plea of insufficiency of the legal means of action which it possessed".[170]

As could be seen from the above, whatever direction the argument goes – dualists or monists, the fact remains that modern international law does, arguably, intrude into the domestic affairs of nation-states particularly, their legislative and law-making activities.

2.3.5 *Enforcement of international law*

As questions have often been raised about the limits of enforcement of international law, the question may also be raised about why do states then need to be cautious of their international law obligations in relation to their domestic legislation. Essentially, the enforcement of rules of international law depends largely on the good-will of states. Nations recognize that the observance of law is in their own interest, and that every violation may also bring undesirable consequences.[171] Although lack of a central authority with powers to enforce rules in a regular and consistent manner is an issue that provokes scepticism about the enforcement of international law,[172] it nevertheless has a number of sanctions for breach of a rule with a view to ensuring compliance.

Chapter VII of the UN Charter gives power to the Security Council to direct its members either individually or collectively to apply force against any state whose violation of its obligations under international law might constitute a threat to international peace and security.[173] For example, by virtue of Resolution 221 of 1966, the Security Council authorized the United Kingdom to use force on the high seas to prevent oil tankers from reaching the port of

168 United States of America v Great Britain, Moore (1872), 1 Int. Arb. 495 at 656.

169 See Harris, D.J., supra note no. 124 at p. 69. See also Triquet v Bath; R. V Keyn; West Rand Central Gold Minning Co. V. R.; Mortensen v Peters; and The Parliament Belge.

170 See e.g. Nicaragua v. The United States of America – Merit Judgment (1986), ICJ, 1.

171 Dixon, M.et al., supra note no. 136 at p. 2.

172 Dugard, J., supra note no. 126 at p. 6.

173 Ibid.

Beira when their oil was destined for Rhodesia. Similarly, by virtue of Resolution 678 of 1990, member states were authorized "*to use all necessary means*" to secure the withdrawal of Iraq's forces from Kuwait, having adopted Resolution 662 of 1990 declaring Iraq's invasion and annexation of Kuwait illegal under international law, despite Iraq's justification of its action under its domestic law.[174]

A respectable body of international lawyers believe that enforceability is a necessary characteristic of any system of law, properly so called, and that international law possessed this characteristic, even if only in a rough and rudimentary form.[175] Kelsen is quoted to have said that international law is true law because, broadly speaking, it provides sanctions, such as the adoption of reprisals, war, and the use of force generally, and makes the employment of these sanctions lawful as a counter-measure against a legal wrong, but unlawful in all other cases...[176] Harris appears as taking exception to this position.[177]

It can be concluded from the above that use of force remains an important means of enforcing the rules of international law. However, the truth is that the real foundation of the authority and enforcement of international law resides in the recognition accorded it by the sovereign states making up the international society and having thus accepted its rules as biding on them regardless of their individual interests,[178] which consequently translates into giving up some of their own domestic sovereign legislative authority.

2.4 The principle of sovereign non-intervention

The principle of sovereign non-intervention is part of customary international law founded upon the notion that the territorial integrity of sovereign states should be respected.[179] It is a corollary of state's right to sovereignty, territorial integrity, and political and legislative independence.[180] Intervention violates the established norms where it bears upon matters that are within the ambit of domestic legislations of sovereign states.[181] Vattel was the first person to formulate a principle of non-intervention.[182] Scholars and jurists of international law have

174 History, 'Iraq invades Kuwait' (02 August 1990), www.history.com/this-day-in-history/iraq-invades-kuwait (accessed 30 July 2020); Peace Resource Center, United Nations Security Council Resolution 660 (Condemning the Invasion of Kuwait by Iraq), S.C. res. 660, 45 U.N. SCOR at 19, U.N. Doc. S/RES/660 (1990), http://hrlibrary.umn.edu/peace/docs/scres660.html (accessed 30 July 2020).

175 Harris, D.J., supra note no. 124 at p. 9.

176 Ibid at p. 10.

177 See Harris for details ibid at p. 10.

178 Ibid at p. 11.

179 *Corfu Channel Case (United Kingdom v. Albania)*, ICJ Reports (1949), p. 4.

180 *Oppeheim's International Law* (edited by R. Jennings and W. Arthur), vol. 1, Oxford: Oxford University Press (2008), p. 428.

181 Shaw, M.N., supra note no. 82 at p. 1148.

182 Vattel, E.D., *Droit des gens ou principes de la loi naturelle* (1758) book IV ch IV (translation by C.G. Fenwick, 1964); also, Vattel, E.D., *The Law of Nations* (translated and edited by Joseph Chitty, bk. 2), Philadelphia, PA: Johnson, Law, 1852), Chapter 4, section 56.

expressed doubt as to whether the principle was reflected in the practice of States well into the nineteenth century.[183]

This principle was enunciated in Article 15(8) of the Covenant of the League of Nations and the Montevideo Convention on Rights and Duties of States of 1933, which prohibited "interference with the freedom, the sovereignty or other internal affairs, or the processes of the Governments of other nations", together with the Additional Protocol on Non-Intervention of 1936.[184] As the Socialist states in the Soviet bloc were insisting on the observance of this principle in the era of the Cold War, so also were the colonial Powers and later the many newly independent States in the early decades of the UN.[185] However, it is significant to note that with the evolution of the right of self-determination and the development of international human rights law, the absolute characteristic of this principle has diminished significantly. It is argued that the notion of "responsibility to protect" may have further paved more inroads in this regard.[186]

In the celebrated *Corfu Channel Case*,[187] the ICJ examined this principle and observed that:

> the alleged right of intervention as the manifestation of a policy force, such as has, in the past, given right to the most serious abuses and as such cannot, whatever be the present defects in international organization, find a place in international law.[188]

The ICJ also stated in its 1986 judgment in the *Nicaragua Case* that:

> [t]he principle of non-intervention involves the right of every sovereign State to conduct its affairs without outside interference; though examples of trespass against this principle are not infrequent, the Court considers that it is part and parcel of customary international law … international law requires political integrity … to be respected.[189]

The principle was also enunciated in the *DRC v Uganda* case where the Court observed that Nicaragua's case had made it clear that the principle of

183 See Holy Alliance in Herberman, C.G. et al. (eds), *The Catholic Encyclopaedia*, Volume 1: Aachen–Assize. New York: Robert Appleton Company (1907).

184 Wood, M., *Non-Intervention (Non-interference in Domestic Affairs)*, Encyclopaedia Princetoniensis, http://pesd.princeton.edu/?q=node/258 (accessed 23 April 2015).

185 Ibid.

186 Ibid.

187 *Corfu Channel Case (United Kingdom v. Albania)*, ICJ Reports (1949) p. 35.
International law, also known as public international law and law of nations, is the set of rules, norms, and standards generally accepted in relations between nations. It establishes normative guidelines and a common conceptual framework to guide states across a broad range of domains, including war, diplomacy, trade, and human rights. International law allows for the practice of stable, consistent, and organized international relations.

188 Ibid.

189 Nicaragua v US, ICJ Report (1986), p. 106, para. 2020; ICJ elaborates further on this principle at parag. 205 of its report.

non-intervention prohibits a State "to intervene, directly or indirectly, with or without armed force, in support of the internal opposition within a State".[190]

2.4.1 The UN and the principle of non-intervention

The UN General Assembly adopted a Declaration on the Inadmissibility of Intervention and Interference in the Domestic Affairs of States in 1965.[191] Similarly, the UN General Assembly Friendly Relations Declaration of 1970 contains a whole section on "The principle concerning the duty not to intervene in matters within the domestic jurisdiction of any State, in accordance with the Charter".[192]

However, it has been argued that the implication of UN membership is that the sovereignty of nation-states members is restricted by and subjected to the provisions of the UN Charter. In other words, they have freedom and possess sovereignty within the prescribed limitations of the Charter,[193] and by extension, they have undertaken upon themselves, in good faith, the duties and responsibilities of membership. However, the residue of sovereign powers remains with states.[194] To preserve this residue of sovereign power of the states, the drafters of the UN Charter included a provision to ensure that the Organization would not be empowered to intervene in matters which were to remain under the control or within the domestic authority of the member states.[195] Thus, the principle of non-intervention was given special recognition and expressed under the provisions of Article 2(7) which states that:

> ...nothing contained in the present Charter shall authorize the United Nations to intervene in matters which are essentially within the domestic jurisdiction of any state or shall require the Members to submit such matters to settlement under the present Charter; but this principle shall not prejudice the application of enforcement measures under Chapter VII.[196]

It has been observed that the dilemma between sovereignty and intervention is reflected in the UN Charter, which contains "two principles that at times, and perhaps increasingly, conflict".[197] It is further observed that the Charter simultaneously prohibits "intervention into matters that are within the domestic

190 DRC v Uganda, ICJ Reports (2005), para. 164.

191 Edward, M., *General Assembly Resolution 2131 (XX) of 21 December 1965*, http://legal.un.org/avl/pdf/ha/ga_2131-xx/ga_2131-xx_e.pdf (accessed 23 April 2015).

192 UN Documents, Gathering a Body of Global Agreements UN A/Res/25/2625 General Assembly, www.un-documents.net/a25r2625.htm

193 Goronwy, J.J., supra note no. 78 at p. 18.

194 Goodrich and Hambro, *Charter of the United Nations, Commentary and Documents*, Boston, MA: World Peace Foundation (1946), p. 64.

195 Goronwy, J.J., supra note no. 78.

196 Charter of the United Nations, Repertory of Practice of United Nations, Codification Division Publications, https://legal.un.org/repertory/art2_7.shtml (accessed 30 July 2020).

197 Finnemore, M., 'Constructing Norms of Humanitarian Intervention', in Katzenstein, P.J. (ed), *The Culture of National Security*, New York: Columbia University Press (1996), p. 181.

jurisdiction of any state",[198] and enshrines "respect for human rights and for fundamental freedoms".[199] It is argued that this apparent "incoherence"[200] of the charter would be less puzzling if sovereignty is seen as relative to state-society relations as well as to interstate relations.[201]

It was in the light of this reality that the former UN Secretary-general, Kofi Annan had once remarked that the Charter is "a living document" and that "its interpretation and implementation should change with the times". He further noted that

> ... [i]t is not the deficiencies of the Charter which have brought us to this juncture, but our difficulties in applying its principles to a new era, an era when strictly *traditional notions of sovereignty*[202] can no longer do justice to the aspirations of peoples everywhere to attain their fundamental freedoms.[203]

Thus, Moses *Moskowitz* notes that the International Atomic Energy Agency is, perhaps, the most dramatic and most recent example of an international cooperative enterprise in which nations have agreed to surrender some other cherished sovereign rights and to submit to international control for the sake of a higher common interest.[204]

Going back to the question of interpretation, there was no indication under the provision of Article 2(7) as to the particular organ or authority to determine whether or not a matter was essentially within the domestic jurisdiction of a state, coupled with the clear omission of international criterion to be adopted.[205] Experts argue that these lacunas were created deliberately to render the question whether or not a matter was essentially within the domestic jurisdiction of a state a subject of controversy when it comes to interpretation.[206] Interpretation of what amounts to intervention had been a subject of controversy even among scholars of international law. Some argue that

> while discussion does not amount to intervention, the creation of a commission of inquiry, the making of a recommendation of a procedural or substantive nature or the taking of a binding decision constitutes intervention under the terms of the paragraph.[207]

198 See UN Charter, Article 2.

199 See UN Charter, Article 1.

200 Robert, H.J., *Quasi-States: Sovereignty, International Relations and the Third World*, New York: Cambridge University Press (1990), p. 180; see Davis, M.C. et al., *International Intervention in the Post-Cold War World*, Armonk, New York and London: M.E. Sharpe (2004), p. 84.

201 Ibid at pp. 84–85.

202 Italics are mine.

203 See Kofi Annan, 'Secretary-General presenting his Annual Report to General Assembly', Press Release, SG/SM/7136 GA/9596, 20 September 1996, www.un.org/News/Press/docs/1999/19990920.sgsm7136.html (accessed 21 March 2003).

204 Moskowitz, M., *Human Rights and World Order, The Struggle for Human Rights in the United Nations*, London: Stevens & Sons Limited (1959), p. 97.

205 Goronwy, J.J., supra note no. 78 at p. 29.

206 Ibid.

207 Goodrich and Hambro, *Charter of the United Nations: Commentary and Documents* (2nd revised edn), Boston, MA: World Peace Foundation (1949), p. 120; see Goronwy, J.J., ibid, footnote no. 43.

Others are of the view that the passing of recommendations on matter of domestic jurisdiction does not amount to intervention arguing that intervention is used in a strictly traditional legal sense in Article 2(7). They further contend that the principle of non-intervention "does not exclude procedures on investigation, studying report and recommendation, all of which do not amount to intervention in the accepted legal connotation".[208] It follows that UN organs are competent to address recommendations that concern not only states generally, but also to individual states on matters of domestic jurisdiction, since such recommendations that do not involve a threat to or recourse to compulsion even if they are not adhered to or observed.[209] These two positions are referred to as "static" and "dynamic" interpretation.[210]

Goronwy holds a contrary view. He argues that the drafters of Article 2(7) had the evident intention that the UN should observe as a strict policy of non-interference in matters traditionally regarded as within the domestic jurisdiction of state, such as a state's form of government, the treatment of its own subjects, which covers the entire spectrum of human rights.[211] He also contends that in the absence of international treaties, issues such as economic policies, questions of immigration and nationality, the size of national armaments and armed forces, internal conflicts within state's territory, and administration of non-self-governing territories, if any, were not invested in the trusteeship system of the UN, rather were exclusively placed within the ambit of state's authority.[212] He asserts that the only recognized exception to this general rule of non-intervention was the competence given to the Security Council to authorize enforcement measures for the maintenance or restoration of international peace and security in the event of imminent conflict arising out of a matter essentially within the domestic jurisdiction of a state, posing a threat to the peace, breach of the peace, or act of aggression.[213]

It should be noted that what constitutes "threat to the peace" was not defined in the Charter. However, the Security Council was empowered under Article 39 to decide whether or not a "threat to the peace" existed.[214] Thus, a lacuna was created such that a situation of international tension arising out of a matter traditionally within the domestic jurisdiction of a state can be interpreted to constitute threat to international peace and security, even when the state accused of such act had not applied force or threat against another state or take steps that undermine territorial integrity or political independence of another state contrary to provisions under Article 2(4) of the Charter.[215] Such acts include issues arising from human rights violation or discriminatory immigration practices by a state.[216]

208 Lauterpacht, H., *International Law and Human Rights*, London: Steven & Sons Ltd., (1950), p. 214.

209 See Goronwy, J.J., ibid at p. 30.

210 Rajan, M.S., *United Nations and Domestic Jurisdiction* (2nd edn), London: Asia Publishing House (1961), pp. 74–75.

211 See Goronwy, J.J., supra note no. 78 at p. 31.

212 Ibid.

213 Ibid.

214 Ibid at p. 32.

215 The UN Charter provides under Article 2(4) that: 'All Members shall refrain in their international relations from the threat or use of force against the territorial integrity or political independence of any state, or in any other manner inconsistent with the Purposes of the Charter'.

216 Goronwy, J.J., supra note no. 78 at p. 32.

In a nutshell, the UN organs were given the loop-hole to affirm their authority in deciding whether or not a question was precluded from their consideration under Article 2(7) of the Charter, and to adopt resolutions on matters that are traditionally within the domestic jurisdiction of the state. This is against the basic intentions of the drafters of the UN Charter and who inserted therein the non-intervention principle.[217]

It is against this background that the debates among the jurists of international law on validity or otherwise of the concept of sovereignty in modern times have continued unabated. For instance, Hans Morgenthau has argued against the obvious *variable* nature of sovereignty in modern times.[218] He defined sovereignty in legal terms as "the appearance of a centralized power that exercised its law-making and law-enforcing authority within a certain territory".[219] He then stressed the continuity of the "doctrine" of sovereignty throughout the modern era (since its origins in the late sixteenth century), and suggested that the idea of popular sovereignty legitimized the contemporary national democratic state.[220]

Carr had also argued that "Few things are permanent in history; and it would be rash to assume that the territorial unit of power is one of them".[221] Carr foresaw the concept of sovereignty "as likely to become in the future even more blurred and indistinct than it is at present".[222]

Intervention is usually exemplified in military, humanitarian, economic (sanction), trade (embargo), political, and diplomatic spheres. Little attention is always paid to the underlined legislative steps and procedures that normally precede practical interventional acts. Similarly, attention is not always focused on UN instruments on human rights issues which have direct bearing on domestic matters of sovereign states.

In the pre-Westphalia era, states were absolutely free to determine the rights which their citizens were entitled to enjoy within their territories, and how those rights were to be protected.[223] But considering the wanton violation of human rights which was prevalent in many parts of the world the issues of human rights and freedom were given prime attentions in the discussions preceding the drafting of the UN Charter in San Francisco. Participants in the Conference insisted on the inclusion of detailed provisions on human rights.[224] That explains why respect for human rights and fundamental freedoms for all without

217 Goronwy, J.J., ibid.

218 Biersteker, T.J., and Weber, C., *State Sovereignty as Social Construct*, Cambridge: Cambridge University Press (1996), p. 4.

219 Morgenthau, H.J., *Politics among Nations*, New York: Alfred A. Knopt (1967), p. 299; Biersteker, T.J., and Weber, C., ibid.

220 Morgenthau, H.J., ibid at p. 300.

221 Carr, E.H., *The Twenty Year Crisis, 1919–1939*, New York: Harper & Row (1964), p. 229.

222 Ibid at p. 230.

223 Goodrich, L.M., *The United Nations in a Changing World*, New York and London: Columbia University Press (1974), p. 160.

224 Ibid at p. 162.

distinction as to race, sex, language, or religion formed a core philosophy of the UN Charter.[225]

This development on human rights marked a dramatic turn in the anal of "law-making" at international level. Since then, the floodgates were open for various instruments in form of treaties, international norm-setting, and the creation of international agencies and commissions.

2.4.2 Nation-states and international law

Benedetto Conforti notes that the proliferation of legal norms has been an extraordinary development in recent years which has led to the transfer from the national to international sphere or regulations concerning economic, commercial, social, and even more "intimate" aspects of national life, including domestic economic policy and the protection of human right.[226] He further notes that the significant increase in the production of international norms has been largely due to the growth of "Soft law", in the form of huge number of resolutions passed by international organizations, particularly the United Nations.[227] The response of modern nation-states to this development confirms the overbearing impact of international norms on the domestic matters of sovereign states. Nation-states reactions to international rules are usually dictated by interests intended to be protected and certainly differently. Among factors attributed to this development is that some States particularly major powers have developed a practice of reneging on agreements to submit their dispute to arbitration when a decision contrary to their interest seems imminent or even after International Arbitral Court have rendered their judgments.[228] US acted this way in the Case Concerning Military and Paramilitary Activities in and Against Nicaragua.[229] The same goes for Argentina in a case with Chile.[230]

US is not a member of the International Criminal Court (ICC) for certain reasons earlier discussed in this chapter.[231] Other countries that have not signed or ratified the ICC include India, Indonesia, and China.[232] In the area of human rights, Saudi Arabia and some other Muslim-majority states that apply Islamic law have not ratified several human rights instruments and ratified some with reservation. It is in the light of this development that the perspectives of Saudi

225 UN Charter, 'Peace, dignity and equality on a healthy planet', United Nations, www.un.org/en/sections/un-charter/un-charter-full-text/ (accessed 30 July 2020).

226 Conforti, B., *International Law and the Role of Domestic Legal Systems*, Leiden: `Martinus Nijhoff Publishers (1993), p. 3.

227 Ibid pp. 3–4.

228 Ibid.

229 See ICJ Report 1986 at p. 17 para. 10.

230 See the Argentina v. Chille (1977) 52 I.L.R. 93.

231 United Nations Treaty Collection, https://treaties.un.org/Pages/ViewDetails.aspx?src=-TREATY&mtdsg_no=XVIII-10&chapter=18&lang=en (accessed 11 July 2015).

232 Shah, A. *United States and the International Criminal Court*, Global Issues, www.globalissues.org/article/490/united-states-and-the-icc (accessed 11 July 2015).

Arabia's application of Islamic law and its adoption and domestication of some international law rules will be examined in this book.

2.5 Conclusion

This chapter has examined a brief historical background of the concept of sovereignty, showing that historically towards the end of the dynastic and imperial struggles of the Middle Ages, monarchical authorities in early modern Europe developed this concept. It was aimed at consolidating their grip on power and to oppose and invalidate the feudal claims by the elites and aristocrats as well as religious pontificating authority of the papacy.

The chapter has also analyzed the relationship of international law with domestic law, showing that individual sovereign states are the basic building blocks of the international system. Although these states are said to be sovereign in the sense that they are juridically independent and can enter into international agreements that promote their interests as they themselves define them. However, legal regime of the contemporary international law has grown beyond that basic norm. Thus, sovereignty of modern nation-state has steadily diminished in value and the concept is called to question.

It has also established that, the principle of non-intervention as part of customary international law was founded upon the notion that the territorial integrity of sovereign states should be respected as a corollary of state's right to sovereignty, territorial integrity, and political independence. The founding members of the UN cherished the sanctity of this principle. However, it is no longer sacrosanct in view of the steady growth of human rights as a universal principle coupled with the sophistication in modern international relations. Thus, the principle of non-intervention has also diminished in value.

Bibliography

Books

Abu al-Wafa al-Afghani, *Introduction to Abu Yusuf, al-Radd 'ala Siyar al-Awza'i* (edited and translated by M.A. Ghazi), Pakistan: IIU (n.d.), p. 1 as quoted by Labeeb, A.B., *International Treaties (Mu'ahadat) in Islam: Theory and Practice in the Light of Siyar (Islamic International Law)*, Montreal: Institute of Islamic Studies, McGill University (2003).

Agenda for Peace – Preventive Diplomacy, Peace-making, and Peace-keeping, Report of the Secretary-general, UN Doc. A/47/277-S/24111, para. 17 (1992), UN Sales No. E.95.1.15 (1995).

Alexandrowicz, C.H., *An Introduction to the History of the Law of Nations*, Oxford: Clarendon Press; Oxford University Press (1967).

Alexandrowicz, C.H., *The European-African Confrontation: A Study in Treaty Making*, Leiden: A.W Sijthoff (1973).

Alina, K., *Public International Law* (4th edn), Oxfordshire: Routledge (2010).

Al-Jurf, T., *Nazariyyat al-Daulah wa Al-Usus al-'Ammah lil Tanzim al-Siyasi*, Cairo: al-Hayah al-Misriyah al-Ammah lil-Kitab (1964).

Anthony, P., 'Victoria: Political Writings', edited by Kant, I. et al., *The History of Political Thought*. Cambridge: Cambridge University Press (1991), pp. 131–176.

Austin, J., *Lectures on Jurisprudence or the Philosophy of Positive Law* (3rd edn, revised and edited by Robert Campbell), London: John Murray, Albemarle Street (1869).

Austin, J., *Province of Jurisprudence Determined*, London: John Murray, Albemarle Street (1832).

Austin, J., 1832, *The Province of Jurisprudence Determined* (edited by W. Rumble), Cambridge: Cambridge University Press (1995).

Bedi, S., *The Development of Human Rights Law by the Judges of the International Court Justice (Studies in International Law)*, Oxford: Hart Publishing (2007).

Biersteker, T.J., and Weber, C., *State Sovereignty as Social Construct*, Cambridge: Cambridge University Press (1996).

Bluntschli, J.K., *The Theory of the State* (translated from German 6th edn, by Ritchie Matheson and Lodge), Oxford: Clarendon; 2nd ed edition (1895).

Boyle, A., and Chinkin, C., *The Making of International Law*, Oxford: Oxford University Press (2007).

Brownlie, I., *Principle of Public International Law* (7th edn), Oxford: Oxford University Press (2008).

Bull, H., *The Anarchical Society: A Study of Order in World Politics*, New York: Columbia University Press (2002), p. 122.

Carr, E.H., *The Twenty Year Crisis, 1919–1939*, New York: Harper & Row (1964).

Charles, E.M., *History of the Theory of Sovereignty since Rousseau*, Kitchener: Batoche Books (2001).

Charles, G., and Michael, Q., *"Ill: The Structure of the Tradition"- Just War: The Just War Tradition: Ethics in Modern Warfare*, London: Bloomsbury Publishing PLC (26 September 2007).

Charlotte, K., and Diehl, P.F., *International Law, Classic and Contemporary Readings* (2nd edn), Boulder, CO and London: Lynne Rienner Publishers (2003).

Chellaney, B., International Law Only for Weaker States? *The Hindu*, www.thehindu.com/opinion/lead/international-law-only-for-weaker-states/article5479314.ece (accessed 25 April 2015).

Conforti, B., *International Law and the Role of Domestic Legal Systems*, Leiden: Martinus Nijhoff Publishers (1993).

Davis, M.C. et al., *International Intervention in the Post-Cold War World*, Armonk, New York and London: M.E. Sharpe (2004), pp. 84–85.

Dixon, M., *Textbook on International Law* (6th edn), Oxford: Oxford University Press (2007), p. 1.

Dixon, M. et al., *Cases and Materials on International Law* (5th edn), Oxford: Oxford University Press (2011), p. 1.

Duchacek, I.D., *Nations and Men: International Politics Today*, New York: Bolt Rinehart and Winston (1966).

Dugard, J., *International Law, A South African Perspective* (3rd edn), Claremont: Jute & Co. (2010), p. 1.

Durga, K.S., *Political Science* (2nd edn), New Delhi: New Age International Publishers (2004).

Edward, M., *General Assembly Resolution 2131 (XX) of 21 December 1965*, http://legal.un.org/avl/pdf/ha/ga_2131-xx/ga_2131-xx_e.pdf (access 23 April, 2015).

Finnemore, M., 'Constructing Norms of Humanitarian Intervention', edited by Katzenstein, P.J., *The Culture of National Security*. New York: Columbia University Press (1996), pp. 153–185.

Fowler, M.R., and Bunck, J.M., *Law, Power, and Sovereign State: The Evolution and Application of the Concept of Sovereignty*, Pennsylvania: Penn State Press (2010).

Franck, T.M., *The Empowered Self*, Oxford: Oxford University Press (1999).

Franck, T.M., *The Power of Legitimacy Among Nations*, Oxford: Oxford University Press (1990).

Frederick Pollock, *First Book of Jurisprudence for Students of the Common Law*, Pennsylvania: The University of Pennsylvania (1897).

Garner, J.W., *Political Science and Government*, American Book Co. (1928).

Ghali, P.P., and 'Isa, M.K., *Mabadi' al-Ulum al-Siyasiyyah* (1st edn), Cairo: Maktabat al- Angelo al- Mesriah (1962).

Ghannouch, R., *Muqarabat fi al-'Ilmaniyyah wa al-Mujtama' al-Madani* [Approaches to secularism and civil society], London: al-Markaz al-Magharibi lil-Buhuth wa al-Tarjamah (1999).

Goodrich and Hambro, *Charter of the United Nations, Commentary and Documents*, Boston, MA: World Peace Foundation (1946).

Goodrich and Hambro, *Charter of the United Nations: Commentary and Documents* (2nd revised edn), Boston, MA: World Peace Foundation (1949).

Goodrich, L.M., *The United Nations in a Changing World*, New York and London: Columbia University Press (1974).

Goronwy, J.J., *The United Nations and the Domestic Jurisdiction of States, Interpretations and Applications of Non-Intervention Principle*, Cardiff: Welsh Centre for International Affairs (1979).

Grotius, H., *On the Land of War and Peace (De iure Belli Ac Pacis)*, Stephen C.N., ed, Prologue Section. Cambridge: Cambridge University Press (2012).

Harris, D.J., *Cases and Materials on International Law* (6th edn), London: Sweet & Maxwell (2004).

Hart, H.L.A., *The Concept of Law (Claredon Law Series)* (2nd edn), Gloucestershire: Claredon Press (1997).

Hinsley, F.A., *Sovereignty* (2nd edn), Cambridge: CUP Archive (1986).

Hinsley, F.H., *Sovereignty* (2nd edn revised), New York: Basic Books (1986).

Holdsworth, G., *A History of English Law*, vol. 5, London: Methuen And Co. Ltd. (1924).

Holy Alliance in Herberman, C.G. et al. (eds), *The Catholic Encyclopaedia*, Volume 1: Aachen–Assize. New York: Robert Appleton Company (1907).

Hoveyda, A., and Ranajay, K., *Political Theory*, London: Dorling Kindersley (2012).

Howland, D., and White, L., *The State of Sovereignty, Territories, Law and Population*, Bloomington: Indiana University Press (2009).

Janis, M.W., *International Law* (5th edn), The Netherland: Wolters Kluwer, Law & Business (2008).

Jennings, R., and Watts, A. (eds), *Oppenheim's International Law* (9th edn), vol. 1 (1992).

Kannan, G.F., *Around the Cragged Hill: A Personal and Political Philosophy*, New York: W.W. Norton (1993).

Kelsen, H., *Principles of International Law* (2nd edn), Van Dyke Ave: Tucker (1966).

Khatab, S., and Gary, D.B., *Democracy in Islam*, Oxfordshire: Routledge (2007).

Kofi Annan, 'Secretary-General presenting his Annual Report to General Assembly', Press Release, SG/SM/7136 GA/9596, 20 September 1996, www.un.org/News/Press/docs/1999/19990920.sgsm7136.html.

Kofi A. Annan, Secretary-General's Speech to the 54th Session of the General Assembly, UN Doc. SG/SM/7136 (1999).

Krasner, S.D., *Sovereignty: Organized Hypocrisy*, Princeton, NJ: Princeton University Press (1999).

Laski, H.J., *A Grammar of Politics*, New Haven: Yale University Press (1925).

Lauterpacht, H., *International Laws* (edited by E. Lauterpacht), Cambridge: Cambridge University Press (1970).

Meron, T., 'The Authority to Make Treaties in the Late Middle Ages', *AJIL*, Vol. 89 (1995), pp. 1–20.

Merriam, E., *History of the Theory of Sovereignty since Rousseau*, New York: Columbia University Press (1900).

Morgenthau, H.J., *Politics among Nations*, New York: Alfred A. Knopt (1967).

Moskowitz, M., *Human Rights and World Order, the Struggle for Human Rights in the United Nations*, London: Stevens & Sons Limited (1959).

Nicholas, T. *Security Council Legislation, Article 2(7) of the UN Charter and the Principle of Subsidiarity*, Adam Smith Research Foundation Working Papers Series 2011:05, (2011).

Nussbaum, A., *A Concise History of the Law of Nations*, London: Macmillan (1954).

Paul, W.W., *Sovereignty, a Study of Contemporary Political Notion*, Oxforshire: Routledge (2010).

Peter, M.A., *Modern Introduction to International Law* (7th revised version), London and New York: Routledge.

Rajan, M.S., *United Nations and Domestic Jurisdiction* (2nd edn), London: Asia Publishing House (1961).

Ray, B.N., *Political Theory: Interrogations and Interventions*, New Delhi: Authors Press (2006).

Robert, H.J., *Quasi-States: Sovereignty, International Relations and the Third World*, New York: Cambridge University Press (1990).

Saikal, A, 'Westphalian and Islamic Concepts of Sovereignty in the Middle East', edited by Jacobsen, T. et al., *Re-Envisioning Sovereignty: The End of Westphalia?* Aldershot: Ashgate Publishing Ltd (2008), pp. 73–81.

Shah, A., *United States and the International Criminal Court*, Global Issues, www.globalissues.org/article/490/united-states-and-the-icc (accessed 11 July 2015).

Sharma, U., and Sharma, S.K., *Principles and Theory of Political Science*, London: Atlantic (2007).

Shaw, M.N., *International Law* (4th edn), Cambridge: Cambridge University Press (1997).

Shaw, M.N., *International Law* (6th edn), Cambridge: Cambridge University Press (2008).

Simpson, G., *Great Powers and Outlaw States, Unequal Sovereigns in the International Legal Order*, Cambridge: University of Cambridge (2004).

Stankiewicz, W.J., *In Defence of Sovereignty*, New York: Oxford University Press (1969).

Steinberg. P.E., *The Social Construction of the Ocean*, Cambridge: University of Cambridge Press (2001).

UN Documents, Gathering a Body of Global Agreements UN A/Res/25/2625 General Assembly, www.un-documents.net/a25r2625.htm.

United Nations, *Oppeheim's International Law* (edited by R. Jennings and W. Arthur), vol. 1, Oxford University Press (2008).

United Nations Conference on International Organisation (UNCIO). Documents, Vol. 13.

United States of America v Great Britain, Moore (1872), 1 Int. Arb.

Vattel, E.D., *Droit des gens ou principes de la loi naturelle* (1758) book IV ch IV (translation by C.G. Fenwick, 1964). Washington, Carnegie institution of Washington.

Vattel, E.D., *The Law of Nations* (translated and edited by Joseph Chitty, bk. 2), Philadelphia, PA: Johnson, Law (1852).

Waltz, K., and Waltz, K., *Theory of International Politics*, New York City: McGraw Hill Inc. (1979).

Watson gives an extensive historical account of this process in his Watston, A., *The Evolution of International Society*, London: Rutledge (1992).

Wood, M., *Non-Intervention (Non-interference in Domestic Affairs)*, Encyclopaedia Princetoniensis, http://pesd.princeton.edu/?q=node/258 (accessed 23 April 2015).

Woods, T.E. (Jr.), *How the Catholic Church Built Western Civilization*, Washington, DC: Regnery Publishing (2005).

Wright, Q., *The Existing Legal Situation as It Relates to the Conflict in the Far East*, New York: Institute of Pacific Relations (1939).

Journals

Bernard, L., 'Islam and Liberal Democracy', *Atlantic Monthly*, Vol. 27, No. 2 (1993), pp. 64–75.

Besson, S., 'Sovereignty, International Law and Democracy', *European Journal of International Law*, Vol. 22, No. 2 (2011), pp. 373–387.

Borchard, E., 'The Relationship between International Law', *Virginia Law Review*, Vol. 27, No. 2 (1940), pp. 137–148.

Bradley, A., and Goldsmith, J.L., 'Customary International Law as Federal Common Law: A Critique of the Modern Position', *The Harvard Law Review Association*, Vol. 110, No. 4 (1997), pp. 815–876.

Burgess, J.W., 'Political Science and Comparative Constitutional Law', *Boston*, Vol. 1 (1890).

Charlesworth, H. et al., 'Deep Anxieties: Australia and the International Legal Order', *Sydney Law Review*, Vol. 25 (2003), pp. 424–465.

Dunning, A., 'Jean Bodin on Sovereignty', *Political Science Quarterly*, Vol. 11, No. 1 (1896), pp. 82–104.

Hathaway, O.A., 'International Delegation and Domestic Sovereignty', *Law and Contemporary Problems*, Vol. 71 (2008), pp. 115–149.

Jackson, J.H., 'Sovereignty – Modern: A New Approach to Out-dated Concept', *American Journal of International Law*, Vol. 97 (2003), pp. 782–802.

Kirgis, F.L., 'Enforcing International Law', *ASIL*, Vol. 1, No. 1 (1996), http://www.asil.org/insight1.cfm.

Nagan, W.P., and Haddad, A.M., 'Sovereignty in Theory and Practice', *San Diego International Law Journal*, Vol. 13 (2011–2012), p. 429.

Nagan, W.P., and Hammer, C., 'The Changing Character of Sovereignty in International Law and International Relations', *Colombia Journal of Transnational Law*, Vol. 43, No. 1 (2004), pp. 141–187.

Nolkaemper, A., and Hey, E., 'The Relationship between International Law and National Law', *International Law FORUM du Droit International*, Vol. 3 (2001).

Szasz, P., 'The Security Council Starts Legislating', *American Journal of International Law (AJIL)*, Vol. 96 (2002), pp. 175–193.

Websites

http://legal.un.org/avl/pdf/ha/ga_2131-xx/ga_2131-xx_e.pdf (access 23 April 2015).
http://pesd.princeton.edu/?q=node/258 (accessed 23 April 2015).
www.globalissues.org/article/490/united-states-and-the-icc
www.mpepil.com
www.thehindu.com/opinion/lead/international-law-only-for-weaker-states/article5479314.ece (accessed 25 April 2015).
https://treaties.un.org/Pages/ViewDetails.aspx?src=TREATY&mtdsg_no=XVIII-10&chapter=18&lang=en

Cases

Corfu Channel Case (United Kingdom v. Albania), ICJ Reports (1949).
DRC v Uganda, ICJ Reports (2005).
Nicaragua v. The United States of America - Merit Judgment (1986), ICJ, 1.
Nicaragua v US, ICJ Report (1986).
Triquet v Bath; R. V Keyn; West Rand Central Gold Minning Co. V. R.; Mortensen v Peters; and The Parliament Belge.
United States of America v Great Britain, Moore (1872), 1 Int. Arb.

3 Islamic law in Saudi Arabia

Between conservatism and moderation

3.1 Introductory remarks

Islamic law is unique in a number of its basic characteristics. Muslim jurists consider it as exhibiting greater relative stability and continuity of values, thought and institutions when compared to some other legal systems.[1] This claim is arguably validated by reference to the respective sources of law in the Islamic and Western legal systems.[2] While rationality, custom, and judicial precedents, which are relatively flexible, constitute the prominent basis of most Western legal systems, religious norms, which are relatively rigid, acquire greater prominence in the former.[3] In its application, there is, on the one hand, a conservative approach that promotes strict textualism (to the exclusion of all rationality) in Islamic law, and which seek to ground the law in the closed cannon of fundamental texts and refuse to accord validity to the law formulated independently of these texts.[4] Traditionally, Saudi Arabia is a notable modern Muslim-majority state that follows a conservative approach to Islamic law based on its adoption of the Hanbali School of Islamic jurisprudence. On the other hand, there is an alternative moderate approach that seeks to construct and produce a considerable body of liberal thought on the re-interpretation and reform of Islamic law and understanding.[5] The methodologies of the alternative liberal approach rest on the interpretation and re-interpretation of the basic sources of the law, namely, the *Qur'an* and the *Sunnah*, through the process of *Ijtihad*.[6] It is through the sustained process of *Ijtihad* that Islamic law has evolved, relatively slowly in comparison with Western legal systems, over the centuries since its inception from the seventh century in Arabia.

This chapter is divided into two parts. The first part examines the theoretical framework and development of Islamic law by analyzing its history and nature as

1 See e.g. Kamali, H.H., *Principles of Islamic Jurisprudence*, Cambridge: The Islamic Texts Society (2003), p. xix.

2 Ibid.

3 Ibid.

4 Weiss, B.G., *The Spirit of Islamic Law*, Athen: University of Georgian Press (2006), p. 38.

5 Safi, O., *Progressive Muslims*, Oxford: One World (2003), p. 8.

6 Aslan, R., *"No God but God" – The Origins, Evolution, and Future of Islam*, London: Arrow Books (2006), p. 165.

a system of law consisting of sources, methods, and principles, while the second part examines its practical evolution and application as a formal legal system in Saudi Arabia. The combination of the two parts of the chapter is an attempt to examine whether Islamic law is capable of evolution and adaptation to changes particularly in a Muslim-majority state like Saudi Arabia where *Hanbalism/ Wahhabism* is the adopted Islamic School of thought.[7]

Part I

The theoretical framework and development of Islamic law

3.2 Basic sources of Islamic law

The *Qur'an* and the *Sunnah* are the two main sources of authority in both Islamic law and theology. Muslims believe that the *Qur'an* is the direct and unaltered word of God which came down by revelation to the Prophet Muhammad through the medium of the archangel Gabriel over a period of about 23 years[8] and was pronounced completed before Prophet Muhammad's death in 632 CE.[9] Generally, Muslims also hold that the *Qur'an* governs all aspects of life and serves as the main source of legislation.[10] This is evidenced by the *Qur'an* itself in different verses, such as:

> "... We have sent down to you the Book [*Qur'an*] explaining all things, a guide, a mercy, and glad tidings to Muslims".[11]

The *Sunnah*, on the other hand, consists of sayings, actions, and tacit approvals of Prophet Muhammad as narrated through his Companions in *Hadith*.[12] The *Qur'an* states that Prophet Muhammad is a model and exemplar to be emulated and followed by Muslims,[13] and confirms his practices (*Sunnah*) also as a source of law, reiterating in many verses that Muslims should "obey God and obey the Messenger".[14]

The *Qur'an* sets forth several general principles regarding how Muslims are to conduct themselves.[15] It is basically an ideal code of behaviour with a wider scope and purpose than a simple legal system. It is the source of the law, whereby

7 Motahari, A.M., *Jurisprudence and Its Principles* (translated by Tawhidi, S., edited by Bakhtiar, L.), New York: Elmhurst, 11373 (1980), pp. 5–6.
8 Iqbal, A., *The Culture of Islam (The Classical Period)* – Lahore: Institute of Islamic Culture (1981), p. 119.
9 Fisher, M.P., *Living Religions: An Encyclopaedia of the World's Faiths*, London: I.B. Tauris (1997), p. 338.
10 Doi, A.R., *Shari'ah: The Islamic Law*, London: Ta Ha Publishers Ltd (2008), p. 21.
11 *Qur'an* 16:89.
12 Motahari, A.M., supra note no. 7.
13 *Qur'an* 33:21.
14 See e.g. *Qur'an* 4:13; 4:59; 4:80; 5:92; 24:54; 33:71.
15 Kamali, M.H., supra note no. 1 at p. 43.

acts are measured by a particular scale of moral evaluation.[16] In classical Islamic legal theory, the *Qur'an* is the revealed will of God, a divinely ordained system preceding and not preceded by the Muslim state, controlling and not controlled by the Muslim state.[17] The legal essence of Islam was rooted in the revelation, as represented by the *Qur'an* and the guidelines of the Prophet.[18] The *Qur'an* establishes a structure putting Allah (God) and Allah alone as the Ultimate Law-giver. His rule is immediate, and His commands, as revealed to Muhammad, embody the Law and Constitution of the *Umma* (Muslim Community).[19] God is the Lawgiver and there can be no room in Islamic political theory for legislation or legislative powers, whether enjoyed by a temporal ruler or by any kind of assembly.[20] There can be no "sovereign state", in the sense that the state has the right of enacting its own law, though it may have some freedom in determining its constitutional structure.[21] The Law precedes the State, both logically and in terms of time; and the State exists for the sole purpose of maintaining and enforcing the Law.[22]

It follows that there are definite limits to speculation on constitutional organization. The function and general form of the State have been laid down once and for all, irrespective of historical circumstances, local traditions, political aptitudes, or other social factors. The minor details of application remain open to discussion, but the main principles of Islamic legislation are conceived as divinely ordained institutions, valid in all circumstances and for all time, and they cannot be questioned on penalty of heresy or sin. Should the Community deviate from these principles, it falls into error and exposes itself to the chastisement of God.[23] Thus, for many conservative Islamic legal theorists (*usulis*), the *Qur'an* represents a body of legal language to be interpreted strictly as commands, prohibitions, tropes, equivocations, and univocal, having only one meaning.[24] However, other scholars such as the renowned fourteenth-century

16 See for example Rahman, F., *The Major Themes of Qur'an* (2nd edn), Chicago: University of Chicago Press (2009); Akhtar, S., *The Qur'an and the Secular Mind: A Philosophy of Islam*, London: Routledge (2008).

17 Coulson, N.J., *A History of Islamic Law* (First Indian Reprint 1997), Edinburgh: Edinburgh University Press, Universal Law Publishing Co., Pvt. Ltd., pp. 1–2.

18 Izzi Dien, M., *Islamic Law from Historical Foundations to Contemporary Practice*, Edinburgh: Edinburgh University Press (2004), p. 1.

19 Gibb, H.A.R., *Constitutional Organization in Law in the Middle East, Origin and Development of Islamic Law* (edited by Khadduri, M., and Liebesny, H.J.) Vol. 1, Washington, DC: The Middle East Institute (1955), pp. 3–4.

20 Al-Muhairi, B.S.B.A., 'Islamisation and Modernization within The UAE Penal Law: Shari'ah in the Pre-Modern Period', *Arab Law Quarterly*, Vol. 10 (1995), p. 289.

21 Gibb, H.A.R, supra note no. 19 at p. 3.

22 Ibid.

23 Ibid.

24 Hallaq, W.B.,'The Primacy of the *Qur'an* in Shatibi's Legal Theory', Islamic Studies Presented to Charles J. Adams, in Hallaq, W.B., *Law and Legal Theory in Classical and Medieval Islam*, Great Britain: Ashgate Variorum (1994), eds Hallaq, W.B., and Little, D.P., Chapter XI, Leiden, 1991, p. 71

Islamic legal theorist Abu Ishaq Al-Shatibi, viewed the *Qur'an* as an integral whole revealed for the common good of humanity and capable of adaptation through *Ijtihad* to meet the welfare of humanity throughout time.[25] Wael Hallaq agrees with al-Shatibi's asserting that constructing *Shari'ah* in its all-embracing characteristics effectively transcends the boundaries set by the strict conservative scholars of *usul*.[26] Building on the views of renowned Islamic legal theorists such as Al-Shatibi, most Islamic jurists today have departed from a strict univocal interpretation of the *Qur'an* to a more contextualist interpretation to meet the needs of time as will be further analyzed in Section 3.2.

The *Sunnah* was a term traditionally and literally used by the Arabs in pre-Islamic era to denote the ancient and continuous practices of the community that were inherited from their forefathers.[27] When the word *Sunnah* is used as an adjunct to Prophet Muhammad in both linguistic and technical senses, it means what emanates from the Prophet in words, action, and whatever he has tacitly approved.[28] *Hadith*, on the other hand, literally means a narrative, communication, or news consisting of the factual account of an event. Although scholars have used *Sunnah* and *Hadith* almost interchangeably, the two terms are not strictly synonymous.[29] *Hadith* is the repository of the *Sunnah*,[30] with the former enshrining the latter.[31] *Hadith* differs from *Sunnah* in that the former is a narration of the conduct of the Prophet whereas the latter is the example or the law that is deduced from it. *Hadith* in this sense is the vehicle or the carrier of *Sunnah*, although *Sunnah* is a wider concept and used to be so especially before its literal meaning gave way to its juristic usage.[32]

The *Sunnah* as a source of law is justified by the *Qur'an* when it commands Muslims to follow Muhammad's words and actions.[33] During his lifetime, the Prophet reiterated that his traditions (along with the *Qur'an*) should be followed after his death.[34] Muslim jurists are unanimous that the *Sunnah* essentially supplements and clarifies the *Qur'an* as it contains rules regulating the behaviour expected of Muslims on which the *Qur'an* does not provide details. Thus, Muslims believe that they can follow the exemplary conducts and way of life or *Sunnah* of Muhammad and his Companions to discover what to imitate and what to avoid.[35]

25 See e.g. Masud, M.K., *Shatibi's Philosophy of Islamic Law*, New Delhi: Kitab Bhavan (2009).
26 Hallaq, W.B., supra, note no. 24 at pp. 71–90.
27 Kamali, M.H., supra note no. 1 at p. 58.
28 Hasaba Allah, A., *Usul Al-Tashri' Al-Islami*, Cairo: Dar Al-Ma'arif, (1985), pp. 253–254.
29 Kamali, M.H., supra note no. 1 at p. 61.
30 Azami, M.M., *Studies in Early Hadith Literature*, Indianapolis: American Trust Publications (1978), p. xvii.
31 Alfred Guillaume, M.A., *The Traditions of Islam*, Beirut: Khayats (1966), p. 10.
32 Kamali, M.H., supra note no. 1 at p. 61.
33 *Qur'an* 5:7.
34 Qadri, A. A., *Islamic Jurisprudence in the Modern World*, New Delhi: Taj Company (1986), p. 191.
35 Ibid.

Despite the well-established nature of the *Sunnah* as a source of Islamic law next only to the *Qur'an*, both classical and modern Islamic jurists appreciate the controversy associated with the authenticity of *Hadith* as the vehicle for the *Sunnah* and its proper ascription to the Prophet Muhammad. This will be further examined in Section 3.2.2.

3.2.1 The Qur'an *as the principal source of Islamic law*

Substantively, *Qur'an*ic injunctions are divided into three main categories, namely, *ahkam 'itiqadiyah* (those that deal with doctrinal matters), *ahkam khulqiyah* (those that deal with ethical matters), and *ahkam 'amaliyah* (those that deal with human conducts).[36] The third category comes under the comprehensive focus of *Qur'an*ic legislation with a view to attain its ultimate end through the mechanism of the Islamic jurisprudence.[37]

The principles that deal with human conducts in the *Qur'an* are divided into two, namely, those that provide guidelines on rituals. The rituals include performance of daily prayers, fasting in the month of Ramadhan, payment the Zakat annual dues, pilgrimage to Makkah and Madinah, devotion and dedication of an action or offer to God and oath-making, etc. These are acts of rituals which are private matters of an individual in maintaining relation with his Lord. The second are those that have to do with human conducts and inter-relations, in social, economic, political, and general human affairs. They also cover criminal, trans-national and international matters, wars, and conflict resolutions, among others. These are outside the purely religious scope. They mainly seek to regulate interaction between individuals and groups in their normal activities known as *Mu'amalaat.* Modern Muslim jurists classify these into *Al-Ahkam Al-Ahwal Al-Shakhasiyah* [Private (family) Law]; *Al-Ahkam Al-Madaniyah* (Municipal Law); *Al-Ahkam Al-Janaiyah* (Criminal and Penal Law); *Ahkam Al-Murafa'at* (Procedural Law); *Al-Ahkam Al-Dusturiyah* (Constitutional Law); *Al-Ahkam Al-Iqtisadiyah Walmaliyah* (Economic and Fiscal Law); and, *Al-Ahkam Al-Dauliyah* (International Law).[38]

There are two important academic points about the role of the *Qur'an* as the principal source of Islamic law, which must be briefly unpacked. The first is in respect of its beginnings as a source of law and the second is in respect of its interpretational approaches. Regarding the first point, there is a view in Western scholarship that the role of the *Qur'an* as the principal source of Islamic law was a later development in Islamic jurisprudence long after the death of Prophet Muhammad. For example Joseph Schacht adduced controversially in his seminal work titled *The Origins of Muhammadan Jurisprudence* that "[t]he Koran taken by itself ... can hardly be called the first and foremost basis of early [Islamic] legal

36 Khalaf, A.W., *'Ilm Usul Al-Fiqh*, Cairo: Dar Al-Qalam (1956), p. 32.
37 Ibid.
38 Ibid.

theory" and that "Muhammadan law did not derive directly from the Koran but developed ... out of popular and administrative practice under the Umaiyads".[39] All classical Muslim jurists and most modern Muslim jurists and non-Muslim Islamic scholars hold a contrary view on this. The role of the *Qur'an* as the principal source of Islamic law right from the time of the Prophet Muhammad is well established in classical Islamic legal and historical sources.[40] For example Wael Hallaq has strongly challenged Schacht and other Western scholar's view on this point arguing strongly on the basis of relevant evidences that "the *Qur'an* was a source of Islamic law since the early Makkah period when the Prophet Muhammad began to receive the Revelation".[41] Zafir Ansari has similarly analyzed in his article on "The Contribution of the *Qur'an* and the Prophet to the Development of Islamic Fiqh"[42] with relevant evidences on how the *Qur'an* had been the principal source of Islamic law from the time the Prophet Muhammad started receiving its revelation.

Regarding the second point, it is obvious that, similar to every source of law, the *Qur'an* despite its divine origin requires interpretation for its application. Prophet Muhammad was the principal source of interpreting the *Qur'an* during his lifetime, which eventually came to form part of the foundation for his *Sunnah*. However, after him the science of *Qur'an*ic interpretation (*ilm al-tafsir*) was initially developed by the early Muslim jurists to ensure consistent rules of *Qur'an*ic interpretation. This was eventually followed by different interpretational approaches under the classical rules of Islamic legal theory (*usul al-fiqh*) which was developed later. Mashood Baderin has noted in that regard that "Islamic legal theory identifies different approaches of *Qur'an*ic interpretation ranging from the literal or textual to the contextual approaches, which are still applicable today for the continued evolution of Islamic law".[43] In relation to the role of the *Qur'an* as the principal source of Islamic law Saeed has observed that today Muslims "are searching for a balance between 'traditional' ways of living and modern conditions" and that how "they approach this balance is often related to the way in which they interpret the *Qur'an*".[44] He then observed that today the interpretation of the *Qur'an* can be loosely grouped into one of main categories, namely, Textualists, Semi-textualists, or Contextualists. Most modern Muslim jurists and scholars today advocate for a contextualist interpretational approach of the *Qur'an* with regard to the different modern challenges

39 Schacht, J., *The Origins of Muhammadan Jurisprudence*, Oxford: The Clarendon Press, 1950, p. 224.

40 See e.g. Kamali, M.H., supra note no. 1 at p. 16.

41 Hallaq, W.B., 'Groundwork of the Moral Law: A New Look at the *Qur'an* and the Genesis of Sharia', *Islamic Law and Society*, Vol. 16 (2009), pp. 239–279 at 239.

42 Ansari, Z.I., The Contribution of the *Qur'an* and the Prophet to the Development of Islamic Fiqh', *Journal of Islamic Studies*, Vol. 3, No. 2 (1992), pp. 141–171.

43 Baderin, M.A., 'Islamic Legal Theory in Context' in Baderin, M.A. (ed), *Islamic Legal Theory*, Vol.1, Surrey: Ashgate Publishing Ltd. (2014), pp. xi–xxxvii, at xxiii.

44 Saeed, A., 'Some Reflections on the Contextualist Approach to Ethico-Legal Texts of the *Qur'an*', *Bulletin of the School of Oriental and African Studies*, Vol. 71 (2008), pp. 221–237, at 221.

facing Islamic law, particularly on issues relating to the application of international law in the Muslim world.[45] It is submitted that this is in conformity with the tradition of debate and scholarship that had characterized the development of Islamic law right from the beginning.[46]

3.2.2 The Sunnah *as the second source of Islamic law*

The *Sunnah* as the second source of Islamic law is based on narrations of the sayings, actions, and tacit approvals of the Prophet Muhammad, which are generally perceived by Muslims jurists as attributed to the Prophet himself on the authority of his Companions. It is however reported that the Prophet had generally discouraged his Companions from writing down his personal sayings and acts, so as not to confuse them with the divine texts of the *Qur'an*. Abu Sa'id Khudri reported that God Messenger said: "Do not take down anything from me, and he who took down anything from me except the *Qur'an*, he should efface that…"[47] Despite this discouragement, he did however instruct his followers to disseminate his sayings orally,[48] and as long as he was alive, any doubtful record could be cross-checked as true or false by simply asking him. There are historical accounts that the Companions did take note and conveyed his sayings and actions and some of them informally recorded them for their own private records.[49] After his death, these were preserved in both written and memorized form.[50] Umar ibn al-Khattab was said to have begun to collect all the *Hadiths* together into one unified volume soon after the Prophet's death, but later gave up the attempt so as to enable the Muslim community to focus its efforts more on the *Qur'an*.[51] There was similar attempt on the part of Umar ibn Abd al-Aziz who took steps to collect all the known *Hadiths* with a view to promote its teachings and to renew the moral fibre of the Muslim community.[52]

After the Prophet's death, ambiguities about his exact sayings and actions arose and in the course of time a great number of fabricated *Hadith* found their way into collections of prophetic sayings. The need then arose to separating genuine traditions from apocryphal material, which led to the emergence of the science of *Hadith (ulum al-Hadith*) as an independent discipline for the sifting

45 See e.g. Abu Sulayman, A.H., *Towards an Islamic Theory of International Relations: New Directions for Islamic Methodology and Thought* (2nd revised edn), Virginia: IIIT (1993).

46 Saeed, A., supra note no 44 at pp. 174–175.

47 Sahih Muslim Book 42, *Hadith* Number 7147.

48 The Prophet is reported to have instructed his companions: "Convey from me even if it is one verse" – Bukhari.

49 Badran, A.B., *Usul al-Fiqh al-Islami*, Alexandria: Mu'assasah Shabab al-Jami'ah (1402/1982), pp. 83–84.

50 Zubayr, S.M., *Hadith Literature*, Oxford: The Islamic Texts Society (1993), p. 6.

51 Ibid.

52 Ibid.

of *Hadiths* in the middle of the second century of Islam.[53] This was a method of textual criticism developed by the early Muslim jurists for determining the veracity of the reports attributed to the Prophet. This was achieved by analysing the text of the report, the scale of the report's transmission, the routes through which the report was transmitted, and the individual narrators involved in its transmission. It was on the basis of these criteria that various *Hadith* classifications developed.

The classification of *Hadith* into *sahih*, sound or authentic; *hasan*, good; and *da'if*, weak, was utilized early in *Hadith* scholarship by Ali Ibn al-Madini (161–234 AH).[54] This historic task was later taken over by al-Madini's student Muhammad al-Bukhari (810–870) who authored a collection, now known as *Sahih Bukhari* which is commonly accepted by Sunni scholars to be the most authentic collection of *Hadith*, followed by that of his student Muslim *ibn* al-Hajjaj.[55] The methodology introduced by Al-Bukhari for testing the authenticity of *Hadiths* and its transmission (*isnad*) are seen by Muslim scholars as exemplary in the development of *Hadith* scholarship.[56] However, Patricia Crone and Michael Cook have expressed some reservation about Al-Bukhari's methodology. They argue that one of the biggest problems with the method of authentication by *isnads* is that the early traditionalists were developing the conventions of the *isnad* simultaneously with the collection of *Hadith*. Thus they (traditionalists) either gave no *isnads* or gave *isnads* that were sketchy or deficient by later standards. They conclude that scholars who adhered strictly to the latest standards might find themselves rejecting or deprecating what was in fact the very earliest historical material, while accepting later, fabricated traditions that clothed themselves with impeccable *isnad*.[57]

Also, similar to his view on the *Qur'an* as the principal source of Islamic law, Schacht has again engaged with the question of the authenticity of *Hadith* as the second source of Islamic law in a 1949 article titled: "A Re-evaluation of Islamic Traditions",[58] which is one of early Western scholarship that critically engages with the subject. Building on earlier arguments of Ignaz Goldziheer, Schacht's advanced the view that *Hadiths* must be presumed unauthentic until proven otherwise. Arguing controversially that *Hadiths* were arbitrarily back-projected

53 Azami, M.M., *Studies in Early Hadith Literature*, American Trust Publication (1992), p. 217; Brown, J.A.C., *Hadith Muhammad Legacy and Modern World*, London: Oneworld Publication (2009), p. 77.

54 Al-Asqalani, A.I.A.H., *al-Nukat ala Kitab Ibn Al-Salah*, vol. 1, Maktabah al-Furqan, Ajman, U.A.E. (2nd edn) (2003), p. 263.

55 Ibn Kathir, *Iktisar Ulum al-Hadith*, published with explanation al-Baith al-*Hadith*, Vol. 1 (1st edn), Riyadh: Maktabah al-Ma'arif, Kingdom of Saudi Arabia (1996), pp. 102–103.

56 Ibid.

57 Crone, P., and Cook, M., *Hagarism: The Making of the Islamic World*, Cambridge, Cambridge University Press (1977), p. 7 ; quoted by Zubayr, S.M., supra note no. 50.

58 Schacht, J. 'A Revaluation of Islamic Traditions', *Journal of the Royal Asiatic Society of Great Britain and Ireland*, Vol. 2 (1949), pp. 143–154.

to Prophet Muhammad in ways that were not theoretically objective or historically reliable, he called for the abandonment of what he called

> the gratuitous assumptions that there existed originally an authentic core of information going back to the time of the Prophet, that spurious and tendentious additions were made to it in every succeeding generation, that many of these were eliminated by the criticism of *isnāds* as practiced by the Muhammadan scholars.[59]

Schacht's propositions about the authenticity of *Hadith* has been challenged by many Muslim and non-Muslim scholars on the subject. For example, in his book titled *On Schacht's Origins of Muhammadan Jurisprudence,*[60] Mustafa Al-Azami challenges Schacht approach and conclusions as untenable based on his own analysis and evidences from the most relevant literature on the subject. Similarly, Wael Hallaq in his article titled "The Authenticity of Prophetic *Hadith*: A Pseudo-problem",[61] observed that the issue of the authentic of *Hadith* constituted the most central problem that had occupied the Muslim specialists since the early classical period of Islamic law. He then challenged Schacht's propositions arguing that three main camps of scholars have emerged in response to Schacht's argument, namely: (i) those attempting to reconfirm Schacht's conclusions, and at times going beyond them; (ii) those trying to refute Schacht's conclusions; and (iii) those "seeking to create a middle, perhaps synthesized, position between the first two".[62] After a detailed analysis of the different academic perspectives on the subject, Wael Hallaq concluded that there is ample evidence from the literature that

> the early and medieval Muslim scholars espoused the view that the Prophetic *Hadīth* literature is substantially genuine, and that despite the relatively large scale forgery that took place in the early period, the literature, at least as it came to be constituted in the six so-called [Sunnī] canonical collections, has been successfully salvaged and finally proven to be authentic.[63]

Considering the arguments on both sides of the debate, and the relevant literature on the subject, it is submitted that the conclusions of Goldziher and Schacht on the authenticity of the *Sunnah* are difficult to sustain academically. And from the practical legal perspective the establishment of the *Sunnah* as a source of Islamic law is now established beyond reproach. Most modern Western scholars

59 Ibid, pp.146–147.

60 Azami, M.M, *On Schacht's Origins of Muhammadan Jurisprudence*, Oxford: OCIS (1996).

61 Hallaq, W., 'The Authenticity of Prophetic *Hadith*: A Pseudo-problem', *Studia Islamica*, Vol. 89 (1999), pp. 75–90.

62 Ibid, p. 76.

63 Ibid, pp. 76–77.

on the subject subscribe to the view that authentic *Hadiths* of the Prophet are established sources for the *Sunnah.*[64]

The effort of the scholars of *Hadith* who engaged in the exercise of verifying the authenticity of *Hadith* should not be under-estimated as they had handed down for posterity, a reliable collection.[65] Norman Anderson had noted that:

> in the course of time it became established that each tradition must include a chain of authorities through which it could be traced back to the actual Companions of the Prophet who were present on the occasion concerned, and traditions were classified and compiled according to the relative certainty with which they could be – or were – accepted as authentic.[66]

Therefore, in the words of Al-Ghunaimi, "the view that the *Hadith* included in the accepted Muslim sources, should be considered genuine until is proved otherwise"[67] should be accepted as a yardstick to determine the authenticity or otherwise of *Hadith.*

To establish the authenticity of a particular *Hadith*, it had to be checked by following the chain of transmission. The reporters had to cite their reference, and their reference's reference all the way back to the Prophet. All the references in the chain had to have a reputation for honesty and possessing a good retentive memory.[68] Biographical analysis (*`asmaʿ al-rijāl*), literally translated as "names of the men"), which contained details about the transmitter are properly investigated. This includes analysing their date and place of birth; familial connections; teachers and students; religiosity; moral behaviour; literary output; their travels; as well as their date of death. Based upon these criteria, the reliability (*thiqāt*) of the transmitter is assessed.[69] Also determined is whether the individual was actually able to transmit the report, which is deduced from their contemporaneity and geographical proximity with the other transmitters in the chain.[70] By this mechanism, *Hadith* are categorized into three, namely, (i) *Hadith* reported by an indefinite number of people in such a way as to preclude the possibility of their agreement to perpetuate a lie[71] (*mutawatir*), which are very widely known, and

64 Nagel, T., "*Hadis ya do Tarihin Imhasi*" [*Hadith* or Destruction of History] translated from German by Ali Dere, *Islami Arastirmalar* [Islamic Researches] X (1–2–3) (1997), p. 166.

65 Ibid at p. 114.

66 Anderson, J.N.D., 'Law as a Social Force in Islamic Culture and History', Chapter 20, *Bulletin of the School of Oriental and African Studies, University of London*, Vol. 20, No. 1/3 (1957), p. 15.

67 Al-Ghunaimi, M.T., *The Muslim Conception of International Law and the Western Approach*, The Hague: Martinus Nijhoff (1968), p. 114.

68 Berg, H. *The Development of Exegesis in Early Islam: The Authenticity of Muslim Literature from the Formative Period*, Richard, Surrey: Curzon (2001), p. 7; Cornell, V., *Voices of Islam*, Praeger Publishers (2007), p. 32.

69 Ibid.

70 Cornell, V., supra note no. 68 at p. 32.

71 Kamali, M.H., supra note no. 1 at p. 93.

backed up by numerous references; (ii) Widespread (*mashhur*), which are widely known, but backed up with few original references; and (iii) Isolated or Single (*wahid*), which are backed up by too few and often discontinuous references.[72]

The classification of *Sunnah* from viewpoint of reliability is divided into two, namely, *Maqbul* (i.e. accepted) and *Mardud* (i.e. rejected).[73] The accepted ones are classified into two, namely, *Sahih* (i.e. authentic) and *Hasan* (i.e. agreeable). *Mardud Hadith* are classified into two, namely, (a) a rejected *Hadith* that may be accepted if it acquires strength from another *Hadith*; and (b) a rejected *Hadith* that cannot be accepted at all.[74] *Da'if* (i.e. weak) *Hadith* is a variety under this category that is said to have inherent weaknesses in the chain of its transmitters or in its textual contents. *Sahih* or authentic is a *Hadith* with a continuous *isnad* all the way back to the Prophet, and whose narrators consist of upright persons who have retentive memories.[75] Hasan or agreeable *Hadith* is that which stands midway between *Sahih* and *Da'if*. Its narrators include people who are truthful and who are not known to have committed forgery or serious errors; or narrators who are though truthful but committed errors; and those whose narrations are accepted implying that there is no proof to the effect that their reports are unreliable.[76] *Da'if* or weak *Hadith* is one in which there are inherent weaknesses in the chain of transmitters or in its textual contents. Its narrator is known to have had a bad memory or his integrity and piety has been subjected to serious doubt.[77] Its varieties include *Mursal, Shadhdh, Munkar, Mudtarib, Mudall,* and *Maqlub*. A variety of *Mardud* can be considered here particularly the one that is rejected and cannot be accepted at all. These can be categorized under the *Da'if* class as: (i) *Mawdu'* which refers to a *Hadith* of an outright forgery and (ii) *Matruk* which is a report whose narrator is accused of lying and whose report is contrary to known principles.[78]

Thus, while the *Qur'an* is accepted by Muslims, *ipso facto,* as an undeniable divine source of Islamic law, the *Sunnah* as a source of Islamic law will depend first on the authenticity and reliability of the *Hadith* conveying any particular *Sunnah* according to the different rules elaborated above.

3.3 Secondary sources or methods of Islamic law

Initially, the period of the orthodox caliphs was governed by legislative procedures that were guided by the *Qur'an* and the *Sunnah*, the sources of that period,

72 Berg, H., *The Development of Exegesis in Early Islam: The Authenticity of Muslim Literature from the Formative Period*, East Sussex: Psychology Press (2000), p. 8.

73 Zubair, A.Q., *The Sunnah between Its Adherents and Adversaries*, Lagos: Madinah Heritage Publication (1995), p. 72 quoting Alfiyat al Suyuti fi 'Ilm al Hadith, (911 A.H.) Beirut: Dar Ibn Hazm Li Taba'a wa Nashr.

74 Ibid.

75 Kamali, M.H., supra note no. 1 at p. 110.

76 Ibid.

77 Kamali, M.H., supra note no. 1 at p. 111, quoting Siba'i, Al-*Sunnah* (n.d.), p. 95.

78 Kamali, M.H., ibid, quoting Isma'il, *Masadir* (n.d.) at pp. 200–201.

which prepared the ground for legislative culture that later led to the emergence of other secondary sources or methods for the consistent articulation of Islamic law.[79] As rules provided for in the primary sources do not explicitly deal with every conceivable eventuality, jurisprudence must refer to other resources and authentic methods to find the correct course of action and avoiding arbitrariness.[80] Consequently, Muslim jurists of the medieval period in a collective rise against arbitrary opinion evolved legal mechanisms known as juristic principles or doctrines to decide on issues over which the primary sources are silent,[81] or how to achieve proper grasp of directives stipulated in general terms in the two primary sources.[82] This move marked the beginning of the emergence of the secondary sources or methods of Islamic law which include, *inter alia*, *Ijma* (consensus), *Qiyas* (analogical reasoning), as well as legal principles such as *Istihisan* (juristic discretion), *Al-Maslahah al-Mursalah* (public interest), *istidlal* (inference), and, *Urf* (custom), and practice of the Muslim community.[83] The combined effects of all these led to the scholastic attempts to identify and analyze the purposes of the *Shari'ah* (*Maqasid Al-Shari'ah*) and, of course, the emergence of Islamic Schools of Jurisprudence.

3.4 Development of Islamic jurisprudence

As could be seen from the above, Islamic law is divine in origin and it is based on the divine command theory.[84] Nevertheless, it is flexible and adaptable to changes and its jurisprudence accommodates a pluralistic interpretation of its sources, which does produce differences in juristic opinions that can be quite significant in a comparative legal analysis. *Al-Shafi'i* remarked that

> *Qiyas* and *Ijtihad* represent the intellectual process whereby a finite body of revealed texts may be rendered relevant to the infinite complexity of human events. Every event has its necessary religious value (*hukm lazim*), and there is evidence as to the true path in that matter. It is incumbent on the Muslim if there is a specific ruling on a matter to follow it. If there is no specific ruling, then evidence as to the true path must be sought by *Ijtihad*.[85]

79 Izzi Dien, M., supra note no. 18 at p. 40.

80 Motahari, A.M., supra note no. 7.

81 John, M., 'Legal Logic and Equity in Islamic Law', *The American Journal of Comparative Law*, Vol. 33, No. 1 (1985), pp. 63–92.

82 Izzi Dien, M., supra note no. 18.

83 Ramadan, H. *Understanding Islamic Law: From Classical to Contemporary*, Rowman Altamira (2006), pp. 6–21; Johansen, B., *Contingency in a Sacred Law: Legal and Ethical Norma in the Muslim Fiqh*, Leiden: Brill Academic (1998), pp. 23–32.

84 Forte, D.F., *Studies in Islamic Law, Classical and Contemporary Application*, Maryland: Austin & Winfield, Publishers (1999), p. 14.

85 Calder, N., *Interpretation and Jurisprudence in Medieval Islam* (edited by Mojaddedi, J., and Rippin, A.), Farnham: Ashgate Variorum (2006), pp. 61–62.

The legislative process that makes Islamic legal system dynamic, its development historically outstanding, and its evolution in changing circumstances possible, is known in Islamic legal terminology as *Ijtihad*.[86] Literally it means "the expending of maximum effort in performance of an act"[87] or "the expending of effort and the exhaustion of all power".[88] In the technical sense however, it means the application by a jurist of all his faculties either in inferring the rules of *Shari'ah* from their sources, or in implementing such rules and applying them to particular issues.[89]

The enunciation of legal theories and principles which later crystalized into Islamic schools of thought demonstrates what *Ijtihad* represents in practical terms. During the formative period, until about the middle of the ninth-century AD, Islamic jurists had unfettered right and freedom to explore Islamic law to solving legal issues through the practice of *Ijtihad*,[90] until the idea of the so-called "closure of the door of *Ijtihad*" surfaced in around the tenth century.

3.5 *Ijtihad* in historical perspective

During the time of Prophet Muhammad, the Companions practiced *Ijtihad* but greater care was observed not to engage in the exercise of *ra'y* (opinion) at the expense of the basic texts.[91] The reason being that the possibility of violating the *Sunnah* at that point in time was greater, especially then, when *Hadith* had neither been compiled nor condensed.[92] Thus, jurists are in agreement that the *fatwa* of the Companions of the Prophet is a binding proof, and represents the most authoritative form of *Ijma'*. They even agreed that a *fatwa* of a single Companion should also be recognized as a proof and given precedence over proofs such as *Qiyas*, or the *fatwas* of other *Mujtahids*.[93] From this, it can be clearly established that the culture of exercising *Ijtihad* must have started right from the inception of Islam itself.

The concept of *Ijtihad* is often validated by reference to a *Hadith* that contains a discourse between the Prophet and one of his Companions, Muadh Ibn Jabl, when the latter was about to be sent to Yemen as a *qadi* (judge). The Prophet is reported to have asked him how he would decide matters that came before him. Muadh's reply was: "I will judge matters according to the *Qur'an*".

> If the Book of God contains nothing to guide me, I will acts on the precedents of the Prophet of God, and if it is not in that either, then I will make a personal effort (*Ijtihad*) and judge according to that.

86 Maududi, S.A.A., *The Islamic Law and Constitution*, New Delhi: Taj Company (1986), p. 76.

87 Ibid at p. 263.

88 Mahmassani, S.R., *Falsafah al-Tashri' fi 'l-Islam: The Philosophy of Jurisprudence in Islam* (translated by Farhat J. Ziadeh), Leiden: E.J. Brill (1961), p. 92.

89 Abu Zahrah, M., *Usul al-Fiqh*, Cairo: Dar al-Fikr al-'Arabi (1973), p. 301; Kamali, M.H., supra note no. 1.

90 Schacht, J., and Schacht, J., *An Introduction to Islamic Law*, Oxford: Clarendon Press (1982), at p. 70.

91 Kamali, M.H., supra note no. 1 at p. 332.

92 Ibid.

93 Ibid at p. 313.

The Prophet is said to have been most pleased at the reply.[94]

This process had continued after the Prophet's death and particularly during the *Khulafa Rashidun*[95] and the *Ummayad* period and was known as *Ijtihad al-ra'y*[96] an expression that occurs frequently in this early period. *Ijtihad* was linked with *ra'y* and was treated as a legitimate activity. The term carried the connotation of exerting one's efforts on behalf of the Muslim community and its interests (*al-Ijtihad fi sabil al-Muslimin*).[97]

From the second century of Islam onward *Ijtihad* was gradually dissociated from *ra'y*. Muhammad Ibn idris al-Shafi, the eponymous of the Shafi school of Islamic jurisprudence, was the first to make a break from *ra'y* and adopted *Ijtihad* as a methodology synonymous with *qiyas*, analogical deduction. Al-Shafi supported the idea of *Ijtihad* by reference to *Qur'an* 2:150 which provides that: "Wherever you go, face the Sacred Mosque, and wherever you are, turn your face towards it". Al-Shafi maintained that this required one to exercise one's intellect in identifying the direction of the Sacred Mosque. "Therefore, Allah Himself indirectly encourages us to exercise our faculty of reasoning, a great gift to mankind, to derive a logical conclusion on certain matters".[98]

Other accounts argue that it was Imam Abu Hanifa, when he started to work on *Usul al-fiqh*, who first found that there were matters on which there were no *Hadiths* or any comment from the Prophet's Companions. He then adopted the method of *Qiyas*.[99] However, other Sunni jurists did not recognize *Ijtihad al-ra'y* as being exclusively *qiyas*.[100] Other characteristics of *Ijtihad* including *Istihsan* (finding the good by one's own deliberation) and *Istislah* (determining what is in the interests of human welfare by one's own deliberations) were introduced later by the jurists. It has been, thus, argued that many of the opinions (*Ijtihad*) held by the Islamic jurists of the past including the Imams of the four Schools of thought were inherited from relevant authorities all going back to the lifetime of the Prophet Muhammad since the basic rule is that *Ijtihad* is inherently exercised within the scope of the *Qur'an* and *Sunnah*.[101]

One important consequence of the development of *Ijtihad* was the emergence of more than 500 different schools of Islamic legal reasoning in the early years after the death of the Prophet, most of which later disappeared and others merged together by the beginning of the tenth century. Subsequently, four main Sunni Schools of Islamic jurisprudence (*Madhahib*) were established in the early tenth century, namely, the Māliki School, named after Imam Malik, the Hanafi School

94 Abu Dawud, *Sunan* (Hasan's trans.), III, 109 *Hadith* no. 3585; see also Glasse, C., *The Concise Encyclopaedia of Islam*, England: Stacey International, New Edition (2003), p. 182.

95 Minhajuddin, M.M., *Islami Fiqh (Mukammal 3 Hissey)*, New Delhi: Al-Hasanat Books (2012), p. 23.

96 Schacht, J., *An Introduction to Islamic Law*, Oxford: Oxford University Press (1983), p. 37.

97 Ibid.

98 Doi, A.R., supra note no. 10 at p. 118.

99 Minhajuddin, M.M., supra note no. 95 at p. 25.

100 Ibid at p. 25.

101 Hallaq, W.B., *Authority, Continuity, and Change in Islamic Law*, Cambridge: Cambridge University Press (2001), p. 26.

named after Imam Abu Hanifah, the Shafi'i School named after Imam Shafi'i, and Hanbali School named after Imam Ibn Hanbal. Different Shi'i schools of jurisprudence also developed consequently. While all these Schools of Islamic jurisprudence acknowledged that the *Qur'an* and *Sunnah* are the main sources of Islamic law, they differed in their interpretational methods of the sources and application of the jurisprudential principles of Islamic law. This resulted in differences in their jurisprudential opinions on different issues in Islamic law, which was also influenced by the different circumstances prevailing in the different provinces where the Schools had developed and flourished at the time.[102] Today different Schools of Islamic jurisprudence prevail as major Schools in different Muslim-majority states, with the Hanbali School prevailing as the major School of Islamic jurisprudence in Saudi Arabia, which is the focus of this study. These will be further analyzed in Section 3.9.

3.6 The so-called closure of the gate of *Ijtihad*

By the late tenth century during the 'Abbasid dynasty, the schools of Islamic jurisprudence had fully emerged and Islamic law itself had approached the end of its formative phase. With active patronage of the government, the whole sphere of Islamic law had been brought to the horizon.[103] Shortly before then the question of *Ijtihad* and who was capable or qualified to exercise it arose contentiously.[104] The state and religious authorities fell apart on this, and thus, majority of jurists and scholars felt that all essential questions had been thoroughly examined and conclusively determined.[105] Another source argues that historically, in the early tenth century, the Islamic schools of law had advanced such that eminent *Sunni* jurists and scholars of that period were unanimous that all major themes of positive law had been thoroughly addressed, while at the same time, the detailed elaboration of the judicial system had grown steady resulting in legal stability that brought a progressive check and control on the scope of *Ijtihād*.[106] It was on account of this development that the general notion was created that jurists had agreed to the "so-called closure of the gate of *ijtihād*" at the time, which became widely prevalent in the narratives of Islamic law by both Muslims and Western scholars.[107] Be that as it may, unanimity unwittingly emerged to the effect that henceforth, no one might be eligible to form independent legal opinion – implying that all subsequent

102 See e.g. Makdisi, G., *The Rise of Colleges: Institutions of Learning in Islam and the West*, Edinburgh: Edinburgh University Press (1981), and Coulson, N., *A History of Islamic Law*, Edinburgh: Edinburgh University Press (1994) for some detailed discussion of the development of the Schools of Islamic Jurisprudence.

103 Schacht, J., supra note no. 96.

104 Ibid at p. 70.

105 Ibid.

106 Schacht, J., supra note no. 96.

107 Ibid.

activity would have to be restricted to the explanation, application, and, at the most, interpretation of the doctrine that had been laid down once and for all under the different established Schools of jurisprudence.[108] This marked the beginning of the notion of the so-called "closure of the door of *Ijtihad*" and implying the adoption of *taqlid*. *Taqlid* itself is a term accustomed to by the *Sunnites* who believe that the legal scholars of the early period were uniquely qualified to derive authoritative legal opinions, binding upon the whole Muslim community, from the basic sources of the law.[109] The term later came to mean the unquestioning acceptance of the doctrines espoused by the main Schools of Islamic law.[110]

Schacht argues that the first indications of this attitude which denied contemporary scholars the same liberty of reasoning as their predecessors had enjoyed are noticeable in *Shafi'i* School. And from about the middle of the third century of the *Hijrah* (ninth-century AD), the idea began to gain ground that only the great scholars of the past who could not be equalled, and not the epigones, had right to "independent reasoning".[111] Anderson, and others, similarly opined that about the end of the ninth century it was commonly accepted that the door of *Ijtihad* had become closed.[112] Gibb argued that the early Muslim scholars held that the door "was closed, never again to be reopened".[113] However, Watt doubted the accuracies in the standard account about this subject without himself suggesting an alternative view.[114] Some historical accounts relate the subject in explaining the immunity of the *Shari'ah* against government interference, while others use it to establish a link between the problem of decadence in Islamic institutions and culture.[115]

Against what appears to be the general and traditional position Wael Hallaq, argues that a systematic and chronological study of the original legal sources reveals that these views on the history of *Ijtihad* after the eighth century are entirely baseless and inaccurate.[116] He first noted that Western accounts of Islamic law is that the "door of *Ijtihad*" was closed in about the tenth century and that since then the *Shari'ah* has been unable to take account of changes through time

108 Hallaq, W.B., 'Was The Gate of Ijtihad Closed?', *International Journal of Middle East Studies*, Cambridge University Press, Vol. 16 (1984), p. 3.

109 The Editors of Encyclopaedia Britannica, *Taqlid: Islamic law*, www.britannica.com/EBchecked/topic/583236/taqlid (accessed 16 April 2015).

110 Hallaq, W.B., ibid.

111 Schacht, J., supra note no. 96.

112 Anderson, N.D., *Law Reform in the Muslim World*, London: University of London, Athlone Press (1976), p. 7. See also M. Khadduri, '*From Religious to National Law*,' in Thompson, J.H., and Reischauer, R.D. (eds), *Modernization of the Arab World*, New Jersey: Van Nostrand Princeton (1966), p. 41; F. Rahman, *Islam*, Chicago, IL (1966), pp. 77–78.

113 Gibb, H.A.R., *Modern Trends in Islam*, Chicago, IL University of Chicago Press (1947), p. 13.

114 Watt, W.M., "*The Closing of the Door of Ijtihad*" Orientalia Hispanica, I, Leiden: E.J. Brill (1974), 675–678.

115 Watt, W.M., *Islam and the Integration of Society*, Illinois: Evanston (1961), pp. 206–207, 242–243; H. Liebesny, 'Stability and Change in Islamic Law,' *Middle East Journal*, Vol. 21 (1967), p. 19; Coulson, supra at pp. 80–81; Schacht, supra at p. 75; Rahman, supra note no. 112 at pp. 77–78.

116 Hallaq, W.B., supra note no. 61 p. 4.

because it has lost its flexibility.[117] Contrary to this traditional view and agreeing with recent research,[118] he explains that *Ijtihad* in reality continued to exist after the tenth century.[119] Benjamin Jokisch holds a similar view.[120] Jokisch notes three interesting *fatawas* of Ibn Taymiyya in which he displays persuasively how the scholar reached new conclusions by employing different analogies and referring to some partial consensuses.[121]

Ijtihad, as a tool of legal development in Islam, brought a renewal to Muslim society over time as it became a religious duty of a *mujtahid* to decide legal rulings for the Muslim society.[122] In fact its exercise became a religious duty to the extent that a *mujtahid* who failed to do it was held to have committed sin.[123] Thus, Islamic law, which had, until the early Abbasid period been eminently adaptable and growing, became subjected to rigidity and put in a stagnating mould.[124] This is very obvious in a comparative assessment of Islamic law with other modern legal systems. Schacht maintains in this regard that taken as a whole, Islamic law reflects and fits the social and economic conditions of the early 'Abbasid period, but has grown more and more out of touch with the reality of later generation of the Muslims.[125] Modern Muslim scholars such as Muhammad Hashim Kamali,[126] Al-Tamawi,[127] and Abdur Rahman Doi[128] have all made the same observation. In dealing with the different challenges posed to Islamic law by the later developments of state and society, the practice of *Ijtihad* is being rejuvenated and modern Muslim scholars are looking back to different classical jurisprudential principles, especially, *Maqasid al-Shari'ah* (objectives of the *Shari'ah*), to liberate the development of Islamic law from the apparent shackles of literalism and stagnation it has fallen into as a consequence of the so-called "closure of the door of *Ijtihad*".

117 Goldziher, I., '*Muhammedanisches Recht in Theoric und Mirklickeit, Zietshrift fur vergleichende* Rechtswissenchaft, 8 (1989), pp. 406–423; Hallaq, W., 'Usul al-*Fiqh*: Beyond Tradition', *Journal of Islamic Studies*, Vol. 3 (1992), pp. 172–202, esp. p. 182.

118 Hallaq, W., ibid.

119 Jokisch, B., *Ijtihad in Ibn Taymiyya's fatawa' in 'Islamic Law, Theory and Practice* edited by Gleave, R., and Kermili, E., London and New York: I.B. Tauris Publishers (2001), p. 119.

120 See generally, Jokisch, B., *Islamic Imperial Law: Harun Al-Rashid's Codification Project*, Berlin: Walter de Gruyter (2007).

121 Jokisch, B. supra note no. 119, pp. 119–137 also, Jokisch, B., *Islamiches Recht in Theorie und Praxis, Analyse einiger kaufrechtlicher Fatawas von Taqi'd-Din Ahmad b. Taymiyyah*, Berlin (1996).

122 Esposito, J. "Ijtihad" *The Islamic World: Past and Present*, Oxford Islamic Studies Online http://oxfordislamicstudies.com/article/opr/t243/e150 (accessed 16 April 2015).

123 Ibid.

124 Schacht, J., supra note no. 59 at p. 75.

125 Schacht, J., ibid.

126 Kamali, M.H., supra note no. 1 at pp. 494–495.

127 Al-Tamawi, S.M., Al-Sultatt al-Thalath fi'l-Dasatir al-'Arabiyyah wa fi'l-Fikr al-Sihasi al-Islami (2nd edn), Cairo: Dar al-Fikr al-'Arabi (1973), p. 307.

128 Doi, A. R., *Basis of Shari'ah (Islamic Law)*, Zaria: Gaskiya Corporation (1983), p. 635.

3.7 The concept of *Maqasid al-Shari'ah*

One of the main goals of Islamic Jurisprudence is to provide a set of guidelines with a view to ensuring that *ra'y* (reason) plays a supportive role to the values of *wahy* (revelation).[129] In other words, it works towards achieving harmony and communality between revelation and reason. *Shari`ah is* fundamentally assertive of the benefits of the individual and that of the community. Rules under its system are thus, designed to protect these benefits with a view to facilitate improvement and perfection of the conditions of human life on earth.[130]

Principally, the inner dynamics of the *Qur'an* and *Sunnah* can be figured out in their assertion on principles of justice and equity, equality and truth; on commanding good and forbidding evil; on the promotion of benefit (*maslahah*) and prevention of harm; on charity and compassion; on fraternity and cooperation (*ta'awun*) among ethnic, tribal groups and nations of the world community; and on consultation (*Shura*) and government under the rule of law, mutual respect, and observance of rights of all.[131] Details of their guidelines expressed as *Shari'ah* are geared towards achieving these objectives. All these relate to the *maqasid* (objectives) of the *Shari'ah* which must always be borne in mind in the understanding and application of Shari'ah rather than mere literalism.

Abu 'Abd Allah al-Tirmidhi al-Hakim (d. 320/932) was first to use the term *maqasid* in his juristic writings in the early tenth century.[132] The term was repeatedly mentioned in works of Imam al-Haramayn al-Juwayni (d. 478/1085) who presumably was the first to classify this concept into the three categories, namely, essential, complementary, and desirable (*darruriyyat, hajiyyat, tahsiniyyat*) and which had enjoyed acceptance since that time.[133] At that early period, the literalists[134] traditional attitude was not much interested in the theory of *maqâsid al-Sharî'ah* and it was not until the time of *al-Ghazâlî* (d. 505/1111) and then *al-Shâtibi* (d. 790/1388) that significant developments were made in the formulation of the theory of *maqâsid*.

Al-Ghazali emphasized the importance of the *Maqasid al-Shari'ah* and the need to consider the revealed texts collectively to benefit from the spirit of the

129 Kamali, M.H., supra note no. 1 at p. 513.

130 Kamali, M.H., ibid.

131 Kamali, M.H., supra note no. 1.

132 Kamali, H.K., 'Maqasid al-Shari'ah Made Simple' (Occasional Papers Series 13), *IIIT*, London, Washington, DC (2008), p. 10.

133 Ibid.

134 Jurists and scholars of Zahiri school. The Early *zahiri* scholars include its founder Abu Dawud az-Zahiri (d. 270 AH) and Ibn Hazm (d. 456 AH). The zahiri school of fiqh is known for its strict adherence to texts and their apparent meanings. They have invalidated *qiyas* (analogy) – let alone other secondary sources of Shari`ah such as *istihsan, al-masalih al-mursalah, `urf*, etc. It is noted that though modern literalists do not accept to be described as "*zahiri*", they rigidly follow the spirit of the *zahiri* school in confining themselves to literal meanings of texts and disregarding their deeper meanings and objectives. See Shihab, W., *The Literalist (Zahiri) School: A Critical Review*, OnIslam, www.onislam.net/english/shariah/contemporary-issues/islamic-themes/449785-literalists-approach-and-complications-part1.html (accessed 15 April 2015).

law.[135] By this he opened an appealing new theory of the law for scholars to explore. Thus, those who followed him in this subject occupied themselves with the refinement of the theory of *maqasid*.[136] Similarly, Sadr al-Shari'ah, in his *al-Tawdih fi Hall al-Ghawamid al-Tanqih*, was fascinated with this theory and tried to assess the Hanafi position with respect to the *maqasid*.[137] It was, however, *al-Shatibi*, a Maliki jurist who built his extensive study on rules of interpretation around the principle of *maqasid al-Shari'ah*.[138] The combined effect of these juristic efforts has come a long way in refining the understanding of the *maqasid al-Shari'ah* and also revealed its significance for the Islamic community as a whole and for taking Islamic law forward progressively.[139]

Generally, the theoretical methodology of Islamic law is arguably explicit. But it is devoid of meaning if it lacks a human face. In other words, its literal rules must be given practical expression which it is fundamentally meant to be. The classification of the *maqasid* according to a number of dimensions demonstrates this practical expression. The dimensions include levels of necessity, scope of the rulings aiming to achieve specific purposes, scope of people included in purposes, and level of universality of the purposes.[140]

Al-Shatibi had advanced the concept of *maqasid al-Shariah* in promoting *maslahah* (human welfare) not only as the "basis of rationality and extendibility of Islamic law to changing circumstances but also presents it as a fundamental principle for the universality and certainty of Islamic law".[141] Against the background of the classical development and intended continued evolution of Islamic law, most modern Islamic jurists and scholars continue to advocate the concept of *maqasid al-Shariah* as one of the most important doctrines of Islamic law for ensuring the viability of the *Shari'ah* in modern times.[142]

3.8 The Schools of Islamic jurisprudence

As earlier mentioned briefly, the emergence of different Schools of Islamic jurisprudence was an important consequence of the early development of *Ijtihad*.

135 Al--Ghazali, A.H., *Al-Mustasfa min 'Ilm al-'Usul*, Vol. 1, Baghdad: Matba'at Muthanna (1870), pp. 286–287.

136 Nyazee, I.A.K., *Theories of Islamic Law*, Islamabad: Islamic Research Institute, International Islamic University, (2009), p. 225.

137 See Al Sadr al-*Shari'ah*, U.A.M.M., *al-Tawdih fi Hall al-Ghawamid al-Tanqih*, Cairo: Dar al-'Ahd al-Jadid li'l-Taba'ah (1377/1957); Nyazee, I.A.K., ibid.

138 See generally Al-Raysuni, A. Nazariyyat Al-Maqasid 'inda Al-Imam Al-Shatibi, Mansoura Egypt: Dar Al-Kalimah, (1997), p. 129.; Nyazee, I.A.K., ibid.

139 Nyazee, I.A.K., supra note no. 136.

140 Auda, J., *A System Approach*, Herndon, VI: IIIT (2008), p. 3.

141 Masud, M.K supra, note no. 25 at p. vi.

142 See e.g. Attia, G.E., *Toward Realization of the Higher Intents of Islamic Law*, Washington, DC: IIIT (2007).

Makdisi identifies three distinct stages in the evolution of these Schools,[143] namely, regional schools (when jurisprudents consciously identified their practice to that of some city or province), then personal schools (when jurisprudents identified their practice with that of some person), and finally guild schools (still personal but now having recognized local chiefs and claiming exclusive authority to regulate the teaching and practice of Islamic law).[144] The notable and surviving four Sunni schools of Islamic jurisprudence, namely, *Hanafi*, *Maliki*, *Shafi'i*, and *Hanbali* are named after jurisprudents of the eighth and ninth centuries AD, namely, Imam Abu Hanifa (d. 767), Imam Malik (d. 795), Imam Al-Shafi'i (d. 820), and Imam Ahmad ibn Hanbal (d. 855). They were the eponyms of the respective schools. Of all these four Sunni schools of Islamic jurisprudence, the *Hanbali* School was the most adhering to the literalist and textualist approach in both Islamic theology and Islamic law,[145] and it is the prevailing major School of Islamic jurisprudence in Saudi Arabia today.

3.8.1 The Hanbali School of Islamic jurisprudence

The importance of Hanbali School of Islamic jurisprudence to this study cannot be overemphasized as it is the officially adopted School in Saudi Arabia. It is therefore pertinent to do a brief appraisal of this School. Its founder was Imam Abu Abdullah Ahmad Ibn Muhammad Hanbal known as Ibn Hanbal and was born in Baghdad in November 780 AD (Muharram, 164AH)[146] He was versed in various Arabic and Islamic sciences as he travelled widely to different parts of the Islamic world searching for knowledge. With this characteristic, coupled with his uncompromising position against the inquisition instituted by the Abbasid al-Ma'mun, he became one of the notable and distinguished personalities of Islam of his time.[147] He studied *Hadith* under the tutelage of Hushaym (d. 183/799) who was known to be his first teacher.[148] Abdul al-Razzaq al-San'ani (d. 211/826) who was one of the most authoritative scholars of *Hadith* at that time was also Ibn Hanbal's teacher.[149] It is noted that Imam Malik's thoughts impacted Ibn Hanbali greatly even though he did not meet him. This is reflected in his works with abundant reference to Malik's treatises, especially his al-Muwatta.[150] He is said to have studied and committed to memory some of

143 Melchert, C., 'How Hanafism Came to Originate in Kufa and Traditionalism in Medina, Islamic Law', in Picken, G.N. (ed), *Critical Concepts in Islamic Studies*, Vol. II London and New York: Routledge Taylor and Francis Group (2011), pp. 311–312.

144 Makdisi, G., *Tabaqat-Biography: Law and Orthodoxy in Classical Islam*, Islamic Studies (Islamabad), xxxii (1993), pp. 371–396.

145 Melchert, C., supra note no. 143 at p. 311.

146 Khan, M.H., *The Schools of Islamic Jurisprudence (a Comparative Study)*, New Delhi: Kitab Bhavan (1997), p. 110.

147 Al-Matroudi, A.H., *The Hanbali School of Law and Ibn Taymiyyah, Conflict or Conciliation*, New York: Routledge (2006), p. 4.

148 Al-Dhahabi, *Tadhkirat al-Huffhz*, vol. 2, Beirut: Dar al-Kutub al-'Ilmiyyah (n.d.), p. 431.

149 Al-Matroudi, A.H., supra note no. 147 at p. 7.

150 Ibid.

Ahl al-Ra'y treatises as their methodology of Islamic law was prevalent in Iraq at his time. But later by reason of his preference for the method of *Ahl al-Hadith*, he abandoned these treatises.[151] Ibn Taymiyyah was quoted to have noted in this regard that: "Although Ibn Hanbal was from al-Basrah, he did not follow the method of this region in studying law; rather he studied according to the method of *Ahl al-Hadith*".[152]

As to whether Ibn Hanbali was a traditionist (Muhaddith) or a jurist, some accounts state that he was only a traditionist not a jurist, meaning that although he was a jurist, he could not be considered an imam in the field of jurisprudence. Ibn Jarir al-Tabari (310/923) subscribed to this viewpoint. This explains why Ibn Jarir did not mention him in his book *Ikhtilaf al-Fuqaha* but rather affirmed him only as a *MuHadith*.[153] Similarly, Qadi 'Iyad (d.544/1149) who was the leading scholar of the Maliki School also considered Ibn Hanbal to be below the rank of *imam* (leadership) in jurisprudence.[154] He was said to have not authored any independent treatise in the field of jurisprudence, whereas he wrote extensively on *Hadith*.[155]

Ibn Hanbali accepted *Ijma'* as a source of law but he rarely used this doctrine due to his strong dependence on the authority of *Hadith*. He held that *Ijma'* was more easy to be achieved in the age of the companions of the Prophet due to proximity and population size.[156] He however admitted that if at any point in time the need for it arises, and the requirements for its exercise are met, it might be possible.[157]

He allowed *Qiyas* merely under sheer necessity and always tried to derive law from traditional sources. In the Hanbali School, *Qiyas* is based on either on the *Qur'an*, *Hadith*, *Ijma*, or *Qiyas* itself.[158] For example, they accept the validity of *Qiyas* generally in matters which are rights of men like appraising the value of property destroyed by a trespasser and are ascertainable by exercise of human senses and reason. They held that any other view of analogy would virtually amount to making law which is the sole privilege of God.[159] Ibn Hanbal's work on *Hadith* is popularly known as "*Musnad Ahmad*" which was actually compiled by his son Abdallah from his lectures and was amplified by supplements (*Zawaid*). The book contained about 29,000 *Hadiths*.[160]

151 Ibid at p. 6.
152 Ibn Taymiyyah, *Majmu' Fatawa Ibn Taymiyyah*, vols. 10 and 20, Beirut: DKI , (n.d.) pp. 362 and 40 respectively.
153 Al-Matroudi, A.H., supra note no. 149 at p. 8.
154 Al-Tabari, M. *Ikhtilaf al-Fuqaha*, Beirut: Dar al-Kutub al-'Ilmiyyah (n.d.), pp. 10–16.
155 Al-Matroudi, A.H., supra note no. 149 at p. 9.
156 Khan, M.H., supra note no. 146 at p. 112.
157 Ibid.
158 Ibid at p. 113.
159 Ibid.
160 Ibid at p. 117.

3.8.2 The Wahhabi movement – a rejuvenating force of the Hanbali School

The *Hanbali* School began in Baghdad and later spread outside Iraq during the tenth century and as far as Egypt during twelfth century.[161] In the thirteenth and fourteenth centuries the school was rejuvenated through the scholastic efforts of Ibn Taymiyah and his pupil Ibn Qayyim al-Jawziyyah and their followers.[162] It was in the eighteenth century that this rejuvenation process began to receive new impetus through the reform movement of Sheikh Muhammad ibn Abdul Wahhab which was launched in Najd. As the movement achieved outstanding success in its reform bids, the Hanbali School spread anew throughout the Arabian Peninsula. It reached its peak during the reign of King 'Abdul Aziz Al-Saud in the first half of the twentieth century. Presently, the Hanbali School is the officially recognized school of jurisprudence in the Kingdom of Saudi Arabia.[163]

The Wahabi Movement emerged as a reformer movement with the aim of ridding Islamic societies of cultural practices and perceived "unorthodox" interpretations of Islamic law that had been acquired over the centuries. The followers of Sheikh Muhammad ibn Abdul Wahab (1703–1792) began it as a movement to cleanse the Arab Bedouins from the influences of Sufism.[164] Thus, they instituted a successful literalist reformist agenda in the religion of Islam in Arabia from the eighteenth century usually referred to as Wahhabism,[165] which continues to significantly influence the literalist interpretation and application of the Hanbali school jurisprudence in Saudi Arabia today.

Muhammad Ibn Abdul Wahhab launched his revivalist movement in Najd, then a thinly populated heart of Central Arabia, calling people to renounce the widespread practices that contradicted the basic tenets of Islamic faith such as "cult of saints", shrine worship and visitation of tombs.[166] In the course of this movement, he entered into a pact with Muhammad Ibn Saud, a local Sheikh and leader, contents of which stated *inter alia* that:

> Ibn Saud would protect and propagate the stern doctrines of the Wahhabi mission, which made the *Qur'an* the basis of government. In return, Abdul Wahhab would support the ruler, supplying him with 'glory and power'. Whoever championed his message, he promised, 'will, by means of it, rule lands and men'.[167]

161 Hallaq, W.B., *The Origins and Evolution of Islamic Law*, Cambridge University Press (2005), p. 177; and also Mahmassani, S., supra note no. 88 p. 32.
162 Mahmassani, S., ibid.
163 Ibid.
164 David, C., *The Wahhabi Mission and Saudi Arabia*, London: I.B. Tauris (2009), p. ix.
165 See al-Faqqi, M.H., *Athar al-Da'wah al-Wahhabiyyah*, Cairo: Al Maktabat Al Shamilat (1354 AH); see also Mahmassani, S., supra note no. 88 at pp. 32–33.
166 David, C., supra note no. 164, p. 7.
167 Robert, L., *Inside the Kingdom: Kings, Cleric, Modernists, Terrorists, and the Struggle for Saudi Arabia,* England: Penguin Books (2010), pp. 10–11.

This pact had been a reference point in the course of history and development of modern Saudi Arabia.

The families of the two men had expanded to become politico-religious empires. The house of Ibn Saud had continued to maintain its alliance with the Wahhabi sect which had grown tremendously beyond the Saudi territory. This alliance had led to the eventual proclamation of the Kingdom of Saudi Arabia in 1932. Also, true to this alliance, the doctrine promoted by Sheikh Abdul Wahhab and his disciples and followers had become state-sponsored and are the official form of Sunni Islam of Saudi Arabia till date.[168]

Consequent to a number of factors[169] coupled with the fortunes of oil boom, it is noted that

> .... the financial clout of Saudi Arabia had been amply demonstrated during the oil embargo against the United States, following the Arab-Israeli war of 1973. This show of international power, along with the nation's astronomical increase in wealth, allowed Saudi Arabia's puritanical, conservative Wahhabite faction to attain a preeminent position of strength in the global expression of Islam.[170]

The financial support of the government had enabled the School to spread rapidly since 1970s and it is said to have become a worldwide religious phenomenon.

It should be noted that the Wahhabi doctrine was based on the theological teachings of Ibn Taymiyyah and Ahmad Ibn Hanbal. This begs the question of what extent has the Wahhabi doctrine impacted the policy and legislation of the Saudi Arabia. Sheikh Abdul-Wahhab postulated that there are three objectives for Islamic rule and society, namely: "to believe in Allah, enjoin good behaviour, and forbid wrongdoing". This postulation had been repeatedly replicated in religious literature, sermons, *fatwa* rulings, and explications of religious doctrine. To that extent, he saw a role for the imam, "responsible for religious matters", and the *Amir*, "in charge of political and military issues".[171] Also, as part of this doctrine, Sheikh Abdul Wahhab postulated that the Muslim ruler is owed unquestioned allegiance as a religious obligation from his people so long as he leads the community according to the laws of God. Therefore, a Muslim must give an oath of allegiance (*bay'a*) to a Muslim ruler during his lifetime to ensure his redemption after death.[172] The scholars (*Ulema*) have the responsibility to

168 Cyril, G., *The New Encyclopedia of Islam*, United Kingdom: AltaMira Press (2001), p. 469.

169 Khaled, A.E.F., *The Great Theft: Wrestling Islam from the Extremists*, California: Harper San Francisco (2005), pp. 70–72.

170 Gilles, K., *Jihad: The Trail of Political Islam*, London: I.B. Tauris (2002), p. 61.

171 DeLong-Bas, N., *Wahhabi Islam: From Revival and Reform to Global Jihad* (1st edn), Oxford University Press (2008), pp. 34–35.

172 Elliott, H.K., *On Saudi Arabia: Its People, Past, Religion, Fault Lines and Future*, N.Y.: Knopf (2012), p. 27.

counsel the ruler and any counsel given in this regard should be private, not through public acts such as petitions, demonstrations.[173]

However, Commins David observes that "while this gives the king wide power, respecting *Shari'ah* does impose limits, such as giving qadis (Islamic judges) independence. This means not interfering in their deliberations, but also not codifying laws, following precedents or establishing a uniform system of law court – both of which violate the qadi's independence".[174] This postulation reflects the legislative policy of Saudi Arabia in its application of Islamic law as will be discussed shortly.

Part II

Application of Islamic law in Saudi Arabia

3.9 Saudi Arabia's legislative and judicial developments

From the above analysis, the question is: to what extent has Saudi Arabia sustained and preserved the classical notion of Islamic law as propounded by its adopted Hanbali/Wahhabi literalist approach, especially in view of the rapid economic and social development that had taken place in the country coupled with the sophisticated international relations it has maintained with Western oriented institutions in the decades following its abundant oil fortunes?

3.9.1 Saudi Arabia during the unification era (1932–1953)

The history of modern Saudi Arabia began with the unification of Hejaz and Nejd to form a new State now known as the Kingdom of Saudi Arabia. The name was given to this new State by its founder Abdulaziz Al-Saud (Ibn Saud). On the 17th of Jumada Al Ula 1351, a Royal Decree[175] was issued declaring all parts of the Kingdom united, under the name "Kingdom of Saudi Arabia".[176] This singular historical event had been the pillar and source of modern Saudi Arabia's basic system of government. It identifies the nature of the state and its goals and responsibilities, as well as the relationship between the government and its citizens. Taking into cognizance the fact that his young nation would need to adapt to the changing times to thrive and prosper, King Abdulaziz built the

173 David, C., supra note no. 164 p. 180; Mordechai, A., *Saudi Arabia: Government, Society and the Gulf Crisis*, London: Routledge (1993), pp. 191–194.

174 Ibid at p. 115.

175 Royal Decree of 23 September 1932.

176 Lewis, B., *The Crisis of Islam: Holy War and Unholy Terror* (1st edn), New York: Modern Library (2003), pp. xx–xxi.

foundation for a constitutional regime, thus establishing a modern government where once tribal rulers had reigned.[177]

As a King with absolute powers he performed three different roles simultaneously. First, he was the country's religious leader having declared himself as 'Imam'. This was the title King Fahd later changed to "the custodian of the two holy sanctuaries" (of Makkah and Medina).[178] Secondly, he performed the role of the traditional tribal chief who was expected to cater for the welfare of his subjects and who was expected to be accessible to them. Finally, he was the secular head of state and thus, he had the responsibility of leading the country in all aspects of life as a modern society that competes in a global economy.[179] In modern political parlance, he was the prime minister (head of the executive branch of the government). But he ruled by decrees in the absence of a parliament, and he influenced the judicial system through his ability to appoint and dismiss judges. As a result, the three branches of the government were not clearly separated.[180] Thus, in the judicial sector, he appointed judges in villages and cities and charged them with the administration of justice "according to *Shari'ah* as espoused in the *Qur'an, Sunnah, Ijma' and Qiyas*".[181] Decisions of the judges on capital punishment, for example, were to be reviewed and ratified by him before their enforcement.[182] It is noted that while the urban areas were observing the *Shari'ah,* the nomads operated the blend of *Shari'ah* and Arab customs. Hijaz's cities had more sophisticated legal structure of courts than those of other parts of the country.[183] Hanbali books of Islamic jurisprudence were officially specified as the authoritative source for the judges in deciding cases.[184]

3.9.2 *Saudi Arabia's oil fortune – a new beginning in foreign policy*

Prior to 1938, Saudi Arabia was one of the poorest nations of the world, relying only on little income derived from the limited agriculture produce and pilgrimage revenues.[185] Shortly afterward, vast oil reserves were discovered in the Al-Ahsa

177 Saudi Ministry of Information, *Government*, www.saudiembassy.net/about/country-information/government/ (accessed 17 April 2015).

178 Faour, M., *The Arab World After Desert Storm*, Washington D.C.: United States Institute of Peace Press (1993), pp. 43–45; Mackey, S., *The Saudis: Inside the Desert Kingdom*, New York: Meridian Book (1987), p. 206.

179 Al-Hamad, H.S., *The Legislative Process and the Development of Saudi Arabia*, A Dissertation Presented for PhD (Political Science) of the University of Southern California (1973), p. 84.

180 Ibid.

181 Ibid at p. 82.

182 Khair al-Din, A.Z., *Shabh al-Jazirah fi Ahd Al-Malik 'Abd al-'Aziz* (The Arabian Peninsula during the Reign of King Abd al-Aziz Al-Saud), Beirut: Dar Al Ilm Lil Malain (1390 AH/1970AD), pp. 421–423.

183 Ibid at p. 87.

184 Mahmassani, S., *Al-Awda' al-Tashriya fi al-Duwal al-'Arabiyyah: Madiha wa Hadiraha* (The Legislative Conditions in the Arab States: Past and Present), Beirut: Dar al-'Ulum Li al-Malayin (1965), pp. 433–434.

185 El Ghonemy, M.R., *Affluence and Poverty in the Middle East*, London: Psychology Press (1998), p. 56.

region along the coast of the Persian Gulf.[186] The full-scale of exploration of the oil fields began in 1941 under the US-controlled Arabian American Oil Company (ARAMCO). This development brought economic fortune and substantial political leverage internationally to Saudi Arabia.[187]

This had introduced a new dimension to Saudi foreign relations which was hitherto largely on the scale of religious brotherhood. It is argued that under King Abdul Aziz, foreigners were guaranteed equal protection under the *Shari'ah* for their lives, their kin, their properties, and their faith as well as keeping agreements with them.[188] From this period onward, Saudi Arabia's foreign relations, especially with West, had assumed a new focus of attention and a subject of academic research.

3.9.3 King Saud bin Abdulaziz Al Saud (1953–1964)

On assumption of power after his father, King Saud established numerous governmental ministries. He promulgated a Royal Decree in 1953 establishing a Saudi Arabia Council of Ministers. Between 1953 and 1964, he appointed eight ministers partly as a practical step to contain the fermenting demands for political participation among members of the royal family.[189] The Council of Ministers, in conjunction with the King, formed the executive and legislative branches of the government.[190] This was the first step taken towards formalizing the long-established Islamic system of popular consultation (*Majlis Al Shura*), which has always been practiced by Saudi rulers. The foreign policy of King Saud was a departure from his father's position of non-involvement.[191] Legislative and judicial systems of Saudi Arabia did not undergo significant development during this period due to political struggles that characterized the regime of King Saud bin Abdulaziz.[192]

3.9.4 King Faisal bin Abdulaziz Al Saud (1964–1975)

Shortly on assumption of power in 1964, King Faisal made a declaration in an emotional speech saying that: "I beg of you, brothers, to look upon me as both brother and servant. 'Majesty' is reserved to God alone and 'the throne' is the

186 See generally, Michael, M.Q., *In the Heart of the Desert: The Story of an Exploration Geologist and the Search for Oil in the Middle East*, Vermont: Green Mountain Press (2006). See also Mirza, M., *The Discovery of Oil in Saudi Arabia – Here Is the Story Presented in a Way You've Never Seen before* (2017), https://destinationksa.com/the-discovery-of-oil-in-saudi-arabia-here-is-the-story-presented-in-a-way-youve-never-seen-before/ (accessed 20 August, 2020).

187 Robert, B.S., *History of Arabia*, Encyclopaedia Britannica, www.britannica.com/EBchecked/topic/31568/history-of-Arabia (accessed 17 April 2015).

188 Anderson, J.N.D., *Changing Law in Developing Countries*, New York: Frederick A. Prager (1963), p. xii.

189 See generally Kechichian, J.A., *Succession in Saudi Arabia*, London: Palgrave Macmillan (2001).

190 Saudi Ministry of Information, *Government*, supra note no. 177.

191 Nehme, M.G., "Saudi Arabia 1950–80: Between Nationalism and Religion", *Middle Eastern Studies*, Vol. 30, No. 4, (1994), pp. 930–943.

192 For details see for example Joseph, K.A., *Succession in Saudi Arabia*, New York, Palgrave (2001).

throne of the Heavens and Earth".[193] In 1967, King Faisal created the post of second prime minister and appointed then Prince Fahd to this post.[194] He also introduced the country's current system of administrative regions, and laid the foundations for a modern welfare system. Another significant policy and legislative matter that King Faisal introduced was the abolition of slavery in 1962 on ground that it was difficult to guarantee the Islamic stipulation that kindness ever be shown to one's slaves.[195]

King Faisal's foreign policy was a continuation of the close alliance policy with the US which was adopted by his father and which relied heavily on the US for the supply of arms and providing training for his armed forces.[196] It was also anti-Communist policy.[197] He also maintained close relationships with western democracies including the United Kingdom.[198] His foreign policy leaned heavily towards the Pan-Arabism and Pan-Islamic movements. He played a significant role in the creation of the then Organization of Islamic Conference[199] having convened a conference in Rabat, Morocco to discuss the issue of Al-Aqsa Mosque in September 1969 which led to the creation of this Pan-Islamic Organization.[200]

When he was the Crown Prince and Prime Minister in 1958, Faisal had transformed the Council of Ministers into a legislative, executive, and administrative body with decision-making abilities. Most of the constitutional basics in the Kingdom were embedded in the Law of the Council of Ministers. Between 1959 and 1960, Faisal made a serious attempt to introduce modern constitutionalism into the Kingdom; however, this attempt did not go beyond the proposal phase.[201] However, many of the country's government ministries, agencies, and welfare administrations were developed during Faisal's reign (1964–1975); the Ministry of Justice is a case in point, having been established by his government in 1970.[202]

193 Zuhur, S. *Saudi Arabia*, California: ABC-CLIO, LLC (2011), p. 52.

194 Safran, S., *Saudi Arabia: The Ceaseless Quest for Security*, Itacha N. Y.: Cornell University Press (1985), p. 217.

195 See generally Nehme, M.G., supra note no. 91.

196 Bruce, R., "Brezhnev in the Hejaz", *The National Interest*, 115, ProQuest Research Library (2011), p. 32.

197 Ibid.

198 Pascal, M., *The Saudi Enigma: A History*, London: Zed Books (2005), p. 22.

199 It now known as Organization of Islamic Cooperation by virtue of 38th meeting of its Council of Foreign Ministers (CFM), which took place on June 28, 2011 in Astana, Kazakhstan.

200 Alexei, V., *King Faisal of Saudi Arabia, Personality, Faith and Times*, London: Saqi Books (2012), pp. 333–334.

201 Ansary, A., *A Brief Overview of the Saudi Arabia Legal System*, Hauser Global Law School Program, www.nyulawglobal.org/globalex/Saudi_Arabia.htm (accessed 19 April 2015); Ahmed H. Dahlan, *The Saudi Arabian Council of Ministers: Its Environment, Its Role and Its Future, in Politics, Administration and Development in Saudi Arabia*, edited by Dahlan, Ahmed H. (1990), 66–67.

202 Kostiner, C.E., et al., "Al-Suʿūdiyya, al-Mamlaka al-ʿArabiyya." *Encyclopaedia of Islam*, edited by Bearman, P., and Bianquis, Th., Brill, Brill Online (2007), http://referenceworks.brillonline.com/?fromBrillOnline=true (accessed 19 April 2015).

3.9.5 King Khalid Ibn Abdalaziz Al-Saudi (1975–1982)

Following the assassination of King Faisal, King Khalid assumed power in 1975.[203] He also became the *de facto* prime minister of Saudi Arabia.[204] King Khalid also introduced some policy reforms which included the creation of the ministry of municipal and rural affairs in 1975.[205] He appointed Prince Saud bin Faisal bin Abdulaziz Al Saud as the foreign affairs minister in 1975.[206]

3.9.6 King Fahd bin Abdulaziz Al Saud (1982–2005)

From the above analysis, it has been shown that Saudi Arabia has passed through developmental stages in term of state policy which covers different political, legislative, and judicial reforms. The combined effects of all these had laid the foundation for some form of modern constitutionalism, which translated into the adoption of the "Saudi Law of Governance" introduced by King Fahd in 1992. This development came to demonstrate a new development in the application of Islamic law in Saudi Arabia in the context of its response to the expectations of the modern nation-state vis-à-vis international law and foreign relations.

On 1 March 1992, King Fahd of Saudi Arabia issued a Royal Decree establishing a basic law of government for the country.[207] Article 1 of the Basic Law provides that the *Qur'an* and the *Sunnah* of the Prophet Muhammad are the Constitution[208] of the Kingdom and that the Islamic *Shari'ah* is the basis of its legal system. It follows that the Saudi Arabian government and the people are all equally bound by the law and the former's powers were derived from and defined by the divine law.[209] The Basic Law then creates several political and legislative organs for the enforcement of Islamic *Shari'ah* in the Kingdom.

3.9.6.1 Saudi King and Council of Ministers

By virtue of the provisions of Article 5 of the Basic Law, Saudi Arabia is a monarchy. The King is both a religious and secular leader. He is the "Imam" and

203 Reed, J., *The Saudi Royal Family*, New York: Infobase Publishing (2009), p. 60.

204 Federal Research Division, *Saudi Arabia: A Country Study*, Montana: Kessinger Publishing (2004), p. 11.

205 See generally Mordechai, A., *Saudi Arabia in the Oil Era: Regime and Elites: Conflict and Collaboration*, Kent, U.K.: Croom Helm (1988).

206 Sabri, S., *The House of Saudi in Commerce*, India: I.S. Publications Pvt., Ltd. (2001), p. 68.

207 Jerichow, A., *The Saudi File, People, Power, Politics*, Surrey: Curzon Press (1998), p. 10.

208 The capitalized version of "Constitution" refers to the fundamental document of Saudi Arabia's polity, i.e. the Holy *Qur'an*. This should not be confused with the lower case version, "constitution", which is the official term used to refer to the constitutive terms of reference establishing and governing the Council of Ministers. See Al-Farsy, F., *Modern and Tradition, the Saudi Equation*, London and New York: Kegan Paul International (1990), p. 39.

209 See Gibb, H.A.R., supra note no. 19, pp. 7–11.

source of power in this Kingdom.[210] It follows that the ultimate power and authority are vested in the King. However, his power is subject to the dictates of Islamic law.[211] The Council of Ministers exists under the Council of Ministers Law. Article 1 of the Law[212] provides that it is an organizational body headed by the King. Articles 7, 9, and 12 of the Law provide for the composition, official sessions, and terms of references of the Council.[213]

3.9.6.2 Saudi Shura (Consultative) Council

The *Shura* Council was created in 1992[214] under Articles 8 and 11 of the Basic Law. In its new form, the Council is an institution intended to exercise oversight functions, allow citizens to participate directly in the administration and planning of country policies, monitor the performance of its agencies, and open up the Saudi decision-making process to greater public scrutiny and accountability.[215] Article 1 of the Council law,[216] provides that it will exercise the duties assigned to it in accordance with the provisions of this Law and of the Basic Law (Constitution); and in so doing it shall observe the precepts of the Book of God and the *Sunnah* of His Apostle and preserve the ties of brotherhood and cooperation to do charity and observe piety. As its name suggests, the *Shoura* Council is the formal advisory body. It cannot pass or enforce laws, a power reserved for the King and the Council of Ministers.[217] However, Articles 17 and 18 suggest that the Council is capable of passing resolutions that can become laws by royal approval to that effect.

3.9.6.3 Council of Senior Ulama' (Religious Scholars)

The Council of Senior Religious Scholars (*Majlis Hay'at Kibar al-'Ulama*), is the highest religious body in Saudi Arabia consisting of Muslim jurists and scholars. It

210 Harari, M., *Government and Politics in the Middle East*, Englewood Cliffs, NJ: Prentice-Hall (1962) at p. 59.

211 Madani, M.O., *The Relationship between Saudi Arabia Domestic Law and International Law: A Study of the Oil Agreement with Foreign Companies*, A Dissertation Submitted to the Faculty of the Law School of The George Washington University in Partial Satisfaction of the Requirements for the Degree of Doctor of Juridical Science (1970), p. 8.

212 Dated 20 August 1992.

213 Article 14 of the Council of Ministers Law.

214 *See* The Basic System of Governance, art. 68. The Basic System of Governance, Royal Order No. A/90 (27/8/1412H, 1 March 1992), O.G. Umm al-Qura No. 3397 (2/9/1412H, 5 March 1992).; The Regional Law, Royal Order No. A/91 (27/8/1412H, 1 March 1992), O.G. Umm al-Qura No. 3397 (2/9/1412H, 5 March 1992); The Shoura Council Law, Royal Order No. A/91 (27/8/1412H, 1 March 1992), O.G. Umm al-Qura No. 3397 (2/9/1412H, 5 March 1992).

215 Ayoub M. al-Jarbou, *Judicial Review of Administrative Actions: A Comparative Study between the United States and Saudi Arabia* 129 – 130 (unpublished S.J.D. dissertation, University of Virginia) (in file with author) (2002), pp. 120–121.

216 Royal Order No. A/19 dated 27 Shaaban 1412 AH.

217 See generally Wilson, P.W., and Graham, D., *Saudi Arabia: The Coming Storm*, Armonk, New York: Routledge (1994).

was established by a Royal Decree of 1971.[218] It advises the King, who is responsible for the appointment of its membership, on religious matters.[219] Members of the Council are on government salary, and as of 2009, the council was made up of 21 members.[220] In 2010, King Abdullah decreed that only members of the Council and a few other Islamic authorities could issue *fataawa* (juristic opinions) in Saudi Arabia.[221] Before its establishment in 1971, the council met informally under the leadership of the Grand Mufti.[222] The Council provides expert opinion in matters of legislations and policies. For example, in 2011, the Council issued a *fatwa* condemning demonstrations describing those involved in such demonstration as "deviant intellectual and partisan connections".[223] Until 2009, membership of this council was restricted to jurists and scholars of the Hanbali School; however, in the first half of that year, its membership was expanded to include jurists and scholars of the other three Sunni Schools, namely, *Shafi'i*, *Hanafi*, and *Maliki*.[224]

3.9.6.4 Supreme Judicial Council

Under Article 51 of the Saudi Basic Law, the Saudi Arabian judiciary is governed by a Supreme Judicial Council.[225] The jurisdiction of this Council is extensive covering varieties of judicial matters. The Judiciary Act conferred upon *Shari'ah* courts general jurisdiction over all judicial matters such as criminal, civil, property and matrimonial claims, etc. The introduction of the Ministry of Justice is a fairly recent development, dating back only to 1970.[226] It is noted that by the time the Ministry came on board, the courts have become strong and autonomous.[227] Traditionally the Minister of Justice is appointed from the body of religious scholars in the Kingdom and thus retains the respect of the *Shari'ah* judiciary.[228] Article 5 of the Law[229] provides for the composition of the judges

218 Royal Decree, No. 137/1 dated 08/07/1391 AH / (29/08/1971 CE).

219 Wilson, P.W., and Graham, D.R., supra note no. 217 at pp. 26–27.

220 Boucek, C., 'Saudi Fatwa Restrictions and the State-Clerical Relationship', *SADA* (2010), http://carnegieendowment.org/2010/10/27/saudi-fatwa-restrictions-and-state-clerical-relationship/6b81 (accessed 01 December 2014).

221 Ibid.

222 Wilson, P.W., and Graham, D.R., supra note no. 217.

223 Saliba, I., 'Saudi Arabia: The Regime Invokes Sharia Law to Prevent Public Protest', *The Law Library of Congress* (2011), www.loc.gov/lawweb/servlet/lloc_news?disp2_l205402565_text (accessed 01 December 2014).

224 Boucek, C., supra note no. 220.

225 See Article 6 of the Royal Decree No.M/64, 14 Rajab 1395 [23 July 1975] Umm al-Qura No.2592, 29 Sha'ban 1395 [5 September 1975.] Brown, N.J., Arab Judicial Structures, A Study Presented To The United Nations Development Program, www.undp-pogar.org/publications/judiciary/nbrown/saudi.html (accessed 16 June 2012).

226 Brown, N.J. (UNDP), ibid.

227 Ibid.

228 Ibid.

229 Royal Decree No.M/64, 14 Rajab 1395 [23 July 1975] Umm al-Qura No.2592, 29 Sha'ban 1395 [5 September 1975.]

of the *Shari'ah* Courts and their general jurisdiction. Article 6 provides for the composition of membership of the Council itself while Article 7 specifies the functions of the Council.

Despite the provisions of Article 1 of the Saudi Basic Law, it can be argued that the establishment and procedures of all the above organs are not based strictly on a textualist approach to Islamic law but takes into consideration the administrative needs of modern governance, which are not necessarily and specifically provided for in classical Hanbali jurisprudence. A similar conclusion can be drawn from the country's legislative enactments and evolution of its legal and judicial system. For example, Article 81 of the Basic Law of Governance provides that: "The enforcement of this law shall not prejudice whatever treaties and agreements with states and international organizations and agencies to which the Kingdom of Saudi Arabia is committed". Some of these treaties and agreements contain some subject matters that are ordinarily considered to be repugnant to Islamic law under classical Hanbali jurisprudence. For example, the International Monetary Fund agreement[230] contains the issue of *Riba,* which ostensibly is considered prohibited in the literal interpretation of the Hanbali School as will be discussed later in Chapter 6 of this book.

3.10 The Saudi Arabian legislative and judicial systems

It has been argued that in spite of the Hanbali School's traditional posture as the most conservative and restrictive of the four main Sunni legal schools, its classical jurisprudence is, in some respects, found to be more liberal than the other schools on certain subject matters.[231] This is evidenced by its far-reaching reliance on consideration of public interest in some situations.[232] For example, Imam Hanbali was said to have issued a verdict making it permissible to compel the owner of a large house to give shelter to the homeless.[233] Similarly, the principle of permissibility under Hanbali law was said to form the basis for unilateral obligation, which means that the individual is free to commit himself or herself in all situations in which this principle is applicable.[234] It follows that a man may validly stipulate in a marriage contract that he will not marry a second wife.[235] The reasoning was that polygyny is only permissible (that is, it is not mandatory)

230 Adopted at the United Nations Monetary and Financial Conference, Bretton Woods, New Hampshire, July 22, 1944 and entered into force December 27, 1945, www.imf.org/external/pubs/ft/aa/pdf/aa.pdf (accessed 19 April 2015).

231 Kamali, M.H., *Law and Society: The Interplay of Revelation and Reason in the Shari'ah.* From Oxford History of Islam, Oxford University Press (2000), www.acc.teachmideast.org/texts.php?module_id (accessed 25 June 2012).

232 Kamali, M.H., ibid.

233 Ibid.

234 Kamali, M.H., *Law and Society: The Interplay of Revelation and Reason in the Shari'ah,* Oxford History of Islam, Oxford: Oxford University Press (2000). http://acc.teachmideast.org/texts.php?module_id=2&reading_id=210&sequence=5 (accessed 19 April 2015).

235 Ibid.

under the *Shari'ah*, the individual is free to make it the subject of stipulation.[236] Some other schools rejected this position arguing that the *Shari'ah* has made polygyny lawful, a position that should not be circumvented or nullified through contractual stipulations.[237] This explains why a cross section of jurists of Hanbali School like Ibn Taymiyyah appeared to have exhibited a degree of liberality in some of their interpretations of Islamic jurisprudence. Therefore, the rigid and conservative posture of the Hanbali School officially applicable in Saudi Arabia can certainly be called to question. That conservative posture has been influenced by the eighteenth-century Wahhabi movement of Sheikh Muhammad Ibn Abd al-Wahab due to some historical factors earlier discussed in this chapter.[238]

With respect of the evolution of Islamic law generally, the reality of modern times, it has been noted, is that liberal legal interpretation of the *Shari'ah* has manifested itself in three ways, namely, statutory legislation, judicial decision and learned opinion (*fatawa)*, and of course, scholarly writings.[239] Coulson referred to this as "neo-*Ijtihad*".[240] This has also manifested itself in modern Saudi Arabia despite the official adoption of the strict *Hanbali* School of Islamic jurisprudence. Generally, the *Hanbali* literalist interpretation of the *Shari'ah* is the applicable law in Saudi Arabia. The interpretations of the other three *Sunni* schools of law could be consulted only under two conditions: 1) where the *Hanbali* School has no specific rule applicable to the situation at hand; or 2) where the available *Hanbali* applicable rules might not do enough justice to the issue at hand or protect the interest of the public.[241] However, despite Saudi Arabia's traditional approach, new developments have made it imperative to introduce modern systems of enacting statutory regulations. This has been through the legislative mechanism of Royal Decrees, Ministerial Resolutions, or Administrative Circulars covering diverse fields of activities including business, banking, labour, social security and arbitration, and even human rights issues, among others.[242]

3.10.1 The Saudi judiciary and freedom of Ijtihad

During the reign of King Abdul Aziz, founder of the modern Saudi Arabia, three categories of courts existed and located in three local regions of the Kingdom, namely, the Hijaz, Najd (around Riyadh), and a number of local tribal areas

236 Ibid.
237 Ibid.
238 See paragraph on 'Saudi Arabia's Oil Fortune – a New Beginning in Foreign Policy.'
239 Kamali, H.H., supra note no. 1 at its note no. 206.
240 See Coulson, N.J., supra note no. 102.
241 Al-Duraibi, S., *Judicial Systemization in the Kingdom of Saudi Arabia*, Riyadh: Hanifa Press (1430H, 1982), at pp. 313–314.
242 Al-Ghadyan, A., 'The Judiciary in Saudi Arabia', *Arab Law Quarterly*, Vol. 13, No. 3 (1998), p. 235.

where dispute resolution was based on their local customs.[243] The court system in the Hijaz region was said to be more organized than in other areas, due partly to modernization carried out by the Turkish Ottoman Kingdom.[244] This reform was sadly checkmated by Sharif Husain, the Hijaz ruler at the beginning of the twentieth century.[245] The Najd region's judicial system followed the traditional method which was based on the prevailing customs and religious laws and which had been handed down by the successive generations.[246] According to this system, which had remained unreformed, dispute resolution was carried out by a judge and *Amir* (King or his descendants who became rulers) in the interests of the disputing parties.[247]

In 1927 the existing three-tier judicial system was abolished.[248] All the courts were merged into one judicial system. The relevant Decree classified judicial institutions into three degrees, namely, Expeditious Courts (*al-Mahakim al-Musta'jilah*), *Shari'ah* Courts (*al-Mahakim Ash-Shari'yyah*), and the Commission on Judicial Supervision (*Hay'ah al-Muraqabah al-Qadha'iyyah*).[249]

As *Shari'ah* is the applicable law in all judicial matters in Saudi Arabia, it is officially specified that it should be applied according to the *Hanbali* School of jurisprudence.[250] In the absence of applicable rule in this school, or if the application of some rules of the school are not in the interest of the public, the other three Sunni schools of jurisprudence (*Hanafi, Shafi'i' and Maliki*) can be consulted.[251] The courts and the single judges were assigned six *Hanbali* books to draw upon in rendering judgments.[252] It was an important move in unifying the judiciary since hitherto, the prevailing schools were the *Hanafi* and the *Shafi'i* in the Hijaz and the *Hanbali* in Najd.[253] It should be noted again that judges could have recourse to the other three schools of law and to their own reasoning in cases where no provisions were provided in the six books.[254]

243 Ka'bah,R.,www.badilag.net/english/DATA/Contemporary%20Islamic%20Court%20System.pdf (accessed 19 September 2012).

244 Az-Zuahaili, M., *at-Tanzhim al-Qadha'l fi al-Fiqh al-Islami*, Damascus: Dar al-Fikr (1423H/2002), p. 218.

245 Ibid.

246 Ibid.

247.Ibid.

248 Royal Decree (*al-Marsum al-Maliki)* dated 4 Safar 1346/1927; Ka'bah, R., supra note no. 243.

249 Majimuat al-Nuzum, Makkah: Umm al-Qura Press (1938), pp. 9–12 and Ka'bah, R., ibid.

250 Al-Ghadyan, A.A., supra note no. 242, p. 235.

251 Saud al-Duraib, *Judicial Systemization in the Kingdom of Saudi Arabia*, Riyadh: Hanifah Press (1430H – 1982), at pp. 313–314.

252 Fuad Hamza, al-Biid al-'Arabiyyah al-Sa'udiyya, Riyadh: Maktabat al-Nasra l-*Hadith*ah (1968), p. 197.

253 Solaim, S.A., Constitutional and Judicial Organization in Saudi Arabia, Unpublished Ph.D. Dissertation, John Hopkins University (1970), pp. 46–68.

254 Ibid and also *Hamza B. Abdu v. Muhammad b. Hassan*, The High Court of Mecca: Case No. 225, vol. 8 (1376 AH 1956 AD) to be discussed shortly.

Judicially, the court was required to apply the *responsa* in certain classical *Hanbali* books.[255] It has been observed that this restriction has not prevented the court from practising some degree of *'Ijtihad* so that a judge may result in adopting the opinion of a *Hanbali* scholar different from the one indicated by the official judicial references.[256] Similarly, Article 6 of the relevant law[257] stated that the Judicial Board of Scrutiny can only object to a decision taken by a court if this decision does not comply with the *Qur'an*, the *Sunnah*, and *'Ijma'*. Thus, the door is wide opened for the possibility of *'Ijtihad,* giving liberty to apply legal opinions of any Islamic School of jurisprudence relevant to the particular case, provided it does not contradict the main sources, namely, the *Qur'an,* the *Sunnah*, and the *'Ijma*.[258]

In the 1956 case of *Hamzah b. Abdu* v. *Muhammad b. Hassan,* the court refrained from applying a classical *Hanbali* rule which stipulates that the father – or in his absence his *wasi,* i.e., executor to marital matters – has the right to conclude the marriage contract of his virgin daughter regardless of her age or consent, for the father is granted the so-called power of compulsion over his virgin daughter in matters of marriage. Consequently, it is merely desirable, but not obligatory for the father to secure the daughter's permission.[259]

Similarly, a classical *Hanbali* rule on child custody was put to test in another 1956 case of *Abdu Qadir v. Suhan.*[260] The court departed from the established *Hanbali* rule and adopted a liberal position of *'Ibn al-Qayyim*, though a jurist of *Hanbali* School of Thought.[261] In the 1960 case of *Bagazi v. 'Awwad,*[262] though, the Saudi court departed from the decision in *Abdul-Qadir v. Suhan* but based its ruling on liberal interpretation.

Another classical Hanbali view stipulates that in the contracts of leases of agricultural land, it is the responsibility of the landlord to provide land, seed, and plants which are indivisible in the contract of *'al-Muzara'a.* This is a contract in which one provides land and seed to a labourer who will work on the land in return for a fixed percentage of its product.[263] The contract becomes void if the seed or the plants are provided by the worker alone or jointly with the landlord.[264] This principle was jettisoned by the Saudi court in *Nura bint*

255 Ahmad 'Ali, M.I., and Abu Sulaiman, A.W., 'Recent Judicial Development in Saudi Arabia', *Journal of Islamic and Comparative Law,* Centre of Islamic Legal Studies, Faculty of Law, Ahmadu Bello University, Zaria, Nigeria, Vol. 3 (1969), p. 12.

256 Ahmad 'Ali, M.I., and Abu Sulaiman, A.W., ibid.

257 Royal Decree dated 20/10/81, Cabinet Decree No. 16-3-3136.

258 Ahmad 'Ali, M.I., and Abu Sulaiman, A.W. supra note no. 255.

259 See Al-Bahuti: Kashshaf: vol 3, p. 23 as quoted by Ahmad 'Ali, M.I., and Abu Sulaiman, A.W., ibid.

260 The High Court of Mecca: Case No. 53, vol. 46 (1375 AH, 1956 AD).

261 See Ibn al-Qayyim: Zad al-Ma'ad, vol. 4, pp. 191–192, also Al-Bahurti, *Sharh Al-Muntaha*, vol. 3, p. 364, Ahmad 'Ali, M.I., and Abu Sulaiman, A.W., ibid.

262 The High Court of Makkah: Case No. 83, vol. 1 (1380 AH, – 1960 AD).

263 Ahmad 'Ali, M.I., and Abu Sulaiman, A.W., supra note no. 255.

264 See al-Muntaha, vol. 2. p. 348; Ahmad 'Ali, M.I., and Abu Sulaiman, A.W., ibid.

Salih al-ʿUmairi and Husn bint Muslih'Imairi v. Abdul-Qadir al-Kiraidimi.[265] The court based its ruling on Ibn Qudama's view that, no matter who provides the seed or the plants, the validity of the contract is not vitiated.[266] A liberal approach was also demonstrated in the case of *Zalikha* and *Barnawi.*[267]

The above cases show that the Saudi Arabian judiciary had identified, as early as the 1950s, the inevitable need to be flexible and proactive in adopting, where necessary, a liberal approach in the interpretation of the basic sources of law if such interpretations do not run counter to the basic sources.[268]

3.11 1975 reform of Saudi Arabian judiciary

The Law of the Judiciary[269] promulgated in 1975 was aimed at reforming the Saudi judicial system. The Act contains sections covering various aspects of the judicial system, such as rules guaranteeing the independence and impartiality of the courts, the hierarchies of courts and their jurisdiction, the judges, their appointment and promotions, the role of the Ministry of Justice, etc.[270] It established a hierarchy of courts including the Supreme Judicial Council (SJC) and others along modern trends.

Under this new law the Supreme Judicial Council (SJC) was conferred with both legislative and judicial powers. Article 8 of the law provides that in addition to the function set forth in this Law, the Council shall (1) look into such *Shari'a*h questions as in the opinion of the Minister of Justice, require the statement of general *Shari'ah* principles; (2) look into issues which, in the opinion of the King, require that they be reviewed by the Council; provide opinions on issue related to the judiciary at the request of the Minister of Justice; and (3) review death, amputation, or stoning sentences. Under its judicial powers, decisions of the SJC on cases referred to it from the Court of Appeal are binding on all other lower courts including the Court of Appeal itself.[271]

Under Article 89 of the Act, a department was created within the Ministry of Justice and saddled with the responsibility of collecting and collating decisions of all hierarchies of courts with a view to study and classify them and refer them to the SJC for proper scrutiny. The latter has the power to ratify or reject or amend such decisions where necessary.

The Law contains 12 articles on the reform of the Appellate Courts.[272] It provides *inter alia* that the Appellate Court shall be composed of a Chief Judge

265 High Court of Makkah: Case No. 258 vol. 7, p. 187.

266 See Al-Mughni, vol. 5, p. 388; Ahmad 'Ali, M.I., and Abu Sulaiman, A.W., supra note no. 255 at p. 19.

267 High Court of Makkah, vol. 1, No. 105, 1963.

268 Ahmad 'Ali, M.I., and Abu Sulaiman, A.W., supra p. 12.

269 Royal Decree No. 64/M dated 14/7/1395H (21/7/1975. See Um Al-~Qura Gazette, issue No. 2592 of 29/8/1395H.

270 Al-Ghadyan, A.A., supra note no. 242 at p. 236.

271 See Article 14 of the Judiciary Act 1395H (1975).

272 Articles 10–21.

and a sufficient number of judges from among whom deputy chief judges shall be designated as needed and in the order of absolute seniority in the service.[273] It also provides that the deputies of the Chief Judge of the Appellate Court shall be appointed by decision of the Minister of Justice on the recommendation of the Supreme Judicial Council.[274]

Other reforms introduced under this new Law include appointment, seniority, and promotion of Judges in Part 3 of the law[275]; transfer, assignment, and vacations of Judges;[276] duties of Judges;[277] disciplining of Judges;[278] and termination of Judges appointment.[279] Part 4 of the law[280] makes extensive provision for the administration of the Ministry of Justice covering the appointment of notaries public and their powers and other employees of the courts, among other things.

3.12 Reforms of Saudi Arabia judiciary 2005–2007

At the behest of the new administration in 2005, a Royal Order was promulgated for judicial reform. The reforms in this instance included the establishment of specialized courts for the first time in the history of the Kingdom.[281] These courts specialize in labour, commercial, domestic, and criminal cases and will have complete jurisdiction in those specialized areas.[282]

As part of government's continued efforts to improve the Saudi judiciary, King Abdullah issued royal decrees in 2007 with the aim of reforming the judiciary and creating a new court system.[283] It is noted that the reforms have not been fully implemented. When it is put into full implementation, it is expected to include, *inter alia*, the creation of a Supreme Court, the transfer of the Board of Grievances' commercial and criminal jurisdictions to a restructured general court system.[284]

Other notable features of the 2007 Law of the Judiciary is the transfer of all relevant administrative prerogatives from the Ministry of Justice to the SJC,

273 Article 10.
274 Article 11.
275 Articles 37–54.
276 Articles 55–57.
277 Articles 58–61.
278 Articles 71–84.
279 Articles 85–86.
280 Articles 87–100.
281 Ansary, A.F., 'Saudi Judicial Reform and the Principle of Independence', www.carnegieendowment.org/sada/2009/05/.../saudi-judicial-reform (accessed 19 September 2012).
282 Ibid.
283 Law of Judiciary (promulgated by Royal Decree No. M/78 on 19 Ramadan 1428H (October 1st, 2007).
284 See generally Van Ejik, E., 'Sharia and National Law in Saudi Arabia', in Otto, J.M. (ed), *Sharia Incorporated: A Comparative Overview of the Legal Systems of Twelve Muslim Countries in Past and Present*, Chapter 4, The Netherlands: Leiden University Press (2010), pp. 139–180.

and all the SJC's judicial prerogatives to the Supreme Court.[285] This new law expatiates on the relationship of the judicial branch with the Minister of Justice and his ministry. The previous judicial system tasked the Minister of Justice with administrative oversight of the courts and judges' affairs, although he was supposed to consult with the SJC. The new law gives these responsibilities to the SJC.[286] The SJC will oversee affairs such as judicial appointments, disciplinary actions, training, leaves of absence, and other matters that had been within the ministry's jurisdiction. The Minister of Justice is also completely absent from the decision-making circle within the proposed Supreme Court.

The Law has also brought improvement to the issue of judicial independence beyond administrative matters by transferring the supervision of the court system from the Ministry of Justice to the SJC. Under the previous law, rulings of the Court of Cassation required the approval of the minister of justice. If the Minister did not approve, the ruling was sent back to the court for reconsideration. If the body's deliberations failed to yield a decision that the minister approved, then the matter was referred to the SJC to render a final judgment. However, under the new law, the Court of Cassation rules by majority decision and its decisions are final.[287]

3.13 Reform of Saudi Arabia judiciary 2011–2013

A number of reforms have been introduced into the Saudi Arabia judiciary between 2011 and 2013. For example, translating court fines from material to monetary values. Generally, the remedies recognized under Islamic law are the right to rescind a contract, restitution, or damages for actual and tangible losses, with no means of recovering compensation for loss of anticipated future profits or loss of business reputation.[288] Where death or accidental personal injury occurs, the responsible party is liable to pay blood money (*diyah*) as compensation to the victim or the victim's heirs. The amount of blood money payable for accidental death was fixed early in the history of Islam at 100 camels, with personal injuries liability pro-rated with reference to this ceiling.[289] From time to time, and location to location, the value of 100 camels has been expressed in a monetary value. Under the new reform, the standard applicable in Saudi Arabia was laid down in a Royal Decree[290] to amount to SAR300,000 which is the equivalent of USD80,000.[291]

285 Ansary, A. F., Saudi Judicial Reform and the Principle of Independence, *SADA (Carnegie Endowment for International Peace)*, http://carnegieendowment.org/2009/05/05/saudi-judicial-reform-and-principle-of-independence/fhpy (accessed 19 April 2015).

286 Ibid.

287 Ibid.

288 Hatem Abbas Ghazzawi & Co., *Saudi Arabia – Law & Practice*. Legal Practice Guide, Litigation 2014–2015. www.chambersandpartners.com/global/person/178973/andreas-haberbeck (accessed 6 July 2015).

289 Ibid

290 Royal Order No. 43108 of 3rd Shawwal 1432 Hejra (1 September 2011).

291 Ibid.

Similarly, before this period, the Board of Grievances, being the tribunal having general jurisdiction over most categories of commercial and administrative disputes, had exclusive jurisdiction to hear applications for the execution of foreign judgments and arbitration awards. By a Royal Decree, a new execution procedure rules have been introduced.[292] Under the new regulation, applications for the enforcement of foreign judgments and arbitration awards are tried by an execution judge. The office of execution judge is a relatively new one which was created by a 2007 Judiciary Regulation.[293] It is noted that the Execution Regulation is the first statute setting out procedures for Execution Judges.[294]

In another development, the concept of the time-barring of substantive rights has been introduced into the Saudi Arabian statute law even though only as procedural devices and not as substantive time bars.[295] It is noted that this concept is alien to Islamic law. It is also noted that these time bars new rules in the Saudi Arabia judicial system are specific rather than general. For example, a 2005 judicial reform covers labour matters.[296] However, in 2012, this judicial innovative reform was brought to matters of carriage of good by sea rules. Under this regulation, cargo claims become time-barred after 365 days from delivery or loss of the cargo.[297]

In 2012, Saudi Arabia also introduced a reform into arbitration matters. A new Arbitration Regulation which was based on the UNCITRAL model was promulgated.[298] This new law removes much of the courts' control. It is now possible to conduct arbitrations in Saudi Arabia in a language other than Arabic, and to appoint non-Muslim arbitrators. The parties are free to agree to the procedures of an international arbitration body or to the procedural rules of another country, or to determine their own procedural rules. Failing such an express choice, the procedural rules applicable under Saudi Arabian law govern the arbitration.[299] Under the old arbitral regime, arbitrations had to be conducted under close supervision of the competent court or judicial tribunal. However, under the new reform no involvement of the courts is necessary in principle until the award is deposited with the competent court by the arbitration tribunal. Prior to that stage, the involvement of the courts will only be necessary if invoked by a party or the arbitrators.[300]

Also, in Saudi Arabia traditional judiciary, court proceedings are treated as confidential such that court records are not open to the public. Court proceedings

292 Execution Regulation, Royal Decree No M/53 of 13th Sha'ban 1433 Hejra (14 July 2012).

293 Judiciary Regulation, Royal Decree No M/78 of 19th Ramadan 1428 Hejra (October 2007).

294 Hatem Abbas Ghazzawi & Co., supra note no. 288.

295 Ibid.

296 Royal Decree No M/51 of 23rd Sha'ban 1426 Hejra (27 September 2005).

297 The Carriage of Goods by Sea Rules, Ministerial Resolution No. 01/12 of 19th Muharram 1434 Hejra (3 December 2012).

298 Royal Decree No M/34 of 25th Jumada Awwal 1433 Hijra (16 April 2012).

299 Hatem Abbas Ghazzawi & Co., supra note no. 288.

300 Ibid.

were open to the public with some restriction for example, as provided under Article 33 of Chapter 3 of the Law of the Judiciary which states that:

> Court hearings shall be public unless the court decides that they be held in a closed session in deference to morals or the sanctity of the family, or for the maintenance of public order. In all cases, judgments shall be pronounced in a public hearing.[301]

However, a reform introduced under the 2013 Civil Procedure Rule of the *Shari'ah* Court[302] stipulates that court hearings are open to the public. It is noted however that in practice courts will only allow parties to a lawsuit and their representatives to enter the courtroom.[303]

3.14 Conclusion

It can be concluded, from this chapter, first, that the *Qur'an* and the *Sunnah,* the two primary sources of Islamic law, can be said to be divine and deal with every conceivable eventuality, but certainly not in explicit details. Practically, the law derived from these two sources are flexible and adaptable to necessary changes from time to time. Second, it was in the course of responding to new issues arising from modernism that leagues of jurists and schools of thoughts began to emerge. The authority of jurists in Islam is exclusively declarative authority, an authority to declare God's law based on an literalist interpretation[304] of underpinning texts. The jurists' roles were to give expression to the wisdom and will of God as revealed in the *Qur'an* and the *Sunnah*. The institutions of schools of jurisprudence arose out of the desire to preserve the pristine nature of the texts and at the same time, ensure their relevance in dealing with unending human novel endeavours. Therefore, the orthodox literalist position that Islamic law could not be interpreted or re-interpreted cannot be absolutely sustained and cannot be said to go unchallenged.

Third, Saudi Arabia was traditionally the cradle of Islam. That perhaps explains why it made *Qur'an* and the *Sunnah* basic sources of its modern Law of Governance. Historical antecedent led to its adoption of a literalist conservative ideology and perspective of Islamic law, but interaction with other cultures and laws of other nations in different spheres of its activities at international levels have led to its swinging between conservative and moderate paradigms. Its legislative and judicial developments have been influenced not only by ideas and

301 Article 33 of the Law of the Judiciary, Royal Decree No. M/64, 14 Rajab 1395 [23 July 1975] Umm al-Qura No.2592, 29 Sha'ban 1395 [5 September 1975].

302 The Civil Procedure Rules of the Shari'a Courts, Royal Decree No M/1 of 22nd Jumada Awwal 1434 Hejra, corresponding to 2 April 2013 CE, and the Civil Procedure Rules of the Board of Grievances, Royal Decree No M/3 22nd Jumada Awwal 1434 Hejra (2 April 2013).

303 Hatem Abbas Ghazzawi & Co., supra note no. 288.

304 An interpretative approach based on the assumption that the meanings of a text are determined mainly by the stated or implied intentions of the author.

doctrines formulated by other Islamic schools of jurisprudence apart from the Hanbali School, but also by other values, including that of international law. What accounts for this development forms the focus of analysis in the subsequent chapters of this book.

Bibliography

Books

Abu Dawud, *Sunan* (Hasan's trans.), III, 109 *Hadith* no. 3585; see also Glasse, C., *The Concise Encyclopaedia of Islam*, Houston: Daru Salaam (2003).

Abu Sulayman, A.H., *Towards an Islamic Theory of International Relations: New Directions for Islamic Methodology and Thought* (2nd revised edn), Virginia: IIIT (1993).

Abu Zahrah, M., *Usul al-Fiqh*, Cairo: Dar al-Fikr al-'Arabi (1973).

Ahmad, H.D., ibid at p. 74; and Ahmad, H.D., *Dirasa fi al-Siyyasah al-Dakhiliyyah li-al-Mamlakah al-Arabiyyah al-Sa'udiyyah [A Study in the Internal Politics of the Kingdom of Saudi Arabia*] (1984) at p. 127.

Ahmad, H.D., *The Saudi Arabian Council of Ministers: Its Environment, Its Role and Its Future in Politics, Administration and Development in Saudi Arabia* (edited by Dalhan, Ahmad) (1990).

Al-Asqalani, A.I.A.H., *al-Nukat ala Kitab Ibn Al-Salah*, vol. 1 (2nd Edn), Maktabah al-Furqan, Ajman, U.A.E. (2003).

Al-Bahuti: Kashshaf: vol 3, p. 23 as quoted by Ahmad 'Ali, M.I., and Abu Sulaiman, A.W., ibid.

Al-Bahurti: *Sharh Al-Muntaha*, vol. 3.

Al-Dhahabi, *Tadhkirat al-Huffhz*, Dar al-Kutub al-'Ilmiyyah, vol. 2, Beirut (n.d.), p. 431.

Al-Duraibi, S., *Judicial Systemization in the Kingdom of Saudi Arabia*, Riyadh: Hanifa Press (1430H, 1982).

Alexei, V., *King Faisal of Saudi Arabia, Personality, Faith and Times*, London: Saqi Books (2012).

Al-Faqqi, M.H., *Athar al-Da'wah al-Wahhabiyyah*, Cairo: Al Zamni Publishing (1354 AH).

Al-Farsy, F., *Modern and Tradition, The Saudi Equation*, London and New York: Kegan Paul International (1990).

Alfred Guillaume, M.A., *The Traditions of Islam*, Beirut: Khayats (1966), p. 10.

Al-~Ghazali, A.H., *Al-Mustasfa min 'Ilm al-'Usul,* Vol. 1, Baghdad: Matba'at Muthanna (1870).

Al-Ghunaimi, M.T., *The Muslim Conception of International Law and the Western Approach*, The Hague: Martinus Nijhoff (1968).

Al-Hamad, H.S., *The Legislative Process and the Development of Saudi Arabia*, A Dissertation Presented for PhD (Political Science) of the University of Southern California (1973).

Al-Matroudi, A.H., *The Hanbali School of Law and Ibn Taymiyyah, Conflict or Conciliation*, Oxfordshire: Routledge (2006).

Al Sadr al-*Shari'ah*, U.A.M.M., *al-Tawdih fi Hall al-Ghawamid al-Tanqih*, Cairo: Dar al-'Ahd al-Jadid li'l-Taba'ah (1377/1957).

Al-Tabari, M. *Ikhtilaf al-Fuqaha*, Beirut: Dar al-Kutub al-'Ilmiyyah (n.d.).

Al-Tamawi, S.M., *Al-Sultatt al-Thalath fi'l-Dasatir al-'Arabiyyah wa fi'l-Fikr al-Sihasi al-Islami* (2nd edn) Cairo: Dar al-Fikr al-'Arabi (1973).

Anderson, J.N.D., *Changing Law in Developing Countries*, New York: Frederick A. Prager (1963).
Anderson, N.D., *Law Reform in the Muslim World*, London: University of London (1976).
Ansary, A., *A Brief Overview of the Saudi Arabia Legal System*, Hauser Global Law School Program (2008). www.nyulawglobal.org/globalex/Saudi_Arabia.htm.
Ansary, A.F., Saudi Judicial Reform and the Principle of Independence, *SADA (Carnegie Endowment for International Peace)* https://carnegieendowment.org/sada/23059.
Aslan, R, *"No God but God" – The Origins, Evolution, and Future of Islam*, London: Arrow Books (2006).
Attia, G.E., *Toward Realization of the Higher Intents of Islamic Law*, Washington, DC: IIIT (2007).
Auda, J., *A System Approach*, Herndon, VI: IIIT (2008).
Ayoub M. al-Jarbou, *Judicial Review of Administrative Actions: A Comparative Study between the United States and Saudi Arabia* 129 – 130 (unpublished S.J.D. dissertation, University of Virginia) (in file with author) (2002).
Azami, M.M, *On Schacht's Origins of Muhammadan Jurisprudence*, Oxford: OCIS (1996).
Azami, M.M., *Studies in Early Hadith Literature*, Indianapolis: American Trust Publications (1978).
Az-Zuahaili, M., *at-Tanzhim al-Qadha'l fi al-Fiqh al-Islami*, Damascus: Dar al-Fikr (1423H/2002).
Baderin, M.A., 'Islamic Legal Theory in Context', edited by Baderin, M.A., *Islamic Legal Theory*, Vol.1, Surrey: Ashgate Publishing Ltd. (2014), pp. xi–xxxvii, at xxiii.
Badran, A.B., *Usul al-Fiqh al-Islami*, Alexandria: Mu'assasah Shabab al-Jami'ah (1402/1982), pp. 83–84.
Berg, H., *The Development of Exegesis in Early Islam: The Authenticity of Muslim Literature from the Formative Period*, United Kingdom: Psychology Press (2000).
Boucek, C., 'Saudi Fatwa Restrictions and the State-Clerical Relationship', *SADA* (2010), http://carnegieendowment.org/2010/10/27/saudi-fatwa-restrictions-and-state-clerical-relationship/6b81.
Brown, J.A.C., *Hadith Muhammad Legacy and Modern World*, London: Oneworld Publication (2009).
Brown, N.J., *Arab Judicial Structures*, A Study Presented to the United Nations Development Program, www.undp-pogar.org/publications/judiciary/nbrown/saudi.html.
Calder, N., *Interpretation and Jurisprudence in Medieval Islam* (edited by Mojaddedi, J., and Rippin, A.) Farnham: Ashgate Variorum (2006).
Cornell, V., *Voices of Islam*, Santa Barbara: Praeger Publishers (2007).
Coulson, N.J., *A History of Islamic Law*, Edinburgh: Edinburgh University Press (1994).
Crone, P., and Cook, M., *Hagarism: The Making of the Islamic World*, Cambridge: Cambridge University Press (1977).
Cyril, G., *The New Encyclopedia of Islam*, Lanham, USA: AltaMira Press (2001).
David, C., *The Wahhabi Mission and Saudi Arabia*, London: I.B. Tauris (2009).
DeLong-Bas, N., *Wahhabi Islam: From Revival and Reform to Global Jihad* (1st edn), Oxford: Oxford University Press (2008).
Doi, A. R., *Basis of Shari'ah (Islamic Law)*, Zaria: Gaskiya Corporation (1983).
Doi, A.R., *Shari'ah: The Islamic Law*, West Norwood, London: Ta-Ha Publishers Ltd. (2008).
El Ghonemy, M.R., *Affluence and Poverty in the Middle East*, United Kingdom: Psychology Press (1998), p. 56.

Elliott, H.K., *On Saudi Arabia: Its People, Past, Religion, Fault Lines and Future*, New York: Knopf (2012).

Esposito, J. "Ijtihad" *The Islamic World: Past and Present*, Oxford Islamic Studies Online http://oxfordislamicstudies.com/article/opr/t243/e150.

Execution Regulation, Royal Decree No M/53 of 13th Sha'ban 1433 Hejra (14 July 2012).

Faour, M., *The Arab World after Desert Storm*, Washington DC: United States Institute of Peace Press (1993).

Federal Research Division, *Saudi Arabia: A Country Study*, Whitefish, Montana: Kessinger Publishing (2004).

Fisher, M.P., *Living Religions: An Encyclopaedia of the World's Faiths*, London: I.B. Tauris (1338).

For details see for example Joseph, K.A., *Succession in Saudi Arabia*, New York: Palgrave (2001).

Forte, D.F., *Studies in Islamic Law, Classical and Contemporary Application*, Maryland: Austin & Winfield, Publishers.

Fuad Hamza, al-Biid al-'Arabiyyah al-Sa'udiyya, Riyadh: Maktabat al-Nasra l-*Hadithah* (1968).

Gibb, H.A.R., *Constitutional Organization in Law in the Middle East, Origin and Development of Islamic Law* (edited by Khadduri, M., and Liebesny, H.J.,) Vol. 1, Washington, DC: The Middle East Institute (1955).

Gibb, H.A.R., *Modern Trends in Islam*, Chicago: University of Chicago Press (1947).

Gilles, K., *Jihad: The Trail of Political Islam*, London: I.B. Tauris (2002).

Goldziher, I., '*Muhammedanisches Recht in Theoric und Mirklickeit, Zietshrift fur vergleichende* Rechtswissenchaft, 8 (1989).

Hallaq, W.B., *Authority, Continuity, and Change in Islamic Law*, Cambridge: Cambridge University Press (2001).

Hallaq, W.B., *The Origins and Evolution of Islamic Law*, Cambridge: Cambridge University Press (2005).

Hallaq, W.B., 'The Primacy of the *Qur'an* in Shatibi's Legal Theory', Islamic Studies Presented to Charles J. Adams, in Hallaq, W.B., *Law and Legal Theory in Classical and Medieval Islam,* Ashgate Variorum, Great Britain (1994), eds Hallaq, W.B., and Little, D.P., Chapter XI, Leiden (1991).

Harari, M., *Government and Politics in the Middle East*, Englewood Cliffs, NJ: Prentice-Hall (1962).

Hasaba Allah, A., *Usul Al-Tashri' Al-Islami*, Cairo: Dar Al-Ma'arif (1985).

Hatem Abbas Ghazzawi & Co., *Saudi Arabia – Law & Practice.* Legal Practice Guide, Litigation 2014–2015.

Ibn Kathir, *Iktisar Ulum al-Hadith*, published with explanation al-Baith al-*Hadith*, Vol. 1 (1st edn), Riyadh: Maktabah al-Ma'arif, Kingdom of Saudi Arabia (1996).

Ibn Taymiyyah, *Majmu' Fatawa Ibn Taymiyyah*, vols. 10 and 20, Beirut: DKI (n.d.), pp. 362 and 40 respectively.

Iqbal, A., *The Culture of Islam (The Classical Period)* – Lahore: Institute of Islamic Culture (1981).

Izzi Dien, M., *Islamic Law from Historical Foundations to Contemporary Practice*, Edinburgh: Edinburgh University Press (2004).

James, W., A Brief History of Saudi Arabia, Infobase Publishing (2010), p. 182; Ansari, A.F., *A Brief Overview of the Saudi Arabian Legal System,* Hauser Global Law School Program, New York University School of Law (2008), www.nyulawglobal.org/globalex/saudi arabia.htm.

Jerichow, A., *The Saudi File, People, Power, Politics*, Surrey: Curzon Press, (1998).

Jokisch, B., *Ijtihad in Ibn Taymiyya's fatawa' in 'Islamic Law, Theory and Practice* (edited by Gleave, R., and Kermili, E.), London and New York: I.B. Tauris Publishers (2001).

Jokisch, B., *Islamic Imperial Law: Harun Al-Rashid's Codification Project*, Berlin: Walter de Gruyter (2007).

Jokisch, B., *Islamiches Recht in Theorie und Praxis, Analyse einiger kaufrechtlicher Fatawas von Taqi'd-Din Ahmad b. Taymiyyah*, Berlin: Walter de Gruyter (1996).

Judiciary Regulation, Royal Decree No M/78 of 19th Ramadan 1428 Hejra (October 2007).

Ka'bah, R., www.badilag.net/english/DATA/Contemporary%20Islamic%20Court%20 System.pdf

Kamail, H.H., *Principles of Islamic Jurisprudence*, Cambridge: The Islamic Texts Society (2003).

Kamali, H.K., 'Maqasid al-Shari'ah Made Simple' (Occasional Papers Series 13), *IIIT*, London, Washington, DC (2008).

Kamali, M.H., *Law and Society: The Interplay of Revelation and Reason in the Shari'ah*. From Oxford History of Islam, Oxford: Oxford University Press (2000), www.acc. teachmideast.org/texts.php?module_id (accessed 25 June 2012).

Kechichian, J.A., *Succession in Saudi Arabia*, London: Palgrave Macmillan (2001).

Khadduri, M., '*From Religious to National Law*', (edited by Thompson, J.H., and Reischauer, R.D.), *Modernization of the Arab World*, Toronto, 1966, p. 41; F. Rahman, Islam, Chicago, IL (1966).

Khair al-Din, A.Z., *Shabh al-Jazirah fi Ahd Al-Malik 'Abd al-'Aziz* (The Arabian Peninsula During the Reign of King Abd al-Aziz Al-Saud), Beirut: Dar Al Ilm Lil Malain (1390 AH/1970AD).

Khalaf, A.W., '*Ilm Usul Al-Fiqh*, Cairo: Dar Al-Qalam (1956). Khaled, A.E.F., *The Great Theft: Wrestling Islam from the Extremists*, San Francisco, CA: Harper (2005).

Khan, M.H., *The Schools of Islamic Jurisprudence (A Comparative Study)*, New Delhi: Kitab Bavahan (1997).

Kostiner, C.E., et al., 'Al-Su'ūdiyya, al-Mamlaka al-'Arabiyya,' (edited by Bearman, P., and Bianquis, Th.), *Encyclopaedia of Islam*, Brill Online, (2007).

Law of Judiciary (promulgated by Royal Decree No. M/78 on 19 Ramadan 1428H (October 1st, 2007).

Lewis, B., *The Crisis of Islam: Holy War and Unholy Terror* (1st edn), New York: Modern Library (2003).

Mackey, S., *The Saudis: Inside the Desert Kingdom*, New York: Meridian Book, (1987).

Madani, M.O., *The Relationship between Saudi Arabia Domestic Law and International Law: A Study of the Oil Agreement with Foreign Companies*, A Dissertation Submitted to the Faculty of the Law School of The George Washington University in Partial Satisfaction of the Requirements for the Degree of Doctor of Juridical Science (1970).

Mahmassani, S., *Al-Awda' al-Tashriya fi al-Duwal al-'Arabiyyah: Madiha wa Hadiraha* (The Legislative Conditions in the Arab States: Past and Present), Beirut: Dar al-'Ulum Li al-Malayin (1965).

Mahmassani, S.R., *Falsafah al-Tashri' fi 'l-Islam: The Philosophy of Jurisprudence in Islam* (translated by Farhat J. Ziadeh), Leiden: E.J. Brill (1961).

Makdisi, G., '*Tabaqat-Biography: Law and Orthodoxy in Classical Islam*', Pakistan: Islamic Studies (Islamabad) (1993), p. xxxii.

Makdisi, G., *The Rise of Colleges: Institutions of Learning in Islam and the West*, Edinburgh: Edinburgh University Press (1981).

Masud, M.K., *Shatibi's Philosophy of Islamic Law*, New Delhi: Kitab Bhavan (2009).

Maududi, S.A.A., *The Islamic Law and Constitution*, New Delhi: Taj Company (1986).

Melchert, C., 'How Hanafism Came to Originate in Kufa and Traditionalism in Medina, Islamic Law', edited by Picken, G.N., *Critical Concepts in Islamic Studies*, Vol. II, London and New York: Routledge Taylor and Francis Group (2011).

Michael, M.Q., *In the Heart of the Desert: The Story of an Exploration Geologist and the Search for Oil in the Middle East*, Jericho Vermont: Green Mountain Press (2006).

Minhajuddin, M.M., *Islami Fiqh (Mukammal 3 Hissey)*, New Delhi: Al-Hasanat Books (2012).

Mirza, M., *The Discovery of Oil in Saudi Arabia – Here Is the Story Presented in a Way You've Never Seen before* (2017).

Mordechai, A., *Saudi Arabia: Government, Society and the Gulf Crisis*, London: Routledge (1993).

Mordechai, A., *Saudi Arabia in the Oil Era: Regime and Elites: Conflict and Collaboration*, Kent, United Kingdom: Croom Helm (1988).

Motahari, A.M., *Jurisprudence and Its Principles* (translated by Tawhidi, S., edited by Bakhtiar, L.) New York: Elmhurst 11373 (1980).

Nagel, T., "*Hadis ya do Tarihin Imhasi*" [*Hadith* or Destruction of History] translated from German by Ali Dere, *Islami Arastirmalar* [Islamic Researches] X (1–2–3) (1997).

Nyazee, I.A.K., *Theories of Islamic Law*, Islamabad: Islamic Research Institute, International Islamic University (2009), p. 225.

O.G. Umm al-Qura No. 3397 (2/9/1412H, Mar. 5, 1992); The Shoura Council Law, Royal Order No. A/91 (27/8/1412H, Mar. 1, 1992), O.G. Umm al-Qura No. 3397 (2/9/1412H, 5 March 1992).

Pascal, M., *The Saudi Enigma: A History*, London: Zed Books (2005).

Qadri, A.A., *Islamic Jurisprudence in the Modern World*, New Delhi: Taj Company (1986).

Rahman, F., *The Major Themes of Qur'an* (2nd edn), Chicago IL: The University of Chicago Press (2009); Akhtar, S., *The Qur'an and the Secular Mind: A Philosophy of Islam*, Oxfordshire: Routledge (2008).

Ramadan, H. *Understanding Islamic Law: From Classical to Contemporary*, Lanham, Maryland: Rowman Altamira (2006), pp. 6–21; Johansen, B., *Contingency in a Sacred Law: Legal and Ethical Norma in the Muslim Fiqh*, The Netherlands: Brill Academic (1998).

Reed, J., *The Saudi Royal Family*, New York: Infobase Publishing (2009).

Robert, L., *Inside the Kingdom: Kings, Cleric, Modernists, Terrorists, and the Struggle for Saudi Arabia*, London: Penguin Books (2010).

Sabri, S., *The House of Saudi in Commerce*, I.S. New Delhi: Publications Pvt., Ltd. (2001).

Safi, O., "*Progressive Muslims*", Oxford: One World (2003).

Safran, S., *Saudi Arabia: The Ceaseless Quest for Security*, Ithaca NY: Cornell University Press (1985).

Sahih Muslim Book 42, *Hadith* Number 7147.

Saliba, I., 'Saudi Arabia: The Regime Invokes Sharia Law to Prevent Public Protest', *The Law Library of Congress* (2011), www.loc.gov/lawweb/servlet/lloc_news?disp2_1205402565_text (accessed 01 December 2014).

Saud al-Duraib, *Judicial Systemization in the Kingdom of Saudi Arabia*, Riyadh: Hanifah Press (1430H – 1982), at pp. 313–314.

Saudi Arabia's Oil Fortune – A New Beginning in Foreign Policy.'

Schacht, J., *An Introduction to Islamic Law*, Oxford: Oxford University Press (1983).

Schacht, J. *The Origins of Muhammadan Jurisprudence*, Oxford: The Clarendon Press (1950).

Schacht, J., and Schacht, J., *An Introduction to Islamic Law*, Clarendon Press, Oxford (1982).

Sabra, A., "Ibn Hazm's Literalism: A Critique of Islamic Legal Theory." Taken from: Ibn Ḥazm of Cordoba: The Life and Works of a Controversial Thinker, pg. 98. Volume 103 of *Handbook of Oriental Studies*, Section 1: The Near and Middle East. Edited by Camilla Adang, Maribel Fierro, and Sabine Schmidtke. Leiden: Brill Publishers (2012).

Solaim, S.A., *Constitutional and Judicial Organization in Saudi Arabia*, Unpublished Ph.D. Dissertation, John Hopkins University (1970), pp. 46–68; Abdul Hakim, A.T., *Al-Malik Faisal wa Al-Alaqat Al-Kharijgiyyah al-Saudiyyah (King Faisal and the Saudi Foreign Relations)* (2002).

The Carriage of Goods by Sea Rules, Ministerial Resolution No. 01/12 of 19th Muharram 1434 Hejra (3 December 2012).

The Editors of Encyclopaedia Britinnica, *Taqlid: Islamic law.*

Van Ejik, E., 'Sharia and National Law in Saudi Arabia', edited by Otto, J.M., *Sharia Incorporated: A Comparative Overview of the Legal Systems of Twelve Muslim Countries in Past and Present*, Chapter 4, The Netherlands: Leiden University Press (2010), pp. 139–180.

Watt, W.M., *Islam and the Integration of Society*, Evanston (1961).

Watt, W.M., "*The Closing of the Door of Ijtihad* Orientalia Hispanica, I, Leiden: Ej Brill (1974).

Weiss, B.G., *The Spirit of Islamic Law*, Athens, Georgia: University of Georgian Press (2006).

Wilson, P.W., and Graham, D., *Saudi Arabia: The Coming Storm*, Armonk, NY: M.E. Sharpe, Inc. (1994).

Zubair, A.Q., *The Sunnah between Its Adherents and Adversaries*, Madinah Heritage Publication, Lagos (1995), p. 72 quoting Al-Suyuti, *Al-Laali Al-Masnn'ah* (n.d.).

Zubayr, S.M., *Hadith Literature*, Oxford: The Islamic Texts Society (1993).

Zuhur, S. Saudi Arabia, California: ABC-CLIO, LLC (2011).

Journal

Ahmad 'Ali, M.I., and Abu Sulaiman, A.W., 'Recent Judicial Development in Saudi Arabia', *Journal of Islamic and Comparative Law*, Centre of Islamic Legal Studies, Faculty of Law, Ahmadu Bello University, Zaria, Nigeria, Vol. 3 (1969), p. 12.

Al-Ghadyan, A.A., 'The Judiciary in Saudi Arabia', *Arab Law Quarterly*, Vol. 1, No. 3, BRILL (1998), pp. 235–251.

Al-Muhairi, B.S.B.A., 'Islamisation and Modernization within the UAE Penal Law: Shari'ah in the Pre-Modern Period', *Arab Law Quarterly*, Vol. 10 (1995), pp. 34–49.

Anderson, J.N.D., 'Law as a Social Force in Islamic Culture and History', Chapter 20, *Bulletin of the School of Oriental and African Studies, University of London*, Vol. 20, No. 1/3 (1957), pp. 14–40.

Ansari, Z.I., 'The Contribution of the *Qur'an* and the Prophet to the Development of Islamic Fiqh', *Journal of Islamic Studies*, Vol. 3, No. 2 (1992), pp. 141–17.

Bruce, R., 'Brezhnev in the Hejaz', *The National Interest*, ProQuest Research Library, Vol. 115, (2011), p. 32.

Hallaq, W.B., 'Groundwork of the Moral Law: A New Look at the *Qur'an* and the Genesis of Sharia', *Islamic Law and Society*, Vol. 16 (2009).

Hallaq, W.B., 'The Authenticity of Prophetic *Hadith*: A Pseudo-problem', *Studia Islamica*, Vol. 89 (1999).
Hallaq, W.B., 'Usul al-*Fiqh*: Beyond Tradition', *Journal of Islamic Studies*, Vol. 3 (1992), pp. 239–279.
Hallaq, W.B., 'Was The Gate of Ijtihad Closed?', *International Journal of Middle East Studies*, Cambridge University Press, Vol. 16 (1984), pp. 75–90.
John, M., 'Legal Logic and Equity in Islamic Law', *The American Journal of Comparative Law*, Vol. 33, No. 1 (1985), pp. 63–92.
Liebesny, 'Stability and Change in Islamic Law', *Middle East Journal*, Vol. 21 (1967), pp. ix. 395.
Nehme, M.G., 'Saudi Arabia 1950–80: Between Nationalism and Religion', *Middle Eastern Studies*, Vol. 30, No. 4 (1994), pp. 30–943.
Saeed, A., 'Some Reflections on the Contextualist Approach to Ethico-Legal Texts of the *Qur'an*', *Bulletin of the School of Oriental and African Studies*, Vol. 71 (2008).
Schacht, J., A Revaluation of Islamic Traditions', *Journal of the Royal Asiatic Society of Great Britain and Ireland*, Vol. 2 (1949), pp. 143–154.

Websites

http://acc.teachmideast.org/texts.php?module_id=2&reading_id=210&sequence=5 /
http://carnegieendowment.org/2009/05/05/saudi-judicial-reform-and-principle-of-independence/fhpy.
http://carnegieendowment.org/2010/10/27/saudi-fatwa-restrictions-and-state-clerical-relationship/6b81
https://destinationksa.com/the-discovery-of-oil-in-saudi-arabia-here-is-the-story-presented-in-a-way-youve-never-seen-before/.
http://referenceworks.brillonline.com/?fromBrillOnline=true.
www.britannica.com/EBchecked/topic/31568/history-of-Arabia.
www.britannica.com/EBchecked/topic/583236/taqlid.
www. *carnegieendowment.org/sada/2009/05/.../saudi-judicial-reform.*
www.chambersandpartners.com/global/person/178973/andreas-haberbeck .
www.imf.org/external/pubs/ft/aa/pdf/aa.pdf.
www.onislam.net/english/shariah/contemporary-issues/islamic-themes/449785-literalists-approach-and-complications-part1.html
https://www.saudiembassy.net/about-saudi-arabia.

Status & judicial rules

Article 14 of the Judiciary Act 1395H (1975).
High Court of Makkah, vol. 1, No. 105, 1963.
High Court of Makkah: Case No. 258 vol. 7.
Ibn al-Qayyim: Zad al-Ma'ad, vol. 4.
Regional Law, Royal Order No. A/91 (27/8/1412H, 1 March 1992).
Royal Decree (*al-Marsum al-Maliki*) dated 4 Safar 1346/1927.
Royal Decree dated 20/10/81, Cabinet Decree No. 16-3-3136.
Royal Decree No.M/64, 14 Rajab 1395 [23 July 1975] Umm al-Qura No.2592, 29 Sha'ban 1395 [5 September 1975.]
Royal Decree No M/34 of 25th Jumada Awwal 1433 Hijra (16 April 2012).
Royal Decree No M/51 of 23rd Sha'ban 1426 Hejra (27 September 2005).

Royal Decree No. 64/M dated 14/7/1395H (21/7/1975. See Um Al-~Qura Gazette, issue No. 2592 of 29/8/1395H.

Royal Decree No.M/64, 14 Rajab 1395 [23 July 1975] Umm al-Qura No.2592, 29 Sha'ban 1395 [5 September 1975.]

Royal Decree of 23 September 1932.

Royal Decree, No. 137/1 dated 08/07/1391 AH / (29/08/1971 CE).

Royal Order No. 43108 of 3rd Shawwal 1432 Hejra (1 September 2011).

Royal Order No. A/19 dated 27 Shaaban 1412 AH.

The Basic System of Governance, art. 68. The Basic System of Governance, Royal Order No. A/90 (27/8/1412H, 1 March 1992), O.G. Umm al-Qura No. 3397 (2/9/1412H, 5 March 1992).

The Civil Procedure Rules of the Shari'a Courts, Royal Decree No M/1 of 22nd Jumada Awwal 1434 Hejra, corresponding to 2 April 2013 CE, and the Civil Procedure Rules of the Board of Grievances, Royal Decree No M/3 22nd Jumada Awwal 1434 Hejra (2 April 2013).

The High Court of Makkah: Case No. 83, vol. 1 (1380 AH, – 1960 AD).

The High Court of Mecca: Case No. 53, vol. 46 (1375 AH, 1956 AD).

Cases

Hamza B. Abdu v. Muhammad b. Hassan, The High Court of Mecca: Case No. 225, vol. 8 (1376 AH 1956 AD) to be discussed shortly.

4 Saudi Arabia between theory and practice of international law

4.1 Introductory remarks

As advanced in Chapter 2, international law has, today, penetrated the once exclusive zone of the domestic affairs of States. It is "no longer limited to the regulation of diplomatic relations between States and the allocation of spaces and competences between countries"[1] but also to regulate the relationships between governments and their own citizens, particularly through the growing bodies of human rights law.[2] The objectives of international law is to try to manage, as consensually as possible, the co-existence and the complex interdependence of states and important non-state actors, although it is widely claimed in the Muslim world that the "international order" often serves the interests of the dominant international Western actors.[3] Contemporary international law, is thus, as Piscatori notes, "conditioned by multistate and multicultural realities. The first suggests difficulties of its enforcement and the second the difficulties of its universalization".[4]

In view of these realities coupled with the controlling tendencies of modern international law, what are the perspectives of Siyar (Islamic international law) and to what extent does it influence a modern Muslim-majority state like Saudi Arabia in their theory and practice of modern international relations? What is the nature of Saudi Arabia's attitude to modern international law, in view of the fundamental role played by Islamic law in its domestic system?

1 Torrijo, Z.F., 'International Law and Domestic Law: Definitely an Odd Couple,' *Revosta Juridoca de la Universidad de Puerto Rico*, Vol. 77 (2008), pp. 483–585.

2 Anne-Marie, S., and, Burke-White, W., 'The Future of International Law Is Domestic (or, The European Way of Law)', *Harvard International Law Journal*, Vol. 47, No. 2 (2006), p. 327.

3 Haynes, J., 'Transnational Religious Actors and International Order', *Perspective: Review of International Affairs*, Vol. 17, No. 2 (2009), p. 44. See generally Bill, B., *The Degradation of the International Legal Order?: The Rehabilitation of Law and the Possibility of Politics*, Oxfordshire: Rutledge-Cavendish (2008).

4 Piscatori, J.P., *Islam and the International Legal Order: The Case of Saudi Arabia*, A Dissertation Presented to the Graduate Faculty of the University of Virginia in Candidacy for the Degree of Doctor of Philosophy, University of Virginia (1976), p. i.

This chapter will engage with the above questions in laying the necessary general foundation for determining, in subsequent chapters, the Saudi Arabia's perspective of the interaction of international law and Islamic law in Muslim States. It starts with a brief history, theory, and practice of *Siyar* followed by an analysis of why Islamic law is so fundamental in Saudi Arabia's domestic system as well as the interplay of international law and Islamic Law in Saudi Arabian foreign policy. This is followed by an examination of Saudi Arabia's policy of domesticating international treaties into its legal system. How this is fitted into the theory of classical *Siyar* and modern international law and how people perceive international law in modern Saudi Arabia will also be examined. A brief examination of Islamic perspective of territorial statehood and nation-state is done to contextualize the Saudi Arabia as a modern nation-state maintaining relations with non-Muslim states.

4.2 *Siyar* (Islamic international law): a variant?

Sirah is an Arabic word which literally expresses specific style of conduct of an exemplary personality and recorded in his biography.[5] In Islamic history and literature, it is a term used to refer to the biography of Prophet Muhammad. Its plural form is *Siyar* which refers to the exemplary lives of saints recorded in biographical dictionaries or to explain and underscore the history of political campaigns.[6] In technical and legal sense, it is used to denote conduct of state in relation to other communities.[7] Nawawi (d. 776/1278) says:

> *Siyar* is the plural of *Sira* which means conduct and [most authors] use the title *Kitab al-Siyar* because its rules are derived from the conduct of the Prophet (PBUH) in his expeditions. And [these authors] discuss the rules of war. Other [authors] use the title '*Kitab al-Jihad*', the title in the book *al-Tanbeeh fi al-Fuqah* [by Imam Abu Ishaq Ibrahim Ibn Ali Al Sherazi] (d. 576/1083) used '*Kitab qital al-Mushrikeen*' (chapter on war with polytheists).[8]

Conceptually, it covers conduct of war, conduct of believers in their relations with nonbelievers in enemy territory, and conduct of believers with whom they have entered into treaties. Today the term refers generally to international law (Arabic *qanun al-dawli*).[9] This technical and legal meaning was popularized in

5 The Oxford Dictionary of Islam, *Siyar*, Oxford Islamic Studies Online, www.oxfordislamicstudies.com/article/opr/t125/e2228 (accessed 29 August 2020).

6 Ibid.

7 Ibid.

8 Muhyyddin Ibn Sharaf al-Nawawi, *Tahzeeb al-Asm'a wa al-Lughat*, vol. 3, Beirut: Dar al-Kutub al-'Elmiya (n.d.) p. 159 as quoted by Munir, M., "Islamic international Law (Siyar): An Introduction", *Hamdard Islamicus*, Vol. XXXX, No. 4 (2012), p. 43.

9 The Oxford Dictionary of Islam, supra note no 5.

the second century of Islam by scholars of Hanafi jurisprudence, particularly al-Shaybani (d. 804).[10]

Western scholars argue that Islam had no system of international law, and so, the so-called *Siyar* and modern international law are different concepts and thus, both systems can better be described as incompatible. Contrary to this position, even a cursory look, shows that Islam is characteristically international and universal in its basic ethos, teachings, and approach.[11] Right from its nascent stage, the Muslim community had started to engage in practices that were potentially universal and international. The message of Islam in the *Qur'an* and *Sunnah* was addressed to humanity rather than being restricted to any group or people. This is evidenced by the expressions such as "*O mankind*"[12] or "*O children of Adam*".[13] It follows that the message of the *Qur'an* was universal and pan-human right from the beginning of revelation in Makkah.[14] It is also argued that contrary to the critics, Islam and Muslims acknowledge diversity and existence of other civilizational norms or cultural values and corollary of their natural rights. *Qur'an* confirms this fact when it refers to the good qualities of other nations including some good qualities of Christians.[15] This was supported by statement credited to Prophet Muhammad where, for example, he was quoted to have said that: '*wisdom was the common heritage (property) of human beings, and, therefore, wherever it was to be found, it should be acquired and availed*'.[16]

For the attainment of universal world peace, based on tolerance, and mutual respect, people of other civilizations particularly the Christians and the Jews were called upon to agree on a common objective of mutual understanding and respect with a view to promote the freedom and equality of mankind and to promote those moral and ethical values which all jointly and commonly shared.[17]

Analysts argue that this historical antecedence explains why the culture of mutual relationship, cooperation, and participation at local and international levels were not alien to Islam and the Muslims. This culture has remained up till now. The same spirit motivated them in the twentieth century to ratify international

10 Ibid.

11 Ghazi, M. A., *Islam International Law and the World Today*, Islamabad: Institute of Policy Studies (2011), p. 66.

12 *Qur'an* 2:21; 4:1; 49:13; etc.

13 *Qur'an* 7:26, 27, 35 etc.

14 Ghazi, M. A., supra note no. 11 at p. 67.

15 See for example *Qur'an* 5:82–83.

16 Tirmidhi, al-Jami', Kitab al-'Ilm, 19; Ibn Majah, al-Sunan, Kitab al-Zahd, p. 15. This Hadith is a good description of what is later known as 'Commonwealth'. The phrase "commonwealth" connotes "public welfare general good or advantage", dating back to fifteenth-century traditional English use of the term for a political community founded for the common good. It has been observed that originally a phrase (the common-wealth or the common-wealth – reflected in the modern synonym "public wealth"). Historically, it comes from the old meaning of "wealth", which is "well-being", and is itself a loose translation of the Latin *res publica* (republic). See *The Monthly Magazine and British Register* (Unknown Author), Vol. 1 (1796), pp. 179–180.

17 See *Qur'an* 3:64.

treaties and join international organizations including, for example, the then League of Nations (now the United Nations), the then Organization of African Unity (now the African Union), and the Non-Aligned Movement.[18]

It is further argued that the *Qur'an* is perhaps the only Divine Scripture in the history of religion that accorded recognition to other faiths and doctrinal cultures.[19] It provides guiding principles on how its adherents would maintain relation with followers of those religions, who enter into agreements with them, those who are not interested in maintaining any relationship with them, who prefer to remain neutral, and those who choose to be belligerents.[20]

The fact that at that early advent of Islam, moral standards of relationship with other civilizations were set, was an indication that the *Qur'an* and the normative practices of Prophet Muhammad (PBUH) contemplated a variety of international relationships and possible channels of interaction and intercourse between Muslims and members of other communities of civilizations.[21] It was based on this reality that Muslim scholars and jurists of the second century (AH) developed an independent legal-historical corpus referred to as *Siyar.*[22]

Al-Sharakhsi attempted a definition of *Siyar* from this historical and classical perspective when he says:

> *Siyar*... describes the conduct of the believers (Muslims) in their relations with the unbelievers of enemy territory as well as with people with whom the believers have made treaties, who may have been temporarily... or permanently... in Muslim land; with apostates... and with rebels...[23]

As stated above, there are several references in the *Qur'an* and *Hadith* pointing to the conduct of Muslims towards non-Muslims trans-nationally. It was from these references that a body of law known as *Siyar* was developed; this, of course, was in the formative period of Islamic Law during the eighth and ninth centuries.[24] There is no consensus of opinion on who originally devised the idea, but it is assumed that the jurists of the legal school of Abu Hanifa were the first to popularize the term in its legal meaning.[25] Al-Shaybani who was

18 Ghazi, M.A., supra note no. 11 at p. 69.

19 Ibid.

20 *Qur'an* 9:4–5, 7; 4:90, 91 etc.

21 Ghazi, M.A., supra note no. 11 at p. 70.

22 Ibid.

23 Khadduri, M.'s introduction to al-Shaybani, *The Islamic Law of Nations – Shaybani's Siyar*, Baltimore, Maryland: Johns Hopkins University Press| (1966), p. 40, quoting Shams al-Din Muhammad Ibn Ahmad Ibn Sahl al-Sarakhsi, *Kitab al-Mabsut* (The Detailed Work of Jurisprudence), Cairo (1980), p. 2.

24 Roader, T., *Traditional Islamic Approach to Public International Law – Historic Concepts, Modern Implications*, Heidelberg: Max-Planck-Institut fur auslandisches offentliches Recht und Volkerrecht (2012), p. 256.

25 Khadduri, M., *The Islamic Law of Nations – Shaybani's Siyar*, Baltimore, Maryland: Johns Hopkins University Press (1966), p. 38.

a notable student of Abu Hanifa is acknowledged to have written the first extensive and systematic work on the subject of *Siyar* at the end of the eighth century.[26] It has been noted that apart from merely systemizing the rules of conduct in war and peacetime between the Muslim realm (*dar al-Islam*) and non-Muslim realm (*dar al-harb*), his works on *Siyar* also covered issues such as the Islamic rules on treaties, territorial jurisdiction, diplomatic relations, and neutrality rules.[27] Essentially, two principal concepts underline the theme of classical *Siyar*, namely, *jihad*, a term that has generated heated controversy in modern times,[28] and the concept of two worlds – *dar al-Islam* and *dar al-harb*. This is a concept which arguably divides the world, politically and legally, between Muslim and non-Muslim communities and could be perceived as being contrary to the concept of developing "friendly relations among nations" under article 1(2) of the UN Charter.[29]

Writing about *Siyar*, Christopher Ford notes that:

> the story of the development of the *Siyar* (Islamic law of nations) is that of the collision between this uncompromising hegemonism and the impossibility of conquering or converting the whole of humanity – in short, of the relationships forced upon Islam by its encounters with powerful non-Muslim states in the world beyond its Arabian heartland.[30]

Christopher then argues that

> [t]o the extent that Islamic law is faithful to its classical traditions, it will remain deeply at odds with international legal norms. From this perspective, a Muslim law of nations that genuinely does conform generally to the structure of modern international law requires Islam's abandonment of much of the bedrock of theocratic principle that make the *Shari'ah* the *Shari'ah*.[31]

Anke Bouzenita advances a similar argument that *Siyar* and modern international law are different concepts having developed from different historical and

26 Ibid at p. 22, and Baderin, M.A., "Muhammad Al-Shaybani (749/50–805)" in Fassbender, B, and Peters, A. (eds), *The Oxford History of International Law*, Oxford: Oxford University Press (2012), pp. 1081–1085.

27 Baderin, M.A., ibid at p.1084.

28 Ali, S.S., and Rehman, J., 'The Concept of *Jihad* in Islamic International Law', *Journal of Conflict and Security Law*, Vol. 10, No. 3 (2005), p. 3.

29 Ibid at p. 9. See however Baderin, M.A., 'The Evolution of Islamic Law of Nations and the Modern International Order: Universal Peace through Mutuality and Cooperation', *The American Journal of Islamic Social Sciences*, Vol. 17, No. 2 (2000), pp. 57–80 for an analysis of what he calls the "traditional hostility view" and "non-hostility view" of the concepts of *Dar al-Islam* and *Dar al-Harb* at pp. 65–70.

30 Ford, C.A., 'Siyar-ization and Its Discontents: International Law and Islam's Constitutional Crisis', *Texas International Law Journal*, Vol. 30, pp. 499–533 at p. 501.

31 Ibid pp. 50–51.

cultural milieus with different objectives and thus concluded that "[b]oth systems can only be described as incompatible".[32]

That line of thought is contentious and had been contradicted on several grounds by other writers. For example, Christopher Weeramantry[33] notes that "part of the Western misrepresentation of Islam was that Islam had no system of international law, no respect for treaties, no concept of human rights and no regard for the rights of neighbouring states".[34] He further questions the early development of international law in Europe whether it was an independent take off or did it draw upon the pre-existing body of knowledge of other civilizations such as Islam. He asserts that it is untenable to conclude that any study of international law proceeds upon the tacit assumption that it was the West which triggered off the development of international law for several reasons. He then reiterates that modern international law could have borrowed from the pre-existing body of Islamic knowledge on the subject on five grounds as follows:

> First, the prior existence of a mature body of international law worked out by accomplished Islamic jurists in textbooks upon the subject is an incontrovertible fact. Second, the flow of knowledge in all departments of science and philosophy from the Islamic to the Western world, commencing from the eleventh century is an indisputable fact. Thirdly, the fundamental rule of Western international law, *pacta sunt servanda,* formulated by Grotius in the seventeenth century is also a fundamental rule of Islamic international law, where it is based upon *Qur'anic* injunction and the *Sunnah* of the Prophet. Fourthly, there had been contact between Christian and Islamic civilizations both in time of war and peace for many centuries dating back to the Crusades. Apart from war times, peaceful relations through trade exposed the West to Islamic concepts of international trade. Thus, it seems unrealistic to suggest that the West remained unaware of the body of international law worked out by the Islamic jurists. Fifthly, Western scholars were not insular in their attitudes when they set off the brilliant and intellectual resurgence which led Europe to world supremacy. In as far as international law are concerned, there was no literature from the great civilizations of Greece and Rome comparable to their literature in private law. Treaties dealing with duties of combatants, the right of non-combatants or the disposal of enemy property were only found in the developed literature of Islamic International law. In Spain and Italy, a knowledge of Arabic was part of the literary equipment of the accomplished fifteenth and sixteenth-century

32 Bouzenita, A.I., "The *Siyar* – An Islamic Law of Nations?" *Asian Journal of Social Sciences*, Vol. 35 (2007), pp. 19–46 at 44.

33 Professor of Law, Monash University, Australia, formerly Justice of the Supreme Court of Sri Lanka, and a former Judge of International Court of Justice (ICJ) (1991–2000).

34 Weeramantry, C.G., *Islamic Jurisprudence – An International Perspective*, New York: Macmillan Press (1988), p. 130.

> scholars. Thus, Arabic literature was not unknown in the days when the first seeds were being sown of what was to become Western International law.[35]

Majid Khadduri adopted a middle ground and observed that while "strictly speaking, there is no Muslim law of nations in the sense of the distinction between modern municipal (national) law and international law based upon different sources and maintained by different sanctions",[36] because *Siyar* is an integral part of the unitary corpus of Islamic law (the *Shari'ah*), nevertheless, the term is taken to mean "the sum total of the principles, rules and practices governing Islam's relationships with the other nations",[37] in a way similar to the principles of modern international law.[38]

Mohammad Al-Ghunaimi has advanced a similar proposition in respect of the similarities and differences between *Siyar* and modern international law.[39] He noted that for international law to exist there must be a combination of three ingredients which include existence of numerous political entities, mutual relations between those entities, and, of course, rules or regulatory principles to manage and control these relations. He then argued that the environment in which *Siyar* developed included these ingredients from the very beginning.[40] Historically, at the dawn of Islam, the Muslims entered into relations, whether peaceful or hostile, with a number of independent states such as Persia, Abyssinia, and Byzantium and later on with other states in Europe, Asia, and Africa. In the course of history, there were principles and rules which Muslims considered as binding in its relations with other independent states.[41]

It is submitted that *Siyar*, despite its Islamic religious foundation, and modern international law, despite its Christian and later secular foundations, are not necessarily incompatible as both focus on the integration of humanity and rules regulating human co-existence. Both the founding fathers of *Siyar* and modern international law were theologians.[42] Like early Christianity, Islam aspires to being a universal faith; thus, the early law relating to dealings with non-Islamic states was thought of as being a passing phase.[43] From the early period of Islam,

35 Ibid at p. 149. Also quoted by Rahmat, M., "International Workshop and Seminar on *Siyar* & Islamic States Practices in International Law" Harmonization of Siyar in International Law: Some Reflections, *Asian-African Legal Consultative Organization*, 18–19 November 2009, Kuala Lumpur, Malaysia, p. 4.

36 Khadduri, M., *War and Peace in the Law of Islam*, Baltimore, MD: The Johns Hopkins Press (1955), p. 46.

37 Khadduri, M., *The Islamic Law of Nations –Shaybani's Siyar* (translated with an Introduction, Notes and Appendices by Khadduri, M.), Baltimore, MD: The John Hopkins (1966), p. 8.

38 Ibid at p. 9.

39 Al-Ghunaimi, M.T., *The Muslim Conception of International Law and the Western Approach*, The Hague: Martinus Nijhoff (1968), p. 28.

40 ibid.

41 Ibid at pp. 29–30.

42 See e.g. Baderin, M.A., 'Religion and International Law: Friends or Foes' *European Human Rights Law Review*, Vol. 5 (2009), pp. 637–658.

43 Weeramantry, C.G., supra note no. 34 at p. 130.

obligations arising from terms of treaties towards non-Islamic states were not only accorded full recognition,[44] but also, observed as religious obligations.[45]

Some of the rules of *Siyar* are based on the treaties between Muslims and non-Muslims,[46] official statements, and instructions of the Caliphs to commanders in the field[47] which were later integrated into Islamic legal corpus.[48] Other sources include the opinions and interpretations of the Muslim jurists on matters of foreign relations.[49] In comparative sense with modern international law, Khadduri observes that the sources of the Muslim law of nations conforms to the same categories defined by modern jurists and the Statute of the International Court of Justice, namely, agreements, custom, reason, and authority.[50] For example, the *Qur'an* and the authentic Hadiths represent authority, the Sunna, embodying the Arabian *jus gentium,* is equivalent to custom; rules expressed in treaties with non-Muslims fall into the category of agreement; and the *fatwas* and juristic commentaries of text-writers as well as the utterances and opinions of the Caliphs in the interpretation and the application of the law, based on analogy and logical deductions from authoritative sources, may be said to form reason.[51]

Generally, classical *Siyar* is theoretically divided into two main themes, namely, War and Peace with specific reference to a number of sub-themes such as the concept of *Dar* or territorial jurisdiction,[52] trading and commercial dealings of non-Muslim with *Dar al-Islam*[53] arbitration,[54] diplomacy,[55] and, the concept of neutrality,[56] all of which are still relevant concepts in modern international law and relations.

4.2.1 Siyar *in the contemporary Muslim worlds*

Relatively, classical *Siyar* has evolved over time. Aside from the classical concept of dividing the world into two abodes, the *Siyar*-rules have eventually evolved to allow for permanent non-violent legal contract with non-Muslim

44 Ibid.

45 See *Qur'an* 16:91–92.

46 Khadduri, M., War and Peace, supra note no. 36 at p. 47.

47 As contained for example, in Tabari, A.J.M.J., *Tarikh ak-Rusul wa al-Muluk*, (edited by M.J. de Geoeje, 15 vols), Leiden: Leiden University (1879–1901), as quoted by Khadduri, M., ibid at p. 102.

48 Khadduri, M., supra note no. 36 at 47.

49 See generally, Hamidullah, M., *The Muslim Conduct of State*, Kazi Publications Inc. (1992), particularly Chapter 15.

50 Rahim, A., *The Principles of Muhammadan Jurisprudence*, Madras: Luzac and Company (1911), p. 68.

51 Khadduri, M., supra note no. 36 at 47.

52 Ghazi, M.A., The Shorter Book on Muslim International Law (*Kitab Al-Siyar Al-Saghir* by Mohammad Ibn al-Hasan al-Shaybani) (edited, translated and annotated by Ghazi, M.H.), Pakistan: Islamic Research Institute, IIU (1998), p. 5.

53 Khadduri, M., supra note no. 36 at p. 225.

54 Ibid at pp. 231–238.

55 Ibid at pp. 239–250.

56 Ibid at pp. 251–267.

political entities – and with Muslim communities of a different persuasion in the form of treaty-making and diplomacy. This is a development that was born out of sheer political and economic exigencies.[57] Under the classical rules, such treaties were understood to be sustainable for a maximum period of ten years.[58] This was later expanded as the Ottoman Empire, for example, concluded treaties with an unspecified duration with European powers.[59] Presently, all Muslim nations are members of the UN which, according to Article 2(1) of its Charter, is based on the principle of the sovereign equality of all its Members and according to Article 1(1) the principle of friendly relations between nations.

On one hand, the Arab-Muslim majority states in their Arab Charter on Human Rights (ACHR) have adopted the basic principles of modern international law, recognizing fundamental rights and values such as self-determination of peoples, national sovereignty, and territorial integrity of States, and the right to life, security, and equality of individuals,[60] but also makes reference to "eternal principles of fraternity, equality and tolerance among human beings consecrated by the noble Islamic religion and other divinely-revealed religions".[61] On the other hand, the Organization of Islamic Cooperation (OIC), whose membership cuts across non-Arab States with commitment to Islamic ethos and values,[62] is founded to *inter alia*, "… unify the efforts of the Member States in view of the challenges faced by the Islamic world in particular and the international community in general", "strengthen intra-Islamic economic and trade cooperation [among the member states] in order to achieve economic integration leading to the establishment of an Islamic Common Market", and "protect and defend the true image of Islam, to combat defamation of Islam and encourage dialogue among civilisations and religions" but also committed to the purposes and principles of the UN.[63] It also issued the OIC Cairo Declaration on Human Rights in Islam in 1990,[64] and has followed this with a couple of other Islamic based human rights instruments.

57 Roader, T., supra note no. 24 at p. 529.

58 Stumpf, C., Völkerrecht unter Kreuz und Halbmond: Muhammad al-Shaybani und Hugo Grotius als Exponenten religiöser Völkerrechtstraditionen, *AVR*, Vol. 41 (2003) at p. 90 as quoted by Roader, T., supra note no 24 at p. 530.

59 Fadel, M., International Law, Regional Developments: Islam, in R. Wolfrum (ed.), MPEPIL, online edition, available at www.mpepil.com; and Mahmoudi, S., Islamic Approach to International Law, in R. Wolfrum (ed.), MPEPIL, online edition, available at www.mpepil.com.

60 See Articles 2,3,4,5,8, and 10 of the Arab Charter on Human Rights.

61 Preamble, Arab Charter on Human Rights 2004.

62 The preamble of the OIC Charter of 2014 states that it is "to be guided by the noble Islamic values of unity and fraternity, and affirming the essentiality of promoting and consolidating the unity and solidarity among the Member States in securing their common interests at the international arena" and committed "to preserve and promote the lofty Islamic values of peace, compassion, tolerance, equality, justice and human dignity".

63 See Charter of the Organisation of Islamic Cooperation (2014).

64 See The Cairo Declaration on Human Rights in Islam, issued by the Member States of the Organization of the Islamic 'Conference' (then) now 'Cooperation', Cairo, 5 August, 1990.

The legislative framework of these two key institutions of Muslim-majority states demonstrates a shift from a strictly traditional *Siyar* approach to an accommodative modern trend in international relations among the Muslim-majority states and the international community generally. It must be recalled that in 1969 when the OIC was founded by Muslim leaders, one of the basic objective of this pan-Islamic Organization was to promote cooperation among Muslim States in political, economic, social, cultural, and scientific matters, and to achieve solidarity in foreign policy goals.[65] The Preamble of old OIC Charter had also reaffirmed Member States' commitment "to adhere ... to the principles of the United Nations Charter ... and [of] international law [in general]".[66] Thus, it was stressed therein that Member States will uphold such values as democracy, good governance, human rights, and the rule of law; that they will respect the sovereignty and territorial integrity of other nations, and settle international disputes through peaceful means; that they will contribute to global peace and security in conformity with the principles of the UN Charter; and that they will work together with the international community in ensuring respect for non-interference in domestic affairs, and in combating aggression and terrorism in all forms.[67] This implies that from the beginning the OIC had confirmed the willingness of Muslim States to enter into relations with non-Muslim nations on the basis of equality, reciprocity, and mutual respect for territorial sovereignty. And thus, the OIC acts as a special institution to enable Muslim States to engage with each other on the common ground of core religio-political precept and at the same time to endorse the secular rule of modern international law on matters of war and peace.[68]

Examples of the practical shift from traditional *Siyar* are reflected in the practice of Muslim-majority states that have adopted diplomacy and modern international law mechanisms in settling international disputes such as the conclusion of a peace treaty between Israel and Egypt;[69] the settlement of territorial dispute between Qatar and Bahrain,[70] Egypt and Israel,[71] Emirates of Dubai and Sharjah,[72] Libya and Tunisia;[73] legal disputes between Algeria, Mauretania, and Morocco,[74] and Libya and the United Kingdom and the United States.[75]

65 Ali, S.S., *Gender and Human Rights in Islam and International Law*, London: Kluwer Law International (2000), pp. 195–196; see also Ali, S.S., & Rehman, J., supra note no. 28 at pp. 321, 343.
66 See Charter of the Organization of the Islamic Conference (1972).
67 Ibid in its Articles 1(3) (6) (14) (18) and 2(3) (4) (5) (7).
68 Bakicioglue, O., *Islam and Warfare, Context and Compatibility with International Law*, Routledge (2014), at p. 169.
69 Peace Treaty between the State of Israel and the Arab Republic of Egypt (26 March, 1979).
70 Maritime Delimitation and Territorial Questions between Qatar and Bahrain (Qatar v Bahrain) ICJ Report (2001) p. 40.
71 Boundary Dispute Concerning the Taba Area (Egypt v Israel) 27 ILM (1988), p. 1421.
72 Boundary Dispute between Dubai and Sharjah (Emirate of Dubai v Emirate of Sharjah), Arbitral Award of 19 October, 1981, ILR Vol. 91, 543ff.
73 Continental Shelf (Tunisia/Libyan Arab Jamahiriya) ICJ Rep. (1982), p. 18.
74 Western Sahara Case, Advisory Opinion, ICJ Rep. (1975), p. 12.
75 Interpretation and Application of the 1971 Montreal Convention Arising from the Aerial Incident at Lockerbie (Libya v UK and Libya v United States of America) ICJ Rep (1998), p. 115.

In summary, the ideal goals set in the traditional *Siyar*, *albeit* to unite the entire Muslim community (*ummah*) and eventually the whole of mankind under an all-encompassing polity, socio-political forces had long compelled Muslims into accommodating the universalist tendencies of Islam with other civilizations. Onder Bakircioglu describes this as "dynamic practical realities".[76] Thus, contemporary *Siyar* has been modified to respond positively to the reality of modern nation-states, and to the "all-encompassing and controlling" tendencies of modern international law.[77] Modern Saudi Arabia, which is the subject of analysis in subsequent paragraphs of this chapter, is reflective of the newly evolving concept of *Siyar* in the contemporary Muslim world.

4.3 Saudi Arabia as a nerve centre of Islamic law

Saudi Arabia stands at the centre of many critical issues of international dimension in relation to the application of Islamic law. On the one hand, it is the cradle of Islam[78] and home to the two holy cities, Makkah, and Madinah[79] which are the nerve centres of Islamic religious rituals and assembly of Islamic socio-political ideas and ideologies. By inference, it is the unnamed "international capital" of the "Muslim World", which is of global spread. The "Muslim World" consists of Muslim states in diverse geographical locations,[80] which consists of a total of more than 1.6 billion people living in about 50 sovereign countries with, significantly, some 10 to 15 million living in the USA and Europe.[81] On the other hand, Saudi Arabia is one of the 51 founding member nation-states of the UN, having signed its Charter in 1945.[82] It therefore plays prominent roles (particularly from the perspective of Middle East generally and Gulf region in particular) in a number of international, regional, and pan-Islamic organizations.

Another strand to Saudi Arabia's international significance is the global dependence on its oil and gas as it holds some 25% of the remaining proven

76 Bakicioglue, O., supra note no. 68 at p. 172.

77 Ibid.

78 See generally Mai, Y., *Cradle of Islam: The Hijaz and the Quest for Identity in Saudi Arabia*, I.B. Tauris (2009), and John, B.R., *Saudi Arabia Exposed : Inside a Kingdom in Crisis*, London: Palgrave (2005), p. 145.

79 Eijk, E.V, 'Sharia and National Law in Saudi Arabia', in Otto, J.M. (ed), *Shari'ah Incorporated, A Comparative Overview of the Legal Systems of Twelve Muslim Countries in Past and Present*, Netherlands: The Leiden University Press Series on Law (2010), p. 139.

80 Muslim states include those states where majority of populations are Muslims. They also include members of the Organization of Islamic Cooperation (OIC). Some of these states may or may not adopt Islam as their official religion or consider Islamic Law an official source of domestic legislations.

81 Cesari, J., *Islam in the West, Modernity and Globalization Revisited*, *Globalization and the Muslim World* (edited by Schalbler, B., and Stenberg, L., Syracuse: Syracuse University Press (2004), p. 2 See also the report of the Population Reference Bureau on Global Muslim Population.

82 UN Member States on the Record, www.un.org/depts/dhl/unms/founders.shtml (accessed 27 April 2015).

oil reserves in the world.[83] For example, Saudi Arabia's leading markets in 2004 were: the United States (18.5% of all exports), Japan (15.2%), South Korea (10.1%), and China (5.7%).[84] Correspondingly, its leading export suppliers within the same period were the United States (9.3%) of all imports), Germany (6.6%), Japan (6.5%), and the United Kingdom (5.3%).[85] Its impact on security issues in the Gulf and the wider Middle East is also significant as all that constitute some of the most crucial dilemma in global affairs generally today.[86]

Saudi Arabia has a dual history – of the Arab origin[87] and of the birth of Islam. Early Arab society was known for nomadic tribal life with no central government.[88] Individual rights were tied strictly to tribal membership which was responsible for protecting such rights and vengeance often applied as the method of punishment.[89] Women were not accorded any rights and were often inherited as ordinary chattels if they were fortunate not to be buried alive at birth.[90] In this lawless situation, endless wars of attrition such as the Basūs War (*harb al-basūs*) or the War of Dāhis and Gabrā' (*harb al-dāhis wa al-gabrā'*) were waged on flimsy and trivial issues.[91]

The advent of Islam transformed Arabia within a generation. It brought to this hitherto fractious and isolated population, significant social order and unity.[92] Right from inception, Islam had been largely a determining factor of the history of the Arabian Peninsula,[93] and consequently embedded its law and unique culture into the system of the region from then on. It was Islam that had led to the emergence and expansion of the Arabian Empire, and unified the Arabs not only in the Arabian Peninsula, but also from Asia to the Atlantic Ocean during the seventh and eighth centuries.[94] Islamic law therefore has a strong traditional hold in most parts of the Arab-Muslim world but particularly in Saudi Arabia.

However, Saudi Arabia, a typical traditional desert society got to a turning point in its history when it discovered oil, marking a new beginning in economic fortune. In the 1950s the production of oil increased beyond all predictions as

83 Niblock, T, *Saudi Arabia – Power, Legitimacy and Survival*, Routledge, London and New York: Taylor and Francis Group (2006), pp. 1–2.

84 Worldmark Encyclopaedia of Nations, *Saudi Arabia*, www.encyclopedia.com/topic/Saudi_Arabia.aspx (accessed 02 May 2015).

85 Ibid.

86 Niblock, T, supra note no. 83.

87 See Encyclopedia Britannica, *History of Arabia, Pre-Islamic Arabia, to the 7th Century CE.*

88 Lewis, B., *The Arabs in History*, Oxford: Oxford University Press (1960), p. 1.

89 Khadduri, M., and Liebesny, H.J., *Law in the Middle East*, Washington DC: Middle East Institute (1960), p. 1.

90 Waheed-Ud-Din, F.S., *The Benefactor*, Lahore: Lion Art Press "Karachi" Ltd. (1965), p. 4.

91 Hitti, P.K., *History of the Arabs* (9th edn), New York: St. Martin's (1968), p. 3.

92 Wynbrandt, J., *A Brief History of Saudi Arabia*, New York: Checkmark Books (2004), p. 24.

93 Al-Farsy, F., *Modernity and Tradition, The Saudi Equation*, London and New York: Kegan Paul International (1990), p. 21.

94 Ibid.

oil revenues began to change the relatively poor and isolated society and by the middle 1970s, the revenues had increased fantastically.[95]

Saud Al-Mishari[96] notes that the oil-boom opened up commercial and industrial activities in the Kingdom in such a way that not only the Saudi citizens were involved but, also, experts and teeming population of foreign workforce coming from many countries of the world. Saudi businessmen emerged at local level and foreign industrialists, investors, and multinational companies and corporations came on board. Consequently, the need arose for creation of Chambers of Commerce and Industry. The Saudi Chamber of Commerce & Industry (JCCI) was first established in 1946 and since then it has been serving the economy of Saudi Arabia and has continuously contributed to its development and progress.[97] However, in 1980, the Saudi authority felt the need to establish a Council of Saudi Chambers of Commerce and Industry whose primary objectives were to act as an institutional body that promotes and protects the interests of regional Saudi Chambers of Commerce and Industry, acting as a voice for them at both the national and international levels.[98] It is noted that the majority of the individual Chambers are much older than the Council, which was created out of a need to coordinate the work of the rapidly growing regional bodies.[99] Functions performed by the Council include, *inter alia,* the monitoring of economic issues affecting the private sector; reinforcing the relationships between the local chambers and facilitation of the communication necessary to prevent duplication of projects.[100] At the initial stage, there were seven such chambers with branches across the Kingdom. At present, there are 28 Chambers with several branches operating under them.[101] As it became rich in oil, it began to acquire more and more material goods and influence, and thus, "an abstemious, austere, and pietistic society suddenly was face-to-face with the values and technology of a comparatively secular and materialistic West".[102]

Against this background, two issues provoke jurisprudential analysis of modern Saudi Arabia as the nerve centre of Islamic law and culture as well as an important player in a secular international community. In 1932 when

95 Ochsenwald, W., and Fisher, S.N., *The Middle East a History* (4th edn), McGraw-Hill Publishing Company (1990), p. 555.

96 Former Assistant Secretary General for Legal Affairs, Council of Saudi Chambers of Commerce and Industry.

97 International Chamber of Commerce, *ICC Saudi Arabia*, www.iccwbo.org/worldwide-membership/national-committees/icc-saudi-arabia/ (accessed 02 May 2015).

98 Council of Saudi Chamber, www.csc.org.sa/English/Pages/default.aspx (accessed 02 May 2015).

99 Ibid.

100 Ibid.

101 Al-Mishari, S.A., in an interview conducted by this author with him in Riyadh on 25 June, 2013.

102 International Context of Major Middle Eastern Events in the Twentieth Century (Posted June 22nd, 2013) by BlackBear, http://historum.com/blogs/blackbear/1705-internationalcontext-major-middle-eastern-events-twentieth-century.html (accessed 28 May 2014).

King Abdulaziz Al-Saudi promulgated a Royal Decree for the unification of Hejaz and Nejd to form a new State now known as Kingdom of Saudi Arabia, a new chapter was opened in the history of political, legislative and judicial history of this new state.[103] Between 1932 and 1992, its legal and judicial systems have undergone several developmental processes introduced by successive administrations after its founder as earlier analyzed in Chapter 2 of this book. However, in 1992, a significant development occurred when King Fahd introduced *quasi*-constitutionalism by promulgating the Basic Law of Governance for the country. Under Article 1 of this law, the *Qur'an* and the *Sunnah* of the Prophet Muhammad were officially declared to be the Constitution of the State and the Islamic *Shari'ah* as the basis of its legal system.[104] It is noted that historically, the *Hanbali* School is the officially recognized Islamic school of jurisprudence in the country, which informs most of its legal conduct.[105] For example, it has been proposed that the *Hanbali* School's jurisprudential interpretation was, apparently, the applicable law in Saudi Arabia oil agreements.[106] It should also be noted that this is the Islamic school of thought whose traditional aversion to opinion *(ra'y)* and strict adherence to the text of the *Qur'an* and the tradition was exceptional.[107] How does Saudi Arabia strike a balance between tradition and modernity? How has it adapted its foreign policy to cope with the different legal systems it had contact with during its development?

4.4 Saudi Arabia foreign policy

Saudi Arabia's foreign policy objectives could be said to be multi-faceted. It is generally focused on cooperation with the Gulf States, the unity of the Arab world, solidarity with Muslim countries, but also support for the UN,[108] based on middle ground and consensus position.[109] Saudi Arabia is a non-aligned state whose foreign policy objectives are to maintain its security and its paramount position on the Arabian Peninsula, defend general Arab and Islamic interests, promote solidarity among Islamic governments and maintain cooperative relations with other oil-producing and major oil-consumer countries.[110]

From the regional perspective, Saudi Arabia's foreign policy specifically emphasizes a number of relation strategies, namely, the security and stability

103 Royal Decree of 23 September 1932.

104 For analysis of this see e.g. Eijk, E.V., supra note no. 79, pp. 139–180.

105 Mahmassani, S., Falsafah al-Tashri' fi al-Islam (*The Philosophy of Jurisprudence in Islam*), Leiden: Brill Archive (1961), p. 32.

106 Madani, M.O., The Relationship between Saudi Arabian Domestic Law and International Law: A Study of the Oil Agreement with Foreign Companies, PhD Dissertation of the Law School of The George Washington University (1970), p. 7.

107 Mahmassani, S., supra, note 105 at p. 30.

108 Saudi Ministry of Foreign Affairs.

109 Quandt, W.B. *Saudi Arabia in the 1980s – Foreign Policy, Security, and Oil*, The Brookings Institution (1981), p. 12.

110 Ibid.

of the Gulf region as an exclusive responsibility of the stakeholders thereon; non-interference in internal affairs of other countries, with modalities to co-operate with these states; strengthening cooperation with member states of the GCC in different political, economic, security, social, cultural fields by deepening and consolidating relations and ties with them; policy coordination with states in the region on issues of international concerns; dispute resolution mechanism based on mutual understanding, brotherhood, and good neighbourliness; adoption of suitable economic policies and integration among states in this region.[111]

Martin Harrison notes that one of the cornerstones of Saudi foreign policy throughout the twentieth century that was laid by Ibn Saud was opposition to the establishment of pan-Arab or pan-Islamic political formations.[112] He argues that Ibn Saud resisted the endorsement of the plans aimed at transforming independent Arab countries into a larger unity. He had little enthusiasm of the pro-unity propaganda of both Arab nationalists in Syria and the Muslim Brotherhood in Egypt in the 1930s. That perhaps explains why Quandt adds that Saudis "still believed that stability in the Middle East would be enhanced if only the Palestinian question could be resolved. ... And Islamic solidarity failed to provide a strong alternative, as fashionable as it might have become in recent years".[113] Ibn Saudi was also opposed to plans for a stronger Arab League in 1945 and refused to be drawn into any integration scheme, insisting that the separate existence of each Arab state be recognized.[114] Jacob Goldberg arguing in the same vain observes that the Saudis' deep anxiety on this point ensures their continued opposition to all unity plans to this day.[115] The cardinal objective of the Saudi foreign policy is thus defensive in nature: securing the independence and integrity of the state, as well as the position of the Saudi royal family, in the fact of a chain of external enemies.[116] Harrison further notes that the evolution of Saudi foreign policy had none of the strong, deep-seated anti-Western sentiments prevalent in other Arab countries such as Egypt, Syria, and Iraq.[117]

The defensive nature of the Saudi foreign policy was demonstrated when the Congress of the Islamic World was convened in 1926. Ibn Sa'ud called for this conference in the midst of his Hijaz conquest expedition at a time when he

111 Saudi Arabia Ministry of Foreign Affairs, The Foreign Policy of the Kingdom of Saudi Arabia, www.mofa.gov.sa/sites/mofaen/KingdomForeignPolicy/Pages/KingdomPolicy34645.aspx (accessed 15 October 2014).

112 Harrison, M., 'Saudi Arabia's Foreign Policy: Relations with the Superpowers', *University of Durham, Centre for Middle Eastern and Islamic Studies, CMEIS Occasional Paper*, No. 46 (1995), p. 7.

113 Ibid at p. 6.

114 Ibid at p. 8.

115 Goldberg, J., *The Foreign Policy of Saudi Arabia – The Formative Years* (1902–1918), Cambridge, Massachusetts: Harvard University Press (1986), pp. 182–183.

116 Harrison, M., supra note no. 112 at p. 8.

117 Ibid.

was still regarded by many in the Muslim world as an intolerant sectarian.[118] In the earlier versions of his invitation, one of the main agendas of the congress was to determine the future of governance of the Hijaz. However as Ibn Saud succeeded in conquering Makkah, Madina, and Jeddah coupled with the endorsement given to his absolute rulership of the territory by the notable leaders of the province, there was nothing left for the congress to discuss.[119] The congress agenda was thus reduced to discussing plans to improve the condition of the pilgrimage; "with the transparent aim of securing formal Muslim acquiescence in the newly installed regime".[120] Ibn Saud later introduced an unequivocal policy prohibiting all activity that could be construed as political during the pilgrimage.[121] Having earlier banned the congress, in 1928, he reopened its building for a tea party of prominent pilgrims, and within a few years, the event had evolved into the pilgrimage banquet, usually held at once of the royal palaces in Makkah.[122]

Ayman al-Yasinni notes that Saudi state policy was based essentially on regional stability and Islam and foreign aid are the instruments.[123] He argues that in using religion as an instrument of foreign policy, Saudi leaders were able to stress the elements in Islam which correspond with their objective; and in the period of territorial shaping, radical *Wahhabism* was the dominant theme.[124]

Despite divergent views, the fact remains that Saudi Arabia is a nation founded on Islamic ethos, upholding Islamic law, and protecting Islamic interests was the cornerstone of its foreign policy right from the era of its founding father – King Abdulaziz. Today, Saudi Arabia is a nation whose views are actively sought and respected by global powers looking for a better understanding of Islamic norms and Arab issues. The Kingdom's diplomacy is considered a central factor in forestalling potential global and regional crises, especially with respect to engagement with Islam and Islamic law in the Muslim world. Its mediation is solicited to resolve disputes that, if unchecked, could have reverberations far beyond the region.[125] It should be noted that the Saudi Arabia foreign policy and international profile took a dramatic turn after the 11 September 2001 attacks that took place in New York City and Washington DC which involved hijacking four airplanes and killing nearly 3,000 people. Following this attack, it was reported that about 15 of the 19 hijackers were from Saudi Arabia. Many countries of the Western hemispheres began to have a review of their relations with

118 Kramer, M., *Islam Assembled – The Advent of the Muslim Congresses*, New York: New York Columbia University Press (1986), p. 106.

119 Ibid.

120 Ibid.

121 Ibid at p. 122.

122 Ibid.

123 Al-Yassini, A., 'Religion and Foreign Policy in Saudi Arabia', *CDAS Discussion Papers No. 2 Department of Political Science, Conordia University* (1983), p. 24.

124 Ibid.

125 Royal Embassy of Saudi Arabia, Washington DC, USA – www.saudiembassy.net/issues/foreign-relations/ (accessed 5 December 2012).

Saudi Arabia. For example, the US began to introduce measures to scrutinize the Saudi teaching of Islam. It also began to reassess its relation particularly on the "oil-for-security" alliance with the Saudi Arabia.[126]

4.5 Incorporation of international treaties and conventions into Saudi Arabian law

Domestication of international treaties and conventions into Saudi local legislation serves as a practical example of its shift from a strict traditional *Siyar* conceptualization of the world into the two spheres of *Dar al-Islam* and *Dar al-Harb*. The Saudi Arabian involvement in political and economic matters of international concern dictates its ratifications of international treaties. This often requires a shift in its domestic legislative policies. It has incorporated a good number of international laws and conventions into its legal system. States that adopt the dualist method of international law require all treaties to be incorporated before they can have any domestic legal effects. Like Britain, Saudi Arabia also adopts the dualist method of domesticating international law to its domestic legislation.[127] Thus, international conventions or agreements are considered to be within the executive competence of "His Royal Majesty's Government" (the Consultative Council and the Council of Ministers). Article 70 of the Basic Law of Governance and Article 20 of the Council of Ministers Law provide that laws were enacted and amended, and treaties, international agreements, and concessions were approved and implemented, by Royal Decrees after having been considered by the Consultative Council and the Council of Ministers, respectively.[128] Thus, under Article 70 of the Basic Law of Governance, Royal Decrees were the legal instrument by which international agreements and treaties were incorporated into domestic law.[129] In accordance with the laid down rules, international agreements and treaties were first referred to the Council of Ministers and the Consultative Council for approval. Upon receiving approval of both bodies, the relevant agreement or treaty became part of domestic law by means of Royal Decree.[130]

It must be noted that most legislations originate in the ministry that has authority over a particular subject matter having submitted the draft law to the

126 Bradley, J.R., *Saudi Arabia Exposed*, California: Macmillan (2005) p. 6; see generally, Michael, R.D., *Wahhabism: Is It a Factor in the Spread of Global Terrorism*? Thesis presented to the Naval Postgraduate School, Monterey, California for Master of Arts in Security Studies, (2009).

127 Bathia, K.L., *Textbook on Legal Language and Legal Writing*, New Delhi: Universal Law Publishing, p. 252.

128 World Trade Organization, *Report of the Working Party on the Accession of the Kingdom of Saudi Arabia to The World Trade Organization*, WT/ACC/SAU/61, 1 November, 2005 (05-5141), Protocols of accession for new members since 1995, including commitments in goods and services (24 August 2012), www.wto.org/english/thewto_e/acc_e/completeacc_e.htm#sau (accessed 18 January 2013).

129 See Royal Decree No. A/90 of 27.8.1412H (1 March 1992).

130 World Trade Organization, supra note no. 128.

Council of Ministers, which assess and evaluate such laws.[131] After the Council's approval, the draft law is sent to the Bureau of Experts, which reviews it to ensure that it would accomplish its purpose and complies with international legal and/or technical norms.[132] If the Bureau gives its approval, it would be submitted to the *Shoura* Council, which determines whether it is compatible with the Saudi Arabia's local and international standards and policies. The *Shoura* Council then sends the law to the Council of Ministers for its approval after which the latter submit the draft to the King for his assent. The King now issues a Royal Decree enacting the law, after which it is returned to the ministry that is responsible for drafting it.[133] It is that Ministry that is responsible for the promulgation and implementation subject to other relevant Royal Decrees.[134] It should be noted that where the Councils of Ministers and the *Shoura* Council have conflicting views on a draft regulations, those views are communicated to the King, who takes final decision on which view should prevail. The final text of the executive regulation is then promulgated into law in the official gazette.[135] It should also be noted that international treaties and conventions do not take precedence over provisions of domestic law, nor do provisions of domestic law take precedent over international agreements or treaties. The conflicts between the two systems are rather resolved in accordance with the same rules of interpretation that are applied to domestic legislation.[136]

The applicable rules of interpretation were as follows: (i) an international agreement could not override a rule of *Shari'ah* (e.g., the prohibition on the importation, sale, or consumption of alcoholic beverages could not be supplanted by an international agreement); (ii) given an apparent inconsistency between an international agreement and domestic law, the text of each would be interpreted so as to avoid any conflict; and (iii) where the text did not resolve the conflict, recourse could be had to the intent and purpose of the agreement and the law. Where a conflict still existed, the conflict would be resolved following the rule that a new law or international agreement to which the Kingdom had agreed was superior to previous laws or international agreements (with the exception noted above that no law or international agreement could overturn a *Shari'ah* rule). This is exemplified by the accession of Saudi Arabia to the Vienna Convention on the Law of Treaties 1969, pursuant to the relevant rules as summarized above.[137]

Under Article 70 of the Basic Law of Governance international agreements entered into, comes to force as domestic laws following their ratification by Royal

131 Al-Bisher, H., et al., *Saudi Maritime Policy integrated Governance*, Oxfordshire: Routledge (2012), p. 33.

132 Ibid.

133 Ibid.

134 Ibid.

135 Ibid at p. 34.

136 Ibid.

137 Council of Ministers Resolution No. 165 of 24.6.1423H (1 September 2002) World Trade Organization, ibid.

Decree and enactment by the Consultative Council and Council of Ministers. As a general rule, should Saudi Arabia's laws or other acts be found to contradict international treaties or agreements, Saudi Arabia would bring its laws or other acts into conformity with such treaties or agreements, and would respond quickly to instances in which inconsistencies were brought to the attention of Saudi officials.[138] However this is not applicable to fundamental religious rules and principles, such as prohibiting the consumption of alcohol and pork, for example.[139]

4.6 Islamic conception of territorial statehood and nation-state

It should be noted from the onset that despite the constitutional separation of church and state, religion has been critical to the evolution of many European national identities as Protestantism played an important role in the formation of the new American nation.[140] Secondly, under modern international law, a sovereign state is a juridical and non-physical entity governed by a centralized authority that possesses sovereignty over a geographically defined area, permanent population, and the capacity to enter into relations with other independent sovereign states.[141] These two characteristics describe the Islamic perspective of territorial statehood and nation-state and particularly the historic "Islamic State of *Madinah*" which arguably serves as a reference point for any aspiration to replicate and re-enact this historic template.

When Prophet Muhammad and his followers migrated from Makkah to Madinah, they met a cosmopolitan city consisting of Jewish, pagan, and Christian groups who had been yearning to have a neutral outsider to serve as the chief arbitrator for the entire community after around a hundred years recurring fights, slaughters, and disagreement among them.[142] He introduced a Charter known as the constitution of Madinah establishing a kind of alliance or federation among the eight Madinah tribes and Muslim emigrants from Makkah specifying rights and duties of all citizens and the relationship among them.[143] Thus, the Muslim Ummah was first recognized as a polity by this development which was a radical departure from the pre-Islamic, chauvinistic, and warmongering attitude of the traditional Arab society. The term "*Ummah*" was used in this Constitution to describe the new polity which, Baderin argues is correct to be referred to as a "city-state" in the context of modern international law.[144]

138 World Trade Organization, supra note no. 128.

139 Ibid.

140 Asad, T., 'Religion, Nation-State, Secularism', Chapter 10, in Van Der Veer, P., and Lehmann, H. (eds), *Nation and Religion Perspective on Europe and Asia*, New Jersey: Princeton University Press (1999), p. 178.

141 Shaw, M.N., *International Law*, Cambridge: Cambridge University Press (2003), p. 178.

142 Watt, W.M., *Muhammad at Medina*, Oxford: Clarendon Press (1956), pp. 227–228.

143 Watt., W.M. *The Cambridge History of Islam*, Cambridge University Press (1977), p. 39.

144 Baderin, M.A., supra note no 29 at p. 60.

It is argued that all essential constituents that qualify a state to be sovereign were extant with the nascent *Madinah* state. It had a population comprising the Muslims and non-Muslims referred to in the Charter as a single political entity (*Ummah*); a defined territory, a government, and the capacity to independently enter into relations with other sovereign states which was subsequently demonstrated by signing treaty relations with other States.[145] This model city-state and its polity later crystalized into a larger *Ummah* from which empires and governments evolved and spread across territories and continents. Like any other human systems, it was influenced by extraneous factors it had contact with during its developmental progression; and at a point in history, it met its own misfortune. It was subjugated and colonized losing its entire cherished glories and the edifice of its Caliphate crumbled and went into oblivion.[146] The abolition of the Caliphate marked the beginning of the emergence of independent Muslim nations under the institution and conception of the modern nation-state.[147]

People's revolt was a significant factor that led to the decline of colonialism after World War II. Islam as a faith and a source of identity and important factor in social relations and politics played significant role in this regard.[148] However, the Muslim world that emerged from this hegemony was divided into independent nation-states and saturated in nationalism bereft of values and ethos of historic *Ummah* under the Caliphate system.[149] This had led to persistent calls for a return to the Islamic heritage of an *Ummah* polity under a single political authority.[150] Anne Mayer observes in this regard that:

> the nation-state… has never been definitely reconciled with Islamic theory, which in its traditional formulation recognized only the *Umma*, or community of believers. There have been Muslim who, despite the entrenched character of the system of nation-states in the modern world, still adhered to the traditional opinion that any political subdivisions of the Islamic *Umma* were inimical to Islam. Other have accepted these divisions or tolerated them on the assumption that they are a temporary phenomenon.[151]

The Muslims' bitter experience of colonialism which had provoked the persistent calls for a rejuvenation of the old system had led to the debate as to whether even if the Muslims were to go back to their political past, would they have

145 Ibid.

146 Ibid at p. 62.

147 Ibid, also Khadduri, M., supra at pp. 19–20; and Al-Ghunaimi, M.T., supra note no. 37 at pp. 38–54.

148 See e.g. Esposito, J.L., The Islamic Threat: Myth or Reality? (3rd edn) New York: Oxford University Press, 1999); Gerges, F.A., *America and Political Islam: Clash of Cultures or Clash of Interests?* Cambridge: Cambridge University Press (1999).

149 Baderin, M.A., supra note no. 29.

150 Ibid.

151 Mayer, A., 'War and Peace in the Islamic Tradition of International Law,' in Kelsey, J., and Turner, J.T. (eds), *Just War and Jihad*, New York: Greenwood Press (1991), pp. 195 and 212.

adopted monist or dualist model of Caliphate. Opinions differ and debate has remained on-going. Baderin observes that the political realities of today's world and the geographical spread of the modern Muslim nations make it even more difficult to think of the Islamic State in a monist perspective under one political authority.[152] This position appears to be justified in view of the metamorphosis of the classical Islamic concept of "*Dar al-Islam*" and "*Dar al-Harb*" as earlier discussed in paragraph 4:2 of this study.

To what extent the practice of modern Saudi Arabia in balancing between Islamic law and international law is influenced by the contemporary reality of the Islamic *Siyar* within the framework of the modern concept of territorial statehood and nation-state as discussed above, this forms the focus of examination in the next paragraph.

4.7 Saudi Arabia – balancing between Islamic law and international law

Saudi Arabia is committed to Islamic law for its domestic interest, but, on the other hand, International law also brings both domestic and international benefits. Saudi Arabia has therefore identified the need to cautiously balance between its commitment to Islamic law and its adherence to international law. Many experts of international law have long asserted the point that: "it really *is* in the best interests of a state to recognize and observe the rules of international law even when it may not seem so at a particular time".[153] Majority of scholars of public international law hold the notion that international law can make the world a "better" place.[154]

Goldberg notes that it has been a general belief that the beginning of the re-establishment of the Saudi entity in 1902 had meant primarily the revival of eighteenth- and nineteenth-century *Wahhabism*, which engender mostly an unchecked, religiously propelled drive for territorial expansionism. Taking this concern into account, stakeholders in Arabian affairs anticipated continuity of the hitherto traditional footsteps. However, in the realm of international order and foreign policy, the twentieth-century Saudi state, has cautiously broken with the strict traditional pattern of *Wahhabi* conduct and thus a turning point in Saudi history.[155] He goes on to state that at that early period of re-establishment of modern Saudi Arabia, three main changes from past *Wahhabi* experience were adopted in Saudi foreign policy, namely, a new strategy toward the mobilization of one power against the other, a new pattern of behaviour toward the Ottoman Empire, and a new attitude toward Britain and her *protégés* along the Persian Gulf coast.[156]

152 Baderin, M.A., supra note no. 29.

153 Shirley, V.S., and Withana, R., 'The Relevance of International Law for Foreign Policy Decision-making When National Security Is at Stake: Lessons from the Cuban Missile Crisis', *Chinese Journal of International Law*, Vol. 2 (2003), p. 163.

154 Ibid.

155 Goldberg, J., supra note no. 115 at pp. 155–156.

156 Ibid.

Abd-Allah al-Munifi, a former legal adviser to the Council of Ministers, had noted that international law as an integral part of the *Shari'ah,* shares the same fundamental sources of the *Qur'an,* the *Sunnah, and Ijma'.*[157] He argued that the imperative of legal obligation is rooted in religious observance as God is the unseen and ultimate authority.[158] His argument goes in line with the Saudi jurists who, at a forum in 1974, emphasized to their European counterparts that good citizenship in Islam is guaranteed by religious obligation.[159] International law according to another Saudi intelligentsia is one with the *Shari'ah* and its roots or *usul*; thus there is no real difference between law and morality in Islam, and thus, there are two distinct though interlinked realms of justice – divine and human.[160]

A Saudi university don had also expressed the view that international law, though less definitive, is still subordinate to God's will and justice. According to him, international law is primarily in the domain of human responsibility in the sense that men through their governments, are called upon to enforce its rules. As far as Islam is concerned, law is subject to God's sanctity since He is the ultimate judge in all matters; human judgments are subject to His divine final decision. It follows that, law generally and international law in particular have both legal and religious connotations. They are guided by exterior and interior rules – the latter being more important because they are bound by conscience.[161]

On the contention that modern international law is predicated upon the superior assessment of peace over war,[162] Saudis are generally and vehemently opposed to the orientalists' common assertion that Islam violates this Western postulation of international law theory. They are unanimous in demurring that the West has so distorted the concept of *Jihad* as to make Islam appear naturally aggressive, belligerent, and combative.[163] Western scholarship has been particularly criticized by the Saudi intelligentsia for absolutizing[164] the concept of *dar al-harb* at the expense of the *dar al-hudna* or sphere of peace (or suspension of hostilities) or (literally "house of calm" – a long-range Islamic strategy for conflict resolution). It is argued that the very religious nature of *Jihad* guarantees

157 Piscatori, J.P., supra note no. 4 at p. 229.

158 Ibid.

159 *Colloques sur le dogme musulman et les droits de l'homme en Islam,* Beirut: Dar al-Kitab al-Lubnani (1974), p. 124 as quoted by Piscatori, J.P., supra note no. 4 at p. 229.

160 Maruf al-Dawalibi, former Prime Minister of Syria and later Adviser to Kings Faysal and Khalid, in an interview with Piscatori on 18th March, 1975; Piscatori, J.P., supra note no. 4.

161 A view expressed by Professor Muhammad al-Mubarak, a former Syrian Minister and Professor at the Faculty of Islamic Studies in Ummu al-Qura University in Makkah. The interview which was conducted by Pisctori took place at the King Abdul Aziz University in Jeddah, Saudi Arabia on 12th June, 1975, Piscatori, J.P., supra note no. 4 at p. 230.

162 Piscatori quoting Bozeman's contention, supra p. 233.

163 Ibid.

164 To render absolute; consider or declare perfect, complete, or unchangeable: Overzealous followers absolutized his theories; see http://dictionary.reference.com/browse/absolutizing (accessed 7 December 2012).

the peacefulness of Islam, as the aim of religion is peace and accordingly is the norm that should govern Islamic relationships.[165]

Khadduri, in this regard, has been sharply criticized for being parochial in his view of Islamic law of nations. He is criticized for being heavily relying only on the *Shafi'i* School. His line of argument is not only selective but restrictive as he ignores a wide variety of opinions that are equally valid and his argument that there is no time limitation to treaties in Islamic law of nations.[166] Abu Sulayman, a former Professor of international relations at the King Saud University in Riyadh criticized Khadduri on several issues. He faulted Khadduri's propositions that there is no time limitation on the issue of treaties; equating polytheists with pagans and suggesting that Islam aspires to expand its territory by defeating the pagans; and presenting his (Khadduri's) views on these issues as representing a general consensus among jurists.[167]

As international law is based essentially on a system of recognized territorial state, the issue of nation-state becomes relevant at this stage. Opinions differ among Saudi scholars and intelligentsia on the compatibility of the classical Islamic notion of state or *Ummah* with the Western notion of modern nation-state. For example, Dean al-Milhan holds that the classical Islamic theory is not antithetical to the concept of state sovereignty because the *Qur'an* urges that measures be taken in self-defence which essentially implies protection of state interest. Secondly, the idea of the *Ummah* is not controverted by the notion of territorial nation-state, because the latter fits easily into the larger framework.[168] Similarly, all Muslims are brothers, and there is no difference among them except in degree of piety. Thus, the existence of separate nation-state does not invalidate this general unity so long all parts of the *Shari'ah* are observed.[169]

On the other hand, Al-Munifi holds a contrary view. According to him, the concept of the nation-state is alien to Islam. It is argued that the *Shari'ah* affirms a single, universal state that contrasts to a system of individual territorial units or entities.[170] It is originally a Western concept with its correlatives, namely, territory, sovereignty, and political liberty and independence. Going down memory lane, Sheikh al-Jabayr[171] asserted that in the classical understanding, Islam was one state, governed by a single *khalifa* until it declined during the Abbasid's era. Consequently, the entire Muslim world was brought under Western colonization which launched and promoted the territorial

165 Opinion expressed by 'Abd al-Latif al-Haymani (Second Secretary of the Saudi Arabia Embassy t Washington, D.C., in an interview with him in June, 1974); Piscatori, J.P., ibid at 234.

166 Piscatori, J.P., supra note no. 4 at p. 234.

167 Abu Sulayman, A.H., *The Islamic Theory of International Relations: Its Relevance, Past and Present*, Ph.D. dissertation, University of Pennsylvanian (1973), pp. 36–42.

168 Piscatori, J.P., supra note no. 4 at pp. 244–245.

169 Ibid at p. 245.

170 Ibid.

171 Sheikh Muhammad al-Jabayr was the Head of the Higher Council of Justice in the Saudi Arabia Ministry of Justice.

divisions of the modern nation-state structure and policy.[172] Be that as it may, majority of modern Saudi intelligentsia accede to the fact that the notion of modern nation-state, though, introduced by the West has come to stay and even adopted or forced upon the Muslim world. Sheikh al-Yamani[173] accepts not only the nation-state but, argues that the Islamic state inherently is the equal in every way to the modern, Western, welfare nation-state; he recommends the example of Saudi Arabia for other Islamic states in the sphere of social and domestic legislation.[174]

Piscatori expressed reservation on the concept of Islamic *Ummah* in the contemporary world politics. Majority of Saudis, however, assert in response to that reservation that its function is spiritual and that the internal divisions of the community have arisen out of political circumstances that have largely left Saudi Arabia unblemished. They further argue that Western colonialism accounted for split and rupture of the hitherto united Muslim *Ummah*. Even after the end of the colonial era, neo-colonialism had perpetually remained with them in different forms and that explains the apparent British, French, and German customs and ways of life, for example, in many Muslim nations up till the present time.[175] Again, on account of the colonization experience, and the divisive mark it left behind, there are wide differences between colonized countries such as Egypt and Iraq and the un-colonized nation such as Saudi Arabia.[176]

Piscatori further observed that the Islamic "nation" is not viewed by the Saudis as a substitute to the present state system, in view of the goal of inter-state cooperation in the present context. But some argue that it is possible to exceed the present order and achieve a real-world community and government.[177] There are others who contend that the idea of world government or a universal system is not realistic, but a one-world or universal order based on Islam is only coveted but could not be anticipated in the contemporary global system that is bedevilled with imperfection and deficiency.[178]

Despite the division of Muslim nations into separate political entities, it is argued that this has not diminished the spirit of brotherhood of the faithful united in their common love and value. In summary, the analysis and logic of Saudis on concept of modern nation-state may differ in one way or the other, the fact remains that all agree that a nation-state system is acceptable to Islam. They also insist that the spiritual unity of the *Ummah* persists with beneficial effects for all men, saying that the Islamic community has potentials to inject into international relations the spirit of tolerance and justice if only the tendencies

172 Piscatori, J.P., supra note no. 4 at p. 246.
173 Former Saudi Arabia Oil Minister.
174 Yamani, A.Z., *Islamic Law and Contemporary Issues*, Jeddah: The Saudi Publishing House (1388 AH), p. 7.
175 Piscatori, J.P., supra note no. 4 at p. 247.
176 Ibid at p. 248.
177 Ibid at p. 253.
178 Ibid at p. 254.

of extremism and radical secularism are avoided in favour of a creative Islamic modernism.[179]

Majority opinion in modern Saudi Arabia tends to suggest that international law and Islamic law and the relevance of the two systems to the contemporary situation in their country, are inherently compatible and reconcilable. Some even are more pungent in articulating the supremacy of the latter over the former. For example, Al-Yamani has argued that Islamic law presents a balance between individual and state rights, an approach, according to him, that can be borrowed by the modern international order.[180] It is also agreed that Islamic *Shari'ah's* ability to be dynamic by changing in application though not in principle is the underlined reason why it acquiesces in the doctrine of modern international law. Thus, the inherent flexibility in Islamic law was on account of a number of factors, namely, the exercise of *Ijtihad,* cultural influences brought to bear on Islamic system from around the Muslim world, and mutual exchange of ideas and communications that usually take place among the Muslims during the yearly pilgrimage gathering.[181]

Therefore, the Saudi Arabia foreign policy should be contextualized within the concept of *Dar al-'Ahd* (House of truce) or *Dar al-Sulh* (House of Conciliation/treaty) rather than *Dar al-Islam* and *Dar-al-Harb.* It is a policy that learns towards the dualist conception of a modern Islamic *Ummah.*

4.8 International law in modern Saudi Arabia

It is almost four decades now that Piscatori and his contemporaries expressed their views on the relationship between Islamic law and international law in Saudi Arabia as previously discussed. It is therefore pertinent to examine the present perceptions on the matter in the Kingdom. Interviews conducted with relevant Saudi and non-Saudi scholars and experts in Saudi Arabia during this study suggest a largely accommodative perception of international law in modern Saudi Arabia. Most of the scholars see the general possibility of balancing the Islamic interest of modern Muslim-majority States, such as Saudi Arabia, with the benefits derivable from inter-state relations under modern international law. The interviews were not restricted to Saudi citizens but also extended to foreign diplomats and scholars who were residents in the Kingdom and who, by virtue of their qualification and experience in international diplomacy and particularly Saudi Arabia foreign policy are experts on the subject.

For example, Abdulqahir Qamar[182] argued that right from inception, Islam has had the culture of relating well with other systems far and near. There had

179 Abu Sulayman, A.H., supra note no. 167 at pp. 197–204.

180 Yamani, A.Z., supra note no. 174 at p. 16.

181 Dawalibi, M., 'The Legal Heritage of Muslims', *The Voice of Islam*, Vol. IX, No. 3 (December, 1960), pp. 1–3 of typescript copy; Piscatori, J.P., supra note no. 4 at p. 266.

182 Dr. Abdulqahir Qamar is a Saudi citizen and Head of Department of Fatwa and Shari'ah Rulings of the Jeddah-based Fiqh Academy of the Organization of Islamic Cooperation.

been a record of steady relations between Muslims and non-Muslims outside Muslim territory right from the advent of Islam and in the course of history, which explains the convenience of modern Muslim nations' membership of modern Western oriented international organizations like the UN, quoting the *Qur'an* in support of his point.[183] He asserted that from the *Qur'anic* point of view, Islam postulates that Muslims and non-Muslims belong to the family of human nations and thus, there must be mutual respect of each other's value and belief.[184] Qamar referred to an official Resolution of the Council of International Islamic Fiqh Academy issued in 2006,[185] which makes abundant provisions for "Relation of the Islamic State with Others and Its Attitude towards International Treaties and Conventions". Details of these provisions were contained in an expert report presented to the Council and was debated. The Council resolved as follows:

1 The relation between the Islamic State and others on international level stands on the concept of peace and rejection of war and mutual respect and cooperation for the benefit of mankind based on the principle and rules of the Islamic *Shari'ah*.
2 The Islamic State does not antagonize other States simply because of differences in religion. It only antagonizes any State that initiates hostility towards it or offends its values and places of worships. In Islam war is the last resort for self-defence and repelling hostility.
3 It is necessary that there should be cooperation and integration between Islamic States in all respects. This is evidenced in the establishment of joint-Islamic market, economic free-zones, and ratification of collaborative pacts in different international spheres.
4 There is no *Shari'ah* principle that specifically prohibits ratification of international pacts that do not violate the principles of Islamic law or lead to preponderant dominance of any world-power over states involved in such pacts. The Islamic *Shari'ah* allows entering all pacts that are in the interest of the Muslims.[186]

Umer Chapra[187] shares this view when he observed that though, Islamic law is classical in nature, it is blending with international law through the mechanism of *Ijtihad*. He cited the example of the Saudi Arabia Monetary Agency (SAMA),

183 Qamar, A., in an interview conducted by this author with him on 2nd June, 2013; quoting *Qur'an* 60:8.

184 Ibid.

185 Resolution No. 160 (17/9) passed by the Council of International Islamic Fiqh Academy at its season held at Oman capital of Jordan between 24 and 28 June, 2006.

186 Fiqh Academy Resolution, ibid.

187 Dr. M. Umer Chapra, a Saudi citizen by adoption is a Research Advisor at the Islamic Research and Training Institute (IRTI) of the Islamic Development Bank (IDB), Jeddah, and a retired senior staff of the Saudi Arabian Monetary Agency (SAMA).

noting that there was nothing like the concept of Central Banking in Islam, but that the concept has now become part of banking and financial practices of Muslim countries including Saudi Arabia. He notes that central banking is deeply rooted and regulated strictly under international law. In this regard, it can be said that international law is impacting on Islamic law in beneficial ways. He noted that Saudi Arabia's central bank is backed by 100% Gold which does not exist in other countries banking and financial systems.[188]

Similarly, Azmi Omar[189] also observed that Islamic Law and international law mutually interact especially in the subject of Sukuk, noting that sometimes there is the problem of resolving which law takes precedent, saying that this is an area which research is still going on.[190]

In his own view Ambassador Yahya Lawal[191] noted that Islamic law has characteristics of universalism right from its inception quoting the last sermon of the Prophet Muhammad. According to him, taking a critical look at that speech reveals that the Prophet's intention was to address all people, regardless of their religions, colours, or times (his time or any time after him until the Day of Judgment). The Prophet's message was to every person everywhere for every moment forward in time.[192] Citing the example of Islamic banking, he observed that the principles of this financial system are universally applicable wherever it is adopted. The system he noted is now being adopted in the West because of its inherent benefits.[193]

Also, Dr Ashraf Dajani[194] started with the observation that the OIC is a permanent observer at the UN. This according to him explains the significant cooperation that exists between the pan-Islamic organization and Western oriented organizations like the UN and EU. According to Dajani, Islamic law and modern international law share similarities in many respects, citing International Humanitarian Law (IHL) and the Geneva Conventions as important examples. IHL or the law of armed conflict is the law that regulates the conduct of armed conflicts (*jus in bello*) and is inspired by considerations of humanity and the mitigation of human suffering. The modern rules of IHL are consolidated in the Geneva Conventions, the Hague Conventions, as well as subsequent treaties, case law, and customary international law.[195]

188 Chapra, U., in an interview held with him by this author on Sunday 2 June, 2013 in his IDB Jeddah office.

189 Professor Azmi, a Malaysian scholar who is currently the Director General of Islamic Research and Training Institute (IRTI), Islamic Development Bank, Jeddah, on attachment from International Islamic University Malaysia (IIUM).

190 Omar, A., in interview with this author held on Sunday 2, June, 2013 in his IDB office in Jeddah.

191 A Nigerian Diplomat serving as Director of African Affairs, Department of Political Affairs in the Jeddah basic Organization of Islamic Cooperation.

192 Lawal, Y., in interview with this author at his Jeddah office on 4th June, 2013.

193 Ibid.

194 An Egyptian Diplomat and Senior Legal Officer of the Department of Legal Affairs of the Organization of Islam Cooperation.

195 Dajani, A., in an interview with him in his office in Jeddah on 4th June, 2014.

From the perspective of human rights, Raouf Salama[196] noted that it could not be said that human rights are universal in view of cultural relativism. For instance, in the West, the rights of homosexual and gays are recognized but such rights are not recognized under Islamic law.[197] They are not also recognized under the rules of some other world religions. According to him, under the Islamic *Shari'ah*, human rights concept is relative.[198] For example, there is no central authority for the interpretation of Islamic law, which enables flexibility through *Ijtihad*. In Tunisia, for example, polygamy is not allowed, whereas in Saudi Arabia and Egypt it is allowed under the law. Yet, the two blocks derived their law from the same sources, the *Qur'an* and the *Sunnah*. Then, how can one define the universality of human rights in this regard? He asked.[199]

From the perspective of Saudi Arabia's membership of international organizations and its ratification of international conventions, Dr Saud Al-Mishari[200] observed that membership of Saudi Arabia in international organization like the World Trade Organization, World Intellectual Property Organization is not against the principles of Islamic law. These organizations are created for the benefit of the people across the globe. Thus, Saudi Arabia's membership of these as well as other international organizations has potential benefits for the country and its people. Apart from the fact that Saudi Arabia has domesticated the conventions, it is also doing its best to ensure the enforcement of those conventions, despite its commitment to Islamic law.[201]

Fahd Al-Matiri[202] argued that Saudi culture is basically rooted in Islamic law but presently is being impacted by international norms. According to him, this impact is evidenced, for example, by Saudi Arabia's ratification of bilateral and multi-lateral treaties. He however noted that where a treaty is bilateral in nature and has negative impact on the cultural and religious values of the Kingdom, such treaty will be rejected out-rightly. But if it is multi-lateral in nature, it will normally enter reservations on areas or items that affect the cultural and religious interests of the Kingdom negatively. In the realm of human rights for example,

196 Egyptian Diplomat and a Legal Officer in the Legal Affairs Department of the Organization of Islamic Cooperation.

197 See however, Rehman, J., and Polymenopoulou, E., 'Is Green a Part of the Rainbow? Sharia, Homosexuality and LGBT Rights in the Muslim World', *Fordham International Law Journal*, Vol. 37, No. 1 (2013) pp. 1–52.

198 See also Donnelly, J., 'International Human Rights: Universal, Relative or Relatively Universal', in Baderin, M., and Ssenyonjo, M. (eds), *International Human Rights Law: Six Decades after the UDHR and Beyond*, Farnham: Ashgate Publishers, 2010, pp. 31–48, for the argument that international human rights are only relatively universal.

199 Salama, R.I., in an interview held with this author in his office on 4 June 2013.

200 A Saudi citizen and former Assistant Secretary General for Legal Affairs, Council of Saudi Chambers of Commerce and Industry.

201 Al-Mihsari, A., in an interview with this author held on 25 June 2013.

202 A Saudi citizen and First Secretary in the Department of Legal Affairs – Saudi Ministry of Foreign Affairs.

Saudi Arabia accepted those provisions that do not conflict with the Islamic *Shari'ah*,[203] as will be further analyzed in Chapter 5 of this book.

Commenting on the classical concept of dividing the world into *Dar Al-Islam* and *Dar A-Harb*, as earlier examined in this chapter, Al-Matiri argued that these terminologies have no place in the Saudi Ministry of Foreign Affairs especially when it comes to Saudi relations with other countries of the world. The concept of dividing the world into two poles is classical in nature and no longer has relevance in the contemporary world. Presently, Muslim countries maintain relations with non-Muslim countries and vice versa. The notion of this concept is a taboo which is better left for debates among scholars and jurists. That explains why Saudi foreign policy of the present is in consonance with the general principles of modern international law. He noted that Saudi Arabia's membership of international organizations conforms to the principles of Islamic law. In practical terms, interests of Saudi Arabia are better protected by its membership in those international organizations. However, this membership is conditional to its culture and Islamic values. He observed that the denial of Saudi women from driving, for example, is not born out of *Shari'ah* rules, but a position dictated by cultural taboo which will eventually fade away[204] as was the case in the areas of employment, education, and politics that were officially adopted in favour of Saudi women over time.[205]

Regarding Saudi Arabia's participation in international organizations, Amin Al-Obeid[206] noted that the participation of Saudi Arabia in international organizations such as the UN, the World Trade Organization, and the World Intellectual Property Rights Organization is in conformity with the Islamic *Shari'ah*. Such participation is for the benefit and interest of humanity and progress.[207]

4.9 Conclusion

In analysing the theory and practice of international law in Saudi Arabia, this chapter has briefly examined the theoretical framework of *Siyar* in relation to modern international law. While religion might have been the common origin of both classical *Siyar* and international law both of which focus on the integration of humanity and rules regulating human co-existence, modern international law is now inherently secular and differs from classical *Siyar* in various ways. It is however noted that modern socio-political factors had long compelled most contemporary Muslim-majority states to find the necessary balance between

203 Al-Matiri, F., in interview with him by this author in his Riyadh office on 1 July 2013.

204 Lina, S., Rights for Women in Saudi Arabia 'Progressing', *BBC New* (4 May 2015), www.bbc.co.uk/news/world-middle-east-32579989 (accessed 5 May 2015).

205 A Saudi Legal Practitioner in The Law Firm of Salah Al-Hejailan in Association with Freshfields Brukhaus Deringer, Riyadh, Saudi Arabia.`

206 Al-Obeid, A., in an interview with this author in Riyadh on 9th July, 2013.

207 Ibid.

their Islamic ethos and modern international law as is necessary. The chapter has also analyzed the position of Saudi Arabia between Islamic law and international law and established that the notion of the modern nation-state and the consequent division of Muslim nations into separate political entities has not diminished the country's strong commitment to Islamic law. While perceptions about the concept of the modern nation-state may differ in one way or the other, the fact remains that there is a general agreement among modern scholars in Saudi Arabia that the modern nation-state system is acceptable to Islam and compatible with Islamic law. This is abundantly demonstrated in its foreign policy and incorporation of international treaties and conventions into its domestic legislations. Therefore, there is a general acknowledgement that the spiritual unity of the Muslim *Ummah* persists with important beneficial effects that can be injected into modern international relations and international law.

It is also evident from the analysis in this chapter that Saudi Arabia perceives the interaction between Islamic law and international law as mutual – that is, the *Shari'ah* can accommodate international law and in its turn the predominately Western international order can also be enhanced by Islamic values. The country has therefore maintained a cautious balance between its commitment to Islamic law, to sustain its domestic interest, and its adherence to international law to draw from the inherent benefits of modern inter-state relations.

These established facts explain why Saudi Arabia is on the membership list of several regional and international organizations, such as the UN today. It is also a party to many international treaties that has been domesticated into its domestic Islamic legal system.

Bibliography

Books

Abu Sulayman, A.H., *The Islamic Theory of International Relations: Its Relevance, Past and Present*, Ph.D. dissertation, University of Pennsylvanian (1973).

Al-Bisher, H. et al., *Saudi Maritime Policy Integrated Governance*, Oxfordshire: Routledge (2012).

Al-Farsy, F., *Modernity and Tradition, the Saudi Equation*, London and New York: Kegan Paul International (1990).

Al-Ghunaimi, M.T., *The Muslim Conception of International Law and the Western Approach*, The Hague: Martinus Nijhoff (1968).

Ali, S.S., *Gender and Human Rights in Islam and International Law*, London: Kluwer Law International (2000).

Asad, T., 'Religion, Nation-State, Secularism', Chapter 10, edited by Van Der Veer, P., and Lehmann, H., *Nation and Religion Perspective on Europe and Asia*, Princeton University Press (1999), pp. 178–196.

Baderin, M.A., 'Muhammad Al-Shaybani (749/50–805)', edited by Fassbender, B., and Peters, A., *The Oxford History of International Law*, Oxford: Oxford University Press (2012).

Bakicioglue, O., *Islam and Warfare, Context and Compatibility with International Law*, Oxfordshire: Routledge (2014).

Bathia, K.L., *Textbook on Legal Language and Legal Writing*, New Delhi: Universal Law Publishing (2010).

Bill, B., *The Degradation of the International Legal Order? The Rehabilitation of Law and the Possibility of Politics*, Oxfordshire: Rutledge-Cavendish (2008).

Bradley, J.R., *Saudi Arabia Exposed*, New York City: Macmillan (2005).

Cesari, J., *Islam in the West, Modernity and Globalization Revisited, Globalization and the Muslim World* (edited by B. Schalbler, and L. Stenberg), Syracuse: Syracuse University Press (2004).

Donnelly, J., 'International Human Rights: Universal, Relative or Relatively Universal', edited by Baderin, M., and Ssenyonjo, M., *International Human Rights Law: Six Decades after the UDHR and Beyond*, Farnham: Ashgate Publishers (2010), pp. 588–605.

Eijk, E.V., 'Sharia and National Law in Saudi Arabia', edited by Otto, J.M., *Shari'ah Incorporated, a Comparative Overview of the Legal Systems of Twelve Muslim Countries in Past and Present*, The Netherlands: The Leiden University Press Series on Law (2010).

Esposito, J.L., *The Islamic Threat: Myth or Reality?* (3rd edn), New York: Oxford University Press (1999).

Fadel, M., International Law, Regional Developments: Islam (edited by R. Wolfrum), MPEPIL, online edition, available at www.mpepil.com.

Gerges, F.A., *America and Political Islam: Clash of Cultures or Clash of Interests?* Cambridge: Cambridge University Press (1999).

Ghazi, M.A., *Islam International Law and the World Today*, Islamabad: Institute of Policy Studies (2011).

Ghazi, M.A., *The Shorter Book on Muslim International Law* (Kitab Al-Siyar Al-Saghir by Mohammad Ibn al-Hasan al-Shaybani) (edited, translated and annotated by M.H. Ghazi), Pakistan: Islamic Research Institute, IIU (1998).

Goldberg, J., *The Foreign Policy of Saudi Arabia – The Formative Years* (1902–1918), Cambridge, MA: Harvard University Press (1986).

Hamidullah, M., *The Muslim Conduct of State*, Kazi Publications Inc. (1992).

Hitti, P.K., *History of the Arabs* (9th edn), New York: St. Martin's (1968).

Khadduri, M.'s introduction to al-Shaybani, *The Islamic Law of Nations*, Baltimore, MD: Johns Hopkins University Press (1966).

Khadduri, M., *The Islamic Law of Nations –Shaybani's Siyar* (translated with an Introduction, Notes and Appendices by M. Khadduri), Baltimore, MD: The John Hopkins (1966).

Khadduri, M., *War and Peace in the Law of Islam*, Baltimore, MD: The Johns Hopkins Press (1955).

Khadduri, M., and Liebesny, H.J., *Law in the Middle East*, Washington, DC: Middle East Institute (1960).

Kramer, M., *Islam Assembled – The Advent of the Muslim Congresses*, New York: New York Columbia University Press (1986).

Lewis, B., *The Arabs in History*, Oxford: Oxford University Press (1960).

Madani, M.O., *The Relationship between Saudi Arabian Domestic Law and International Law: A Study of the Oil Agreement with Foreign Companies*, PhD Dissertation of the Law School of The George Washington University (1970).

Mahmassani, S., *Falsafah al-Tashri' fi al-Islam (The Philosophy of Jurisprudence in Islam)*, Leiden: E.J. Brill (1961).

Mahmoudi, S., Islamic Approach to International Law (edited by R. Wolfrum), MPEPIL, online edition, available at www.mpepil.com.

Mai, Y., *Cradle of Islam: The Hijaz and the Quest for Identity in Saudi Arabia*, I.B. Tauris (2009), and John, B.R., *Saudi Arabia Exposed: Inside a Kingdom in Crisis*, London and New York: Palgrave (2005).

Mayer, A., 'War and Peace in the Islamic Tradition of International Law', edited by Kelsey, J., and Turner, J.T., *Just War and Jihad*, New York: Greenwood Press (1991).

Michael, R.D., *Wahhabism: Is It a Factor in the Spread of Global Terrorism?* Thesis presented to the Naval Postgraduate School, Monterey, California for Master of Arts in Security Studies (2009).

Muhyyddin Ibn Sharaf al-Nawawi, *Tahzeeb al-Asm'a wa al-Lughat*, Beirut: Dar al-Kutub al-'Elmiya, Vol. 3 (n.d.).

Niblock, T., *Saudi Arabia – Power, Legitimacy and Survival*, Routledge, London and New York: Taylor and Francis Group (2006).

Ochsenwald, W., and Fisher, S.N., *The Middle East a History* (4th edn), New York City: McGraw-Hill Publishing Company (1990).

Piscatori, J.P., *Islam and the International Legal Order: The Case of Saudi Arabia*, A Dissertation Presented to the Graduate Faculty of the University of Virginia in Candidacy for the Degree of Doctor of Philosophy, University of Virginia (1976).

Quandt, W.B., *Saudi Arabia in the 1980s – Foreign Policy, Security, and Oil*, Washington D.C.: The Brookings Institution (1981).

Rahim, A., *The Principles of Muhammadan Jurisprudence*, London: Luzac (1911).

Roader, T., *Traditional Islamic Approach to Public International Law – Historic Concepts, Modern Implications*, Heidelberg, Allemagne: Max-Planck-Institut fur auslandisches offentliches Recht und Volkerrecht (2012).

Shams al-Din Muhammad Ibn Ahmad Ibn Sahl al-Sarakhsi, *Kitab al-Mabsut* (The Detailed Work of Jurisprudence), Beirut: Dar Al-Kotob Al-Ilmiya (2002).

Shaw, M.N., *International Law*, Cambridge: Cambridge University Press (2003).

Tabari, A.J.M.J., *Tarikh ak-Rusul wa al-Muluk* (edited by M.J. de Geoeje, 15 vols), Leiden: Brill (1879–1901), p. 266.

The Monthly Magazine and British Register (Unknown Author), Vol. 1 (1796).

Imam Al-TirmidhiJami', Jami' Al-Tirmidhi By Imam Al-Tirmidhi: Arabic Only, Riyadh: Darussalam (n.d); Imam Ahmad Ibn Hanbal, Kitab al-Zuhd, Beirut: Dar Al-Kitab Al-Ilmiyah (2007).

Waheed-Ud-Din, F.S., *The Benefactor*, Lahore: Lion Art Press "Karachi" Ltd. (1965).

Watt, W.M., *Muhammad at Medina*, Oxford: Clarendon Press (1956).

Watt, W.M., *The Cambridge History of Islam*, Cambridge: Cambridge University Press (1977).

Weeramantry, C.G., *Islamic Jurisprudence – An International Perspective*, New York City: Macmillan Press (1988).

Wynbrandt, J., *A Brief History of Saudi Arabia*, New York: Checkmark Books (2004).

Yamani, A.Z., *Islamic Law and Contemporary Issues, Jeddah*, Saudi Arabia: The Saudi Publishing House (1388 AH).

Journals

Ali, S.S., and Rehman, J., 'The Concept of Jihad in Islamic International Law', *Journal of Conflict and Security Law*, Vol. 10, No. 3 (2005), pp. 321–343.

Al-Yassini, A., 'Religion and Foreign Policy in Saudi Arabia', CDAS Discussion Papers No. 2 Department of Political Science, *Conordia University* (1983).

Anne-Marie, S., and, Burke-White, W., 'The Future of International Law Is Domestic (or, The European Way of Law)', *Harvard International Law Journal*, Vol. 47, No. 2 (2006), pp. 327–352.

Baderin, M.A., 'The Evolution of Islamic Law of Nations and the Modern International Order: Universal Peace through Mutuality and Cooperation', *The American Journal of Islamic Social Sciences*, Vol. 17, No. 2 (2000), pp. 57–80.

Baderin, M.A., 'Religion and International Law: Friends or Foes', *European Human Rights Law Review*, Vol. 5 (2009), pp. 637–658.

Bouzenita, A.I., 'The Siyar – An Islamic Law of Nations?' *Asian Journal of Social Sciences*, Vol. 35 (2007), pp. 19–46.

Ford, C.A., 'Siyar-ization and Its Discontents: International Law and Islam's Constitutional Crisis', *Texas International Law Journal*, Vol. 30 (1995), pp. 499–534.

Harrison, M., 'Saudi Arabia's Foreign Policy: Relations with the Superpowers', University of Durham, *Centre for Middle Eastern and Islamic Studies*, CMEIS Occasional Paper, No. 46 (1995).

Haynes, J., 'Transnational Religious Actors and International Order', *Perspective: Review of International Affairs*, Vol. 17, No. 2 (2009), pp. 308–322.

Lina, S., 'Rights for Women in Saudi Arabia 'Progressing', *BBC New* (4 May 2015).

Munir, M., 'Islamic international Law (Siyar): An Introduction', *Hamdard Islamicus*, Vol. XXXX, No. 4 (2012), pp. 33–58.

Rahmat, M., 'International Workshop and Seminar on Siyar & Islamic States Practices in International Law, Harmonization of Siyar in International Law: Some Reflections', *Asian-African Legal Consultative Organization*, Kuala Lumpur, Malaysia (2009).

Rehman, J., and Polymenopoulou, E., 'Is Green a Part of the Rainbow? Sharia, Homosexuality and LGBT Rights in the Muslim World', *Fordham International Law Journal*, Vol. 37, No. 1 (2013), pp. 1–14.

Samuel, H., 'Islam in Saudi Foreign Policy: The Case of Maʿruf al-Dawalibi', *The International History Review*, Vol. 42, No. 3 (2020), pp. 449–464.

Shirley, V.S., and Withana, R., 'The Relevance of International Law for Foreign Policy Decision-making When National Security Is at Stake: Lessons from the Cuban Missile Crisis', *Chinese Journal of International Law*, Vol. 2 (2003), pp. 163–188.

Stumpf, C., 'Völkerrecht unter Kreuz und Halbmond: Muhammad al-Shaybani und Hugo Grotius als Exponenten religiöser Völkerrechtstraditionen', *AVR* Vol. 41 (2003).

Torrijo, Z.F., 'International Law and Domestic Law: Definitely an Odd Couple', *Revosta Juridoca de la Universidad de Puerto Rico*, Vol. 77 (2008), pp. 187–206.

Websites

http://historum.com/blogs/blackbear/1705-international-context-major-middle-eastern-events-twentieth-century.html.

www.bbc. co.uk/news/world-middle-east-32579989.

www.csc.org.sa/English/Pages/default.aspx.

www.encyclopedia.com/topic/Saudi_Arabia.aspx.

www.iccwbo.org/worldwide-membership/national-committees/icc-saudi-arabia/.

www.mofa.gov.sa/sites/mofaen/KingdomForeignPolicy/Pages/KingdomPolicy34645.aspx.

www.oxfordislamicstudies.com/article/opr/t125/e2228.

www.saudiembassy.net/issues/foreign-relations/.
www.un.org/depts/dhl/unms/founders.shtml.
www.wto.org/english/thewto_e/acc_e/completeacc_e.htm#sau.

Cases

Continental Shelf (Tunisia/Libyan Arab Jamahiriya) ICJ Rep. (1982).
Egypt v Israel) 27 ILM (1988).
Emirate of Dubai v Emirate of Sharjah, Arbitral Award of 19 October, 1981, ILR Vol. 91, 543ff.
Qatar v Bahrain, ICJ Report (2001).
Western Sahara Case, Advisory Opinion, ICJ Rep. (1975). Libya v UK and Libya v United States of America) ICJ Rep (1998).

Statutes, regulations, reports, and resolutions

Council of Ministers Resolution No. 165 of 24.6.1423H (1 September 2002).
Report of the Working Party on the Accession of the Kingdom of Saudi Arabia to the World Trade Organization; World Trade Organization (WTO) - Working Party on the Accession of the Kingdom of Saudi Arabia (2005); https://publicintelligence.net/report-of-the-working-party-on-the-accession-of-the-kingdom-of-saudi-arabia-to-the-world-trade-organization/
Resolution No. 160 (17/9) Passed by the Council of International Islamic Fiqh Academy at Its Season held at Oman capital of Jordan (2006).
Royal Decree of 23 September 1932.
Royal Decree No. A/90 of 27.8.1412H (1 March 1992).
Saudi Arabia to the World Trade Organization, WT/ACC/SAU/61 (1 November 2005).

5 International human rights law and Islamic law in Saudi Arabia

5.1 Introductory remarks

> "...We prefer world law in the age of self-determination to world war in the age of mass extermination"; and "... we cannot expect that all nations will adopt like systems, for conformity is the jailer of freedom and the enemy of growth".[1]
>
> "Any concept of human rights that is to be universally accepted and globally enforced demands equal respect and mutual comprehension between rival cultures".[2]

The above statements touch on the important issues of international human rights but also on the question of internationalism and the enforcement of international rules in this polarized world of cultural diversity. More than that, they are vindications of the argument that modern internationalism is a paradox. It is thus argued that while internationalism has led to a greater number and density of universally applicable norms, it has also kindled a strong cultural consciousness and identity assertion, particularly from Muslim-majority states such as Saudi Arabia in relation to the application of international human rights law.[3] Samuel Huntington had also remarked in this regard, albeit controversially, that people's cultural and religious identities would be the primary source of conflict in the post-Cold War world, as culture and cultural identities (including Islam and Islamic law), which at the broadest level are civilizational identities,

1 John Fitzgerald "Jack" Kennedy (May 29, 1917–November 22, 1963). He was the 35th President of the United States, serving from 1961 until his death in 1963. The two statements were contained in President J. F. Kennedy's address to the United Nations. The address captioned: "The Role of the United Nations" was presented before the General Assembly of the United Nations in New York City on 25 September, 1961.

2 An-Na'im, A., 'What Do We Mean by Universal?' *Index on Censorship* Vol. 4, No. 9 (1994), pp. 120–128.

3 Baderin, M.A., 'A Macroscopic Analysis of the Practice of Muslim State Parties to International Human Rights Treaties: Conflict or Congruence?' *Human Rights Law*, Vol. 1, No. 2 (2001), p. 265.

are shaping the patterns of cohesion, disintegration, and conflict in the post-Cold War world.[4]

The starting point of the international human rights debate is the question of its universality as the first UN human rights instrument adopted in 1948 is referred to as the *Universal Declaration of Human Rights* (UDHR). This is a clear indication that the international human rights agenda was meant to be a universal one from the beginning,[5] and this has continued to be emphasized ever since. However, the scope of the universality of international human rights norms is often contested especially by Muslim State Parties to international human rights treaties, on grounds of Islamic norms.[6] Thus begging the question of whether the universalization of international human rights law has had any significant impact on the Islamic legal systems of modern Muslim-majority states, with particular reference to Saudi Arabia.

Within the context of identified paradox of internationalism versus cultural consciousness and identity assertion,[7] to what extent the principles of international human rights have impacted on the domestic policies and legislations of modern Saudi Arabia is arguably contentious. It is intended in this chapter to explore possible answers to pertinent questions arising from these contentious issues. This chapter examines human rights from international law perspective with a view to link its theory and practice to Islamic jurisprudence and Saudi Arabian's state practice of human rights. This is underscored by the provisions of the Saudi Basic Law which stipulates that the *Qur'an* and the *Sunnah* are the dual Grundnorm of its law. In this chapter, attempt will be made to discuss detailed account of Saudi Arabia's participations in the international forums on human rights. Principally, attempt will be made to determine the extent of the impact of international human rights law on the domestic legislation and application of Islamic law in the Kingdom of Saudi Arabia.

5.2 Theoretical debates on human rights and Islamic law

As already noted in Chapter 3, the *Shari'ah* determines the boundaries of legal and ethical conduct for Muslims generally. It is said to be a universal system of law and ethics and claimed to regulate every aspect of public and private life in Muslim societies.[8] It influences individual and collective behaviour in Muslim communities through its role in the socialization processes of such nations

4 Huntington, S.P., *The Clash of Civilizations and the Remaking of World Order*, New York, London, Toronto, and Sydney: Simon & Schuster (1996) paperback (2002), p. 20.

5 Baderin, M.A., *Islam and Human Rights*, Selected Essays of Abdullahi An-Na'im (edited by Masood A. Baderin), Farnham: Ashgate Publishers (2010), p. xv.

6 Ibid at p. 266.

7 Ibid.

8 An-Na'im, A., 'Human Rights in the Muslim World: Socio-Political Conditions and Scriptural Imperatives', *Harvard Human Rights Journal*, Vol. 3 (1990), pp. 13–14.

regardless of its status in their formal legal systems.[9] Conversely, the Vienna Declaration on human rights states that all human rights are universal and indivisible in theory and practice everywhere.[10]

Against this background, the International Commission of Jurists (ICJ) argued in 1974 that, if human rights are to be accepted as universal, they must be presented in the context of cultures other than that of the West.[11] It is thus argued that although the UDHR is called "Universal", it "was articulated along the lines of historical trends of the Western world during the last three centuries, and a certain philosophical anthropology of individualistic humanism which helped justify them".[12] Nevertheless, the basic assumptions underlying the Declaration were (a) a universal human nature common to all the peoples, (b) the dignity of the individual, and (c) a democratic social order.[13]

The conceptualization of the universality of human rights continues to be an important element of the debate on the relationship between human rights and Islamic law. There have been different academic perspectives to the understanding of universality of human rights generally. For example, Jack Donnelly is a protagonist of universality of human rights who propounds what he calls conceptual or relative universality of human rights.[14] He argues that while human rights are indeed universal in some standard and important senses of the term, they are also relative in some relevant standard senses of the term. He observes that the real issue is not whether human rights are universal or relative but how these universalities and relativities interact in theory and practice.[15] This perspective can serve as a useful dimension in the debate on the interaction between human rights and Islamic law.

Goodheart Michael contests this proposition and identified that "some difficulties with the relative universality of human rights become apparent when considering Donnelly's arguments about the different types of universality".[16] He argued that what Donnelly calls conceptual universality is really a formal feature of some accounts of human rights that is not common to all account of human rights.

9 Ibid.

10 Vienna Declaration and Programme of Action, UN GAOP, World Conf. on Hum Rts. 48th Sess., 22nd Plen. Mtg., part1, 5, U.N. Doc. A/ Conf.157/24 (1993), reprinted in 32 I.L.M.1661, 1665 (1993).

11 'Editorial', The Review, International Commission of Jurists, No. 12 (June, 1974), p. 1.

12 Panikkar, R., 'Is the Notion of Human Rights a Western Concept?' in Little, D., , Kelsay, J., and Sachedina, A.A. (eds), *Breakthrough*, New York: Global Education Associates, Spring (1989), p. 31.

13 Ibid.

14 Donnelly, J., 'The Relative Universality of Human Rights', *Human Rights Quarterly*, Vol. 29 (2007), p. 282.

15 See generally Donnelly, J., 'International Human Rights: Universal, Relative of Relatively Universal' in Baderin, M.A., and Ssenyonjo, M. (eds), *International Human Rights Law: Six Decades after the UDHR and Beyond*, Farnham: Ashgate Publishing Ltd. (2010), pp. 31–48.

16 Michael, G., 'Neither Relative nor Universal: A Response to Donnelly', *Human Rights Quarterly*, Vol. 30 (2008), pp. 185–186.

Louis Henkin had also noted earlier in this regard that there is universally a common contemporary moral intuition that responds to, and will not reject, most of the provisions in the UDHR, those that constitute the core of human rights, for example, right to life and physical integrity, freedom from torture, slavery, and arbitrary detention and due process of law and right not to suffer cruel punishment.[17] He then noted, however, that some rights in the UDHR are not universally favoured and may meet cultural resistance, giving examples such as freedom of expression, freedom of conscience and religion, and so on.[18] He argued that freedom of expression, religion, and the equality of women appear not yet to be accepted in fact in a number of societies and in that sense, those rights were not yet universal.[19]

Most Muslims are of the view that Islam certainly accommodates most basic assumptions underlying international human rights but that the *Qur'an* is the *magna carta* of human rights in Islam. A large part of the *Qur'an* is concerned with freeing human beings from the bondage of traditionalism, authoritarianism (religious, political, economic, or any other), tribalism, racism, sexism, slavery, or anything else that prohibits or inhibits human beings from actualizing the *Qur'anic* vision of human destiny and dignity embodied in the classic proclamation: "And verily unto thy Lord is the limit".[20]

Historically before Islam, the way of life of the Bedouin Arabs was primitive, crude, and rudimentary.[21] Lawlessness and the mentality of *asabiyyah*, or the tribal kin feeling accounted for continual bloodshed and lack of security. Self-help, rather than established rules of human rights, was the dominant principle.[22] Islam came with social and legal norms that imparted into the Arab converts the sense of brotherhood, human rights, and positive human relations.[23] Islam thought them to respect the rights of others, refrain from negative tendencies such as bloodshed and robbery. Islam laid down guidelines for individual and collective rights. Under these guidelines, human rights, it is argued, may be classified into two main headings, namely, private, and public rights.[24] Private rights are those that concern the individual as a member of the community, and public rights are those that concern the Muslim community at large.[25] The latter

17 Henkin, L., 'The Universality of the Concept of Human Rights', *American Academy of Political and Social Science*, Vol. 506 (1989), p. 15.

18 Ibid.

19 Ibid.

20 Iqbal, M., *The Reconstruction of Religious Thought in Islam*, Lahore: Sheikh Muhammad Ashraf (1971), p. 57 in Iqbal translation and commentary on relevant excerpts of the *Qur'an* (53:42) on the subject.

21 Thomas Hobbes, *Leviathan* (edited by Richard Tuck), Cambridge: Cambridge University Press (1996).

22 Khadduri, M., 'Human Rights in Islam', *Annals of the American Academy of Political and Social Science*, Vol. 243, Essential Human Rights (1946), p. 77.

23 Ibid.

24 Ibid.

25 Ibid.

are called rights of God, owing to the magnitude of the risk involved in their violation and of the general good which would result from their observance.[26]

Against this background, Piscatori observes that it was not quite clear whether the traditional Islamic legal order was compatible with the prevailing outlook of international human rights norms.[27] Academic perspectives may be categorized into three main groupings according to their line of thought on human rights and Islam. A group consists of scholars such as Anderson, Bonderman, and Coulson as well as Ann Elizabeth Mayer who maintain that the Islamic classical order *per se* was incompatible with the modern view of human rights.[28] Anderson, citing discrimination of rights between Muslims and non-Muslims, the absolute prohibition on Muslim apostasy and the reliance on force to coerce infidels, finds Islamic principles and practice inconsistent with the UDHR.[29] Coulson agreed with him, arguing that classical *Shari'ah* does not incorporate fundamental human rights as part of the law because wide powers are given to the ruler and no separate judicial body existed.[30] Mayer identifies two views of Muslims who favour and those who oppose adherence to international human rights standards, namely, in her words, the *liberal* and *conservative*.[31] Liberal Muslims, according to her, are those who favour adherence to democratic principles and human rights, and conservative Muslims are those who oppose democratization and resist human rights insofar as they appear to threaten established Islamic institutions.[32] She contends that generally speaking, the Universal Islamic Declaration of Human Rights (UIDR) approach to equality is more similar to the models of Mawdudi, Tabandeh, and the Azhar draft constitution.[33] She's emphatic in concluding that "reference to Islamic criteria on rights is not likely to result in respect for the principles of equality and equal protection of the law as mandated in international human rights law"[34] as long as the notion of superiority of Islamic criteria remains.

Contemporary scholars including Abul A'la Mawdudi, Mashood Baderin, Javaid Rehman, Muhammad Hamidullah, Muhammad Khalafallah Ahmad, Mufti M. Mukarram Ahmad, Khalid Ishaq, Katerina Dalacoura, and several others maintain that the *Shari'ah* is compatible with human rights. For example, Abul A'la Mawdudi in one of his famous treatises reiterates that human rights in

26 Ibid.

27 Piscatori, J.P., *Islam and The International Legal Order: The Case of Saudi Arabia*, A Dissertation Presented to the Graduate Faculty of the University of Virginia in Candidacy for the Degree of Doctor of Philosophy (1976), p. 296.

28 Ibid.

29 Anderson, J.N.D., *Islamic Law in the Modern World*, New York: New York University Press (1959), pp. 97–98.

30 Coulson, N.J., 'The State and Individual in Islamic Law', *International and Comparative Law Quarterly*, Vol. 6 (1957), pp. 49–60.

31 Mayer, A.E., *Islam and Human Rights, Tradition and Politics*, Boulder, USA: Westview Press (2007), p. 29.

32 Ibid.

33 Ibid at p. 107.

34 Ibid at p. 108.

Islam are those that have been granted by God; they have not been granted by any king or by any legislative assembly which can be withdrawn in the same way they are conferred.[35]

Mashood Baderin argues that there is certainly a human rights discourse in Islamic law. He calls to question the theory of incompatibility of human rights and Islamic law and argues that the theory is squarely challenged. According to him, there exists a common ground between international human rights law and Islamic law.[36] Despite that, he observes, there exist some areas of differences in scope and application, and thus, recommends positive basis for managing such differences through the development of complementary methodologies between the two legal regimes.[37]

Javaid Rehman also maintains that the *Shari'ah* and human rights are not incompatible with each other. According to him, *Shari'ah* may compliment human rights norms so long as the domains of operation of both systems of law are properly contextualized and an effort is made to preserve both within their respective spheres of authority.[38] He recalls that Islam was a positive force of change in seventh-century Arabia and produced many positive features including an egalitarian model of rights. Thus, Islam's contribution to human rights must be viewed within these historical, social, and political contexts.[39]

Katerina Dalacoura agrees with Baderin and Javaid. She contends that some interpretations of Islam make room for human rights principles and this, according to her, will re-enforce the argument that it is not necessary to reject religion altogether – and Islam in particular – in order to secure human rights.[40] She asserts that there are some ideas in the religious doctrine and even in the *Shari'ah* which can provide building blocks for a conciliation of Islam and human rights, among which are equality of believers, respect for minorities and the belief that the ruler must obey the law. Duties, she argues, can imply correlative rights. The position of the individual is central, and the human being is valued, to a degree, for his or her humanity. Even the slave is considered a person in Islamic law, *albeit* not a fully responsible one.[41]

35 Mawdudi, A.A., *Human Rights in Islam*, Lahore: Islamic Publications Ltd. (2nd edn) (1995), p. 12.

36 Baderin, M.A., *International Human Rights and Islamic Law*, Oxford: Oxford University Press (2005), p. 219.

37 Ibid.

38 Javaid, R., 'Islam and Human Rights: Is Compatibility Achievable between the *Shari'ah* and Human Rights Law?' A paper presented at an *International Conference in Konya, Turkey* (30 November–1 December, 2013), http://papers.ssrn.com/sol3/papers.cfm?abstract_id=2373930 (accessed 2 December 2014).

39 For further debate in this regard see Javaid, R., 'The *Shari'ah*, Islamic Family Laws and International Human Rights Law: Examining the Theory and Practice of Polygamy and Talaq', *International Journal of Law, Family and Policy*, Vol. 21, No. 1 (2007), p. 108.

40 Dalacoura, K., *Islam, Liberalism and Human Rights, Implications for International Relations*, London and New York: I.B. Tauris (2003), p. 39.

41 Ibid at p. 48.

Mufti Mukarram Ahmad like Mawdudi is theologically blunt. He argues that all citizens (Muslims and non-Muslims) are guaranteed certain fundamental rights. These include security of person, property, and honour; freedom of opinion and association; freedom of conscience including the freedom to apostatise after accepting Islam; the right to offer advice and criticism; equal treatment under law without discrimination; protection against one's religion, ideology, or person being reviled; right of privacy. Other rights include freedom from surveillance by secret services; freedom from unlawful detention; economic security, productive and remunerative work, free and compulsory education, free medical and health services; and the free provision by the state of the necessities of life to the disabled and deprived on account of illness, old age, and childhood, and to widows and unemployed.[42] Both Muhammad Khallafah Ahmad[43]and Khalid Ishaq[44] agree with this line of thought.

The third group that maintains a middle course include Majid Khadduri, K.K. Nawaz, al-Ghunaimi,[45] Abdullah An-Na'im, and others. Khadduri argues, for example, that the treatment meted to the *Ahl al-Dhimmah* is discriminatory, ambivalent, and debatable. It is true that they are guaranteed the rights to property, life, and unhindered travel but, they are prohibited from marrying Muslims, engaging in certain business activities, inheriting Muslims, and practicing their religion in an obviously public manner. He then concludes that they are protected though second-class citizens.[46] Khadduri also notes that Islam, on the one hand, presents a crusading side that may be insensitive to the rights of its ideological opponents, but, on the other, is protective of the individual to a greater extent than in the prevailing legal order and is admirably tolerant in warfare due to its moral content.[47] Al-Ghunaymi agrees with him, but prefers to describe *Ahl-al-Dhimmah* as non-citizens, arguing that they are protected non-believers with bifurcated restrictions and rights.[48] K.K. Nawaz argues that Islam enshrines some human rights but that it discriminates on the basis of religion, thereby giving rise to inequality of rights.[49]

Muhammad Hamidullah who, though, belongs to the second group disagrees. He argues that the practice under the classical *dhimmah* system whereby

42 Ahmad, M.M., *Human Rights in Islam*, New Delhi: Anmol Publications PVT. Ltd. (2008), p. 91.

43 Ibid.

44 Khalid, M.I., 'Human Rights in Islamic Law', *The Review, International Commission of Jurists*, No. 12 (1974) , Ed. MacDermot, N., pp. 30–39.

45 Ghunaimi, M.T., *The Muslim Conception of International Law and the Western Approach*, The Hague: Martinus Nijhoff (1968), pp. 214–215.

46 Khadduri, M., *War and Peace in the Law of Islam*, Baltimore: The John Hopkins Press (1955), pp. 177, 195–198.

47 Khadduri, M., supra note no. 46; also Khadduri, M., 'The Islamic System: Its Competition and Co-existence with Western System', *Proceedings of the American Society of International Law*, 53rd Annual Meeting, Washington, DC: April 30–May 2 (1959), p. 52.

48 Ghunaimi, M. T., supra note no. 45 at pp. 82, 151, 186–187.

49 Nawaz, K.K., 'The Concept of Human Rights in Islamic Law', *Howard Law Journal*, Vol. 11, No. 2 (1965), pp. 326–332.

non-Muslims were disallowed to imitate Muslims in dress or other social traits within the Islamic State, was not really a discriminatory treatment against them, as usually misrepresented by critics, but it was out of "share considerateness in protecting their interest" to boost their communal culture and assist them to feel proud of their own cultural and social values within the Islamic State.[50] Similarly some jurists are of the view that Muslims living as minorities outside *dār al-Islām* should also maintain a distinctive appearance to sustain their own culture amongst the non-Muslim majority where they live.[51]

Be that as it may. Khadduri agrees that Islam recognizes private rights which include the right to personal safety; rights to respect of personal reputation (*hurma*); right to equality;[52] right to justice;[53] and right to feelings of brotherhood.[54] Public rights on the other hand include, *inter alia*, rights of *ibadat*, i.e. observance of rituals and acts of worship as prescribed by Islam. These rights of devotion are known in the modern term as "freedom of religion".[55] Al-Ghunaimi argues in similar vein when he says that many verses of the *Qur'an* do cover most of the rights guaranteed under the UDHR and other human rights instruments.[56]

An-Na'm observes that some Muslims claim that the historical formulations of *Shari'ah* have always secured human rights in theory, though such a situation may not have always materialized in practice. He noted that by securing a relatively advanced degree of protection for the rights of women and non-Muslims, historical formulations of *Shari'ah* did provide for better protection of human rights than other normative systems in the past.[57] For example, from the very beginning, *Shari'ah* was understood to require an independent legal personality for women, and the protection of certain minimum rights for them in inheritance and family relations, beyond what was possible under other major normative systems until the nineteenth century.[58] Similarly, the *Shari'ah* guarantees specific rights for the so-called People of the Book (mainly Christians and Jews) more than what had been provided for under other major normative systems in the past.[59] However, the rights of women and non-Muslims under the *Shari'ah* are not sufficient when judged by the standards set by the UDHR, which require

50 Hamidullah, M., *The Muslim Conduct of State*, Lahore: Sh. Muhammad Ashraf (1977), pp. 117–118.

51 See e.g. *Al-Fatāwā Al-Hindiyyah*, Vol. 6, Bulaq: al-Matba'ah al-Kubrā al-Amīriyyah, 1310AH), p. 311.

52 See generally the Prophet Mohammed's last Pilgrimage sermon (Tabari, *Tarikh al-Russul wa al-Muluk* (Leiden, 1890), Series I, Vol. IV, p. 1754.

53 *Qur'an* 5:153; 22:42; and 28:25; see also Arnold, T., *The Caliphate*, Oxford: Oxford University Press (1924), p. 72.

54 *Qur'an* 49:10.

55 Khadduri, M., supra note no. 22.

56 Ghunaimi, M.T., supra note no. 45 at p. 215.

57 An-Na'im, A.A., 'Islam and Human Rights: Beyond the Universality Debate', *American Society of International Law Proceeding*, Vol. 94, No. 96 (2000), p. 98.

58 Ibid.

59 Ibid.

equal rights for all human beings, without distinction on such grounds as sex, religion, or belief.[60]

In summary, the proposition of incompatibility of international human rights norms and Islamic law is ostensibly challengeable. While it can be argued that the practices of some Islamic authorities in the past and present violate basic norms of international human rights, this may not be ascribed to the prescriptions under the Islamic law *per se*. This fact is deductible particularly from the arguments of pro-compatibility jurists as stated above.[61]

The attention should be focused on finding a common ground between the two systems in the light of the observation made by An Na'im that any concept of human rights that is to be universally accepted and globally enforced demands equal respect and mutual comprehension between rival cultures.[62] Although, this might arguably be doubtful presently, for example, in the light of observations made by some renowned jurists of international law who noted that a Western representative bias can be detected in recent years, with over half of the Human Rights Council (HRC) members serving from 1998 to 2000 coming from the United States, Canada, Australia, the United Kingdom, France, Italy, Israel, Finland, Germany, and Poland.[63] While it is appreciated that the situation has relatively improved in the past 14 years since this observation was made, yet there still remains a need for the reflection of a more "equitable distribution of membership" not only of the HRC but also of all the UN human rights treaty bodies, as noted by Baderin. It is also of utmost importance that both international human rights and Islamic law jurists and scholars adopt an accommodative and complementary attitude and overture towards the promotion of human rights in the contemporary world.[64] With reference to the application of Islamic law Baderin maintains that its evolutionary nature makes it complementary with human rights regime.[65]

5.3 Saudi Arabia and the international human rights regime

In analysing Saudi Arabia's participation and interaction in the UN human rights system, two distinctive phases are significant. The first phase spanned between the late 1940s to the early 1990s, while the second phase spanned from

60 See generally, An-Na'im, A.A., *Towards an Islamic Reformation: Civil Liberties, Human Rights and International Law*, Syracuse, NY: Syracuse University Press (1990), particularly Chapter 3.

61 For example Dalacoura, K., supra note no. 40 at p. 48.

62 See generally An-Na'im, A., 'What Do We Mean by Universal?' *Index on Censorship*, The Magazine for Free Speech (September/October 1994).

63 Joseph, S., Schulz, J., and Castan, M., *The International Covenant on Civil and Political Rights, Cases and Materials, and Commentary* (2000) p. 10, as quoted by Baderin, M.A., supra note no. 36 at p. 221.

64 Baderin, M.A., supra note no. 36.

65 Baderin, M.A., 'Islam and Human Rights in the Muslim World: A Reflection on Approaches', A paper presented at Conference on Reframing Islam: Politics into Law, *Irish Centre for Human Rights, National University of Ireland, Galway*, 10–11 September 2005, p. 5.

the early 1990s to 2008 and to date.[66] The first phase could be described as formative and rudimentary while the second could be described as contemporary and tempestuous.

It is pertinent to first briefly examine the relevant international instruments on human rights and throw light on the general participation of Saudi Arabia in debating and negotiating those international instruments. Three documents establish the bedrock of international human rights standards, and international human rights law. They are the Universal Declaration of Human Rights (UDHR), the International Covenant on Civil and Political Rights (ICCPR), and the International Covenant on Economic, Social and Cultural Rights (ICESCR).[67] While the ICCPR and ICESCR are legally binding treaties, the UDHR is considered an initial, primarily declaratory statement designed to establish broad benchmarks for the international community to observe certain standards of human rights.[68] Together, these three documents comprise the International Bill of Rights. Many other international human rights treaties and standards build on this foundation.

Traditionally, the UDHR was believed to have arisen directly from the experience of the Second World War and represents the first global expression of rights to which all human beings are inherently entitled.[69] Accuracy of this historical account has been challenged[70] by several authorities.[71]

UN records reveal the active participation of delegations from the Muslim world in the 20-year negotiation of international human rights standard, bearing

66 Alwasil, A.M., 'Saudi Arabia's Engagement in, and Interaction with, the UN Human Rights System: An Analytical Review', *The International Journal of Human Rights*, Vol. 14, No. 7 (2010), p. 1072.

67 Universal Declaration of Human Rights, *adopted* 10 Dec. 1948, G.A. Res. 217A (III), U.N. GAOR, 3d Sess. (Resolutions, pt. 1), at 71, U.N. Doc. A/810 (1948), *reprinted in* 43 AM. J. INT'L L.SUPP. 127 (1949) [hereinafter UDHR]; International Covenant on Economic, Social and Cultural Rights, *adopted* 16 Dec. 1966, G.A. Res. 2200 (XXI), U.N. GAOR, 21st Sess., Supp. No. 16, U.N. Doc. A/6316 (1966), 993 U.N.T.S. 3 (*entered into force* 3 Jan. 1976) [hereinafter ICESCR]; International Covenant on Civil and Political Rights, *adopted* 16 Dec. 1966, G.A. Res. 2200 (XXI), U.N. GAOR, 21st Sess., Supp. No. 16, U.N. Doc. A/6316 (1966), 999 U.N.T.S. 171 (*entered into force* 23 Mar. 1976) [hereinafter ICCPR].

68 Alwasil, A.M., supra note no. 66 at p. 1073.

69 Waltz, S., Universal Human Rights: The Contribution of Muslim States, *Human Rights Quarterly*, Vol. 26, No. 4 (2004), pp. 799–844.

70 See generally Waltz, S., 'Universalizing Human Rights: The Role of Small States in the Construction of the Universal Declaration of Human Rights', *Human Rights Quarterly*, Vol. 23 (2001), p. 44; Waltz, S., 'Reclaiming and Rebuilding the History of the Universal Declaration of Human Rights', *Third World Quarterly*. Vol. 23, No. 3, pp. 437–448; Waltz, S., 'Human Rights Standards and the Human Rights Movement in the Global South: The UDHR and Beyond', in Andreopoulos, G. (ed), *Concepts and Strategies in International Human Rights*, New York: Peter Lang (2002), pp. 51–71.

71 See generally Farrokh, J., 'The Drafting of the Human Rights Provisions of the UN Charter', *Netherlands International Law Review*, Vol. 44 (1997), p. 3; Korey, W., *NGOS and The Universal Declaration of Human Rights: "A Curious Grapevine"*, New York: St. Martin's Press (1998), pp. 29–42; Farrokh, J., ibid at pp. 1–31; also, Lauren, P.G., *The Evolution of International Human Rights*, Visions Seen (1998), pp. 223–25.

in mind, the issues that appeared most salient to them.[72] Writers and commentators on international affairs argue that by the provisions they actively promoted, the ideas they argued against, and the various proposals to which they lent political support, Muslim delegates helped give shape to international human rights instruments.[73]

5.3.1 Saudi Arabia and the adoption of the UDHR

The first phase of Saudi Arabia's involvement in the international human rights development began right from the inception. Saudi Arabia along with other Muslim countries was actively involved in the debates and negotiations on the UDHR and proposed Covenants in the General Assembly Third Committee.[74] Jamil Al-Baroody was Saudi Arabia's representative to the UN.[75] He actively participated in the discussions and his vocal, vigorous, and logical arguments attracted the attention of other states delegates.[76] For example, he made the general observation that the proposed draft of the UDHR was saturated in Western culture, itself often at conflict with the world's other cultures.[77]

Saudi Arabia's position was clearly articulated on a number of draft articles. For example, the Kingdom strongly supported the then Soviet Union proposal to qualify draft article 11 (final article 13) so that freedom of movement would be dependent on local laws. Here Saudi Arabia argued that the right of internal and external travels could be qualified in times of emergency, asserting that its government would act in accordance with its own domestic legislations and traditions.[78] Thus, Saudi Arabia was disposed to argue that it does not feel obligated to allow unfettered freedom of movement and residence within and outside its boundaries, a policy that its Communist allies at that period have later agreed to abandon in Helsinki.[79] The Saudi position here, it is argued, must have been motivated by obvious steps to prohibiting non-Muslims entry to the holy cities of Makkah and Madinah.[80]

Article 12 (final article 14) was also of concern to Saudi Arabia. This article would grant the right of asylum in cases of political crime. In its motion for amending this article, it sought the omission from the draft the section which

72 Waltz, S., supra note no. 69.

73 Ibid.

74 Ibid at pp. 799–844.

75 Jamil Al-Baroody was originally Lebanese who worked in the United Kingdom as an Arab political and economic observer (1929, 1935–1939). He lived in Saudi Arabia for a few years. He was part of the Saudi delegation to the San Francisco Conference in 1945. He served as the Saudi representative to the UN for over 20 years; see also Waltz, S., ibid at p. 811.

76 Alwasil, A.M., supra note no. 66 at p. 1073.

77 Piscatori, J.P., supra note no. 27 at p. 299.

78 United Nations, General Assembly, Official Records, 3rd Session, Third Committee, Lake Success, New York: 21 September–8 December, 1948, pp. 324–326.

79 Piscatori, J.P., supra note no. 27 at p. 300.

80 Ibid.

promised that asylum "be granted". It argued that the article, as it stood, promised much at the expense of state sovereignty. It further argued that the right to seek asylum is itself acceptable, but states must not be coerced into accepting the persecuted without adequate study of their psychological state and potential dangers involved. The amendment was adopted, and Saudi Arabia went on to support the British proposal which became the text article: "Everyone has the right to seek, and to enjoy, in other countries, asylum from persecution".[81] The idea behind Saudi Arabia's position in this regard, was informed by its concern for unbridled power and possibly its fear that it might be obligated to accept refugee hostile to the regime.[82]

Saudi Arabia's concern was also manifested in its opposition to the draft of Article 13 (final Article 15). This article deals with the right of nationality. Here the Kingdom again went along with the Soviet Union in denouncing a provision dealing with right to change nationality. The Soviet representatives noted that it is wrong for the UN to encourage what may be an unpatriotic action. Saudi also advanced argument calling for deleting the offending section because the amendment made clear that the legislation of states in this issue is an area outside UN jurisdiction and competence.[83] The objection was rejected and the objectionable provision was retained.[84] It is noted that the Saudi delegate in the UN debate relied only on the argument that state sovereignty would be violated by passage of the article in question coupled with share aim of protecting the traditional value.[85] Saudi's concern was also visible over draft Article 14 (final Article 16) dealing with marriage and the family. The article states *inter alia* that, "men and women of full age, without any limitation due to race, nationality or religion, have the right to marry…". It also establishes the principles of consent to marriage and equal rights in marriage, gender equality in marriage, and the banning of restrictions on marriage due to nationality or religion.

Saudi Arabia and some other states objected to the unspecified concept of gender equality. Their opposition was based on the argument that the authors of the draft text had shown excessive propensity for the standards recognized by Western civilization in an unreserved disregard for the heritage of more ancient civilizations.[86] The Saudi amendment to the article proposed that men and women should be "entitled to the full rights as defined in the marriage laws of their countries".[87] UN records of the proceedings on the debate of Article 16 indicate that the Saudi position was that "it was not for the Committee to proclaim the superiority of one civilization over all others or to establish uniform standards

81 UN General Assembly, Official Records, supra at pp. 331, 343–344.
82 Piscatori, J.P., supra note no. 27.
83 UN General Assembly, Official Records, supra at pp. 344, 361–362.
84 Ibid.
85 Piscatori, J.P., supra note no. 27 at pp. 301–302.
86 UN document, GA Third Committee.
87 UN document, GA Third Committee, 3rd Session (1948), p. 370.

for all the countries in the world".[88] In articulating the point, Al-Baroody explained that a Muslim woman could own, inherit, and dispose of property and, in the event of a divorce, was entitled to a pre-determined indemnity.[89] The Saudi proposed amendment was unanimously rejected because, according to the reports, it would undermine the concept of the universality of human rights.[90] Again on the same article, Saudi Arabia argued that the phrase that accorded marriage rights to men and women did not take cognisance of the notion of physiological development of sexes. Thus, it proposed rephrasing "legal matrimonial age" to "legal age of marriage".[91] It is noted that the age of marriage in traditional mainstream Islamic jurisprudence is linked to physical signs of a person having attained the age of puberty. Consequently, Saudi Arabia favoured a substitute phrase "mature age" proposed by Syria, in deference to objections raised by other delegations, which was rejected.[92]

Another point of concern to Saudi Arabia in Article 16 is the prohibition of restrictions on marriage due to race, nationality, or religion. It thus proposed amendment to that provision on the argument that a Muslim woman is not allowed to marry a non-Muslim man. Also, under Saudi domestic law, neither a male nor a female is allowed to marry a non-Saudi without obtaining a permit from the government. The Saudi proposed amendment in this regard was rejected.[93]

As could be seen from the above analysis, Saudi positions on a number of human rights issues were rejected during the UDHR debate and negotiation. However, Saudi Arabia's participation in the debates and negotiations prove two points. One, the intrusion of international law into domestic affairs of states and two, its overbearing impact on modern nation-states generally and Muslim-majority states in particular. Ordinarily, Saudi Arabia traditionalists approach to *Shari'ah* was not likely to accommodate participation and debate of such issues.

5.3.2 Saudi Arabia's ratification of ICERD and CAT

The International Convention on the Elimination of All Forms of Racial Discrimination (ICERD) is a UN convention and second-generation human rights instrument.[94] The Convention commits its members to the elimination of racial discrimination and the promotion of understanding among all races.[95] The Convention also requires its parties to outlaw hate speech and criminalize

88 UN document, GA Third Committee, 3rd Session (1948), ibid.
89 Alwasil, A.M., supra note no. 66 at p. 1074.
90 Ibid.
91 UN document, GA Third Committee, 3rd Session (1948), ibid at p. 371.
92 Alwasil, A.M., supra note no. 66.
93 Ibid.
94 Natán, L., *The U.N. Convention on the Elimination of All Forms of Racial Discrimination*, Wilhelminalaan: Sijthoff & Noordhoff International, (1980), p. 1.
95 See ICERD, Article 2.1.

membership in racist organizations.[96] The Convention against Torture and Other Cruel, Inhuman or Treatment or Punishment (CAT) adopted in 1984 is an international human rights instrument that aims to prevent torture around the world. The Convention requires states to take effective measures to prevent torture within their borders and forbids states to transport people to any country where there is reason to believe they will be tortured.[97]

Saudi Arabia was among the states that voted for the adoption of ICERD.[98] It is noted that the debate on this piece of international legislation was not so controversial and Saudi Arabia had previously ratified some international treaties that were part of the UN efforts to combat various forms of discrimination.[99] It is noteworthy that historically, Saudi Arabia abolished slavery in the early 1960s under international pressure mounted mainly from two directions – President John Kennedy and the UN.[100] Thus, it ratified the Slavery Convention of 1926 only on 5 July 1973.[101] Also, Saudi Arabia is said to have come closer to the legally binding labour standards when it ratified, at the same time, four international labour conventions, namely, International Labour Convention No. 29 of 1930 concerning forced labour,[102] International Labour Convention No. 100 of 1951 concerning equality of opportunity and treatment of men and women,[103] International Labour Convention No. 105 of 1957 concerning abolition of forced labour,[104] and International Labour Convention No. 111 of 1958 concerning discrimination in respect of employment and occupation.[105]

The General Assembly Third Committee unanimously approved CAT and was later adopted without a vote in General Assembly Resolution 39/46 at the GA Plenary Meeting of 10 December 1984.[106] Saudi Arabia's position on this piece of legislation was limited to casting its vote mostly in favour of certain articles, while abstaining from voting on articles that established procedures for

96 See ICERD, Article 4.

97 United Nations Treaty Collection: Convention against Torture and Other Cruel, Inhuman or Degrading Treatment or Punishment. Retrieved on 13 September 2012, http://treaties.un.org/Pages/ViewDetails.aspx?src=TREATY&mtdsg_no=IV-9&chapter=4&lang=en (accessed 13 February 2013).

98 Alwasil, A.M., supra note no. 66, at pp. 1077.

99 Ibid.

100 Simons, G., *Saudi Arabia: The Shape of a Client Feudalism*, New York, St. Martin's Press (1998) p. 63; Long, D.E., *The Kingdom of Saudi Arabia*, Gainesville: University Press of Florida (1997), p. 36; Wilson, P.W., and Graham, D.F., *Saudi Arabia: The Coming Storm*, New York: M.E. Sharpe (1994), p. 62; Alwasil, A.M., supra note no. 66.

101 UN Document, States Parties to the Slavery Convention, http://untreaty.un.org/English/sample/EnglishInternetBible/partI/chapterXVIII/treaty2.htm (accessed 11 July 2007).

102 ILO Document, Ratification of Convention No 29, www.ilo.org/ilolex/eg-lex/ratifice.pl?C029 (accessed 11 July 2007).

103 Ibid ILO Document, Ratification of Convention No 29.

104 Ibid.

105 Ibid.

106 UN Document, Yearbook of the United Nations (1989), p. 675.

monitoring or arbitration. Thus, Saudi Arabia ratified CAT on 23 September 1997.[107]

Saudi's ratification of ICERD, its casting votes in favour of certain articles and particularly its abstention from some other articles of CAT are again proofs of its conscious understanding of the fact that those international instruments would necessarily have some impact on its domestic legislation.

5.4 The Universal Islamic Declaration of Human Rights (UIDHR)

The year 1981 was a landmark in the history of Saudi Arabia's involvement in human rights issues as the Universal Islamic Declaration of Human Rights (UIDHR) was launched. UIDH was an Islamic human rights instrument prepared and adopted by Islamic Council in Paris[108] and London in 1981.[109] UIDH was prepared by representatives of several Muslim countries, including Saudi Arabia, under the auspices of the Islamic Council, a private group affiliated with the Makkah based Muslim World League, which has strong patronage of the Saudi Arabian government.[110] Eva Brems notes that although the UIDHR was drafted by a private organization and not an intergovernmental document, it "has been granted a credible international status by UNESCO, to which it was solemnly presented by representatives of the Islamic Council in 1981".[111] It was stated in the forward of its Secretary General that accompanied the text, that it was "compiled by eminent Muslim scholars, jurists and representatives of Islamic movements and thought".[112]

In a comparative assessment of UIDHR, some commentators have been critical of it for what has been described as "its apologetic tones and for the fact that it does not offer the same protection as international human rights text".[113] Yet, some others have acknowledged it as a positive initiative, noting that it is important that the UIDHR attaches the authority of Islamic tradition to human rights.[114] In fact, Sinaceur, a UNESCO functionary, expressed the view that the

107 "Parties to the Optional Protocol to the Convention against Torture and Other Cruel, Inhuman or Degrading Treatment or Punishment". United Nations Treaty Collection. Retrieved 4 September 2012, http://treaties.un.org/Pages/ViewDetails.aspx?src=TREATY&mtdsg_no=IV-9-b&chapter=4&lang=en (accessed 13 February 2013).

108 Azzam, S., Universal Islamic Declaration of Human Rights, *The International Journal of Human Rights*, Vol. 2, No. 3 (1998), pp. 102–112.

109 Halliday, F., 'Relativism and Universalism in Human Rights: The Case of the Islamic Middle East', *Political Studies*, Vol. 43 (1995), pp. 152–167.

110 Mayer, A.E., 'Islam', in Forsythe, D.P. (ed), *Encyclopaedia of Human Rights*, Oxford: Oxford University Press (2009), p. 240.

111 Brems, E., *Human Rights: Universality and Diversity*, Leiden: Martinus Nijhoff Publishers (2001), p. 242.

112 Ibid.

113 Ibid.

114 Arkoun, M., Declaration Islamique Universelle des droits de l'homme", in Frene, A. (ed), *Droits de l'homme, droits des peuples*, Paris: P.U.F. (1982), p. 226 as quoted by Brems, E., supra note no. 111.

UIDHR might serve as motivation for doing *Ijtihad*[115] which is of particular importance in the contemporary times.

UIDHR which arguably is an Islamic response to the UDHR outlines a wide range of rights which include rights in criminal cases, marriage, inheritance, divorce, and economic activities, and supports freedom of religion based on traditional Islamic law.[116] For example, it provides for right to life;[117] right to freedom;[118] right to equality and prohibition against impermissible discrimination;[119] right to justice;[120] rights to fair trial;[121] right to protection against abuse of power;[122] right to protection against torture;[123] right to protection of honour and reputation;[124] and right to asylum.[125]

Of particular note are rights of minorities[126] which is ostensibly based on *Qur'anic* text that (a) the *Qur'anic* principle "There is no compulsion in religion" shall govern the religious rights of non-Muslim minorities, and (b) in a Muslim country religious minorities shall have the choice to be governed in respect of their civil and personal matters by Islamic law, or by their own laws; the right to freedom of belief, thought and speech;[127] and right to freedom of religion.[128] It also provides for rights of married women to receive the means necessary for maintaining a standard of living which is not inferior to that of her spouse … seek and obtain dissolution of marriage (*Khul'a*) in accordance with the terms of the law … in addition to her right to seek divorce through the courts … inherit from her husband, her parents, her children and other relatives according to the Law…".[129]

It is noted however that the UIDHR is silent on gender equality as provided for in the UDHR. It is also silent on the freedom of thought, conscience, and religion, which covers freedom to change one's religion or belief as provided for in UDHR.[130] That perhaps explains why Eva Brems describes the instrument as

115 Sinaceur, M.A., Declaration Islamique Universelle des droits de l'homme", in Frenet, A. (ed), *Droits de l'homme, droits des peuples*, Paris: P.U.F. (1982), p. 226, as quoted by Brems, E., supra note no. 111.

116 Oxford Islamic Studies Online, The Oxford Dictionary of Islam, *Universal Islamic Declaration of Human Rights* (UIDHR), www.oxfordislamicstudies.com/article/opr/t125/e2435?_hi=0&_pos=8054 (accessed 9 May 2015).

117 Article I.

118 Article II.

119 Article III.

120 Article IV.

121 Article V.

122 Article VI.

123 Article VII.

124 Article VIII.

125 Article IX.

126 Article X.

127 Article XII.

128 Article XIII.

129 Article XX.

130 Article 18 of UDHR.

apologetic and of lower standard to the UDHR.[131] These have been two contentious issues upon which Saudi Arabia based its refusal to adopt the UDHR in 1948 and upon which it adopted some UN human rights conventions with reservation.

5.5 Saudi Arabia's human rights commitments: a new beginning

The UN human rights system had faced series of challenges across the globe from 1990 to date. For example, the OIC, in which Saudi Arabia plays a major role, adopted the Cairo Declaration on Human Rights in Islam (CDHRI) in 1990, the Cold War came to an end in 1991, the Gulf War raged between 1990 and 1991, and the 11 September attacks occurred in 2001. This was followed by the consequential upsurge of the war against terrorism. The cumulative effect of all these has had profound impact on Saudi Arabia's political and legal systems. This period marked a new beginning and, of course, a second phase of Saudi's active involvement in the international human rights system. In this second phase, Saudi Arabia has taken remarkable and very conscious steps towards fuller participation in the UN human rights system.[132]

5.5.1 The Cairo Declaration on Human Rights in Islam (CDHRI)

The year 1990 was another landmark in the anal of Saudi Arabia's involvement in human rights issues at international level. That year, the member states of the OIC, in which Saudi Arabia plays a major role, adopted the Cairo Declaration on Human Rights in Islam CDHRI in Cairo.[133] The OIC was established upon a decision of the historical summit which took place in Rabat, Kingdom of Morocco on 25 September 1969 consequent to the arson at Al-Aqsa Mosque in occupied Jerusalem.[134] This instrument provides an overview of the Islamic perspective on human rights, and affirms Islamic Shari'ah as its sole source. It also declares its purpose to be "general guidance for Member States in the field of human rights".[135]

Unlike the UIDHR, the CDHRI was adopted by an intergovernmental organization and is arguably seen as an Islamic response to the UDHR by the OIC member states, guaranteeing many of the same rights as the latter, while at

131 Brems, E., supra note no. 111 at p. 242.

132 Alwasil, A.M., supra note no. 66 at p. 1078.

133 The Nineteenth Islamic Conference of Foreign Ministers (Session of Peace, Interdependence and Development), held in Cairo, Arab Republic of Egypt, from 9 to 14 Muharram 1411H (31 July to 5 August 1990).

134 Organization of Islamic Cooperation, *About OIC*, www.oic-oci.org/oicv2/page/?p_id=52&p_ref=26&lan=en (accessed 9 May 2015).

135 Brems, E., supra note no. 111.

the same time upholding what some argue to be "inequalities inherent in Islamic law and tradition" in terms of religion, gender, sexuality, political rights, and other aspects of contemporary society at odds with Islamic law and traditions.[136]

The CDHRI contains 25 Articles providing for a wide range of rights. For example, Article 1 states *inter alia* that all men are equal in terms of basic human dignity and basic obligations and responsibilities, without any discrimination on the grounds of race, colour, language, sex, religious belief, political affiliation, social status, or other considerations. True faith is the guarantee for enhancing such dignity along the path to human perfection. Article 2 provides for right to life. Article 6 provides that "woman is equal to man in human dignity and has rights to enjoy as well as duties to perform; she has her own civil entity and financial independence, and the right to retain her name and lineage". Article 22 provides for freedom of opinion subject to *Shari'ah*; while Article 24 states specifically that all the rights and freedoms stipulated in this Declaration are subject to the Islamic *Shari'ah*. Similar notion is expressed under the provision of Article 25 which states that "the Islamic *Shari'ah* is the only source of reference for the explanation or clarification of any of the articles of this Declaration".

The CDHRI has been sharply criticized. An example is its Section 22 which provides that: "Everyone shall have the right to express his opinion freely in such manner as would not be contrary to the principles of the *Shari'ah*",[137] Dacey Austin and Koproske Colin have argued that this permits limitations on freedom of expression that clearly are not permitted by the UDHR, whose Article 19 simply states, "Everyone has the right to freedom of opinion and expression; this right includes freedom to hold opinions without interference and to seek, receive and impart information and ideas through any media and regardless of frontiers". Also, the CDHRI mentions *Shari'ah* 15 times, mostly to qualify various rights by stipulating that they must be exercised within the limits of *Shari'ah*.[138] They argue quoting Ann Mayer[139] that the Cairo Declaration contains no endorsement of equality of rights, and instead says that all human beings "are equal in terms of basic human dignity and basic obligations and responsibilities"[140] noting that equality in "dignity" and "obligations" does not necessarily signify equality in rights.[141]

The CDHRI has also been criticized for failing to guarantee freedom of religion, in particular the right of each and every individual to change their religion, as a fundamental and non-negotiable right.[142] Also its provisions that: "All the rights and freedoms stipulated in this Declaration are subject to the Islamic

136 Mayer, A.E., supra note no. 31.

137 CDHRI, Article.

138 Austin, D., and Colin, K., *Islam and Human Right*, Butterflies & Wheels, www.butterfliesandwheels.org/2008/islam-and-human-rights/ (accessed 9 May 2015).

139 Mayer, A.E., supra note no. 31 at p. 102.

140 Article 1 of CDHRI.

141 Austin, D., and Colin, K., supra note no. 138.

142 Kazemi, F., Perspectives on Islam and Civil Society, in Hashmi, S.H. (ed), *Islamic Political Ethics: Civil Society, Pluralism and Conflict*, New Jersey: Princeton University Press (2002), pp. 50.

Shari'ah"[143] and, "There shall be no crime or punishment except as provided for in the *Shari'ah*"[144] are all restrictive and negotiable.[145]

Commenting on the CDHRI, Adama Dienga, a member of the International Commission of Jurists, argues that the instrument gravely threatens the inter-cultural consensus on which the international human rights instruments are based. In other words, it introduces "intolerable discrimination against non-Muslims and women".[146] It is however noted that the CDHRI has been linguistically secular than the UIDHR and less biased against Shi'ite Muslims.[147]

5.5.2 *Arab Charter on Human Rights (ACHR)*

It is significant to note that as part of Saudi Arabia's participation in human rights issues at international level, it also played an active role in the adoption of the first Arab Charter on Human Rights in 1994 and the subsequent revised Charter of 2004 which came into force in March 2008 and ratified by 10 of the 22 League of Arab States (LAS) members, namely, Algeria, Bahrain, Jordan, Libya, Palestine, Qatar, Saudi Arabia, Syria, the United Arab Emirates, and Yemen.[148]

The ACHR affirms the principle contained in the UDHR, the International Covenants on Human Rights, and the CDHR. The ACHR provides for a wide range of rights including the right to liberty and security of persons, equality of person before the law, protection of person from torture, the right to own private property, freedom to practice religious observance, and freedom of peaceful assembly and association. It is noted that although the Charter recognizes key rights that conform to international human rights law as reflected in treaties, jurisprudence, and opinions of UN expert bodies,[149] "it also authorizes the imposition of restrictions on the exercise of freedom of thought, conscience, and religion far beyond international human rights law", subjecting many important rights to national legislation.[150]

5.6 Saudi Arabia's adoption of CRC, CAT, ICERD, and CEDAW

In 1996 Saudi Arabia acceded to the Convention on the Rights of the Child (CRC) even though, this was conditioned by a generalized reservation that it

143 Article 24 of CDHRI.

144 Article 19 of CDHRI.

145 Kazemi, F., supra note no. 142.

146 David, L., Universal Human Rights and 'Human Rights in Islam', *Midstream Journal*, New York (1999), www.dhimmitude.org/archive/universal_islam.html (accessed 9 May 2015).

147 Ali, M., *Islam Encountering Globalization*, Oxfordshire: Routledge (2002), p. 114.

148 Norman, H., In the Name of God, Faith-based Internet Censorship in Majority Muslim Countries, in Monroe, E.P., et al. (eds), *Routledge Hanbook of Media Law*, Oxfordshire: Routledge (2013), p. 255.

149 Ibid.

150 See generally, Rishmawi, M., The Arab Charter on Human Rights, *Arab Reform Bulletin*, Carnegie Endowment for International Peace (2009).

would not be bound by articles of the Convention which might conflict with Islamic law.[151] However, this implies that Saudi is under obligation to submit periodic reports on steps taken to giving effect to rights recognized in the CRC in accordance with its Article 4. Accordingly, Saudi Arabia submitted initial report in 2000 and subsequent report in 2006.[152]

The Committee on the Rights of the Child made several observations and recommendations on this report. It observed that narrow interpretations of Islamic texts hinder the realization of the human rights guaranteed under the CRC. For example, persons under 18 could be liable for prosecution and punishment for crimes in the same manner as adults.[153] Secondly, "the right recognized by the CRC were still not reflected in the Saudi Arabia basic laws; lack of systematic data collection and planning and a low level of awareness among the stakeholders particularly, those professionals responsible for children affairs".[154] It then recommended that Saudi Arabia review relevant domestic laws and administrative regulations in order to ensure equality between boys and girls.[155]

In its response Saudi Arabia explained that the *Shari'ah* fundamentally protects children and guarantees their rights.[156] It argued that Islam gives children a privileged position and views the family as the basic unit of society and the natural environment in which every child should grow up and develop.[157] It, however, noted that measures and institutions had been put in place in conformity with the CRC, accepting that customary practices derived from popular traditions rather than from the *Shari'ah*, and which might be considered discriminatory, still existed.[158] The commitment to address at least some of the issues raised by the CRC Committee will necessarily require Saudi Arabia to re-evaluate its narrow interpretations of the *Shari'ah* that hinder the realization of the human rights of children as guaranteed under the CRC as noted by the Committee.

151 UN Document, Office of the UN High Commissioner for Human Rights (OHCHR), Ratification and Reservation, www.ohchr.org/english/countries/ratification/11.htm (accessed 15 March 2005).

152 Committee on the Rights of the Child, *Second Periodic Reports of States Parties Due in 2003: Saudi Arabia*, U.N. Doc. CRC/C/136/Add.1 (April 21, 2005), www.unhchr.ch/tbs/doc.nsf/(Symbol)/bfff4a8b21a0a267c125703c004a0025?Opendocument, *and also as* .pdf Document; (accessed 12 September 2014).

153 UN document, CRC/C/15/Add.148 of 22 February 2001, Concluding Observations of the Committee on the Rights of the Child: Saudi Arabia; Alwasil, A.M., supra note no. 66 at pp. 1079.

154 UN Document, ibid.

155 Committee on the Rights of the Child, *Initial Reports of States Parties Due in 1998: Saudi Arabia*, U.N. Doc. CRC/C/61/Add.2 (March 29, 2000), available at www.unhchr.ch/tbs/doc.nsf/(Symbol)/fa46e24ca2ecc709c1256918004525b9?Opendocument, *and also as* .pdf Document, CRC/C/SAU/CO/2, para. 28; (accessed 12 September 2014).

156 UN Document, CRC/C/SR.687 of 1 February 2002, Summary Record of the 687th Meeting: Saudi Arabia.

157 UN Document, CRC/C/SR.687, ibid.

158 Alwasil, A.M., supra note no. 66.

Although Saudi Arabia acceded to Convention Against Torture (CAT) in 1997 it was not until 2001 that it presented its initial report which was due for presentation in 1998. It stated in the introductory paragraph of the report that it endorsed the UDHR and subsequent human rights covenants, conventions, and protocols, noting at the same time, that the *Shari'ah* guaranteed human rights and explaining how the Convention's articles were incorporated in its local legislations. The report also highlighted numerous laws relevant to the Convention, including the rules prohibiting torture during investigations, which required that "confessions should result from thorough and careful investigation without torture".[159] During the presentation of this report, the Saudi delegations noted that the Committee against Torture did not have proper grasp of the basic sources of the Saudi legal systems – the *Qur'an* and the *Sunnah* which could not be amended *per se*.[160] That explained the use of corporal punishment for certain crimes as dictated by the *Qur'an* which could neither be abrogated nor amended as they are essentially divine. The State, it was argued, was bound not to take any decision that ran counter to this divine law, and moreover, those corporal punishments were not forms of torture as defined in Article 1 of CAT, which excluded pain arising from, inherent in, or incidental to lawful sanctions.[161]

The Committee appreciated the competence of the Board of Grievances to hear allegations of violations of human rights and described it as a welcomed positive development in the Kingdom. It however expressed reservations over a number of matters, particularly the allegations of prolonged pre-trial detention of some individuals and the "sentencing to, and imposition of, corporal punishment by judicial and administrative authorities, including, particularly flogging and amputation of limbs, that were not in conformity with the Convention".[162] It thus made a number of recommendations for implementation including incorporation of the crime of torture into Saudi domestic legislation and re-examination of corporal punishment, which were noted to be in violation of the Convention.[163]

In the year 2000, the Saudi government took a giant stride by implementing the obligation stipulated under the CAT rules. In that year, Saudi Arabia officially established a committee to investigate allegations of torture.[164] Similarly, in the newly promulgated Code of Criminal Procedure, which came into force in

159 UN Document, CAT/C/42/Add.2 of 20 September 2001, Initial Reports of States Parties: Saudi Arabia.

160 UN Document, CAT/C/SR.519 of 17 May 2002, Summary Record of the First Part of the 519th Meeting: Saudi Arabia.

161 UN Document, CAT/C/SR.519 of 17 May 2002, ibid.

162 UN Document, CAT/C/CR/28/5 of 12 June 2002, Conclusions and Recommendation of the Committee against Torture: Saudi Arabia.

163 Alwasil, A.M., supra note no. 66 at p. 1080.

164 Saudi Arabia (official document), Saudi Arabia's Statement delivered by Turki Bin Muhammad Bin Saud Al-Kabeer at the 56th Session of the Commission on Human Rights on 6 April 2000.

May 2002, Saudi Arabia addressed its obligations under CAT by specifying legal procedures and due process rights.[165]

In acceding to International Convention on the Elimination of All Forms of Racial Discrimination (ICERD) along CAT in 1997, Saudi Arabia asserted a general reservation to the effect that it would implement the provisions therein as long as they were not in conflict with mandates of the *Shari'ah* and also not to be bound by Article 22 concerning the referral of disputes to the International Court of Justice.[166] In 2001, Saudi Arabia submitted its initial and second periodic reports to the Committee on the Elimination of Racial Discrimination highlighting the legal framework through which it would implement the provisions of the Convention, while the third report was submitted in 2003. Commenting on the reports, the Committee acknowledged some positive reforms in the field of human rights in the Kingdom, particularly the enactment of new codes relating to the judicial system and expressed optimism that Saudi Arabia would soon accede to the International Covenant on Civil and Political Rights (ICCPR) and International Covenant on Economic, Social and Cultural Rights (ICESCR).[167]

Saudi Arabia also acceded to Convention on the Elimination of All Forms of Discrimination Against Women (CEDAW) in the year 2000,[168] again, with a general reservation against the background of Article 1 of CEDAW, that it would not be obliged to observe provisions that were in conflict with the *Shari'ah*. Similarly, it would not be bound by Article 29, paragraph 1 which stipulates instituting disputes with other states before the International Court of Justice; and that it would not be bound by Article 29, paragraph 2, which granted women equal rights with men in respect to the nationality of their children.[169]

By virtue of its commitment to the Convention, it was under obligation to comply with its provisions and to submit reports on measures taken with its treaty obligations.[170] Thus, it submitted its initial and second reports, in late 2007 which were due in October 2001. In these reports, Saudi Arabia responded to issues raised by the Committee on the Elimination of Discrimination against Women. The Committee acknowledged the significant progress made in women's education. It however expressed concerns over the non-inclusion of the principle of equality between women and men and absence of a definition of

165 Alwasil, A.M., supra note no. 66.

166 UN Document, Office of the UN High Commissioner for Human Rights (OHCHR), Ratification and Reservation, www.ohchr.org/english/countries/ratification/2.htm (accessed 15 March 2005).

167 UN Document, CERD/C/62/CO/8 of 21 March 2003, Concluding Observations of the Committee on the Elimination of Racial Discrimination: Saudi Arabia.

168 CEDAW, art.2. Saudi Arabia's accession to the convention was formalized through the adoption of Royal Decree No. 25 of 28/5 [Concerning the kingdom's accession to the Convention on the Elimination of All Forms of Discrimination against Women] on 28 August 2000.

169 UN Document, Declarations, Reservations, and Objections to CEDAW, www.un.org/womenwatch/daw/cedaw/reservations-country.htm (accessed 25 May 2005).

170 Alwasil, A.M., supra note no. 66.

discrimination against women in neither the Constitution nor other local legislations. The Committee thus recommended practical steps to increase women's participation in the workforce substantial measures to accelerate the increase in the participation and presentation of women in all elected and appointed governmental bodies, including the *Majlis Al-Shoura* (Consultative Council).[171]

5.7 Saudi Arabia's refusal to ratify ICCPR and ICESR

Eighteen years after the adoption of UDHR, both the International Covenant on Economic, Social and Cultural Rights (ICESCR) and the International Covenant on Civil and Political Rights (ICCPR) got a widespread consensus evidenced by 105 and 106 votes respectively at the time of their adoptions. It is argued that this was due to the fact that in the two instruments, the controversial provisions in Article 18 of the UDHR had been reconsidered against the background of the specificities and sensitivities of religion, particularly Islam.[172] Thus, references to religious matters in both Article 18 concerning the right to change one's religion and Article 16 concerning the right to marry and to found a family under the provisions of the UDHR were removed from the ICCPR concerning the two issues.[173] Thus, Article 18 of ICCPR acknowledges freedom of thought, conscience and religion, the right to have or adopt a religion or belief and to manifest one's religion or belief, without a specific citation on the right to change one's religion.[174] Also, Article 23 of ICCPR acknowledges the right to marry and found a family but omits sensitive stipulations (based on religion) which would most likely lead to reservation from Muslim countries on this point.[175]

Despite these changes in the two instruments, Saudi Arabia had maintained its refusal to ratify either of them. During the debate of the two instruments, Saudi Arabia reiterated its objection as based on the grounds of Islamic considerations.[176] Saudi Arabia argued that the provision under Article 18 of ICCPR had a tendency that "it would raise doubts in the minds of ordinary people to whom their religion [is] a way of life". Regarding Article 9 of ICESCR which provides for "the right of everyone to social security including social insurance", Saudi Arabia vehemently objected to this provision arguing that the provision under the *Shari'ah* rules for such goes beyond what was deemed as inferior Western requirements,[177] and accordingly refused to ratify this instrument.

171 UN Document, Declarations, Reservations, and Objections to CEDAW, ibid.

172 Abiad, N., *Sharia, Muslim States and International Human Right Treaty Obligations: A Comparative Study*, London: British Institute of International and Comparative Law (2008), p. 61.

173 Ibid.

174 Ibid at p. 62.

175 Ibid.

176 Ibid.

177 Piscatori, J., 'Human Rights in Islamic Political Culture', in Thompson, K. (ed), *Moral Imperatives of Human Rights*, Washington, DC: University Press of America (1980), p. 151.

5.8 The challenge of implementation of ratified human rights treaties

Saudi Arabia faces the challenge of maintaining a balance between strict adherence to its "hardline" interpretations of the *Shari'ah* and the practical implementation of the international human rights treaties it has ratified. This fact was confirmed in Saudi Arabia's 2009 human rights report to the UN Human Rights Council where it is specifically stated that among the challenges that face Saudi Arabia in complying and implementing international treaties are terrorism[178] and factors of inherited conventions, customs and traditions that had been historically endemic and are still prevalent in the Kingdom.[179] Also, Saudi Arabia is placed in an impossible situation, by which it cannot ratify and honour international human rights treaties without reviewing its strict "hard-line" interpretations of the *Shari'ah*. This fact is reflected in a number of reports presented by several organs of the UN as well as in reports presented by Saudi Arabia itself.

5.9 Critical appraisal of Saudi Arabia's human rights record

In the 2009 Human Rights Council Working Group report,[180] the Committee on the Elimination of Discrimination against Women (CEDAW), though welcomed Saudi Arabia's accession to the Protocol to Prevent, Suppress and Punish Trafficking in Persons, especially Women and Children (Palermo Protocol),[181] it expressed concern over the general reservation of Saudi Arabia upon ratification of the Convention urging it to consider the withdrawal of its general reservation.[182] It also requested it to withdraw its reservation concerning Article 9 of the Convention.[183] Similarly, the Committee on the Rights of the Child (CRC) reiterated its earlier call on Saudi Arabia to review the general nature of its reservation with a view to withdrawing it, or narrowing it.[184] In similar vein, the Committee on the Elimination of Racial Discrimination (CERD) was also concerned about the broad and imprecise nature of Saudi Arabia's general reservation and encouraged it to review the reservation with a view to formally

178 National Report Submitted in Accordance with Paragraph 15 (A) of the Annex to Human Council Resolution 5/1United Nations General Assembly, Human Rights Council Working Group on the Universal Periodic Review (Fourth Session), Geneva, 2–13 February 2009, para. 64.

179 National Report Submitted in Accordance with Paragraph 15 (A) of the Annex to Human Council Resolution 5/1United Nations General Assembly, Human Rights Council Working Group on the Universal Periodic Review (Fourth Session), Geneva, 2–13 February 2009, para. 73.

180 Human Rights Council, Working Group on the Universal Periodic Review (Fourth Session) Geneva, 2–13 February 2009.

181 CEDAW/C/SAU/CO/2, para. 23.

182 Concluding comments of the Committee on the Elimination of Discrimination against Women (CEDAW) (CEDAW/C/SAU/CO/2), paras. 9–10.

183 Ibid at para. 28.

184 Concluding observations of the Committee on the Rights of the Child (CRC/C/SAU/CO/2), para. 8.

withdrawing it.[185] CEDAW expressed satisfaction that in practice, Saudi Arabia gave precedence to international treaties over domestic law.[186] However, it encouraged the Kingdom to amend its legislation to confirm that international treaties have precedence over domestic laws, to redouble its efforts to raise awareness about the Convention among the general public and to enact a comprehensive gender equality law.[187] Also, an International Labour Organization (ILO)'s Committee of Experts has once observed that the new Saudi Labour Code which came into force in 2006 contains no reference to equal remunerations for men and women for work of equal value, and that women are restricted in the types of job they may do.[188]

Like the Committee on the Elimination of Racial Discrimination (CERD), the Committee on the Rights of the Child (CRC) expressed concerns that the mere statement of the general principle of non-discrimination in domestic law may not be taken to be enough response to the requirements of the Convention.[189] It thus recommended that Saudi Arabia review relevant domestic laws and administrative regulations to ensure equality between boys and girls.[190]

In another development, a UN Special Rapporteur on the independence of judges and lawyers on a visit to Saudi Arabia in 2002, welcomed the issuance of the Law on Criminal Procedure and particularly the inclusion of provisions prohibiting torture and other cruel, inhuman, or degrading treatment, and guaranteeing the right to have access to a lawyer at all stages of the legal process. He however expressed concern that sometimes the provisions of the code favour the interests of an investigation over the rights of the accused.[191] Also, in 2002, the Committee Against Torture (CAT) urged Saudi Arabia to expressly incorporate into its domestic law the crime of torture, as defined in Article 1 of the Convention. This is necessary to signal the fundamental importance of this prohibition.[192]

CRC also hailed Saudi Arabia's bold step in creating the National Human Rights Association (NHRA) and took note of its mandate to receive complaints regarding alleged human rights violations. However, it expressed concern about the fact that NHRA has not been able to attain a fully independent status.[193] CEDAW also commended Saudi Arabia in this regard,[194] but urged the Kingdom

185 Concluding Observations of the Committee on the Elimination of Racial Discrimination (CERD/C/62/CO/8), para. 9.
186 CEDAW/C/SAU/CO/2, para. 11.
187 Ibid at para. 12.
188 ILO Committee of Experts on the Application of Conventions of Conventions and Recommendations, Doc.092007SAU100, paras. 1 and 3.
189 CRC/C/SAU/CO/2, para. 27, CERD/C/62/CO/8, para. 10.
190 CRC/C/SAU/CO/2, para. 28.
191 E/CN.4/2003/65/Add.3, para. 96.
192 Concluding Observations of the Committee against Torture (CAT/C/CR/28/5), para. 4 (a).
193 CRC/C/SAU/CO/2, para. 13.
194 See the list of national human rights institutions with accreditation status granted by the International Coordinating Committee of National Institutions for the Promotion and Protection of Human Rights (ICC), see A/HRC/7/69, annex VIII, and A/HRC/7/70, annex I.

to ensure that the national machinery for the advancement of women has the necessary visibility and decision-making, as well as coordination powers to enable it effectively to fulfil its mandate in promoting gender equality.[195] CEDAW also urged Saudi Arabia to ensure that the Convention becomes an integral part of the legal education and training of judicial officers, and to enhance women's awareness of their rights.[196] It also advocated a Saudi Arabia national action plan for the promotion of gender equality.[197]

On the issue of prolonged pre-trial detention beyond the prescribed statutory limits CAT raised serious concern especially on the limited degree of judicial supervision of pre-trial detention[198] as well as the issue of *incommunicado* detention.[199] Thus, the Working Group on Arbitrary Detention indicted the Government saying that it deprives individuals of their liberty in contravention of the Universal Declaration of Human Rights.[200]

CRC commended Saudi Arabia for establishing special juvenile courts and that persons under 18 years of age were held in separate detention facilities and entitled to be represented by a lawyer.[201] It also took note of Saudi Arabia's intention to raise the minimum age of criminal responsibility but expressed concern that it was still seven years. CERD noted[202] and CAT welcomed the establishment of a standing commission to investigate accusations concerning the subjection of any person to torture or other cruel, inhuman, or degrading treatment or punishment during the arrest, detention, and investigation of suspects. However, it urged Saudi authority to take the necessary steps to immediately suspend the execution of all death penalties imposed on persons for having committed a crime before the age of 18, and to take the appropriate legal measures to convert them into penalties in conformity with the Convention.[203]

CEDAW urged Saudi Arabia to prescribe and enforce a minimum age of marriage of 18 years for both women and men, and to introduce legislative reforms to provide women with equal rights in marriage, divorce, the custody of children, and inheritance, and called upon the government to end the practice of polygamy.[204] Similarly, CERD commended Saudi government for taking

195 CEDAW/C/SAU/CO/2, para. 20.
196 CEDAW/C/SAU/CO/2, para. 12.
197 Ibid at paras. 17 and 18.
198 CAT/C/CR/28/5, para. 4 (d).
199 Ibid at para. 4 (e).
200 Opinions adopted by the Working Group on Arbitrary Detention, E/CN.4/2006/7/Add.1, Opinion No. 25/2004, pp. 16–20; No. 34/2005, pp. 90–92; No. 35, pp. 92–95. Opinions adopted by the Working Group on Arbitrary Detention, A/HRC/4/40/Add.1, No. 9/2006, pp. 54–55; and No. 12/2006, pp. 63–65. Opinions adopted by the Working Group on Arbitrary Detention, A/HRC/7/4/Add.1, No. 36/2006, pp. 10–12; No. 37/2006, pp. 12–14; No.4/2007, pp. 64–65; No. 9/2007, pp. 78–81.
201 CEDAW/C/SAU/CO/2, para. 24; CRC/C/SAU/CO/2, para. 73.
202 CERD/C/62/CO/8, para. 4.
203 Ibid at para. 33.
204 CEDAW/C/SAU/CO/2, para. 36.

measures to put an end to the practice of employers retaining the passports of their foreign employees, in particular domestic workers.[205]

The International Commission of Jurists (ICJ) called on the Human Rights Council to urge the Government of Saudi Arabia to accede to the International Covenant on Civil and Political Rights (ICCPR) and its Protocols, the International Covenant on Economic, Social and Cultural Rights (ICESCR), the Optional Protocol to the Convention against Torture (OP-CAT); the International Convention on the Protection of the Rights of All Migrant Workers and Members of Their Families; and to the International Convention for the Protection of All Persons from Enforced Disappearance.[206] Also, the ICJ urged the Saudi authority to ensure that its Law of Criminal Procedure comply with the international human rights standards, particularly by allowing detainees to challenge the lawfulness of their detention before a competent, independent, and impartial court and by protecting their right to be presumed innocent.[207] It noted that lack of a codified penal law continues to endanger the rights of citizens and residents, often implicating arbitrary arrest or detention, and unfair trials, is also in contravention of the principle of legality of offences, *nullum crimen sine lege*, which is one of the cornerstones of contemporary criminal law, as well as a principle of international human rights law.[208] It also called for an amendment to the criminal law prohibiting imprisonment merely on the grounds of indebtedness and make sure that no one is adjudged guilty for an act which did not constitute a penal offence under national or international law at the time when it was committed.[209]

Amnesty International (AI), on the other hand, noted that the government's human rights pledges prior to Saudi Arabia's election to the HRC in 2006 continue to be undermined by serious and deeply rooted patterns of human rights violations, exacerbated by government policies and actions, including those adopted on the pretext of fighting terrorism.[210]

Commending the Kingdom for the establishment of two human rights organizations, the National Human Rights Commission (NHRC) and the National Human Rights Society (NHRS), Amnesty International (AI) noted that this step marked a beginning of giving visibility to human rights in the country.[211]

205 CERD/C/62/CO/8, para. 6.

206 International Commission of Jurists UPR submission, p. 4; see para 2 of the Human Rights Council Working Group on the Universal Periodic Review (Fourth Session) Geneva, 2–13 February 2009, p. 2.

207 International Commission of Jurists UPR submission, p. 4; para 21, Human Rights Council Working Group on the Universal periodic Review, p. 6.

208 International Commission of Jurists UPR submission, p. 3; ibid Human Right Council Working Group.

209 Ibid at p. 4.

210 Amnesty International UPR submission, p. 4; supra para. 2 Human Rights Council Working Group.

211 Ibid at p. 6; see para. 8 Human Rights Council Working Group, p. 3.

5.10 Impacts of international human rights instruments on Islamic law in Saudi Arabia

Saudi Arabia is known for its adherence to the *Hanbali/Wahhabi* strict interpretation of Islamic law. It is also known for its reservation for perceived Eurocentric international norms that are contrary to the *Shari'ah*. Despite these, and the criticisms against its human rights records as previously highlighted, there has been significant and practical shift towards the adoption of the prevailing international human rights legal norms through resorting to relevant Islamic principles that facilitate a less hard-line interpretation and application of the *Shari'ah*. This is evidenced by several developments that had taken place during this second phase of its participation in the human rights systems. It is pertinent at this juncture to consider some of these developments which include constitutionalism, institutional frameworks, participatory engagements, legislative and judicial reforms, and responses to voices of reason on several issues of international law concern.

5.10.1 Constitutionalism

Following the turbulent events that occurred in the Arabian Gulf which include the Iraqi invasion of Kuwait and the First Gulf War coupled with vociferous international clamours for human rights reform in the Kingdom, King Fahd issued a royal decree promulgating a Basic Law of Governance in 1992.[212] This step was a turning point in the history of human rights and constitutionalism in Saudi Arabia. Micheal Tarazi observes that it was the first extensive written constitutional system toward modernization.[213]

In a 2009 report to the Human Rights Council, Saudi Arabia argued that under this Basic Law of Governance, due regard is given to the principle of the equality of all citizens before the law as governance is based on justice, consultation, and equality in accordance with the Islamic *Shari'ah*".[214] This law specifically provides that "the State shall protect human rights in accordance with the Islamic *Shari'ah*",[215] and that "the State shall guarantee the rights of the citizens and his family in emergencies, sickness, disability, and old age, and shall support the social security system and encourage institutions and individuals to participate in charitable work".[216] It further argued that the government duly observes the doctrine of separation of power as governmental power is assigned to the judicial, executive, and regulatory/legislative authorities, all of which must cooperate in the exercise of their functions, the King being the arbiter between

212 Royal Decree No. A/90 dated 27/8/1412 AH (1 March 1992).

213 See generally, Tarazi, A.M., 'Recent Development: Saudi Arabia's New Basic Laws: The Struggle for Participatory Islamic Government', *Harvard International Law Journal*, Vol. 34, No. 1 (1993), pp. 258–275.

214 Article 8, Part Two, Royal Decree, ibid.

215 Article 26, Part Five, Royal Decree, ibid.

216 Article 27, Part Five, Royal Decree, ibid.

these authorities.[217] According to this report, equal rights of the citizens and resident to seek legal remedy are guaranteed under this law;[218] and that "laws and international treaties, conventions and concessions shall be promulgated and amended by Royal Decrees".[219]

The law also provides for the protection of civil, political, economic, social, and cultural rights of the citizens;[220] and the freedom and inviolability of private property rights, specifying that "no one shall be deprived of his property except in the public interest and on condition that the owner receives fair compensation".[221] State shall facilitate the provision of job opportunities for every person capable of working and "shall enact laws to protect workers and employers".[222] Also, "the State shall provide public education and shall be committed to combating illiteracy".[223] The law also provides for personal freedoms, stipulating that "homes shall be inviolable and shall not be entered without permission from their occupants, nor shall they be searched except in the circumstances in which such is permitted by law".[224] The law provides that "telegraphic, postal, telephone and other communications shall be confidential and shall not be censored, delayed, inspected or overheard except in the circumstances in which such is permitted by law".[225]

On the elimination of discrimination against migrant workers, the Basic Law of Governance[226] and the Council of Ministers Decision[227] were quoted. The former provides that: "The right to seek legal remedy shall be guaranteed, on an equal footing, to all citizens and residents of the Kingdom"; and the latter regulates relations between migrant workers and their employers such that employers shall no longer retain the passports of migrant workers or the passports of members of their families; shall be entitled to freedom of movement within the Kingdom of Saudi Arabia provided that they hold a valid residence permit; may apply to governmental and other bodies to avail themselves of the services needed to ensure a decent life for themselves and their families, such as the issuance of driving licenses, the purchase of motor vehicles, telephone connections, etc., without being obliged to obtain the consent of their employers.[228] Similarly,

217 Article 46, Part Five, Royal Decree, ibid, see National Report Submitted in Accordance with Paragraph 15 (A) of the Annex to Human Council Resolution 5/1United Nations General Assembly, Human Rights Council Working Group on the Universal Periodic Review (Fourth Session), Geneva, 2–13 February 2009, para. 9.

218 Article 47, Part Six, Royal Decree, ibid.

219 Article 70, Part Six, Royal Decree, ibid and National Report para. 10, supra note no. 178.

220 Article 18 Part Four, Royal Decree, ibid.

221 Article 27 Part Five, Royal Decree, ibid.

222 Article 28, ibid.

223 Article 30, ibid.

224 Article 37, ibid.

225 Article 40, ibid.

226 Article 47, Part Six, Royal Decree, ibid.

227 Council of Ministers Decision No. 166 of 12/7/1421 AH.

228 National Report para 35, supra note no. 178.

the new Saudi Labour Law, according to this report, protects the rights of these set of people.[229] This Law does not differentiate between Saudi and non-Saudi workers or between males and females.[230]

The enactment of the Saudi Basic Law of Governance and the different rights guaranteed under it are clearly a shift from the previous traditional practice by Saudi Arabia in respect of its domestic application of Islamic law.

5.10.2 Legislative reforms

As part of steps taken by the Kingdom in the promotion of human rights by legislation, its report to the UN Human Rights Council stated that it has promulgated numerous new legislations while it has amended existing ones in a manner consistent with the obligations arising from its accession to various international conventions. Some of these amended laws and new legislations include the following:[231] The Statutes of the Judiciary and the Board of Grievances;[232] The Code of *Shari'ah* (Civil) Procedure;[233] The Code of Criminal Procedure;[234] and The Code of Practice for Lawyers.[235]

The code of *Shari'ah* (Civil) Procedure and the Code of Criminal Procedure are particularly significant because they are aimed at facilitating fair trial and due process within the *Shari'ah* courts and the traditional application of Islamic law in Saudi Arabia. These legislations are very novel regarding the application of Islamic law in the Kingdom and they provide very comprehensive procedural rules that did not exist previously under the traditional application of Islamic law in the Kingdom.

5.10.3 Participation and cooperation

The report also noted that Saudi Arabia was among the founding member states that participated in the drafting of the UDHR and has consequently ratified numerous international human rights instruments.[236] The Kingdom expressed its eagerness to fulfil its international obligations and cooperation with all various international human rights agencies, such as treaty bodies, special rapporteurs, working groups, and complaints procedures, in several instances. For example, replying to all allegations received from the Office of the UN High Commissioner for Human Rights and its special rapporteurs; facilitating the tasks of special rapporteurs wishing to visit the Kingdom, and responding to their requests

229 Labour Law, promulgated on 23/8/1426 AH corresponding to 27/9/2005; National Report para. 36, supra note no. 178.
230 Labour Law promulgated on 23/8/1426 AH corresponding to 27/9/2005.
231 National Report para. 12–18, supra note no. 178.
232 Royal Decree No. M/78 of 19/9/1428 AH, corresponding to 30/9/2007.
233 Royal Decree No. M/21 of 20/5/1421 AH, corresponding to 20/8/2000.
234 Royal Decree No. M/39 of 28/7/1422 AH, corresponding to 15/10/2001.
235 Royal Decree No. M/38 of 28/7/1422 AH, corresponding to 15/10/2001.
236 National Report Submitted in Accordance with Paragraph 15 (A) of the Annex to Human Council Resolution 5/1United Nations General Assembly, Human Rights Council Working Group on the Universal Periodic Review (Fourth Session), Geneva, 2–13 February 2009, para. 19.

in the light of the appointments and circumstances of the authorities concerned; presenting the Kingdom's treaty-specific reports and discussing them before the committees concerned; cooperating with non-governmental human rights organizations including, for example, Human Rights Watch which has visited the Kingdom in the recent past; and playing an active participatory role in its capacity as a member of the Human Rights Council.[237] It reiterated its readiness to collaborate with every institution seeking to defend, guard, protect, and promote human rights. It is committed to the continuation and furtherance of purposeful and constructive dialogue at all levels, believing that this will guarantee the promotion and propagation of these rights among all mankind in accordance with the divine dictates[238] as contained in the *Qur'an*.[239]

5.10.4 Institutional frameworks

Saudi Arabia asserted that it is committed to human rights by establishing a number of institutions. These include the Human Rights Commission[240] and the formation of a committee within this Commission to explore the extent to which Saudi legislation is compatible with human rights instruments as a first step towards harmonization of the Kingdom's existing laws with its obligations under international treaties and conventions and amendment of any legal provisions that might conflict with those obligations. This Committee is also charged with exploring the possibility of accession to instruments to which the Kingdom is not yet a party.[241] This Commission has also set up a unit consisting of experts charged with trial hearing of cases with a view to strengthen this right. About 350 cases in several Saudi courts were heard by this unit in the year 2012 alone. The trials were conducted in the presence of representatives of National Society for Human Rights,[242] the media, and individuals interested in human rights issues.[243] One interesting case in this regard was an accused person brought to the courtroom with shackled feet and two others who have remained indefinitely in detention without trial.[244] The unit treated such cases expeditiously. Other institutions include the King Abdul Aziz Centre for National Dialogue[245] and the National Strategy to Preserve Integrity and Prevent Corruption.[246]

237 National Report, para. 28, supra note no. 178.

238 Ibid at para. 6.

239 *Qur'an* 17:70 and 4:58.

240 Council of Ministers Decision No. 207 of 8/8/1426 AH, corresponding to 12/9/2005.

241 National Report para. 62; supra note no. 178.

242 A Non-governmental Saudi Human Rights Body, Human Rights Council, Working Group on the Universal Periodic Review (Seventeenth Session), Geneva, 21 October-1 November 2013 – National Report Submitted in Accordance with para. 5 of the Annex to Human Rights Council Resolution 16/21 – Saudi Arabia, Part III, para. 31, p. 8.

243 Supra, Human Rights Council, Working Group on the Universal Periodic Review, para. 31.

244 Ibid.

245 Royal Decree promulgated on 24/5/1424 AH, corresponding to 23/7/2003; Council of Ministers Decision No. 43 of 1/2/1428 AH.

246 Council of Ministers Decision No. 43 of 1/2/1428 AH.

5.10.5 Judicial reforms

In 2007 some legislative rules relating to various sections of the judiciary and judicial process were promulgated, as the Ministry of Justice produced a strategic plan for speeding up the tempo of litigation and enforcement of courts decisions. It also prepared several draft laws, which include the Code of *Shari'ah* (Civil) Procedure, as amended; the Code of Practice for Lawyers, as amended; the Alternative Penalties Act; the Bar Association Act; the Experts Act; the Notarization Act; the Regulation on judges' assistants; and the Statute of the Alimony Fund. Numerous measures were also taken at the Ministry of Justice to develop its administrative and technological structure and procedural *modus operandi*. Approval of all these was under consideration.[247] Similarly, the Ministry of Justice has maintained its blueprint in building judicial capacities through training for judges, whose enrolment in training programmes amounted to 35% of their number in 2011 and 25% thereof in 2012. The targeted figure for their enrolment in training programmes in 2013 is 90%. The Ministry is executing this blueprint in collaboration with some institutions including the Higher Institute for Judicial Studies, the Human Rights Commission, and the Naif Arab University for Security Studies. It has also been organizing training courses and workshops with a focus on judicial matters, including 12 human rights seminars and workshops, held in Riyadh, Jeddah, Jawf, Abha, Dammam, and Baridah, and 5 workshops on strengthening the role of the judiciary.[248]

As part of efforts to strengthen arbitration and the practice of law in enhancing due process, about 1,513 courts were registered with the Ministry of Justice in 2013, while 2,700 lawyers were licensed to practice, and 1,300 trainees were signed up. Judicial personnel had also participated in several regional and international programs and various meetings with official delegations and international organizations took place. The Ministry of Justice had embarked on the publication of a peer-reviewed scientific journal (e.g. *al- Qada'iyah*) on contemporary judicial research and studies, together with a journal dealing with justice-related matters (e.g. *al-'Adl*) and a series of information booklets on the judicial culture. All these serve as medium of enlightenment to show-case the activities of the judiciary, and as capacity-building mechanism for judges, court officials, legal practitioners, experts in arbitration, and other stakeholders.[249]

5.10.6 Proactive responses to voices of reason

Capital punishment, rights of juvenile offenders, torture of accused people under detention, and freedom of faith had been some challenging issues for Saudi Arabia from the perspective of international human rights law. In its 2013 report to the Human Rights Council, Saudi Arabia stated that capital punishment is

247 National Report (2013) para. 28, supra note no. 210.
248 Ibid at para. 29.
249 Ibid at para. 30.

imposed only in most serious crimes and in the narrowest circumstances after it must have passed through all levels of judicial trials. For example,

> the case must have been heard jointly in the court of first instance by three judges, whose ruling must be unanimous. It is then taken to the court of appeal, where the ruling, even if uncontested, is scrutinized by a criminal division composed of five judges. If the ruling is upheld by the court of appeal, it must go to the Supreme Court to be scrutinized by five judges. If the Supreme Court upholds the ruling, the stages of the judicial process are complete.[250]

Even then, as part of liberality and breadth of the *Shari'ah* applicable in the Kingdom, a person convicted of murder may be pardoned by the authorities (the King) in the case of *ta`zir* offences (for which the penalties are discretionary) or, in the case of *qisas* offences, by the next of kin, it being an irrevocable personal right of theirs to do so.[251] It is further noted that a person convicted of murder may, if the next of kin are minors, request that their wishes concerning enforcement of the sentence be determined only after they have attained the age of majority. It also takes only one of the next of kin, irrespective of their numbers, to issue a waiver for the death penalty to be set aside on the strength of the words of the *Qur'an* which stipulates that: "If anyone saves a life, it shall be as if he saved the lives of all humankind".[252] The institutionalization of committees attached to provincial authorities is part of reforms in this regard. These committees are charged with the responsibility of appealing to the relatives of a victim of murder to pardon the accused person.[253] Where offences involve banditry (*hirabah*), the death penalty is not a requirement *per se* and may be substituted by exile, i.e., imprisonment.[254]

On the rights of juvenile accused persons, special divisions have been created within the criminal court system to ensure the protection of their rights. These judicial divisions are composed of three judges, as opposed to one judge under the old conventional system that was operating prior to enactment of the new Judiciary Act.[255]

> In establishing whether or not a person has attained puberty, court judgements rely on the person having one of the evident physical signs of puberty that qualifies him as competent to perform religious obligations, dispose of assets and be held criminally accountable, which is consonant with the provisions of the Convention on the Rights of the Child and the Kingdom's obligations thereunder.[256]

250 Supra, Human Rights Council, Working Group on the Universal Periodic Review, para. 35.
251 Ibid at para. 37.
252 *Qur'an* 5:32.
253 Royal Decree No. KH/8/547 of 8 February 2000.
254 Supra, Human Rights Council, Working Group on the Universal Periodic Review, para. 37.
255 Supra, Human Rights Council, Working Group on the Universal Periodic Review, para. 39.
256 Ibid.

Theoretically, establishing puberty of a juvenile offender is a doctrinal matter in which the most appropriate interpretation is permitted, considering circumstances and factors arising from the perspective of modern-day development. It is noted however that, under the new child protection law a child is defined as "anyone who is under 18 years of age".[257] This law also stipulates that a juvenile offender must be taken care of in an observation centre (juvenile home) immediately on arrest; may not be detained except by the order of a juvenile court judge; during the time of arrest, the security officers must be in mufti (plain or ordinary clothes); use of handcuffs or any other mechanical restraints is absolutely forbidden; investigations and trials of a juveniles must be conducted at the observation centre and in the presence of his parents/guardian and an expert; medical and psychological tests must be conducted as soon as the juvenile is placed in the observation centre and a report of his health, psychological and social condition must be submitted to the case supervisor before any trial begins; and, must be enrolled in appropriate school and training programmes at the observation centre.[258]

On torture and impunity against an accused person, it is argued in the report that it is against the Saudi Code of Criminal Procedure[259] which provides *inter alia* that persons under arrest must not be subjected to any physical or mental harm, or to any torture or degrading treatment. It also provides that interrogation must be carried out in such a manner as not to affect the will of the accused person in making his statements. He may not be made to take oath, nor be subjected to any coercive measures ...".[260] Competent officers from the Bureau of Criminal Investigation and Prosecution regularly visit prisons, listen to complaints from prisoners and detainees, and take statutory measures against any violation of prisoners' rights.[261] About 20,301 visits were conducted into prisons and places of detention in 2011.[262] The Human Rights Commission makes regular and unannounced visits to prisons, places of detention and observation centres, for which no authorization is required from the competent authority.[263] The Internal Security Forces Act is another regulatory rule in this regard[264] which provides *inter alia* that anyone proven to have inflicted ill-treatment or engaged in coercion in his line of duty, including by carrying out any kind of torture or mutilation, or to have denied personal liberties or administered an exemplary punishment, is liable to be disciplined by dismissal from service or imprisonment for a term of up to six months, or both, depending on the seriousness of the act. Any person with a private or personal injury claim arising out of the above violations may seek redress from the culprit before the competent bodies.[265]

257 Ibid.

258 Ibid at para. 40.

259 Article 2 of Criminal Procedure Code.

260 Article 102 of Criminal Procedure Code.

261 Articles 38 & 39 of Saudi Arabia Criminal Procedure Code, Royal Decree No. (M/39), 28 Rajab 1422 – 16 October 2001.

262 Supra, Human Rights Council, Working Group on the Universal Periodic Review, para. 42.

263 Ibid at para. 43.

264 Supra, Human Rights Council, Working Group on the Universal Periodic Review, para. 45.

265 Articles 171 and 172 of the Internal Security Forces Act.

Freedom of faith is another topical issue in this regard. The report revealed that non-Muslims residents are free to worship in private places. This is assured by law and in practice. Accordingly, non-Muslims have been officially permitted to engage in worship in their homes and within the premises of diplomatic missions.[266] These directives have been circulated to all concerned agencies. It is noted that residential complexes are also regulated in a manner that enables non-Muslim residents to engage in worship. This is in line with the provision of the Basic Law of Governance[267] as well as the Code of Criminal Procedure.[268]

5.10.7 Rights of women

There has also been significant improvement in women participation in politics, social activities, and public sector employment. For example, approval has been given for women to stand for and be elected to membership of municipal councils as from 2014.[269] Women are involved in several civic bodies and NGOs, such as chambers of commerce, literary clubs, and social services associations. Various girl-scout groups have been established and are actively involved in providing several humanitarian services during the main pilgrimage season and throughout the year in the case of the minor pilgrimage. Several women's sports clubs have likewise been established and the Red Crescent Society has provided skills-development training for nearly 12,000 women in voluntary field activities.[270] The number of women employed in public sector rose by 7.95% within 2010–2011, while the number of women employed in education sector alone stands as 228,000, as against 224,000 men. The number of women employed as lecturers at the Saudi Universities has increased from 11,000 to 13,000. Similarly, women's sections have recently been established in several government departments.[271]

Official approval has been given to the sponsorship of children of Saudi women married to foreigners to be transferred to their mother if they are resident in the Kingdom.[272] If they are abroad, their mother is entitled to send for them, and the State shoulders the cost of their resident permits. They receive the same schooling and medical treatment as any Saudi citizen and are included in the Saudization percentages for the private sector. Saudi women married to non-nationals are further permitted to bring their spouse to the Kingdom if he is abroad or, if he is resident in the Kingdom and so wishes, to have his sponsorship

266 Supra, Human Rights Council, Working Group on the Universal Periodic Review, para. 22.
267 Article 37.
268 Article 41.
269 Supra, Human Rights Council, Working Group on the Universal Periodic Review, para. 49.
270 Ibid at para. 51.
271 Ibid at para. 52.
272 Ibid at para. 56.

transferred to her. The spouse is also permitted to work in the private sector, if he has a recognized passport.[273]

Saudi Arabia, though, committed to its policy of gender segregating; it has planned to build an entire city just for women to work in all by themselves. The women-only industrial city, to be built within the Eastern Province city of Hofuf, is just the first of what could be many zones that the Gulf kingdom aims to create to maintain gender segregation while still getting the maximum level of productivity out of its educated female population.[274]

In another development, it is reported that Saudi women's uphill battle for access to positions of power has seen another victory, with positions in the General Directorate for Investigations now open to them. Potential female secret service agents will be selected from a pool of students already abroad on scholarships. The qualities that *Al Mabahith Al Amma* (the name of Saudi intelligence services in Arabic) is seeking in the new recruits will be an advanced academic level as well as managerial and foreign language skill.[275]

5.10.8 30 Saudi women sworn in as members of Shoura *Council*

Another Saudi Arabia's perspective of interaction of Islamic law and international norms was exemplified by the appointment of 30 women into the *Shoura* Council. When the first *Majlis al Shoura* was founded by King Abdulaziz in 1926, it could not be imagined that a time would come when women would later in history take practical participation in such a traditional male dominated body. As a sign of what was coming in the Kingdom, in 2006, women were appointed as advisers only. But the inclusion of such a number of women in the hitherto traditional male dominated forum, "came as a response to rights advocates" demands to give a voice to women, many of whom have been challenging the country's religious establishment, which adheres to Wahhabism, one of the strictest interpretations of *Shari'ah* law in Islam'.[276]

The Royal Decree that established the *Shoura* Consultative Council were amended in this regard.[277] The amendments specifically involved Articles 3 and 22 of the *Shoura* Council.

273 Cabinet Decision No. 406 of 12 November 2012.

274 Barry, D., Thanks to Workplace Segregation, Saudi Women Are Getting Their Very Own 'Cities' to Work in, *JEZEBEL* (2013), http://jezebel.com/5934111/thanks-to-workplace-segregation-saudi-women-are-getting-their-very-own-cities-to-work-in (accessed 16 February 2013).

275 ANSAmed, Saudi Arabia: secret service positions open up to women (31 January 2013), www.ansamed.info/ansamed/en/news/nations/saudiarabia/2013/01/31/Saudi-Arabia-secret-service-positions-open-up-women_8169484.html (accessed 20 February 2013); www.theguardian.com/world/2013/jan/11/saudi-king-allows-women-advisory-council (accessed 12 September 2014).

276 'Saudi King Allows Women on Top Advisory Council', *Associated Press, Riyadh* (11 January 2013).

277 Royal Decree No. A/91 of 27 Sha'ban 1412/ I March 1992 Published in Umm-al-Qura Gazette, No.3397, 2 Ramadan 1412 / 5 March 1992.

Meanwhile, a cross-section of Saudi scholars has earlier shown approval for this new development as the orthodox hard-liners were asked to present conclusive evidence to the contrary.[278] In a report, Saudi religious scholars were said to have held up the view that women are entitled to become members of the *Shoura* (Consultative) Council and challenged those opposing the move to produce religious evidence to the contrary. The decision by the monarch, seen as a leading reformer, was hailed as a positive step and was warmly welcomed by the society.[279] However, a small group of hard-liners expressed scepticism about the merits of appointing women to the council and claimed that religion did not condone allowing women to take up high positions.[280] The Saudi scholars who support this development include Sheikh Abdullah Al-Munai, Abdullah Fadaaq, a senior member of a religious think tank, and Abdullah Al Sahreef, a researcher in religion.[281]

This is a practical shift from strict traditional to a more liberal position and a response to clamours of the "rights advocates" across the globe and as a practical impact of international human rights instruments such as CEDAW, which Saudi Arabia has acceded to even though with some reservations.

5.10.9 Saudi women's right to drive: a 2017 new development

Before 2017, Saudi Arabia was the only country in the world where the right of women to drive a vehicle was outlawed.[282] It is noted that morality police was set up in Saudi Arabia as an informal institution in the 1930s to enforce public morals according to the strict interpretation of *Shari'ah* in the Kingdom's official Wahhabi school of Sunni Islam.[283] As far back as1957 women were barred from driving a car and the Saudi Interior Ministry strictly enforced this rule. That explains why in those days, women who violated the prohibition rules were arrested by the country's regular police department and charged with offences such as causing public disturbance.[284] This raises questions whether the banning can be attributed to the strict interpretation of Islamic law or a tenacity to the observance of custom. It is noted that there is no specific written legal code to

278 Habib, T., Bureau Chief, Saudi Scholars Support Role for Women in Shoura, *Gulfnew.com* (26 January 2013), http://gulfnews.com/news/gulf/saudi-arabia/saudi-scholars-support-role-for-women-in-Shoura-1.1137765 (accessed 20 February 2013).

279 Ibid.

280 Ibid.

281 Ibid.

282 Roberts, R., 'Saudi Women in Silent Walking Protest over Right to Drive in the Kingdom' Independent (2017), www.independent.co.uk/news/world/middle-east/saudi-arabia-women-silent-protest-walking-right-drive-kingdom-middle-east-only-country-world-theresa-may-a7667646.html (accessed 22 October 2020).

283 McDowall, A., et al., 'Saudi Women Driving Ban Not Part of Sharia-morality Police Chief' (2013), www.reuters.com/article/us-saudi-women-driving-idUSBRE98I0LJ20130919 (accessed 20 October 2020).

284 Ibid.

go with the texts making up the Islamic *Shari'ah* on the issue of banning women from driving. However, the police and judiciary have long enforced a prohibition on women driving based purely on old, acknowledged customs.[285]

In 2013, Sheikh Abdulatif Al Al-Sheikh told Reuters that the official ban placed on women driving in the Kingdom was not mandated by any text in the *Shari'ah* which is the Islamic legal code that forms the basis for most Saudi law.[286] Sheikh Abdulatif who was then the head of Saudi morality police but now, the Minister of Islamic Affairs, Endowment and Propagation stressed that he has no authority to change Saudi policy on women driving. He noted that his role as head of the morality police did not qualify him to make policy but implemented the rules and laws of the Kingdom. He said that the morality police had not pursued or stopped any women for driving since he was made head of the organization and said he was not aware of such cases before his appointment.[287] Analysts noted that his comment may feed into a national discussion in Saudi Arabia, where women have in the past been arrested for defying the ban.[288]

In 2014, Sheikh Ayed Al-Qarni, a prominent Saudi Islamic scholar, has argued that Islam does not prohibit women from driving but that the matter must be seriously discussed. According to him, it is preferable to allow a woman driving her car herself rather than being driven by a stranger without a legal escort. "There is no definite text (either in the *Qur'an* or *Sunnah*) that bans women driving". He challenged other Saudi prominent scholars to engage in debating the issue.[289]

Agreeing with this view, Dr. Rashid Al-Rajeh, deputy chairman of a women workshop which took place in Madinah and where 30 Saudi women were participants in that year stated that "the prohibition of women driving is not an established religious rule".[290]

Arguing in the same vein, Faisal Ahmad, a postgraduate student in Islamic studies at Imam Muhammad ibn Saud Islamic University in Riyadh, said scholars must take decisions on important issues with responsibility. According to Faisal,

> permitting and prohibiting things shouldn't be done lightly. When one permits or prohibits something in Islam, it is applicable to all Muslims. So, when driving for women is prohibited, it means that all our Muslim sisters in the world are committing a sin when they drive,

285 Ibid.

286 McDowall, A., et al., 'Saudi Women Driving Ban Not Part of Sharia-morality Police Chief', Reuters (19 September 2013), www.reuters.com/article/us-saudi-women-driving-idUS-BRE98I0LJ20130919 (accessed 26 October 2020).

287 Ibid.

288 Ibid.

289 Somayya, J., and Akeel, M., 'Women Not Prohibited from Driving in Islam, Says Al-Qarni', *Arab News* (11 January 2004), www.arabnews.com/node/242826#:~:text=JEDDAH%2C%20 11%20January%202004%20%E2%80%94%20Sheikh%20Ayed%20Al-Qarni%2C,driven%20 by%20a%20stranger%20without%20a%20legal%20escort (accessed 23 October 2020).

290 Ibid.

he pointed out.[291] Going back to memory lane, Faisal notes that: "I cannot but help thinking that the Prophet Muhammad (pbuh) never prohibited women from riding horses or whatever in those times...so what is the difference now?"

> I can understand some of us do not want our sisters, daughters, mothers or wives to drive but it's not due to their being unable to drive. In fact, many of them drive abroad, but here in the Kingdom, many men in the streets and in cars do not practice Islamic conduct,

he told Arab News.[292]

Reacting to the view expressed by Sheikh Al Qarni's, Rana Abdul Aziz, a religious education teacher in a girls' school, stressed the need to separate tradition from religion. According to her, "what is culturally or socially rejected is different from what is religiously acceptable".[293]

Dr. Afaf Al-Bar, associate professor of Arabic at King Abdul Aziz University, agrees with Al-Qarni that Islam does not prohibit women from driving. She noted that "the problem is that our society is not ready for women driving yet". Even though she can drive abroad, she does not think that the social environment in the Kingdom is suitable for women driving. "There are also problems such as lack of parking facilities, bad road conditions and reckless driving".[294]

In his response to a question whether a Muslim woman is permitted to ride a bicycle for her work and other places, Sheikh Muhammad Saalih al-Munajid[295] said that: "The basic principle is that it is permissible for a woman to ride animals, just as women used to ride camels and so on at the time of the Prophet (blessings and peace of Allah be upon him)".[296] He noted that some jurists forbade women to ride horses except in cases of necessity such as jihad or Hajj, and they gave as the reason for that the fact that it is an imitation of men, and because of the reports that the women who do that are cursed, but that is a *Hadeeth* that is not *Saheeh*.[297]

It was a turning point for women's rights in Saudi Arabia when in 2017 King Salman ordered that women be allowed to drive vehicles. This order was expressed in a Royal Decree titled: "Royal Order to Adopt the Provisions of the Traffic Law and Its Executive Regulation, Including the Issuance of Driving

291 Ibid.
292 Ibid.
293 Ibid.
294 Ibid.
295 A Saudi Scholar.
296 Al-Bukhaari (5365) and Muslim (2527) narrated from Abu Hurayrah (may Allah be pleased with him) that the Messenger of Allah (blessings and peace of Allah be upon him) said: "The best women who ride camels are the women of Quraysh".
297 Shaykh Muhammad Saalih al-Munajid, https://islamqa.info/en/answers/152058/ruling-on-women-riding-bicycles-in-western-countries (accessed 26 October 2020).

Licenses for Males and Females Alike".[298] The decree refers to what the King described as "negative consequences" of not allowing women to drive vehicles and the positive aspects of allowing them to do so. It also states that most of the senior religious scholars have endorsed the concept of women driving. The decree states further that the Kingdom will take all necessary measures to preserve the security and the safety of Saudi society. To that effect, a committee consisting of representatives from the Ministries of Interior, Finance, Labour, and Social Development will be set up to oversee the implementation of the decree in accordance with Islamic Law.[299]

This development ended the age-long unwritten rule denying women the right to drive vehicles which was seen by some as a major social dilemma within Saudi society. Not long after this announcement, the first car showroom for women only opened in a Jeddah shopping mall as the first driving licenses were issued to 10 Saudi women in the Kingdom.[300] It was reported that on the first day when women were allowed to drive on the Kingdom's roads many female drivers, including Shoura Council member Leena Almaeena, hit the roads after midnight. Traffic police handed out flowers to female motorists in the morning.[301]

5.10.10 Conclusion

Human rights issues form an important debate in Islamic law. The debate is principally about the compatibility of Islamic law or otherwise with human rights principles. Modern Muslim scholars argue that the incompatibility theory does stand scrutiny under a proper understanding and application of Islamic law. They argue further that although differences in scope and application may exist there is certainly a wide positive common ground between international human rights law and Islamic law. Moreover, there is a general acknowledgement of the importance of international human rights law by Muslim States that apply Islamic law.

Saudi Arabia is active in the international human rights project. Its participation has been seen by some as an attempt to prove some points. Saudi Arabia wants to prove, *inter alia* that human rights as observed in the Kingdom are not only in accordance with Islamic *Shari'ah* but also compatible with, or at least not in violation of, internationally recognized human rights standards. What forms the Saudi Arabian attitude to the international human rights regime are, among

298 Royal Order to Adopt Provisions of Traffic Law, Executive Regulations, Including Issuance of Driving Licenses for Males, Females, Alike [English translation of the Decree], SAUDI PRESS AGENCY (26 September 2017).

299 Global Legal Monitor, Saudi Arabia: Royal Decree Allows Women to Be Issued Driving Licenses (3 October 2017), www.loc.gov/law/foreign-news/article/saudi-arabia-royal-decree-allows-women-to-be-issued-driving-licenses/ (accessed 26 October 2020).

300 Arab News, 'Key Moments in the Driving History of Saudi Women', www.arabnews.com/node/1515186/saudi-arabia Updated 25 June 2019 (accessed 20 October 2020).

301 Ibid.

other things, a sense of cultural superiority that translates into a belief that Islamic law principles go further than international human rights covenants; a belief that Islamic norms need to be protected against alien encroachments; and the need to protect its state sovereignty from an unrestricted encroachment of international law. Therefore, it may be incorrect to conclude that Saudi Arabia's Islamic ethos constitutes a hindrance to adhering to international human rights norms.

It can be argued that being signatory to many international human rights treaties, Saudi Arabia, despite reservations and some resistance has come to clearly demonstrate a practical shift from its traditional strict position to modern reality. Its moves to fulfil its obligations under the international instruments it has ratified are clear manifestations of the impact of the international law regime on its local legislations including its application of Islamic law as has been demonstrated in the analyses of this chapter. Putting this in perspective shows an international law consciousness bearing strong influence on the domestic legal framework in Saudi Arabia but ensuring the protection of its domestic interest while also enjoying the benefits of international law. The next chapter examines another important area of international law.

Bibliography

Books

Abiad, N., *Sharia, Muslim States and International Human Right Treaty Obligations: A Comparative Study*, London: British Institute of International and Comparative Law (2008).

Ahmad, M.M., *Human Rights in Islam*, New Delhi: Anmol Publications PVT. Ltd. (2008).

Al-Fatāwā Al-Hindiyyah, Vol. 6, Bulaq: al-Matba'ah al-Kubrā al-Amīriyyah, 1310AH.

Ali, M., *Islam Encountering Globalization*, Oxfordshire: Routledge (2002).

Anderson, J.N.D., *Islamic Law in the Modern World*, New York: New York University Press, (1959).

An-Na'im, A.A., *Towards an Islamic Reformation: Civil Liberties, Human Rights and International Law*, Syracuse, NY: Syracuse University Press (1990).

Arkoun, M., 'Declaration Islamique Universelle des droits de l'homme', edited by Frene, Alain, *Droits de l'homme, droits des peuples*, Paris: P.U.F. (1982), pp. 49–56.

Baderin, M.A., *International Human Rights and Islamic Law*, Oxford: Oxford University Press (2005).

Baderin, M.A., 'Islam and Human Rights', edited by Baderin, Masood A., *Selected Essays of Abdullahi An-Na'im*, London: Routledge (2016), pp. 3–360.

Brems, E., *Human Rights: Universality and Diversity*, Leiden: Martinus Nijhoff Publishers (2001).

Dalacoura, K., *Islam, Liberalism and Human Rights, Implications for International Relations*, London and New York: I.B. Tauris (2003).

Donnelly, J., 'International Human Rights: Universal, Relative of Relatively Universal' edited by Baderin, M.A., and Ssenyonjo, M., *International Human Rights Law: Six Decades after the UDHR and Beyond*, Farnham: Ashgate Publishing Ltd. (2010), pp. 588–605.

Ghunaimi, M.T., *The Muslim Conception of International Law and the Western Approach*, The Hague: Martinus Nijhoff (1968).

Hamidullah, M., *The Muslim Conduct of State*, Lahore: Sh. Muhammad Ashraf (1977).

Hobbes, T., *Leviathan* (edited by Tuck, Richard), Cambridge: Cambridge University Press (1996).

Huntington, S.P., *The Clash of Civilizations and the Remaking of World Order*, New York, London, Toronto, and Sydney: Simon & Schuster (1996) paperback (2002).

Iqbal, M., *The Reconstruction of Religious Thought in Islam*, Lahore: Sheikh Muhammad Ashraf (1971).

Joseph, S. et al., *The International Covenant on Civil and Political Rights, Cases and Materials, and Commentary*, Oxford: Oxford University Press (2000).

Kazemi, F., 'Perspectives on Islam and Civil Society', edited by Hashmi, S.H., *Islamic Political Ethics: Civil Society, Pluralism and Conflict*, New Jersey: Princeton University Press (2002), pp. 38–55.

Khadduri, M., *War and Peace in the Law of Islam*, Baltimore, MD: The John Hopkins Press (1955).

Korey, W., *NGOs and The Universal Declaration of Human Rights: "A Curious Grapevine"*, New York: St. Martin's Press (1998).

Lauren, P.G., *The Evolution of International Human Rights*, Pennsylvania: Visions Seen (1998).

Long, D.E., *The Kingdom of Saudi Arabia*, Gainesville, Florida: University Press of Florida (1997).

Mawdudi, A.A., *Human Rights in Islam* (2nd edn), Lahore: Islamic Publications Ltd. (1995).

Mayer, A.E., *Islam and Human Rights, Tradition and Politics*, Boulder, CO: Westview Press (2007).

Mayer, A.E., 'Islam', edited by Forsythe, D.P., *Encyclopaedia of Human Rights*, Oxford: Oxford University Press (2009).

Natán, L., *The U.N. Convention on the Elimination of All Forms of Racial Discrimination*, Wilhelminalaan: Sijthoff & Noordhoff International (1980).

Norman, H., 'In the Name of God, Faith-based Internet Censorship in Majority Muslim Countries', edited by Monroe, E.P. et al., *Routledge Handbook of Media Law*, Routledge, (2013).

Oxford Islamic Studies Online, The Oxford Dictionary of Islam, Universal Islamic Declaration of Human Rights (UIDHR). http://www.oxfordislamicstudies.com/article/opr/t125/e2435

Panikkar, R., 'Is the Notion of Human Rights a Western Concept?' edited by Little, D., Kelsay, J., and Sachedina, A.A., *Breakthrough*, New York: Global Education Associates, Spring (1989), p. 31.

Piscatori, J., 'Human Rights in Islamic Political Culture', edited by Thompson, K., *Moral Imperatives of Human Rights*, Washington, DC: University Press of America (1980), pp. 144–146.

Piscatori, J.P., *Islam and The International Legal Order: The Case of Saudi Arabia*, A Dissertation Presented to the Graduate Faculty of the University of Virginia in Candidacy for the Degree of Doctor of Philosophy, (1976).

Prophet Mohammed's last Pilgrimage Sermon (Tabari, Tarikh al-Russul wa al-Muluk), Leiden (1890), Series I, Vol. IV.

Rishmawi, M., *The Arab Charter on Human Rights, Arab Reform Bulletin*, Washington D.C.: Carnegie Endowment for International Peace (2009).

Simons, G., *Saudi Arabia: The Shape of a Client Feudalism*, New York: St. Martin's Press, (1998).

SInaceur, M.A., 'Declaration Islamique Universelle des droits de l'homme', edited by Frenet, Alain, *Droits de l'homme, droits des peuples*, Paris: P.U.F. (1982), p. 226.

Waltz, S., *Human Rights Standards and the Human Rights Movement in the Global South: The UDHR and Beyond, in Concepts and Strategies in International Human Rights*, 51 (edited by New York: Andreopoulos, George) (2002), pp. 51–71.

Wilson, P.W., and Graham, D.F., *Saudi Arabia: The Coming Storm*, New York: M.E. Sharpe (1994).

Online materials

Arab News, *Key Moments in the Driving History of Saudi Women*, (24 June 2019), https://www.arabnews.com/node/1515186/saudi-arabia.

Austin, D., and Colin, K., *Islam and Human Right*, Butterflies & Wheels, http://www.butterfliesandwheels.org/2008/islam-and-human-rights/.

Barry, D., Thanks to Workplace Segregation, Saudi Women Are Getting Their Very Own 'Cities' to Work in, *JEZEBEL*, (2013), http://jezebel.com/5934111/thanks-to-workplace-segregation-saudi-women-are-getting-their-very-own-cities-to-work-in.

David, L., 'Universal Human Rights and 'Human Rights in Islam'', *Midstream Journal*, New York, (1999), http://www.dhimmitude.org/archive/universal_islam.html.

Global Legal Monitor, *Saudi Arabia: Royal Decree Allows Women to Be Issued Driving Licenses*, (3 October 2017), https://www.loc.gov/law/foreign-news/article/saudi-arabia-royal-decree-allows-women-to-be-issued-driving-licenses/

Habib, T., *Bureau Chief, Saudi Scholars Support Role for Women* in Shoura, Gulfnew.com (26 January, 2013), http://gulfnews.com/news/gulf/saudi-arabia/saudi-scholars-support-role-for-women-in-Shoura-1.1137765.

ILO Document, Ratification of Convention No 29, http://www.ilo.org/ilolex/eg-lex/ratifice.pl?C029.

Javaid, R., 'Islam and Human Rights: Is Compatibility Achievable between the Shari'ah and Human Rights Law?', a paper presented at an *International Conference in Konya, Turkey* (30 November – 1 December, 2013), http://papers.ssrn.com/sol3/papers.cfm?abstract_id=2373930.

McDowall, A. et al., '*Saudi Women Driving Ban Not Part of Sharia-morality Police Chief*' Reuters (19 September 2013), https://www.reuters.com/article/us-saudi-women-driving-idUSBRE98I0LJ20130919.

Roberts, R., '*Saudi Women in Silent Walking Protest over Right to Drive in the Kingdom*' Independent, (2017), https://www.independent.co.uk/news/world/middle-east/saudi-arabia-women-silent-protest-walking-right-drive-kingdom-middle-east-only-country-world-theresa-may-a7667646.html.

Journals

Al Wasil, A.M., 'Saudi Arabia's Engagement in, and Interaction with, the UN Human Rights System: An Analytical Review', *The International Journal of Human Rights*, Vol. 14, No. 7 (2010), pp. 1072–1091.

An-Na'im, A., 'Human Rights in the Muslim World: Socio-Political Conditions and Scriptural Imperatives', *Harvard Human Rights Journal*, Vol. 3 (1990), pp. 13–52.

An-Na'im, A.A., 'Islam and Human Rights: Beyond the Universality Debate', *American Society of International Law Proceeding*, Vol. 94 (2000), p. 96.

An-Na'im, A., 'What Do We Mean by Universal?' *Index on Censorship, the Magazine for Free Speech*, (September/October 1994).

Azzam, S., 'Universal Islamic Declaration of Human Rights', *The International Journal of Human Rights*, Vol. 2, No. 3 (1998), pp. 120–128.

Baderin, M.A., 'A Macroscopic Analysis of the Practice of Muslim State Parties to International Human Rights Treaties: Conflict or Congruence?' *Human Rights Law*, Vol. 1, No. 2, (2001), pp 265–303.

Baderin, M.A., 'Islam and Human Rights in the Muslim World: A Reflection on Approaches, A paper presented at Conference on Reframing Islam: Politics into Law', *Irish Centre for Human Rights, National University of Ireland, Galway*, (10–11 September 2005), pp. 1–25.

Brems, E., ibid. Somayya, J., and Akeel, M., 'Women Not Prohibited from Driving in Islam, Says Al-Qarni', *Arab News*, (11 January 2004).

Coulson, N.J., 'The State and Individual in Islamic Law', *International and Comparative Law Quarterly*, Vol. 6 (1957), pp. 49–60.

Donnelly, J., 'The Relative Universality of Human Rights', *Human Rights Quarterly*, Vol. 29 (2007), pp. 281–306.

Farrokh, J., 'The Drafting of the Human Rights Provisions of the UN Charter', *Netherlands International Law Review*, Vol. 44 (1997), pp. 1–31.

Halliday, F., 'Relativism and Universalism in Human Rights: The Case of the Islamic Middle East', *Political Studies*, Vol. 43 (1995), pp. 152–167.

Henkin, L., 'The Universality of the Concept of Human Rights', *American Academy of Political and Social Science*, Vol. 506 (1989), pp. 10–16.

Khadduri, M., 'Human Rights in Islam', *Annals of the American Academy of Political and Social Science*, Vol. 243, Essential Human Rights (1946), pp. 77–81.

Khadduri, M., 'The Islamic System: Its Competition and Co-existence with Western System', *Proceedings of the American Society of International Law, 53rd Annual Meeting*, Washington, DC: April 30 – May 2, (1959), pp. 49–52.

Khalid, M.I., 'Human Rights in Islamic Law', *The Review, International Commission of Jurists*, Vol. 12 (June, 1944), pp. 30–39.

Javaid, R., 'The Shari'ah, Islamic Family Laws and International Human Rights Law: Examining the Theory and Practice of Polygamy and Talaq', *International Journal of Law, Family and Policy*, Vol. 21, No. 1 (2007), pp. 108–127.

Michael, G., 'Neither Relative nor Universal: A Response to Donnelly', *Human Rights Quarterly*, Vol. 30 (2008), pp. 183–193.

Nawaz, K.K., 'The Concept of Human Rights in Islamic Law', *Howard Law Journal*, Vol. 11, No. 2 (1965), pp. 326–332.

Tarazi, A.M., 'Recent Development: Saudi Arabia's New Basic Laws: The Struggle for Participatory Islamic Government', *Harvard International Law Journal*, Vol. 34, No. 1 (1993).

Waltz, S., *Reclaiming and Rebuilding the History of the Universal Declaration of Human Rights, Third World Quarterly*, Vol. 23 (2002), pp. 437–448.

Waltz, S., 'Universal Human Rights: The Contribution of Muslim States', *Human Rights Quarterly*, Vol. 26, No. 4 (2004), pp. 799–844.

Waltz, S., 'Universalizing Human Rights: The Role of Small States in the Construction of the Universal Declaration of Human Rights', *Human Rights Quarterly*, Vol. 23 (2001), pp. 44–72.

Statutes, regulations, reports and resolutions

Committee on the Rights of the Child, Initial reports of States parties due in 1998: Saudi Arabia, U.N. Doc. CRC/C/61/Add.2 (29 March 29, 2000).

Committee on the Rights of the Child, Second periodic reports of States parties due in 2003: Saudi Arabia, U.N. Doc. CRC/C/136/Add.1 (21 April 2005).

Convention on the Elimination of All Forms of Discrimination against Women] on 28 August 2000.
Council of Ministers Decision No. 166 of 12/7/1421 AH.
Council of Ministers Decision No. 207 of 8/8/1426 AH, corresponding to 12/9/2005.
Council of Ministers Decision No. 43 of 1/2/1428 AH.
Human Rights Council, Working Group on the Universal Periodic Review (Fourth Session) Geneva, (2–13 February, 2009).
ILO Committee of Experts on the Application of Conventions of Conventions and Recommendations, Doc – Reports from 1932 to 2017 and Report since 2018. https://www.ilo.org/global/standards/applying-and-promoting-international-labour-standards/committee-of-experts-on-the-application-of-conventions-and-recommendations/lang--en/index.htm
John Fitzgerald "Jack" Kennedy "The Role of the United Nations" was presented before the General Assembly of the United Nations in New York City on 25th September, 1961.
National Report Submitted in Accordance with Paragraph 15 (A) of the Annex to Human Council Resolution 5/1United Nations General Assembly, Human Rights Council Working Group on the Universal Periodic Review (Fourth Session), Geneva, (2–13 February 2009).
Opinions adopted by the Working Group on Arbitrary Detention, E/CN.4/2006/7/Add.1, Opinion No. 25/2004, pp.16–20; No. 34/2005.
Opinions adopted by the Working Group on Arbitrary Detention, A/HRC/4/40/Add.1, No. 9/2006, pp. 54–55; and No. 12/2006.
Royal Decree No. A/90 dated 27/8/1412 AH (1 March 1992).
Royal Decree No. A/91 of 27 Sha'ban 1412/ I March 1992 Published in Umm-al-Qura Gazette, No.3397, 2 Ramadan 1412 / 5 March 1992.
Royal Decree No. KH/8/547 of 8 February 2000.
Royal Decree No. M/21 of 20/5/1421 AH, corresponding to 20/8/2000.
Royal Decree No. M/38 of 28/7/1422 AH, corresponding to 15/10/2001.
Royal Decree No. M/78 of 19/9/1428 AH, corresponding to 30/9/2007.
Royal Decree promulgated on 24/5/1424 AH, corresponding to 23/7/2003 – Council of Ministers Decision No. 43 of 1/2/1428 AH.
Royal Order to Adopt Provisions of Traffic Law, Executive Regulations, Including Issuance of Driving Licenses for Males, Females, Alike [English translation of the Decree], SAUDI PRESS AGENCY (26 September 2017).
Saudi Arabia (official document), Saudi Arabia's Statement delivered by Turki Bin Muhammad Bin Saud Al-Kabeer at the 56th Session of the Commission on Human Rights, (6 April 2000).
Saudi Labour Law, promulgated on 23/8/1426 AH corresponding to 27/9/2005.
UN Document, CAT/C/42/Add.2 of 20 September 2001, Initial Reports of States Parties: Saudi Arabia.
UN Document, CAT/C/CR/28/5 of 12 June 2002, Conclusions and Recommendation of the Committee against Torture: Saudi Arabia.
UN Document, CAT/C/SR.519 of 17 May 2002, Summary Record of the First Part of the 519th Meeting: Saudi Arabia.
UN Document, CERD/C/62/CO/8 of 21 March 2003, Concluding Observations of the Committee on the Elimination of Racial Discrimination: Saudi Arabia.
UN document, CRC/C/15/Add.148 of 22 February 2001.
UN Document, CRC/C/SR.687 of 1 February 2002, Summary Record of the 687th Meeting: Saudi Arabia.

UN Document, Office of the UN High Commissioner for Human Rights (OHCHR), Ratification and Reservation, http://www.ohchr.org/english/countries/ratification/11.htm (accessed 15 March 2005).

UN Document, Office of the UN High Commissioner for Human Rights (OHCHR), Ratification and Reservation, http://www.ohchr.org/english/countries/ratification/2.htm (accessed 15 March 2005).

UN Document, States Parties to the Slavery Convention, https://legal.un.org/avl/ha/sc/sc.html

UN Document, Yearbook of the United Nations (1989), Volume 43, Department of Public Information, United Nations, New York.

United Nations Treaty Collection: Convention against Torture and Other Cruel, Inhuman or Degrading Treatment or Punishment. Retrieved on 13 September 2012.

United Nations, General Assembly, Official Records, 3rd Session, Third Committee, Lake Success, New York: (21 September – 8 December, 1948).

Universal Declaration of Human Rights, adopted 10 Dec. 1948, G.A. Res. 217A (III), U.N. GAOR, 3d Sess. (Resolutions, pt. 1), at 71, U.N. Doc. A/810 (1948), reprinted in 43 AM. J. INT'L L.SUPP. 127 (1949) [hereinafter UDHR]; International Covenant on Economic, Social and Cultural Rights, adopted 16 Dec. 1966, G.A. Res. 2200 (XXI), U.N. GAOR, 21st Sess., Supp. No. 16, U.N. Doc. A/6316 (1966).

The Nineteenth Islamic Conference of Foreign Ministers (Session of Peace, Interdependence and Development), held in Cairo, Arab Republic of Egypt, from 9–14 Muharram 1411H (31 July to 5 August 1990).

Vienna Declaration and Programme of Action, UN GAOP, World Conf. on Hum Rts. 48th Sess., 22nd Plen. Mtg., part1, 5, U.N. Doc. A/ Conf.157/24 (1993), reprinted in 32 I.L.M.1661, 1665 (1993).

Working Group on Arbitrary Detention, A/HRC/7/4/Add.1, No. 36/2006, pp. 10–12; No. 37/2006.

Working Group on the Universal Periodic Review (Fourth Session) Geneva, (2–13 February 2009).

6 International economic relations and Islamic law in Saudi Arabia

6.1 Introductory remarks

Trans-national economic and trade policies are the fundamental indices of international economic law. Nation-states observe rules even when they do not want to on the notions of reciprocity and a desire to depend on other nations' observances of rules. The importance of operational functions of rules cannot be over-emphasized in the context of economic behaviour, and particularly when that behaviour is set in circumstances of decentralized decision-making, as in a market economy. Such rules provide the only predictability, practicality, and, of course, stability to a potential climate of investment or trade opportunity. It is argued that international rules and policies that determine the *modus operandi* of trans-national economic and trade activities tend to reduce potential risks and stimulate entrepreneurs to enter international transactions.[1]

This chapter will focus on two important international institutions regarding Saudi Arabia's international economic relations and the impact on its domestic application of Islamic law, namely, the International Monetary Fund (IMF) and the World Trade Organisation (WTO). These are two important institutions that are responsible for the regulation of international economic cooperation among modern nation-states. The IMF was conceived at the conference of representatives of 45 countries convened in Bretton Woods in the United States of America in July 1944. The aim was to build an international framework for economic cooperation that would avoid a repetition of the vicious circle of competitive devaluations that had contributed to the Great Depression of the 1930s.[2] Thus, the Fund was aimed at fostering international monetary cooperation, securing financial stability, facilitating international trade, promoting high employment and sustainable economic growth, and reducing poverty around the world.[3] The IMF's primary objectives are to ensure the stability of the international

1 Jackson, J.H., *The World Trade Organization, Constitution and Jurisprudence*, London: The Royal Institute of International Affairs (1998), pp. 9–10.

2 International Monetary Fund, Factsheet, *The IMF at a Glance*, August 22, 2010, www.imf.org/external/np/exr/facts/glance.htm (accessed 24 January 2013).

3 Ibid.

monetary system – the system of exchange rates and international payments that enable countries (and their citizens) to transact with one other. This system is essential for promoting sustainable economic growth, increasing living standards, and reducing poverty.[4]

The WTO was founded in 1995 (replacing the former General Agreement on Tariffs and Trade (GATT) to administer a set of international agreements governing international trade. In its passionate efforts to foster freer trade between nations, it does promote one key element of the "Washington Consensus"[5] but, in principle, it does so only to the extent that its members have agreed to reduce barriers to trade and subject themselves to a rule-governed trading system.[6]

As a developing economy, a world leading oil producer, and a focal point of the Muslim world, Saudi Arabia's participation in trans-national economic and trade activities, is certainly momentous. Saudi Arabia's economy is petroleum-based; roughly 75% of budget revenues and 90% of export earnings come from the oil industry. The oil industry comprises about 45% of Saudi Arabia's nominal gross domestic product, compared with 40% from the private sector. Saudi Arabia officially has about 260 billion barrels of oil reserve comprising about one-fifth of the world's proven total petroleum reserves.[7]

Islamic law, which is officially applicable in Saudi Arabia, it is argued, provides general guidelines on how to regulate economic and trading activities. These guidelines are generic in terms, capable of interpretations and adapting to circumstances based on relevant excerpts of the *Qur'an* and the *Sunnah*. Discussing the development of medieval Islamic economic thought, Ghazanfar has noted that "a substantial body of Greek economic thought was subsequently integrated into and further refined by Arab-Islamic scholarship, as the latter attempted to build its own structure of social thought, inspired and bonded by their young faith".[8] He further noted that Greek economic thought loomed large in the writings of some of Muslim scholars over the period 700–1400 AD, saying that four "representative" names whose commentaries on economic issues could be readily available were: Abu Yusuf (731–798); Ahmad Bin Hanbal (780–855); Abu Hazm (d. 1064); and, Al-Ghazali (1058–1111).[9] The principles laid down by these and some other medieval scholars have continued to serve as reference points in the writings of modern scholars on Muslim economic thought.

4 Ibid.

5 The term '*Washington Consensus*' refers to a set of broadly free-market economic ideas, supported by prominent economists and international organizations, such as the IMF, the World Bank, the EU, and the US.

6 The Open University – OpenLearn, 'Playing By the Rules? Developing Countries in the World Trade Regime', www.open.edu/openlearn/society/politics-policy-people/geography/developing-countries-the-world-trade-regime/content-section-1.1 (accessed 29 December 2012).

7 Roger, O., *State, Power and Politics in the Making of the Modern Middle East* (3rd edn), London and New York: Routledge (2000), p. 56.

8 Ghazanfar, S.M., *Medieval Islamic Economic Thought*, New York: Routledge Curzon (2003), p. 146.

9 Ibid at p. 147.

Muhammad Siddiqi, for example, argues that international economic relations begin on the premise of the universality of Islam and the universal mission of the Muslim *Ummah*.[10] Therefore, the pursuit of economic interest of the Muslim *Ummah* must always be in conformity with the principles of the *Shari'ah* which do not allow selfishness or neglect of moral values in its relation with others.[11] Those *Shari'ah* rules which cover inter-personal economic relations do also govern international economic relations.[12]

As noted in Chapter 4 of this book, Saudi Arabia has attempted to harmonize its traditional Islamic culture and the perceived Western-oriented modern international law values through creative accommodation, seeking modernization without secularization.[13] Against this background and in spite of all odds, it has been a story of successful harmonization in a number of sectors including modern communications, transportation, information technology, healthcare, and adoption of modern economic and financial standards and norms.[14]

But as Saudi Arabia adheres strictly to the orthodoxy of the Hanbali School of Islamic jurisprudence and the Wahhabi doctrine, how then, does it blend and harmonize, its economic and trade policies and regulations with various legal regimes it has had contacts with, particularly, the multinationals in the Western hemisphere and world trade institutions and organizations? This forms the central point of analysis in this chapter. The chapter will examine issues relating to the prohibition of *riba* under Islamic law and the rule of trademarks law in Saudi Arabia against its membership of international organizations concerned with international finance and trade matters. The chapter starts with a brief history of trading activities in the classical period before Islam; the international dimension brought to trade and economic activities of the region by Islam; the basic theory of economic and trade regulation under Islamic law; the participation of Saudi Arabia in trans-national economic and trade activities; and of course the impacts of various legal regimes it has been having contacts with on its Islamic law-based domestic regulations.

6.2 Theory of economics and trade in Islamic jurisprudence

Khallaf has noted that the *Qur'an* contains guidelines on economic and fiscal policies which he refers to as "*Al-Ahkam Al-Iqtisadiyah Wa Al-ma'liyah*" (Economic and Fiscal Rules). According to him, this branch of *Qur'anic* law deals with the rights of the needy and less-privileged members of the society.

10 Siddiqi, M.N., *Principles of International Economic Relations in Islam* (edited by M.L. Mannan et al.), *International Economic Relations from Islamic Perspectives*, Jeddah: Islamic Development Bank, Islamic Research and Training Institute (1992), p. 9.

11 Ibid.

12 Ibid.

13 Long, D.E., *Culture and Customs of Saudi Arabia*, California: Greenwood Press (2005), p. 30.

14 Ibid.

It also regulates importing and exporting transactions as well as monetary matters between the rich and the poor, between sovereign states and individual citizens living under sovereign governments. About ten verses of the *Qur'an*, he argues, serve as the general foundation of Islamic law on such matters.[15]

Kay, on the other hand, contends that the *Qur'an* is silent in respect of business law, but agrees that there are many references in the *Qur'an* relevant to business practice.[16] According to him, in a society where the moral standards are so high, these practices are frequently regarded as being more binding than legislative restraint.[17] He quotes several verses of the *Qur'an* and goes further to explain that these verses are perhaps the most relevant to modern business as they concern *riba*, which includes usury as well as interest, witnessing of documents, and pledge.[18] He explains further that the *Qur'an* draws a distinction between trading and usury – in trade, risk of loss is taken along with the expectation of profit, in money lending, on usury basis, the entire loss is taken by one person while the other takes a profit even though the project suffers an overall loss.[19]

As stated above, Islam provides general guidelines on how to regulate economic and trading activities. These guidelines are generic in terms capable of interpretations and adaptation to specific circumstances. Thus, Wright observes that the dialogue over the adaptability of Islamic economic precepts to commercial business practices is relatively new.[20] Baderin identifies two main broad principles in this regard, namely, positive and negative principles. According to him, positive principles relate to those that must be promoted, while the negative principles relate to those that must be prevented in Islamic banking and finance,[21] and, of course, in other trading and business transactions. He notes that these principles must be understood in the context of the well-known dictum of permissibility articulated in the maxim: "*Al-asl fi al-ashya' ibahah*". This means that the primary rule in all acts is that of permissibility under Islamic law.[22] This is based on *Qur'anic* texts which indicate that God has created everything on earth for the use of mankind,[23] and that God has subjected everything that is in the heavens and earth to the use of mankind.[24]

15 Khallaf, A.W., '*Ilm Usul Al-Fiqh*, Cairo: Dar Al-Qalam (1956), pp. 32–35.

16 Kay, E., *Legal Aspects of Business in Saudi Arabia*, London: Graham & Trotman Limited(1979), p. 9.

17 Ibid.

18 Ibid at p. 11.

19 Ibid.

20 Wright, J.W. (Jr), *Islamic Banking in Practice: Problems in Jordan and Saudi Arabia*, Washington College, United State, Centre for Middle Eastern and Islamic Studies, Durham and Stockton-on-Tees: University of Durham (1995), p. 5.

21 Baderin, M.A., 'Islamic Banking in Theory and Practice: An Analysis of the Fundamental Principles, Legal and Regulatory Framework in Relation to Nigeria', *Paper presented at the Annual General Conference of the Nigeria Bar Association* at The Civic Centre, Port Harcourt, River State, Nigeria (23rd August, 2011) p. 10.

22 Ibid.

23 *Qur'an* 2:29.

24 *Qur'an* 45:13.

The positive principles include: permissibility and encouragement of trade and finance; sanctity and validity of contracts in accordance with Islamic law; mutual cooperation, human benefit and social responsibility; all financial transactions must be asset-backed; and profit and loss sharing between parties. The negative principles on the other hand include: prohibition of *ribā* (usury/interest); prohibition of *gharar* (excessive speculation) and *maysir* (gambling); prohibition of trading in prohibited sectors, such as alcohol, armaments, gambling, pork, and pornography; and prohibition of corruptive or unfair dealings such as short-selling.[25]

Prohibition of *ribā* (usury/interest) is a fundamental relevant principle in this instance. The *Qur'anic* philosophy of trade supports free-market systems in which all resources, human and natural, are employed to full capacity, making it the duty of every Muslim to pursue productive and fair business activities.[26] The *Qur'an* counsels businessmen that: "let there be amongst you traffic and trade, by mutual goodwill".[27] They are, on the other hand, warned that miserly and selfish behaviour, hoarding, usury, monopolies, hedonism, exploitation, and foreclosure in bankruptcy are banned. These warnings are specifically stated in several excerpts of the *Qur'an*.[28]

Riba (usury) which is described as an exploitative business practice is expressly prohibited. However, this does not go to the point of preventing the operations of a commercial financial system.[29] Wright cites an example of the Prophet Muhammad and his Companions accepting money from fellow tribesmen for safekeeping and for recirculating capital among the tribe's entrepreneurs. However, rather than accepting the money as deposit, they promised to reinvest funds with an entrepreneur who in return promised to share his profits with the intermediary, who would then divide his part of these revenues with the original owner of the capital.[30] The intermediary's charge was to find the best investments available for his clients, but he could make no guarantees as to the safety of the loans or about the amount or timing of the expected returns.[31]

25 Baderin, M.A., supra note no. 21.

26 El-Bdour, R., 'Problems of Research in Islamic Economics', The Proceedings of the 1986 Symposium of the *Islamic Research and Training Institute and the Islamic Development Bank on Problems of Research in Islamic Economics*, Jeddah, Saudi Arabia (1986), pp. 110–144.

27 *Qur'an* 4:29.

28 *Qur'an* 2:275–276 and 278–279; 53:39–40.

29 Wright, J.W. (Jr), supra note no. 20 at p. 7 quoting Wilson in *Arab Law Quarterly* and adopting N.N. Dawood's translation of the *Qur'an*, London: Penguin Books (1956) pp. 70–73.

30 Ibid.

31 A-Qatamin, M.M., *Islamic and Conventional Banks: A Comparative Study*, M.B.A. Thesis, University of Nottingham (1990), pp. 23–25; He cites three sources: Al-Sharkhasi, S., *Kitab Al-Mabsout*, Cairo: Al-Sa'ada Press (1903); Al-Maqdesi, A.Q., *Al-Muganni*, Cairo: Dar Al-Manor (1946), and Ben Abdullah Yaqut, *Mu'jam Al-Udabba*, Cairo: Issa Al-Babi El-Halabi Library (n.d.); Abderrahman, D.B., 'A Contribution to the Study of the Koranic Sources of Saudi Arabia Law', *Arab Law Quarterly* Vol 3, No. 2 (1988), pp. 132–150; Wright, J.W. (Jr), supra note no. 20.

6.2.1 Prohibition of riba *under Islamic law*

Muslim jurists recognize two broad paradigms by which rulings (*Ahkam*) of the *Shari'ah* operate. The first involves all activities connected to rituals or worship (*ibadaat*) which covers the relationship of a person with God. The second involves his disposition or dealings with other beings (*Mu'amalat*). This second paradigm covers all mundane and temporal transactions including trade and economic transactions. Economic transactions under Islamic law come under the second paradigm, meaning that all types of business transactions are permissible except that which has been expressly and clearly forbidden by the *Shari'ah*. It is about this proposition that Ibn Al-Qayyim Al-Jawziyya was quoted to have said that: "There is nothing prohibited except that which God prohibits... To declare something permitted prohibited is like declaring something prohibited permitted".[32]

Riba is declared expressly prohibited in both the *Qur'an*[33] and the *Sunnah*.[34] But what exactly constitutes *riba* has remained controversial among Muslim jurists and economic analysts over time.[35] There are two contradictory perceptions of *riba* among Muslim jurists: one is that *riba* means only "usury" but not ordinary interest, while the other insists that *riba* means any form of interest.[36]

Umar Ibn Al-Khattab was quoted to have remarked that: "We wished that we had more light from the Prophet about the *riba*, *khilafah* and *kalalah*".[37] Later, when jurists from the different schools of jurisprudence looked into the question of

32 Quoted in Abdulkader Thomas (ed.) *Interest in Islamic Economics: Understanding Riba*, Routledge, 2006, p. 63.

33 *Qur'an* 2:275, 276, 278 and 279; *Qur'an* 3:130; *Qur'an* 4:161 etc.

34 Some *Sunnah* authorities include the following: (1) from Jabir: The Prophet cursed the receiver and the payer of interest, the one who records it and the two witnesses to the transaction and said: "They are all alike [in guilt]" (Muslim, Kitab al-Musaqat, Bab la'ni akili al-riba wa mu'kilihi; also in Tirmidhi and Musnad Ahmad). (2) Jabir ibn 'Abdallah, giving a report on the Prophet's Farewell Pilgrimage, said: The Prophet addressed the people and said "All of the riba of Jahiliyyah is annulled. The first riba that I annul is our riba, that accruing to 'Abbas ibn 'Abd al-Muttalib [the Prophet's uncle]; it is being cancelled completely" (Muslim, Kitab al-Hajj, Bab Hajjati al-Nabi, ; may also in Musnad Ahmad). (3) From 'Abdallah ibn Hanzalah: The Prophet, said: "A dirham of riba which a man receives knowingly is worse than committing adultery thirty-six times" (Mishkat al-Masabih, Kitab al-Buyu', Bab al-riba, on the authority of Ahmad and Daraqutni). Bayhaqi has also reported the above hadith in Shu'ab al-iman with the addition that "Hell befits him whose flesh has been nourished by the unlawful", www.ibrahimm.com/Islamic%20Banking/RIBA%20IN%20HADITH.htm (accessed 6 May 2014).

35 Bakar, M. D., *Riba and Islamic Banking and Finance* (40th Islamic Banking and Finance (unpublished article), International Islamic University, Malaysia (2009), p. 5.

36 Samad, A., and Hassan, M.K., 'Riba and Islamic Banking', *Journal of Islamic Economics, Banking and Finance*, http://ibtra.com/pdf/journal/v3_n1_article1.pdf at page 10 online (accessed 6 May 2014).

37 Sunan Ibn Majah, Book of Inheritance, Vol. 4, #2727; Ibn Majah adds: "According to al-Zawa'id, the authorities of its isnad are reliable, but it has *munqata* chain of transmission", p. 113; *munqata* means an interrupted, broken or discontinuous chain; Samir, M.K., *Riba and Paper Money-Riba in The Shari'ahh (the Islamic Law)*, Syria: Islamic Business Research Centre, www.kantakji.com/fiqh/Files/Riba/Y417.pdf (accessed 5 January 2013).

riba from within the sources of Islamic law in order to develop their contemporary rulings, they all found that the earlier quoted *Hadith* of the Prophet on the six commodities stands out more than any other in defining the scope and kinds of *riba*.

6.2.2 The question of riba *among different schools of Islamic jurisprudence*

Muslim jurists have done extensive analysis of *riba* in the light of a well-known *Hadith* on the subject. The Prophet was quoted to have stated that: "Sell gold in exchange of equivalent gold, sell silver in exchange of equivalent silver, sell dates in exchange of equivalent dates, sell wheat in exchange of equivalent wheat, sell salt in exchange of equivalent salt, sell barley in exchange of equivalent barley, but if a person transacts in excess, it will be usury (*riba*). However, sell gold for silver anyway you please on the condition it is hand-to-hand (spot) and sell barley for date anyway you please on the condition it is hand-to-hand (spot)".[38]

Generally, jurists of the Hanafi, Hanbali, and Shi'a Schools have divided the six commodities mentioned in the Prophet's *Hadith* into two categories, namely, (a) Commodities that are measured by weight such as gold and silver and (b) Commodities that are measured by volume such as wheat, barley, dates, and salt. They ruled that *riba* applies only to commodities that fall under these two categories and by analogy, they added other commodities that can be measured by weight or volume such as rice, beans, seeds, iron, raisins, copper, etc. They exempted from *riba* all other commodities that are not measured by weight or volume.[39] Also, all the four *Sunni* schools of Islamic jurisprudence excluded from *riba* money that is made of materials other than gold and silver called *(fulus)*.[40]

Regarding the Islamic jurisprudential ruling on contracts involving *riba*, Abu Hanifa while drawing a distinction between void (*batil*) and voidable (*fasid*) contracts, contended that contracts of usury fell into the category of valid contracts. Such contracts, in his view, were valid in essence and only vitiated in their usurious element. That is, ownership of the basic commodity concerned duly passed, but the forbidden extra quantity was expunged.[41] The Malikis and Shafi'is disagreed with him on the ground that the essential agreement which constituted the contract was only reached on the usurious basis and thus, with the Hanbalis, they held such contracts wholly void.[42] It is important to reiterate that Saudi Arabia follows the Hanbali School, a point which we will return to shortly.

38 Sahih Bukhari, Vol. 4, Hadith No.385, www.nur.org/en/nurcenter/nurlibrary/Sahih_Bukhari_Hadith_Collections_86958?pg=293 (accessed 7 May 2014).

39 Al-Jaziri, A.R., *Islamic Jurisprudence According to the Four Sunni Schools: Al-Fiqh 'Ala Al-Madhahib Al-Arba'a*, Fons Vitae, US (2009), Vol. 2, Section on Selling and Exchange 710 pages, as quoted by Samir, M.K., supra note no. 37.

40 Ibid.

41 Anderson, J.N.D., 'Invalid and Void Marriages in Hanafi Law', *Bulletin of the School of Oriental and African Studies*, Vol. 13, No. 2 (June 1950), p. 358.

42 Ibid.; see also al-Qarrafi, *al-Furuq*, vol. II p. 82; and Ibn Hazm, A.A., *Al-Muhalla*, Dar al-Fikr, Beirut, vol. 9, p. 498.

6.3 A historical overview of trade and commerce in pre-Islam Arabia

Historically, Makkah was the epicentre of economic and trade activities in the Arabian Peninsula before Islam. The genesis of Makkah trade is conventionally explained with reference to the fact that Makkah was a *haram* or sanctuary,[43] which was the focus of an annual pilgrimage making it a pilgrims fair, "a typical … combination of pilgrim center and marketplace".[44] Also, Makkah was inviolable, no bloodshed being permitted within it, thus, attracting settlers and visitors all the year round.[45] It became a commercial centre because it was a place "to which men could come without fear of molestation".[46]

At the advent of Islam, Makkah remained the centre of a far-flung trading empire. According to an oriental narrative, it plays a role of some importance in all orthodox accounts of the rise of Islam.[47] It is not an exaggeration that at that point in time, the volume of international trading activities of Makkans had become significant. Trade and commerce played a key role in the expansion of Islam – although, of course, the structure of economic relations during early Islamic history varied significantly from the modern economic system.[48] In previous centuries, economic exchange centred on principles of kinship, tradition, and communal relationships.

The city of Makkah, the birthplace of Islam, was therefore a market and centre for commerce.[49] The early Arab Muslims not only maintained the pre-Islam trans-border trading activities but also extended same to other continents. It was through such trading activities that Islam reached East and West Africa, as well as South and East Asia through Muslim merchants who travelled to those areas. The Prophet Muhammad was himself a successful and honest merchant. After his return to Makkah from Medinah, commerce continued a pace, although trade was structured under a type of chiefdom with taxes allocated to provide care for the poor and strangers, in accordance with Islamic principles.[50] Illustrating the importance of trade during the founding of Islam, it is an often overlooked fact that the Prophet Muhammad (pbuh) and his adherents continued to trade while in exile in Medinah.[51] That explains why there are numerous Islamic teachings and instructions in the area of trade, commerce, and business ethics. Indeed, there are extensive and specific collections of *Hadith* narrations

43 Crone, P., *Makkah Trade and the Rise of Islam*, Oxford: Basil Blackwell Ltd. (1987), p. 168.
44 Donner, F.M., *The Early Islamic Conquests*, New Jersey: Princeton University Press (1981), p. 51.
45 Crone, P., supra note no. 43.
46 Watt, W.M., *Muhammad at Makkah*, Oxford: Oxford University Press (1953), p. 3.
47 Crone, P., supra note no. 43 at p. 3.
48 Khan, A.A., and Laura, T., *An Islamic Perspective of Fair Trade*, Birmingham: Islamic Relief Worldwide (2008), pp. 5–6.
49 Wolf, E. 'The Social Organization of Makkah and the Origins of Islam', *South-western Journal of Anthropology* (1951), p. 332.
50 Khan, A.A., and Laura, T., supra note no. 48.
51 Wolf, E. supra note 49 at p. 349.

attributed to the Prophet Muhammad that deal exclusively with sales, trade, and commercial transactions.[52]

The advent and spread of Islam brought another dimension to the international facet of the economic and trade pattern of the Arabian Peninsula. Economy and trade are integral parts of the general Islamic social order in which various aspects of Islamic social affairs are closely inter-related.[53] In Islamic theory of economics and trade, the roles of the buyer and seller, and thus supply and demand, are transfused with certain moral and ethical values founded in Islamic ideals of honesty, sincerity, and forbearance from exploiting asymmetric information advantages.[54] The aims, *inter alia*, are to provide a level playing ground by introducing as much transparency to economic transactions as possible through relevant regulations under Islamic law.[55]

6.3.1 Saudi Arabia and the theory of riba

There was no formal money and banking system in Arabia until the mid-twentieth century.[56] In practical terms and to the degree that money transactions were adopted, Saudis primarily used coins having a metallic content equal to their value (full-bodied coins) for storing value and limited exchange transactions in urban areas.[57] Foreign coins had been the medium of exchange serving the local inhabitants' monetary needs. It is argued that the development of banking was constrained by the *Qur'anic* prohibition of *riba*. A few financial functions existed, such as money changers (largely for pilgrims visiting Makkah), who had informal connections with international currency markets.

A foreign bank was established in Jeddah in 1926, but its importance was minor.[58] Following the discovery of oil, foreign and domestic banks were formed as oil revenues began to increase. Their businesses consisted mostly of making short-term loans to finance imports, commercial trading, and businesses catering for pilgrims. In 1952, Saudi Arabian Monetary Agency (SAMA) was established as technical assistance was provided by the US in this regard.[59] SAMA was designed to serve as the central bank within the framework of Islamic value; thus,

52 Khan, A.A., and Laura, T., supra note no. 48.

53 Satoshi, I., *A New Approach to Human Economics: A Case Study of an Islamic Economy*, The Institute of Middle Eastern Studies, Niigata: International University of Japan (1985), p. 50; Naqvi, S.N.H., *Ethics and Economics: An Islamic Synthesis*, London: The Islamic Foundation (1981), p. 6.

54 Karim, S.A., *A Study of Islamic Money and Financial Instruments*, Boca Raton, FL: Brown Walker Press (2010), p. 2.

55 Ibid.

56 The Library of Congress Country Studies; CIA World Factbook, *Saudi Arabia: Money and Banking*, www.photius.com/countries/saudi_arabia/economy/saudi_arabia_economy_money_and_banking.html (accessed 14 May 2015).

57 Ibid.

58 Ibid.

59 Ibid.

its charter stipulated that it would conform to Islamic law.[60] The Saudi Arabian monetary system had undergone several developmental stages until 1992 when King Fahd promulgated the Basic Law of Governance. Thus, a new chapter in theory and practice of banking and finance was opened.

Article 1 of the Saudi Arabia Basic Law of Governance, as noted in Chapter 2 of this book, provides that Saudi Arabia's "constitution is Almighty God's Book, The Holy *Qur'an* and the *Sunnah* (Tradition) of the Prophet (pbuh)".[61] By implication, *riba* is prohibited in economic transactions in the Kingdom and not enforceable there.[62] Secondly, the *Shari'ah* which is the applicable law in all judicial matters in Saudi Arabia, as officially specified, is required to be generally applied according to the Hanbali School of jurisprudence.[63] However, in the absence of applicable rules in this School, or if the application of some rules of the school are not in the public interest, the other three *Sunni* Schools of Islamic jurisprudence (*Hanafi, Shafi'i, and Maliki*) can be consulted.[64] It follows that the position of the Hanbali School on *riba* is officially applicable in the Kingdom, but, arguably, the rule of the other *Sunni* Schools of Islamic jurisprudence on *riba* may also be adopted, in the public interest.

It has been proposed by one of the leading law firms in Saudi Arabia that

> the teachings of the Hanbali school of Islamic Law as interpreted in the Kingdom of Saudi Arabia leave no room for doubt that agreements for the receipt or payment of interest are void and forbidden to believers. In this context, it is irrelevant whether interest is referred to as such, or by some synonym, such as "commission" or "service charge".[65]

Thus, Article 6 (a) of the Charter of the Saudi Arabian Monetary Agency (SAMA)[66] provides *inter alia* that SAMA "shall not undertake any of the following functions: (a) acting in any manner which conflicts with the teachings

60 Ibid.

61 Basic Law of Governance (Royal Order No. (A/91), 27 Sha'ban 1412H – 1 March 1992, *Umm al-Qura* Gazette No. 3397, 2 *Ramadan* 1412H – 5 March 1992.

62 Vogel, F.E., and Hayes, S.L., *Islamic Law and Finance Religion Risk and Return*, Leiden: Koninklijke Brill NV (2006), p. 87; see also Sfeir, A., and Tirado, J., "The International Comparative Legal Guide To: International Arbitration 2010", *Global Legal Group*, Vogel and Hayes, p. 87, "Saudi Arabian Law Overview", Hatem Abbas Ghazzawi & Co. "Law of the Board of Grievances," Royal Decree No. M/51, 17 Rajab 1402 [10 May 1982]; Information Office of the Royal Embassy of Saudi Arabia.

63 Al-Ghadyan, A.A., 'The Judiciary in Saudi Arabia', *Arab Law Quarterly*, Vol. 1, No. 3, BRILL (1998), p. 235.

64 Saud, A. D., *Judicial Systemization in the Kingdom of Saudi Arabia*, Riyadh: Hanifah Press (1430H – 1982), pp. 313–314.

65 Hatem Abbas Ghazzawi & Co. (formerly Abbas F. Ghazzawi & Co.), Saudi-legal – Saudi Arabian Law Overview, www.saudilegal.com/saudilaw/02_law.html. Hatem Abbas Ghazzawi & Co. (formerly Abbas F. Ghazzawi & Co.).

66 Issued by Royal Decree No. 23 (dated 23-5-1377H) and Council of Ministers' Resolution No. 103 (dated 20/05/1377H).

of the Islamic Law. The Agency shall not charge any interest on its receipts and payments…".

Commenting from the perspective of professional and practical experience however, Hatem Abbas Ghazzawi & Co., a Saudi based legal firm, notes that although agreements for the receipt or payment of interest are considered invalid and unenforceable through the Saudi Courts, Saudi banks pay and charge interests. Thus, the term "interest" is usually avoided and instead referred to as "commission", "service charge" or similar expressions even though interest as known under conventional banking is meant by such terms. It further argues that all Saudi Arabian banks operate under strict Saudi Arabian Monetary Agency supervision and thus, there cannot be any suggestion that such interest-related transactions are conducted illicitly. It follows, therefore, that interest-related transactions are not illegal in Saudi Arabia. Rather, they are void and unenforceable. To bring the point home, it maintains that the Saudi Arabian courts and judicial tribunals, including the Board of Grievances, do not award interest in any manner or form; however, interest provisions in an agreement are severable, and a contract will not be ruled invalid solely because it includes interest-related provisions.[67]

Umer Chapra[68] notes that SAMA's Charter does not permit taking of interest but in practice, all banks in Saudi Arabia charge and pay interest. He argues that in principle, Islamic law prohibits taking interest; thus, in the 1970s Islamic financial system emerged in Pakistan. The Islamic system is about sharing both risks and benefits. He recalled that in 2011 the International Monetary Fund (IMF) and the World Bank (WB) came out to accept that it is not possible to realize financial development without risk-sharing.[69] He also noted that Islam prohibits sale of debt and to that extent, debt cannot be sold to another person. This restriction according to him has come to check excessive lending. The sale of debt, which resulted in excessive lending, was the underline cause of the economic crisis which was witnessed in the United States of America in 2008. Sale of debt leads to incident of fraud as has been the case in many countries in the West.

How liquid funds received as subscription from members will be placed in accordance with the *Shari'ah* was the first major challenge that faced the Islamic Development Bank (IDB) well before commencing operation. It was later decided that the cumulative interest proceeds from these deposits should be held separately.[70] After consultation with the *Ulama*, it was concluded that under

67 Hatem Abbas Ghazzawi & Co., supra note no. 65.

68 Chapra M.U. is a Research Advisor at the Islamic Research and Training Institute (IRTI) of the Islamic Development Bank (IDB), Jeddah. Former Senior Economic Advisor at the Saudi Arabian Monetary Agency Associate Professor of Economics at the University of Wisconsin (Platteville) and the University of Kentucky, Lexington; a Senior Economist and Associate Editor of the Pakistan Development Review at the Pakistan Institute of Development Economics; and as Reader (Associate Professor) at the Central Institute of Islamic Research, Pakistan.

69 Chapra, M.U., in an interview conducted with him by this author in Jeddah on Sunday 2 June, 2013.

70 Meenai, S.A., *The Islamic Development Bank – A Case Study of Islamic Co-operation*, London: Kegan Paul International (1989), p. 195.

the rule of "necessity" these interest proceeds could be utilized for assistance to the poor in member and non-member countries and to assist Islamic communities in non-member countries to maintain their Islamic identity and legitimate rights.[71] Thus, the IDB, in accordance with its rules of operation, supports Islamic communities by providing scholarships and training facilities.[72] Through the Islamic Research Training Institute (IRTI), it conducts research on Islamic topics having modern day relevance. It also mobilizes technical capabilities within member countries to promote exchange of expertise and experience. Science and Technology development are in the forefront of the strategic agenda of the IDB which forms an integral part of project financing. Additionally, the IDB provides scholarships for high technology to Muslim scholars for pursuing doctorate programmes and post-doctoral research in centres of excellence in the world.[73]

In what appears as a confirmation of the above arguments, a circular issued by SAMA in 1979 addressed to Saudi banks stated as follows:

> SAMA has conducted a comprehensive study of the fees charged by the banks for their services. The study covers fees charged by banks in various parts of the world. A considerable time has elapsed since SAMA issued the schedule of tariff for banks. Hence, it became necessary to make this study, keeping in view the rapid economic growth witnessed by the Kingdom and the expansion of banking business which SAMA encourages to promote banking habit among the public. In the light of the said study, SAMA has introduced a new tariff for banking services (a copy is enclosed herewith), which supersedes the old tariff issued under SAMA's circular No. 115288/71 dated 22.12.1379. The new tariff shall be effective as from 10.10.1399. SAMA has kept in view that the new tariff should reflect the state of our economy and be moderate and reasonable as well as the need to spread the banking habit.[74]

Ernest Kay notes that there is justification in Saudi Arabia for charging interest and many arguments are put forward to limit the *Qura'nic* prohibition to those rates of interest which are excessive, i.e. *riba*, as opposed to a reasonable rate of interest, i.e. *fai'da*. It is because of this distinction that in some Muslim countries interest was frequently restricted to below 10%. However, in Saudi Arabia, no limitation of this nature now exists, provided the rate is not penal.

71 Ibid.

72 Islamic Development Bank, *Principles of Operations*, www.isdb.org/irj/portal/anonymous?NavigationTarget=navurl://91b765e29a0bbf4da579f0c9bbf5f83f (accessed 14 May 2015).

73 Ibid.

74 Saudi Arabia Monetary Agency Circular No. M/A/1/291 dated 19-9-1390 (12-8-1979), www.sama.gov.sa/sites/samaen/RulesRegulation/BankingSystem/Pages/BankingSystemFD08.aspx (accessed 5 May 2014).

Despite the acceptance of interest in Saudi Arabia, for commercial expedience it is advisable to avoid the use of the word "interest" and instead to use words such as "handling charges" or "special commission".[75]

Rodney Wilson makes similar observation when he notes that in the face of financial difficulties following the decline in oil revenues, the Saudi authority resulted into moving away from Islamic finance and encouraged the emergence of conventional financing instruments.[76] Thus, SAMA issued government development bonds in 1988 on behalf of the Ministry of Finance and National Economy. The return on these was theoretically linked to the profits on unspecified investment projects, but in practice directly linked to the returns on US treasury bonds, with a 0.2% premium on two-year issues and a 0.5% premium for long issues. According to him, in November 1991, SAMA issued treasury bills with maturities running up to one year, which effectively paid interest, even though the term was not used because of Islamic sensitivities.[77]

He further notes that SAMA's attitude to Islamic finance was also exemplified by the difficulties faced by Al-Rajhi which earlier in 1983 applied for a licence to become the Kingdom's first designated Islamic bank as it wanted to diversify into accepting deposits and undertaking financing.[78] The exchange and remittance businesses involved charging fees rather than interest, but Al-Rajhi's out of commitment to Islamic compliance, wanted the new bank to avoid *riba* transactions. SAMA presumably maintained that if Al-Rajih was to be granted a licence and designated an Islamic bank, this would create an impression that the other existing financial institutions were non-Islamic. Thus, it refused the application, but eventually in 1988, and after an underground persuasion, granted a licence on condition that Al-Rajhi refrained from using "Islamic" in its title.[79]

It is noted that ever before Saudi Arabia's membership of international organizations such as IMF and WTO, there had been an attempt to shift from the strict Hanbali classical to a more liberal position on issue of *riba*, perhaps due to peculiar circumstances dictated by economic and political exigencies. Thus, under its Commercial Regulations 1931,[80] loans with interest were recognized. When later Saudi Arabia joined international commercial and trading organizations and its participation in trans-national economic and commercial activities increased, it introduced new dimension to its legal system, reflecting an impact of the international legal order on its local legislations as will analyzed later below.

75 Kay, E., *Legal Aspects of Business in Saudi Arabia*, London: Graham & Trotman Limited (1979), p. 35.

76 Wilson, R., Al-Salamah, A., Malik, M., and Al-Rajhi, A., *Economic Development in Saudi Arabia*, London and New York: Routledge Curzon, Taylor & Francis Group (2004), p. 60.

77 Wilson, R., *Banking and Finance in the Middle East*, London: Financial Times Publication, pp. 234–235.

78 Wilson, R., Al-Salamah, A., Malik, M., and Al-Rajhi, A., supra note no. 76 at p. 61.

79 Ibid at p. 238.

80 Kay, E., supra, note no. 75.

It should also be noted that the 1931 Commercial Regulation avoided the use of the word "interest" but uses "profit" or "commission". For example, commercial transactions are described as including "everything related to all money receipts, exchange and commission". Kay cites, as examples, that a merchant is obliged to keep a daybook in which articles "borrowed, lent, received, paid in money, effects and commercial bills" must be entered. A sea loan must be repaid "together with sea profits which resulted from the agreement and this profit must be paid in full if it exceeded the amount agreed". The agreement for the sea loan must include "the amount of money lent with percentage of profit agreed upon". He then remarked that in the context of this provision in the Regulation, profit, used in conjunction with percentage, would indicate the rate of interest stated in the loan agreement.[81] In a similar vein, Anders Jerichow notes that in Saudi Arabia the charging or paying of interest by banks is prohibited as un-Islamic but banks have exploited the device of selling "shares" in a bank's profits as an equivalent, legal means of paying for the use of money.[82]

6.3.2 Saudi Arabia jurists (Ulama') on riba

The *Hanbali* School of law officially adopted in Saudi Arabia is arguably the most liberal among the four Sunni schools when it comes to the freedom of persons to contract.[83] However, this freedom is governed and restricted in degree by two *Qur'anic* prohibitions, namely, *riba* (usury) and *gharar (speculation)*.[84] Thus, Saudi Arabian *Ulama'* and jurists are unequivocal in declaring *riba* (interest in banking transactions) and *gharar* (speculation in the insurance business) prohibited. For example, in a *fatwa* issued by the Saudi Arabian Standing Committee for Scholarly Research and Fatwa it was stated that:

> The profits that the bank pays to those who make deposits, adding them to the sums of money that the people deposit in it, are considered *Riba* (usury). It is not permissible for the person to benefit from these profits. .... He (the depositor) must also withdraw the money that he deposited and its *Riba* profit. Then, he keeps the capital sum and, he spends whatever is more than that in the ways of righteousness, such as on the poor, the needy, helping to make the public utilities better and so forth.[85]

81 Ibid at pp. 35–36.

82 Jerichow, A., *The Saudi File, People, Power, Politics*, London: Curzon Press (1998), p. 68.

83 Nicholas, K.P., "Influence of Islamic Law on Contemporary Middle Eastern Legal Systems: The Formation and Binding Force of Contracts", *Columbia Journal of Transnational Law*, Vol. 9 (1970), p. 429.

84 Ibid.

85 Fataawa Islamiyyah, No. 2/404 of the Saudi Arabian Standing Committee for Scholarly Research and Fatwa, see also Fataawa No. 4/30, 31 of Sheikh Abdulaziz Bin Baz; see also Obligation of Disapproving of Usurious Transactions, Chairman of Departments of Scholarly Research, *Portal of the General Presidency of Scholarly Research and Ifta'*, www.alifta.net/Fatawa/FatawaChapters.aspx?languagename=en&View=Page&PageID=3695&PageNo=1&BookID=14 (accessed 9 July 2015).

It is noted, however, that in several of their *fatawa*, they acknowledged some exceptions. For example, Sheikh Abdulaziz Ibn Baaz in one of his *fatawa* stated that:

> If there is a need to protect money by means of the bank, there is nothing wrong with that … because God says (interpretation of the meaning): "He has explained to you in detail what is forbidden to you, except under compulsion of necessity".[86] Undoubtedly making transfers via the bank is a widespread necessity nowadays, as is putting money in the bank without stipulating that interest be paid. If interest is paid … without … stipulating that or agreeing to it, there is nothing wrong with … taking it and spending it on charitable causes, such as helping the poor and debtors and so on, not to keep it and make use of it. Rather it comes under the heading of money that, if left (unclaimed)… will bring harm upon the Muslims, even though the way in which it is acquired is not permissible, so spending it in ways that will benefit the Muslims is better than leaving it … to (be) use(d) in ways that help … do things that God has forbidden. If it is possible to transfer money through Islamic banks or other permissible means, then it is not permissible to transfer it through the *riba*-based banks. The same applies to depositing money, if it is possible to deposit it in Islamic banks or businesses; it is not permissible to deposit it in *riba*-based banks, because this is no longer a case of necessity. It is not permissible for a Muslim to deal … in a *riba*-based transaction, even if he does not want to keep the interest, rather he wants to spend it on charitable causes, because dealing in *riba* is haram (prohibited) according to the texts and scholarly consensus, so it is not permissible to do it, even if that is with the aim of not making use of the interest himself.[87]

In instances where the bank charges on services provided to depositors in transferring money, the Saudi Scholars declared that:

> … With regard to transferring money to another bank, even if that is in return for an extra amount taken by the bank, that is permissible, because the extra amount that is taken by the bank is a fee in return for making the transfer…[88]

These positions are reflected in the Charter that established the SAMA[89] which provides, *inter alia* that:

> The Saudi Arabian Monetary Agency shall not pay nor receive interest, but it shall only charge certain fees on services rendered to the public and to the

86 *Qur'an* 6:119.

87 Abdulaziz bin Baz, *Al-Fataw,Mu'assasat Al-Da'wa* (2nd edn) (1408); Majmoo' Fatawaa al-Sheikh Abdulaziz Ibn Baaz No. 19/194; also in Fataawa al-Lajnah al-Daa'imah (13/369).

88 Fatwa No. 13/369 of the Saudi Arabian Standing Committee for Scholarly Research and Fatwa.

89 Charter of the Saudi Arabian Monetary Agency Royal Decree No. 23 dated 23-5-1377AH (15-12-1957).

> Government, in order to cover the Agency's expenditures. Such fees shall be charged in accordance with a regulation passed by the Board of Directors and approved by the Minister of Finance.[90]

The Saudi banking and financial system operates generally on the above Islamic law principles as articulated by the Saudi scholars, often relying on the principle of necessity in some cases or using terms such as "service charges" or "commissions" as the case may be.

6.4 The International Monetary Fund (IMF)

The IMF was formally established under the aegis of the UN in 1945 and started operating in 1947. The underlined objectives of this world monetary institution were to promote international monetary cooperation and the growth of international trade, and to facilitate multilateral payment arrangements among member states.[91] It is an organization which currently has 188 member states including Saudi Arabia. It works "to foster global monetary cooperation, secure financial stability, facilitate international trade, promote high employment and sustainable economic growth, and reduce poverty around the world".[92]

Decision-making powers of the IMF are based on a proportional system of evaluating a member nation's quota. The quota is related to national income, monetary reserves, trade balance and other economic indicators.[93] Besides being the factor which decides how much voting power a nation will carry, it also decides how much that nation must contribute to the Fund.[94]

One important portfolio of the IMF is the provision of short-term (one to three years) loans, which are made contingent on the imposition of structural adjustment programs (SAPs).[95] These are usually designed to correct a deficit, and can involve a number of measures including, abolishing or liberalizing foreign exchange and import controls; reducing growth in the domestic money supply; increasing taxes and reducing government spending; abolishing food, fuel, and transportation subsidies; cutting government wages and seeking wage restraint from labour unions; dismantling price controls; privatizing publicly owned firms; reducing restrictions on foreign investment; and depreciating the currency.[96]

Through the operational mechanism of the IMF, its members define the value of their currencies in terms of the dollar instead of gold because the US had

90 Article 2 of Charter of SAMA Royal Decree.

91 Khan, S.N., *Money, Riba, Usury and Interest - Part 2*, www.paklink.biz/articles/riba2.html (accessed 21 January 2013).

92 International Monetary Fund (IMF), www.imf.org/external/np/sec/memdir/memdate.htm (accessed 22 January 2013).

93 Model United Nations of the Far West (MUNFW), IMF and the World Bank, 45th Session Issues, www.munfw.org/archive/45th/ecosoc3.htm (accessed 22 January 2013).

94 Ibid.

95 Ibid.

96 Ibid.

conventionally agreed to convert all dollars held by foreign governments into gold on demand. The US dollar, accordingly, had become the world's currency.[97] The IMF used to operate in US dollars linked to gold. But since 1972 the IMF has used the special drawing right (SDR) as its standard unit of account, valued in terms of a weighted "basket" of currencies. Since 1971, IMF rules have been progressively adapted to floating exchange rates that are controlled by the big economic powers. It is alleged that the liabilities of the third world countries are inflated and the liabilities of the G7 countries[98] are reduced by manipulation of exchange rates.[99]

It is observed that as IMF obliged its members to follow a managed monetary system without any gold or commodity base, this has a consequence on what is referred to by Muslim experts in banking, finance, trade and economic transactions generally, as a new kind of '*riba*'.[100] It is also argued that the IMF operates other drawing facilities, including several other means designed to provide preferential credit to developing countries with liquidity problems.[101]

6.4.1 Membership obligations and special drawing rights

Members of the IMF are obliged to observe terms as spelled out in its Articles of Agreement.[102] For example, Article VIII of the Agreement which contains seven sections specifies the general obligations of members. It provides for, among other things, avoidance of restrictions on current payments; avoidance of discriminatory currency practices; convertibility of foreign-held balances; furnishing of information; consultation between members regarding existing international agreements; and obligation to collaborate regarding policies on reserve assets. It is significant to note that in compliance with provisions under this Article, Saudi Arabia, in March 1961, converted to the Saudi Riyal.[103] In the 1970s and early 1980s, the SAMA focused on controlling inflation as the economy boomed, expanding the banking system, and managing foreign exchange

97 Khan, S.N., supra, note no. 91.

98 Seven leading industrial nations consist of the US, Japan, Germany, France, the UK, Italy, and Canada that formed this group ostensibly with the aim of coordinating international management of exchange rates after the collapse of the old system of fixed rates. It is however argued that the real motive behind its formation of this group is suspected to be to offset the impact of increase in oil prices. With inclusion of Russia it is now G8.

99 Khan, S.N., supra note no. 91.

100 Ibid.

101 Ibid.

102 Adopted at the United Nations Monetary and Financial Conference, Bretton Woods, New Hampshire, July 22, 1944; see International Monetary Fund, www.imf.org/external/pubs/ft/aa/#art20 (accessed 22 January 2013).

103 See generally Krause, Chester L., and Mishler, C., *Standard Catalogue of World Coins: 1801–1991* (18th edn) (1991); Krause Publications and Pick, Albert, *Standard Catalogue of World Paper Money: General Issues*. Colin R. Bruce II and Neil Shafer (editors) (7th edn), Krause Publications (1994).

reserves. From mid 1980s, SAMA's priorities have been to introduce financial market reforms.

Specific attention must be paid also to Article XX of the Agreement titled "Special Drawing Rights Department Interest and Charges". This Article contains five sections relating to interests and charges and provides as follows:

> Interest at the same rate for all holders shall be paid by the Fund to each holder on the amount of its holdings of special drawing rights. The Fund shall pay the amount due to each holder whether or not sufficient charges are received to meet the payment of interest.[104]

It also provides that "charges at the same rate for all participants shall be paid to the Fund by each participant on the amount of its net cumulative allocation of special drawing rights plus any negative balance of the participant or unpaid charges".[105] It also provides that "the Fund shall determine the rate of interest by a seventy per cent majority of the total voting power. The rate of charges shall be equal to the rate of interest".[106] The Article also provides for payment of interest, charges, and assessments in special drawing rights of IMF members.[107]

The concept of Special Drawing Right (SDR) was an International financing instrument introduced in 1970 by the IMF to coincide with the disfavour of the US dollar as the principal currency of the world trade.[108] SDR is also referred to as paper gold which is neither paper nor gold but an accounting entry. It is not backed by any currency or precious metal, and is used only among governments and the IMF for balance of payments settlements.[109] SDRs are technically a measure of a country's reserve assets with the IMF and, whereas not "money" in the strict sense, have several characteristics of money as interest bearing assets, store of value, and means of settling indebtedness. They are allocated to all member states of IMF in proportion to each member's quota of IMF dues based on the member's market value of all the products and services produced in one year by labour and property supplied by the citizens of a country otherwise call the Gross National Product (GNP).[110] SDRs values are determined on the basis of the value of a basket of 16 major currencies with periodically adjusted weightage reflecting each currency's importance in global trade.[111]

The provisions under this Article XX raise important questions about the prohibition of *riba* under Islamic law, Saudi Arabia's membership of the IMF vis-à-vis its economic and trade relations with non-Muslim countries and institutions.

104 Section 1 on 'interest'.

105 Section 2 on 'Charges'.

106 Section 3 on 'Rate of interest and charge'.

107 Section 5 on 'Payment of interest, charges, and assessments'.

108 Business Dictionary, *Special Drawing Rights (SDR)*, www.businessdictionary.com/definition/special-drawing-rights-SDR.html#ixzz317tkYTu9 (re-accessed 16 September 2020).

109 Ibid.

110 Business Dictionary, *Special Drawing Rights (SDR)*, supra note no. 108.

111 Ibid.

6.5 Saudi Arabia's membership of the IMF

On assumption of membership of the IMF, a member country is expected to cooperate with all other member countries in handling international monetary challenges. Members are obliged to "agree to the code of conduct found in the IMF Articles of Agreement; pay a quota subscription; refrain from restrictions on exchange of foreign currency; and, strive for openness in economic policies affecting other countries".[112] A member of IMF has opportunity to influence members' economic policies, financial support in times of payment difficulties, and increased opportunity for trade and investment.[113] It is noted that Saudi Arabia's journey to the membership of the IMF began with its admission into the UN on 24 October 1945.[114] By assuming membership of the IMF a member country automatically becomes a member of International Bank for Reconstruction and Development (IBRD) members and vice versa. It was in realization of the significance and benefits of its membership that Saudi Arabia officially joined IMF on 26 August 1957.[115]

6.5.1 Saudi Arabia's IMF special drawing rights (SDRs)

Apart from being a supplementary reserve asset, the SDR serves as a medium of payment within the IMF, as well as the unit of account for the IMF and several other international organizations. SDRs may be exclusively held by the official sector – IMF member countries and specific institutions authorized by the IMF as prescribed holders.[116] It is noted that the SDR has a variable interest rate, calculated on weekly basis and published on the IMF's information channels as a weighted average of short-term interest rates of the SDR basket of currencies.[117] The SDR interest rate is adopted to determine the interest charged on the IMF's non-concessional loans, interest earned on IMF members' reserve positions in the IMF, interest paid to members on SDR holdings, and interest charged on members' SDR allocations.[118]

A US Congressional report shows a breakdown of Saudi Arabia's SDRs between 2009 and 2010 as $6,682,495,468 representing Cumulative SDR Allocations through September 2009; $5,661,398,099 representing its SDR holdings as of

112 Obligations and Benefits of IMF Membership, International Monetary Fund, www.imf.org/external/np/exr/center/mm/eng/mm_bnfts.htm (accessed 7 May 2014).

113 Ibid.

114 Member State, *Member States of the United Nations*, www.un.org/en/members/index.shtml (accessed 9 May 2014).

115 International Monetary Fund, *List of Members*, www.imf.org/external/np/sec/memdir/memdate.htm (accessed 9 May 2014).

116 Prescribed holders currently include the Arab Monetary Fund, the Bank for International Settlements, the Bank of Central African States, the Central Bank of West Africa, the European Central Bank, and the Islamic Development Bank.

117 'Special Drawing Rights', *International Monetary Fund*, www.imf.org/external/np/exr/facts/sdr.htm (accessed 4 May 2014).

118 Ibid.

August 2009; $6,969,947,160 representing its SDR Holdings as of September 2009; and $6,971,070,156 representing its SDR Holdings as of June 2010. Thus, there was 1,122,996 SDR use by Saudi Arabia since September 2009.[119] It is argued that Saudi Arabia's exercise of the SDR as a *bona fide* member of IMF is quite significant despite that this arrangement is based on interest, which according to strict classical Hanbali jurisprudence is prohibited under Islamic law. This certainly indicates a shift from the strict traditional Hanbali position of Islamic law to a more liberal trend by getting involved in international transactions that involves interest (*riba*) within the regulations of the IMF.

6.5.2 Saudi Arabian jurists (Ulama'), SAMA, and the IMF

Umer Chapra notes that the concept of Central Banking is a new development in Islamic jurisprudence. But the concept has become part of banking and financial practices of modern Muslim countries. He notes further that Saudi Arabia's central bank is backed by 100% Gold which does not exist in other countries' banking and financial systems.[120] The Saudi authority is always conscious of the influence of the Saudi jurists which is derived from the central role of religion in Saudi society. That perhaps explains why Saudi Arabia is almost unique in the Islamic world in giving the jurists a direct role in government. Not only is royal succession subject to the approval of the jurists, so are all new laws (Royal decrees) which of course, are the product of the *Tanzima*.[121] It is noted that the institution of jurists, which has historically been led by the Al ash-Sheikh family, has also influenced major executive decisions, such as the imposition of the oil embargo in 1973 and the invitation of foreign troops to Saudi Arabia in 1990. It plays a major role in the judicial and educational systems and has a monopoly in the sphere of religious, social, and morals principles.[122]

Therefore, it is not an overstatement to argue that the Saudi jurists must have had religious input in the establishment of SAMA as well as Saudi Arabia's membership of the IMF. In the case of SAMA, Saudi Scholars and jurists' position on the issue of *Riba* and *Gharar* are adequately reflected in the official Charter that established SAMA.[123]

To that extent, it is debatable to argue that Saudi Arabia has compromised its orthodox hardline position on the issue of *riba* as regards its monetary transactions in its membership rights of the IMF. This is against the background of the fact that if SDR has a variable interest rate, calculated on weekly basis

119 Report to Congress on the Use of Special Drawing Rights by IMF Member Countries, August 2010.

120 Chapra, M.U., supra note no. 69.

121 The Kingdom of Saudi Arabia: An Overview, *Macro Insight*, Issue No. 14 of September, 2012, www.ca-suisse.com/c12575de004f6944/lkpresources/mi_14_ksa/$file/mi_14_ksa.pdf (accessed 5 May 2014).

122 Ibid.

123 See Article 2 of SAMA Charter.

and, according to the above US Congressional report, Saudi Arabia as a member of the IMF had exercised its special drawing rights between 1999 and 2010, it follows that it has involved itself in the issue of interest as analyzed under Article XX of IMF Agreement. What happened to the interest-based proceeds of these Special Drawing Rights is another issue entirely. The Kingdom's membership of the IMF and its consequent international obligations in that regard has without doubt impacted on the scope of application of its traditional Islamic law rules with respect to economic policies within its domestic legal system in various ways as will be analyzed below.

Fahd Al-Matiri[124]argues that Saudi Arabia's membership of international organizations such as the IMF conforms to the principles of Islamic law. In practical terms, the interests of Saudi Arabia are better protected by its membership in those international organizations. He argued however that, this membership is based on the overall interest of its Islamic values, whereby consideration is normally first given to the dictates and guidelines of the *Shari'ah* as laid down in the *Qur'an* and the *Sunnah* of the Prophet Muhammad.[125]

Amin Al-Obeid[126] agrees with Fahd as he notes that participation of Saudi Arabia in international organizations such as the UN, the WTO, and the World Intellectual Property Organization (WIPO) is in conformity with the Islamic *Shari'ah*. Such participation is for the interest of humanity and progress of the country.[127]

6.6 The World Trade Organization (WTO), and intellectual property rights

There are basically four levels of international trade relationships: unilateral measures,[128] bilateral relationships,[129] plurilateral agreements,[130] and multilateral arrangements such as the WTO.[131] Objects of international trade law include a wide range of trade issues, such as customs duties, dumping, embargoes, free trade zones, intellectual property, quotas, and subsidies.[132] The WTO was

124 First Secretary, Department of Legal Affairs – Ministry of Foreign Affairs – Saudi Arabia.

125 Al-Matiri, F., in an interview conducted with him by this author on 1st July, 2013.

126 A Legal Consultant in the Law Firm of Salah Al-Hejailan in Association with Freshfields Brukhaus Deringer.

127 Al-Obeid, A., in an interview conducted by this author with him on 9 July, 2013.

128 Through national laws.

129 For example, Canada/United States Free Trade Agreement.

130 A plurilateral agreement as commonly used in the World Trade Organization (WTO) circle implies that member countries would be given the choice to agree to new rules on a voluntary basis. This differs from the multilateral WTO agreement, where all WTO members are party to the agreement. The Agreement on Government Procurement is a good example of plurilateral agreement. See Deardirffs' Glossary of International Economics, www-personal.umich.edu/~alandear/glossary/p.html (accessed 7 May 2014).

131 BerkeleyLaw Library, University of California, www.law.berkeley.edu/library/dynamic/guide.php?id=60 (accessed 17 January 2013).

132 Legal Information Institute, International Trade, Cornell University Law School, www.law.cornell.edu/wex/international_trade.

founded with aims of, among other things, supervising and liberalizing international trade.[133] The organization officially began operation in 1995 under the Marrakech Agreement, replacing the General Agreement on Tariffs and Trade (GATT), which commenced in 1948.[134] Before its advent, there was no multilateral or international organization that dealt with trade issues between countries. For almost 50 years, the international trading system had functioned without such an organization under the auspices of the General Agreement on Tariffs and Trade through which the rules of trans-border business ventures had been evolved and duly observed.[135]

The organization deals with regulation of trade between participating countries; it provides a framework for negotiating and formalizing trade agreements, and a dispute resolution process aimed at enforcing participants' adherence to WTO agreements.[136] The WTO objective is specifically to "facilitate the implementation, administration, and operation as well as to further the objectives" of the WTO agreements.[137] Its *modus operandi* is based on four core functions, namely, to provide a forum for negotiations among Members both as to current matters and any future agreements; to administer the system of dispute settlement; to administer the Trade Policy Review Mechanism; and to cooperate as required by the IMF and the World Bank, the two other Bretton Woods institutions.[138] The WTO portfolio include, provision of framework for administration and implementation of agreements; creation of forum for further negotiations; trade policy review mechanism; and promoting greater coherence among members economics policies. Its principles include (a) non-discrimination (most-favoured-nation treatment obligation and the national treatment obligation); (b) market access (reduction of tariff and non-tariff barriers to trade); (c) balancing trade liberalization and other societal interests; and (d) harmonization of national regulation (TRIPS agreement, TBT agreement, SPS agreement).[139]

The Agreement on Trade Related Aspects of Intellectual Property Rights (TRIPS) is an international agreement administered by the WTO which lays down minimum standards for many forms of intellectual property (IP) regulation as applied to nationals of other WTO Members.[140] It was a piece of legislation

133 'Understanding The WTO', *Who We Are*, www.wto.org/english/thewto_e/secre_e/budget_e.htm (accessed 17 January 2013).

134 Ibid.

135 Krueger, A.O., *The WTO as an International Organization* (edited by Anne O. Krueger), Chicago IL: The University of Chicago Press (1998), p. 1.

136 Understanding WTO, *Who We Are*, supra note no. 133; see also Malanczuk, P., 'World Trade Organization' *Encyclopaedia Britannica* 442 (1999), pp. 305.

137 See Article III:1.

138 See Article III.

139 Matushita, M., et al, P.C., *The World Trade Organization, Law, Practice, and Policy*, Oxford: Oxford University Press, (2003), p. 7.

140 Article 1(3) of the General Provisions and Basic Principles of Agreement on Trade Related Aspects of Intellectual Property Rights (TRIPS), www.wto.org/english/docs_e/legal_e/27-trips_03_e.htm (accessed 7 May 2014).

negotiated at the end of the Uruguay Round of the General Agreement on Tariffs and Trade (GATT) in 1994.[141]

The concept of Intellectual property rights has become an international issue regarding Saudi Arabian foreign policy and international relations for a number of reasons. One, it might be argued that intellectual property rights as a concept may not be totally new to Muslim jurists and Islamic jurisprudence. But the fact remains that not until it assumed international dimension did Muslim jurists began to consider the propriety of its legislation in relation to Islamic law.

6.6.1 WTO and intellectual property rights

The large number of foreign and local investors and volume of trades, industrial and commercial activities that compete in a fast growing economy like Saudi Arabia, usually prove the importance of intangible assets, often equalling or surpassing the value of physical assets for a company. It is noted that the state of the intellectual property of a company defines their share and corresponding influence on the market.[142]

Intellectual property right as a concept is concerned with creation of the mind for which exclusive rights are acknowledged and recognized.[143] Under the relevant legal regime that regulates intellectual ownership claims, certain exclusive rights are conferred on owners of certain intangible assets. These assets include ***inter alia***, musical, literary, and artistic works; discoveries and inventions; and words, phrases, symbols, and designs.[144] Common types of intellectual property rights include copyright, trademarks, patents, industrial design rights, and, in some jurisdictions, trade secrets.

The WTO's Agreement on Trade-Related Aspects of Intellectual Property Rights (TRIPS), negotiated during (1986–1994) Uruguay Round, introduced intellectual property rules into the international multilateral trading system for the first time.[145] In contrast to most other Uruguay Round agreements, the TRIPS agreement is not an elaboration of a subject covered in GATT 1947 which was clearly devoid of any mention of intellectual property rights.[146] The Agreement on trade-related aspect of the TRIPS agreement which came into force on 1 January 1995 along with other WTO agreements is largely an

141 Understanding WTO, *Who We Are*, supra note no. 133.

142 O'Connell, D., Why Intellectual Property Matters, *Intellectual Property Research Centre, Imperial College, London*, www3.imperial.ac.uk/intellectual-property-research/aboutus/why-ip (accessed 9 May 2014).

143 Raysman, R., Piscareta, E.A., and Adler, K.A., 'Intellectual Property Licensing: Forms and Analysis', *Law Journal Press* (1998–2008), pp. 2–10.

144 Ibid.

145 World Trade Organization (WTO), The Agreements Intellectual Property: Protection and Enforcement; www.wto.org/english/thewto_e/whatis_e/tif_e/agrm7_e.htm (accessed 23 January 2013).

146 Matushita, M., et al., supra note no. 139 at p. 397.

affirmation of the position of the industrialized world in the trade and intellectual property right debate.[147]

Under the general principles of the TRIPS Agreement, WTO members are required to observe the standards specified in the Paris Convention regardless of whether or not they are parties to the Convention.[148] The Agreement also requires observance of certain other multilateral conventions governed by World Intellectual Property Organization (WIPO) rules.[149] Thus, WTO Members, as a matter of principle, must create and operate governmental offices for the acquisition and maintenance of all forms of intellectual property rights, and procedures for approving and registering of intellectual property rights must be seen to be reasonable.[150] Members are required to provide appropriate *inter partes* procedures, such as opposition, revocation, and cancellation.[151]

TRIPS addresses seven types of intellectual property rights, namely, (1) copyright and related rights; (2) patents; (3) trademarks and service marks; (4) geographical indications; (5) undisclosed information or trade secret; (6) industrial designs; and (7) layout designs of integrated circuits.[152] Members are required to provide minimum standards that must be adhered to by all for each category of IP rights mentioned above.

In a nutshell, the TRIPS Agreement is a transformational novel instrument that breaks new ground covering field related directly to international trade that is not covered in the GATT Agreement of 1994. It is noteworthy, however, that the Ministerial Declaration adopted at Doha, Qatar in 2001 signals that the TRIPS may be significantly modified.[153]

The questions that arise from the above theoretical and historical frameworks are: Does intellectual property rights as a concept occupy a position in the realm of Islamic jurisprudence and what is the present position of this concept in relation to the application of Islamic law in Saudi Arabia?

6.6.2 Intellectual property rights in Islamic jurisprudence

The concept of intellectual property rights is a new subject in Islamic jurisprudence. It cannot be said to be directly and expressly mentioned in the *Qur'an* or the *Sunnah*. Thus, the argument as to finding proof for it in the *Qur'an* and the *Sunnah* is a question of interpretation. Generally, in doing this, there are bound to be differences of opinions. Since it is a modern concept, the predominant view on it can only be attributed to the modern Muslim

147 Ibid.
148 TRIPS Agreement Art. 2:1.
149 Arts. 1, 2, 3, 4, 5, 9, 10, 14, 15, 16, 22, 35 and 39.
150 TRIPS Agreement Art. 62. 1–2.
151 Art. 62.4.
152 Matushita, M., et al., supra note no. 139 at pp. 399–400.
153 Ibid at p. 437.

jurists.[154] Before examining the opinions of Muslim scholars, it is pertinent to briefly discuss the *Maqasid Shari'ah* due to its relative connection to the subject of intellectual property rights.

Muslim scholars have classified the entire scope of *masalih*-cum-*maqasid* into three categories in order of importance, namely, the essential *masalih*, or *daruriyyat*, followed by the complementary benefits, or *hajiyyat*, and then the embellishments or *tahsiniyyat*.[155] The essential interests are categorized under five values, namely, faith, life, lineage, intellect, and property.[156] They maintain that these five values are essential to normal order in society as well as to the survival and spiritual well-being of individuals, while neglecting or annihilating them will cast doom over the entire society. Thus, the *Shari'ah* seeks to defend and promote the advancement of these values with a view to preserve the existence and survival of the society.[157] The *Shari'ah*, for example, prohibits theft, adultery, and alcoholic drinking and makes them punishable offenses as they constitute danger and menace to the protection of private property, the well-being of the family, and the integrity of human intellect, respectively.[158]

In Islamic law, property acquisition and ownership, is an inherent right of every human beings. This right remains exclusive to the owner of the property so long he uses it properly to the extent that the property is not utilized to harm others. Ownership of such property can be transferred only through legitimate methods.[159]

Although Islam holds that all property belongs to God,[160] thus, private owners are considered as trustees or agents of God in this regard. Nonetheless, Islam acknowledges and upholds the inviolability of private ownership of property. For example the *Qur'an* provides that "… do not eat up your property among yourselves for vanities, nor use it as bait for the judges, with intent that you may eat up wrongfully and knowingly a little of (other) people's property".[161] In his farewell pilgrimage, Prophet Muhammad was quoted to have said that: "no property of a Muslim is lawful to his brother except what he gives him from the goodness of his heart, so do not wrong yourselves".[162] It is in the light of this that the *Shari'ah* maintains equilibrium between communal property rights

154 Beltrametti, S., 'The Legality of Intellectual Property Rights under Islamic Law', in Mach, T. et al. (eds), *The Prague Yearbook of Comparative Law*, Prague: The Prague Centre for International and Comparative Law (2009), pp. 55–94.

155 Kamali, M.H., *Maqasid al-Shari'ah Made Simple* (Occasional Papers Series 13), London: The International Institute of Islamic Thought (n.d.), p. 4.

156 Ibid.

157 Ibid.

158 Ibid.

159 Laluddin, H., et al, 'Property and Ownership Right from an Islamic Perspective', *Advances in Natural and Applied Sciences*, Vol. 6, No. 7 (2012), pp. 1125–1129, at p. 1126.

160 *Qur'an* 3:129.

161 *Qur'an* 2:188.

162 See generally, Muhammad Al-Ghazali, *Fiqh-Us-Seerah: Understanding the Life of the Prophet Mohammad*, Riyadh: International Islamic Publication House (2nd edn) (1999).

and personal rights to property.[163] It is also in the light of that that majority of Muslim jurists recognize intellectual property as a species of property, with the exception of the Hanafi School.[164]

There are three main views on the concept of intellectual property rights under Islamic law. One view argues that such a practice is in conformity with the *Shari'ah*. According to this view, copy rights law, for example, implies that Muslims should respect and observe the rights of others. Leading modern Muslim jurists who hold this view include Sheikh Bakr Abu Zaid, Taqi al-din Usmani, Abdullah ibn Manee, Wahbah al-Zuhaili, Sheikh Muhammad ibn al-Uthaymeen at-Tamimi, Salmaan al-Audah, and numerous others.[165] This view is supported by the *Majma al-Fiqhi* (Fiqh Council) of the Organization of Islamic Cooperation (OIC)[166] as well as the Standing Committee of Religious Scholars of Saudi Arabia.[167]

It is interesting to note that Sheikh Bakr Abu Zayd is a Saudi Arabian jurist, a leading proponent of the Salafi form of Islam and a member of both the Saudi Council of Senior Scholars and the Permanent Committee for Islamic Research and Issuing Fatwa.[168] Sheikh Abdullah bin Suleiman al-Manee is also a Saudi jurist, a member of the Board of Senior Ulama and Adviser to the Royal Court.[169] Sheikh Muhammad ibn al-Uthaymeen at-Tamimi was one of the most prominent Saudi jurists of his time.[170] As a contemporary of Abd al-Aziz ibn Baz, he was considered one of the two leading representatives of the conservative Saudi Arabian religious establishment.[171] These are the jurists of the strict textualist Hanbali School that are very restrictive in their interpretation of basic sources of Islamic law. However, they are now the pioneers in the campaign for intellectual property rights interpreting the *Qur'an* and the *Sunnah* as proofs of its validity as a concept.

According to the Fiqh Council of the OIC, writing or inventing something is a private right that belongs to the individual owner. In the contemporary world, it adds material value to it that people can make money from. These rights are

163 Malkawi, B.H., 'The Alliance between Islamic Law and Intellectual Property: Structure and Practice', *University of St. Thomas Law Journal*, Vol. 10, No. 3 (2012–2013), p. 623.

164 Ibid.

165 Zarabozo, J.D., The Copyright Issue, *Save on Delicious digg*, www.islamicawakening.com/viewarticle.php?articleID=1351 (accessed 11 January 2013).

166 The Fiqh Council of the OIC is the ....

167 Zarabozo, J.D., supra note no. 165.

168 'His Eminence Shaykh Bakr ibn 'Abdullah Abu Zayd'. *This Occasion's Fatwas*, www.alifta.com/Search/MoftyDetails.aspx?Type=Mofty&section=tafseer&ID=9&languagename=en (accessed 8 May 2014).

169 Saudi Cleric Allows Visits to non-Muslim Place of Worship, social Media Use, *Al-Arabiya News* (9 October, 2012), www.alarabiya.net/articles/2012/10/08/242630.html (accessed 8 May 2014).

170 Murphy, C., 'A Kingdom Divided', *Global Post* (15 July 2010), http://islamdag.info/story/415 (accessed 8 May 2014).

171 See generally Nielsen, N.J., and Christoffersen, L. (eds). *Legal Traditions and the Encounter with Europe*, p. xv. Part of the *Cultural Diversity and Law* series. Farnham: Ashgate Publishing (2010).

therefore to be respected from the perspective of Islamic *Shari'ah*. It follows that it is unlawful to violate these rights.[172]

Those who hold contrary view include Muhammad Shafee (the former mufti of Pakistan), Abdul-Razzaaq Afeefi, and Muhammad Mukhtaar al-Shinqeeti.[173] However, there are those who maintain a middle course position on the subject. They include Abdullah ibn Bayyah and Muhammad Abdul-Lateef al-Furfoor.[174] According to these jurists, copy rights should be respected and observed, except regarding material related to the religion.

In response to questions as to the position of Islamic law on a personal property which had been copyrighted, and whether it would make any difference if it were from a Muslim or non-Muslim company, the Standing Committee of Religious Scholars of Saudi Arabia stated that: "It is illegal to reproduce a copyrighted work of others unless there is an explicit authorization to do so". Their contention was based on some *Hadiths*, one of which states that: "The Muslims must abide by conditions that they lay down".[175] It is argued here that when a person buys a book or software which is copyrighted, they are essentially agreeing to the conditions of that copyright which is clearly stated on the product that they are purchasing and which is not something new or strange to the purchaser. Hence, the purchaser must observe the condition that he has agreed on. They quoted another *Hadith* which states that: "No wealth of a Muslim can be taken except with his approval".[176] They explained that it is irrelevant whether the creators of the work were Muslims or non-Muslims, as "the rights of a non-Muslim are to be respected like that of a Muslim".[177]

As regards the illegal act of pirating tapes and books, the Saudi jurists quote a *Hadith* which states that: "That which you have the most right to take wages/reward for is the Book of Allah".[178] They argue that the Prophet was quoted to have made this statement in response to some Companions who objected to another Companion receiving sheep as wages for reciting the *Qur'an* as an incantation. It is thus noted that the wording used by the Prophet is both general and unreserved. The statement was made in response to those who argue that one cannot benefit from religious knowledge in any way and, thus, copyright on books or other material related to the religion is forbidden.[179]

172 *Majallah Majma al-Fiqh al-Islaami*, volume no. 5, part 3, p. 2267; Resolutions and Recommendations of the Council of Islamic Fiqh Academy 1985–2000, Resolution No. 43 at 89 (Research and Training Institute 2000), www.irtipms.org/OpenSave.asp?pub=73.pdf; Zarabozo, J.D., supra note no. 165.

173 Zarabozo, J.D., supra note no. 165.

174 Ibid.

175 Recorded by Abu Dawood and al-Haakim; Al-Albaani says it is authentic. See al-Albaani, *Saheeh al-Jaami al-Sagheer* No. 6714.

176 Recorded by Abu Dawood and al-Albaani authenticates it. See al-Albaani, *Saheeh al-Jaami al Sagheer* No.7662.

177 Fatwa No.18453 signed by Sheikh Abdul-Azeez ibn Baaz (late), Abdul-Azeez Aali-Shaikh, and Saalih al-Fauzaan and Bakr Abu Zaid.

178 Sahih Bukhari.

179 Zarabozo, J.D., supra note no. 165.

In another *Hadith* the Prophet was quoted to have told a man who had virtually nothing to offer as a marriage dower to his bride. The Prophet asked him if he knew any of the *Qur'an* which was answered in the affirmative, the Prophet then said, "I marry her off to you for what you have of the *Qur'an*".[180] This proves that book knowledge is a type of wealth or property and can be treated as such.[181]

In line with the trends of these arguments, Ibn Uthaimeen[182] explained that if Saudi Arabia has accepted the concept of copyright as a rule and has made violation of this rule actionable, it follows that one must comply with such rules. He stated that "If the country prohibits that, then it becomes sanction-able, as God has ordered that those in authority are to be obeyed in any matter that is not disobedience to God and this is not disobedience to God".[183]

Proponents of intellectual property rights law also argue from the perspective of convention (known as *urf*). According to them, it has become a recognized convention not to violate the copyrights of others when it comes to dealing with books and other such material. This is to protect the work of the original author and to make the work available to the public through the proper and right channel.[184] Such convention or *urf* cannot be said to violate any command in the texts of *Qur'an* and the *Sunnah* unless it could be proved otherwise. Therefore, this legal novel has its place in Islamic Law as a basis for law and practice.[185]

Opponents of the concept on the other hand, argue that the *Qur'an* and the *Sunnah* contain no clear textual ruling on the subject. They insist that nowhere in the two primary sources of Islamic law are intangible properties expressly treated as subject matter of private ownership. Intangible rights can be implied but they are never explicitly mentioned, and this may suggest that property can be uniquely intended as tangible property.[186] Secondly, this kind of legislation amounts to concealment of knowledge; and from Islamic perspective, no one possesses knowledge to the extent of laying personal or exclusive claim to it and thus copyrights legislation must be forbidden.[187]

It is argued in response that new issues may arise that are not covered explicitly by the texts of the *Qur'an* and the *Sunnah*. Muslim scholars have a duty to derive legislation for such issues in the light of the *Qur'an* and the *Sunnah*. Thus, it is asserted that the mere fact that something is not directly mentioned

180 Recorded by al-Bukhari and Malik; Zarabozo, J.D., supra note no. 165.

181 Zarabozo, J.D., supra note no. 165.

182 He was a notable and respected member of the Saudi Arabia Standing Committee of Jurists.

183 Sheikh Ibn Uthaimeen in *alLiqaa al Maftoohah*, Session No.178; Zarabozo, J.D., supra note no. 165.

184 Zarabozo, J.D., supra note no. 165.

185 Ibid.

186 Khoury asserts that this is in fact the view adopted by the *Hanafi* School. The *Shafi* and *Maliki* Schools, according to him, have no objection to possession of intangible properties. The *Hanbali* school requires that the possession of intangibles is somehow linked to tangible items; Khoury, A., ibid at p. 172.

187 Zarabozo, J.D., supra note no. 165.

or alluded to in the texts, does not necessarily mean that it is either prohibited or permissible.[188] As to the objection to copyright law on grounds of promoting concealment of knowledge, it is argued that copyright is, in fact, a means of providing for the means of spreading of knowledge. Without such a law and protection for the work of an individual, whereby he can earn an income via such work, the individual would not have the means and wherewithal to do research. This is especially true in modern times when cost of living and pursuance of knowledge can be awfully expensive.

It is then argued that copyright must be seen in the light of the bigger picture of the overall goals of the *Shari'ah* (*maqasid al-Shari'ah*) which essentially stand to protect the overall interests of humanity. This has been discussed in detail in Chapter 3 of this book.[189]

6.7 Saudi Arabian government and jurists on IPR agreements

The position of the Muslim jurists who uphold the concept of intellectual property rights arguably conforms to the spirit and letter of WTO's TRIPS Agreement which introduced intellectual property rules into the international multilateral trading system.[190] Saudi Arabian commercial and trading activities had assumed international dimensions such that issues relating to intellectual property rights cannot be ignored if the rights of nationals and foreign partners in businesses and investors are to be duly protected.

The 1883 Paris Convention for the Protection of Industrial Property is one of the first intellectual property treaties.[191] It established a Union for the protection of industrial property. The Convention is still in force.[192] The Berne Convention for the Protection of Literary and Artistic Works, usually known as the Berne Convention, is an international agreement governing copyright, which was first accepted in Berne, Switzerland, in 1886.[193] The Convention requires its signatories to recognize the copyright of works of authors from other signatory countries (known as members of the *Berne Union*) in the same way as it recognizes the copyright of its own nationals.[194] In addition to establishing a system of equal treatment that internationalized copyright among signatories, the agreement also requires member states to provide strong minimum standards

188 Ibid.
189 Ibid.
190 Ibid.
191 Dr Al Oufi Law Firm, *Trademarks*, www.aloufilawfirm.com/tm.htm (accessed 28 May 2012).
192 *Paris Convention, Accession by Brunei Darussalam*, PCT Newsletter, December 2011, No. 12/2011, page 2.
193 Fitzgerald, B. F., Shi, S. X., Foong, C., and Pappalardo, K. M., 'Country of Origin and Internet Publication: Applying the Berne Convention in the Digital Age', *Journal of Intellectual Property* (NJIP) Maiden Edition (2011), pp. 38–73.
194 Ibid.

for copyright law.[195] Saudi Arabia is a signatory to these two intellectual property rights conventions. Saudi Arabia ratified both the Paris Convention for the Protection of Industrial Property and the Berne Convention on 11 December 2003 which came into force on 11 March 2004 respectively.[196] Thus, it is argued that regardless of whether Islamic law is understood and interpreted in a more modern and reformist way or in a more fundamentalist tradition, intellectual property rights can have its place in Islamic legislation.[197] This was reflected in interviews conducted with different members of the intelligentsia in Saudi Arabia during this research.

For example, Hani Zedan[198] noted that intellectual property rights concept is widely acknowledged in Saudi Arabia. The position is that owners of a particular product, industrial, commercial, or academic materials should have rights over their property. He, however, notes that this right may cease after a period of 35 years when the products or academic materials become free and accessible to the public.[199]

Similarly, Mohammad Saleh Otaishan[200] noted that the concept of intellectual property rights is not new in Saudi Arabia, it dates back to about 40 years ago. According to him, there has been debate among Saudi scholars on the validity or otherwise of this concept. A cross-section of the scholars argued at the initial stage that, if the concept is adopted, it would amount to allowing rights to monopolize things against the interest of the people. But later, it was unanimously agreed that the concept is to compensate the owner of particular inventions or authorship of particular books.[201]

Also, Amin Al-Obeid[202] stated that basically, respect for rights of others is fundamental in Islam. The same applies to individual right of ownership to inventions, trademarks, books, and other types of intellectual property. Under the Islamic *Shari'ah* observance of rights of others in possessing intellectual property such as inventions, trademarks, copyrights, and academic books is mandatory. That explains why intellectual property rights law has now occupied a special position in Saudi legislative enactments.[203] The arrival of multi-national companies and corporations to invest in various economic sectors of the Kingdom need arose to adjust Saudi Arabia legislative rules in commercial and intellectual property rights laws.[204] According to him, the intellectual property rights law developed along commercial and industrial laws in the Kingdom.

195 Ibid.

196 WIPO-Administered Treaties, WIPO, www.wipo.int/treaties/en/ShowResults.jsp?lang=en&treaty_id=15 (accessed 8 May 2014).2

197 Beltrametti, S., supra, note no. 154.

198 An Associate in Abdulaziz Algasim Law Firm, a Riyadh-based Law Firm.

199 Zedan, H., in an interview conducted with him by this author on 7 July 2013.

200 Senior Partner in Mohammad Saleh Otaishan Law Office, a Riyadh-based Law Firm.

201 Otaishan, M.S., in an interview conducted with him by this writer on 8 July, 2013.

202 A Legal Consultant in the Law Firm of Salah Al-Hejailan in Association with Freshfields Brukhaus Deringer.

203 Al-Obeid, A., in an interview conducted with him by this author on 9 July, 2013.

204 Ibid.

6.8 Intellectual property rights law in Saudi Arabia

Signatories to the Berne Convention are required to recognize the copyright of works of authors from other signatory countries (known as members of the *Berne Union*) in the same way as it recognizes the copyright of its own nationals.[205] In addition to establishing a system of equal treatment that internationalized copyright among signatories, the agreement also requires member states to provide strong minimum standards for copyright law.[206] Despite Saudi strict literalist approach to Islamic law, it has taken steps to comply with the international rules with regards to its local IPR legislation. Thus, it has introduced several intellectual property rights laws in this regard as discussed in the following paragraphs.

6.8.1 Copyrights law

Saudi Arabia has enacted a new Copyrights Law[207] which arguably is in full conformity with the provisions of the TRIPS Agreement.[208] The main features of the new Law are: (i) more explicit protection for computer software and data bases; (ii) more specific protection to audio-visual works and sound recordings, including protection for 50 years after first public display or publication; (iii) legal use of foreign works such as translations and copying had been clarified according to the TRIPS Agreement; (iv) duration of protection of all artistic and literary works had been provided according to the requirements of the Berne Convention.[209] In the area of enforcement, the new Law details all types of infringements and piracies and strengthened penalties, including provisions for: (i) imprisonment of up to six months (which can be doubled for repeat offenders); (ii) a maximum fine of SAR 250,000 (which can be doubled for repeat offenders); and (iii) compensation for damages and defamation due to the conduct of the violator) to meet the requirements of the TRIPS Agreement.[210]

6.8.2 Patents law

Local legislation on patentable subject matter in Saudi Arabia is also consistent with the requirements of Section 5 of the TRIPS Agreement. Processes (methods of manufacturing) were patentable and were protected against its violation.

205 Fitzgerald, B. F., Shi, S. X., Foong, C., and, Pappalardo, K. M., supra, note no. 193.

206 Ibid.

207 See Royal Decree No. M/41 of 2.7.1424H (30 August 2003).

208 The WTO's Agreement on Trade-Related Aspects of Intellectual Property Rights (TRIPs), particularly Article 27, is occasionally referenced in the political debate on the international legal framework for the patentability of software, and on whether software and computer-implemented inventions should be considered as a field of technology.

209 World Trade Organization, *Report of the Working Party on the Accession of the Kingdom of Saudi Arabia to The World Trade Organization*, WT/ACC/SAU/61, 1 November, 2005 (05-5141), Protocols of accession for new members since 1995, including commitments in goods and services (24 August 2012), www.wto.org/english/thewto_e/acc_e/completeacc_e.htm#sau (accessed 18 January 2013).

210 Ibid.

Plant varieties currently were patentable and protected by the New Patents Law. The protection of plant varieties had been provided for in accordance with the provisions of Article 27(3)(b) of the TRIPS Agreement. Patent holders in Saudi Arabia had been accorded the rights mentioned in Article 28 of TRIPS. A patent holder is no longer required to make full industrial use of the patent in Saudi Arabia within two years. Although the old Patent Law conferred a term of protection of 15 years with the possibility of a five-year extension, the representative of Saudi Arabia stated that, according to Article 19 of the New Patents Law, the term of protection would be 20 years.[211]

Regarding compulsory licensing, the Patent Law has been amended to conform to the requirements of Article 31 of the TRIPS Agreement. The review of the Patent Law had showed that, in comparison with Article 27(3) of the TRIPS Agreement, the exclusion of patentability contained in paragraphs (a) and (b) of Article 8 was in accordance with Article 27(1) of the TRIPS Agreement, which limits the patentable inventions to those which were related to products or processes; paragraph (c) of Article (8) was in full compliance with sub-paragraph (b) of Article 27(3) of the TRIPS Agreement, except that paragraph (c) did not exclude "micro-organisms" from "plants and animals" and did not include "non-biological processes" as processes excluded from "biological processes for the production of plants and animals"; paragraph (d) of the Patent Law was in full compliance with sub-paragraph (a) of Article 27(3) of the TRIPS Agreement.[212] It is noted that Saudi Arabia in this regard was cooperating with the Patent Office of the Government of Germany to take advantage of its experience and further streamline the Saudi system.[213]

6.8.3 *Trademark law*

Under Saudi Arabia's Trademarks Law, geographical names could not be registered as trademarks if their uses can lead to misunderstanding as to the source of products or services, or their origin.[214] As regard some inconsistencies of Saudi local legislations with certain rules under the WTO regime on Trademarks, a new Saudi local legislation has been promulgated with a view to conforming to provision of the TRIPS Agreement.[215] Some of the salient points addressed by the new Trademarks Law and Implementing Regulations include increase and imposition of harsher punishments on infringement of trademarks rules; the right of the injured party to compensation in proportion to the damages suffered by the injured party due to infringement; determination of all disputes

211 Ibid.

212 Ibid.

213 World Trade Organization Report, supra note no. 209.

214 Ibid.

215 See Trademarks Law, issued pursuant to Royal Decree M/21 of 29.5.1423H (7 August 2002); and the implementing regulations for the new Trademarks Law issued on October 4, 2002, by Ministerial Order No. 1723.

arising as a result of trademark infringements is put within the jurisdiction of the Board of Grievances; the right to file an appeal before the Board of Grievances against the decision of the Ministry of Commerce and Industry denying registration of a trademark; as well as protection of well-known trademarks, even if not registered.[216]

The new Saudi Trademarks Law to be implemented by the King Abdulaziz City for Science and Technology (KACST) protects the industrial designs under the industrial design provisions of the Law. However, the conditions for obtaining design protection were that the design must be new, have specific features and not be contrary to the *Shari'ah* (public order); and the term of protection was ten years from the date of filing. Articles 48 and 51 of the Trademarks Law complied with TRIPS Agreement provisions regarding damages and compensation.[217]

Regarding provisional measures, a right holder could obtain an order for precautionary and preventive measures under specific intellectual property laws. Articles 49–51 of the Trademarks Law permitted a trademark owner to seek precautionary measures from the Board of Grievances based on a petition and official certificate of trademark registration. Articles 22 and 24 of the Copyrights Law and Articles 27 and 28 of the Implementing Regulations of the Copyrights Law provided for provisional measures to stop printing the infringing work, seize copies, extracts, and printed matter as a precaution or to apply such other precautionary seizure that the Committee responsible for determining violations of the Copyrights Law deemed necessary to protect copyrights. Article 34 of the Law on Patents, Layout Designs of Integrated Circuits, Plant Varieties and Industrial Designs authorized the Committee responsible for adjudicating disputes and appeals to take such prompt measures as the Committee deemed necessary to avoid the damages arising from infringement. Article 55 of the Implementing Regulations of this Law provided that the Committee may, upon submission of a statement of the case, order that precautionary and preventive measures be taken against the defendant.[218]

It can be concluded from the above analysis that intellectual property rights law is a new development emanating from the West. But, regardless of the traditional strict literalist Hanbali approach to Islamic law in Saudi Arabia, the international rules on the protection of intellectual property rights and its membership of the WTO and the inherent benefits derivable therefrom, have made it irresistible for Saudi Arabia to accept and find justification for the propriety of intellectual property rights law in the application of Islamic law within its domestic legal system.

216 World Trade Organization Report, supra, note no. 209.

217 Ibid.

218 Ibid.; see also Ministerial Decision No. 1277 of 15.5.1425H (3 July 2004) and by Copyrights Law and the Trademarks Law. In his view, these provisions fully complied with Section 4 of Part III of the TRIPS Agreement.

6.9 Conclusions

In conclusion, legislation in a country cannot be said to be totally independent without some degree of influence from other nations' legal systems, especially now that the trans-national economic and trade activities have assumed sophisticated and global dimensions. International treaties and conventions constrain domestic political sovereignty through the assumption of external obligations. However, the benefits of reciprocal obligations involved outweigh the costs associated with any loss of political sovereignty. Moreover, notions of reciprocity and a desire to depend on other nations' observances of rules lead many nations to observe rules even when they do not want to.

In the face of these global dynamics, Islamic law has proven in most cases that it is a legal system capable of adapting to changes. In monetary and banking matters, as could be seen, *riba* is basically and expressly forbidden in the basic sources. But what amounts to *riba* remains a contentious issue. It is through *Ijtihad* that modern Muslim jurists have drawn a line between what they term as "*Qur'anic* and *Sunnah riba*" from the issue of interest in the modern conventional banking practices. It thus creates a chance for having a second thought over the practices of the present-day banking system. The fact remains that jurist debates over the issue is a clear proof that Islamic law is not static. It is capable of interpretation and re-interpretation.

Saudi Arabia's assumption of membership of a Western-oriented international institution like the IMF and the WTO, which recognizes and tolerates *Riba* is *ab initio* a shift from its traditional hardline to a more liberal position. This itself is evidence of significant impact of international law on the Saudi Arabia local legislative policy, in this area of law. Also, in the exercise of its Special Drawing Rights as a *bona fide* member under Article XX of IMF, Saudi Arabia has arguably and unwittingly compromised its hardline position on the issue of *Riba* to a more liberal attitude even though this is not clearly pronounced, and this reality may be contested and even denied by the concerned authority.

This fact also manifests itself in the modern concept of intellectual property rights. Ordinarily, one would have thought that Islamic law would have nothing to do with the concept since it is essentially a Western-oriented novel idea that has no direct authority from the *Qur'an* and the *Sunnah*. By virtue of *Ijtihad*, Muslim jurists have come out to prove the validity of the concept in the light of the two basic sources of Islamic law. Interestingly, Saudi Arabia's renowned jurists were in the forefront in the campaign for legislative sensibility of the concept.

The above analyses demonstrate that Saudi Arabia has virtually been able to accommodate these perceived Eurocentric international economic law and legislative norms due to its membership of both the IMF and the WTO. Its jurists and scholars had, in one way or the other, found justification for those norms from the basic sources of law applicable in the Kingdom through *Ijtihad*. This is certainly due to derivable economic and international relations benefits from those international norms.

Bibliography

Books

Abdulaziz bin Baz, Al-Fataw, *Mu'assasat Al-Da'wa* (2nd edn) (1408); Majmoo' Fatawaa al-Sheikh Abdulaziz Ibn Baaz No. 19/194.

Abu Dawood and al-Albaani authenticates it. See al-Albaani, *Saheeh al-Jaami al Sagheer* No. 7662.

Abu Dawood and al-Haakim; Al-Albaani says it is authentic. See al-Albaani, *Saheeh al-Jaami al-Sagheer* No. 6714.

Al-Jaziri, A.R., *Islamic Jurisprudence According to the Four Sunni Schools: Al-Fiqh 'Ala Al-Madhahib Al-Arba'a*, Fons Vitae, US, Vol. 2 (2009).

Al-Maqdesi, A.Q., *Al-Muganni*, Cairo: Dar Al-Manor (1946).

Al-Sharkhasi, S., *Kitab Al-Mabsout*, Cairo: Al-Sa'ada Press (1903).

A-Qatamin, M.M., *Islamic and Conventional Banks: A Comparative Study*, M.B.A. Thesis, University of Nottingham (1990).

Baderin, M.A., 'Islamic Banking in Theory and Practice: An Analysis of the Fundamental Principles, Legal and Regulatory Framework in Relation to Nigeria', *Paper presented at the Annual General Conference of the Nigeria Bar Association* at The Civic Centre, Port Harcourt, River State, Nigeria (23rd August, 2011).

Bakar, M.D., *Riba and Islamic Banking and Finance* (40th Islamic Banking and Finance (unpublished article), International Islamic University, Malaysia (2009).

Bakr ibn 'Abdullah Abu Zayd'. *This Occasion's Fatwas*, 'Special Drawing Rights', International Monetary Fund. https://www.imf.org/en/About/Factsheets/Sheets/2016/08/01/14/51/Special-Drawing-Right-SDR

Beltrametti, S., 'The Legality of Intellectual Property Rights under Islamic Law', edited by Mach, T. et al., *The Prague Yearbook of Comparative Law*, Prague: The Prague Centre for International and Comparative Law (2009), pp. 55–94.

Ben Abdullah Yaqut, *Mu'jam Al-Udabba*, Cairo: Issa Al-Babi El-Halabi Library (n.d.).

BerkeleyLaw Library, University of California, BusinessDictionary, Special Drawing Rights (SDR), www.businessdictionary.com/definition/special-drawing-rights-SDR.html#ixzz317tkYTu9.

Crone, P., *Makkah Trade and the Rise of Islam*, Oxford: Basil Blackwell Ltd. (1987).

Dawood, N.N.'s *Translation of the Qur'an*, London: Penguin Books (1956).

Deardirffs' Glossary of International Economics, www-personal.umich.edu/~alandear/glossary/p.html.

Donner, F.M., *The Early Islamic Conquests*, New Jersey: Princeton University Press (1981).

Dr Al Oufi Law Firm, Trademarks, www.aloufilawfirm.com/tm.htm.

El-Bdour, R., 'Problems of Research in Islamic Economics', The Proceedings of the 1986 Symposium of the *Islamic Research and Training Institute and the Islamic Development Bank on Problems of Research in Islamic Economics*, Jeddah, Saudi Arabia (1986).

First Secretary, Department of Legal Affairs – Ministry of Foreign Affairs – Saudi Arabia. https://www.mofa.gov.sa/sites/MofaEN

General Provisions and Basic Principles of Agreement on Trade Related Aspects of Intellectual Property Rights (TRIPS), www.wto.org/english/docs_e/legal_e/27-trips_03_e.htm.

Ghazanfar, S.M., *Medieval Islamic Economic Thought*, New York: Routledge Curzon (2003).

Hatem Abbas Ghazzawi & Co. (formerly Abbas F. Ghazzawi & Co.), Saudi-legal – Saudi Arabian Law Overview, www.saudilegal.com/saudilaw/02_law.html. Hatem Abbas Ghazzawi & Co. (formerly Abbas F. Ghazzawi & Co.).

Jackson, J.H., *The World Trade Organization, Constitution and Jurisprudence*, London: The Royal Institute of International Affairs (1998).
Jerichow, A., *The Saudi File, People, Power, Politics*, London: Curzon Press (1998).
Kamali, M.H., *Maqasid al-Shari'ah Made Simple* (Occasional Papers Series 13), London: The International Institute of Islamic Thought (n.d.).
Karim, S.A., *A Study of Islamic Money and Financial Instruments*, Boca Raton, FL: Brown Walker Press (2010).
Kay, E., *Legal Aspects of Business in Saudi Arabia*, London: Graham & Trotman Limited (1979).
Khallaf, A.W., *'Ilm Usul Al-Fiqh*, Cairo: Dar Al-Qalam (1956), pp. 32–35.
Khan, A.A., and Laura, T., *An Islamic Perspective of Fair Trade*, Birmingham: Islamic Relief Worldwide (2008).
Khan, S.N., Money, Riba, Usury and Interest - Part 2, www.paklink.biz/articles/riba2.html.
Krause, Chester L., and Mishler, C., *Standard Catalogue of World Coins: 1801–1991* (18th edn) (1991); Krause Publications and Pick, Albert, Standard Catalogue of World Paper Money: General Issues. Colin R. Bruce II and Neil Shafer (editors) (7th edn), Krause Publications (1994).
Krueger, A.O., *The WTO as an International Organization* (edited by Anne O. Krueger), Chicago IL: The University of Chicago Press (1998).
Legal Information Institute, International Trade, Cornell University Law School. https://www.law.cornell.edu/.
Long, D.E., *Culture and Customs of Saudi Arabia*, California: Greenwood Press (2005).
Majallah Majma al-Fiqh al-Islaami, volume no. 5, part 3; Resolutions and Recommendations of the Council of Islamic Fiqh Academy 1985–2000, Resolution No. 43 (Research and Training Institute 2000), www.irtipms.org/OpenSave.asp?pub=73.pdf.
Matushita, M. et al., *The World Trade Organization, Law, Practice, and Policy*, Oxford: Oxford University Press (2003).
Meenai, S.A., *The Islamic Development Bank – A Case Study of Islamic Co-operation*, London: Kegan Paul International (1989).
Model United Nations of the Far West (MUNFW), IMF and the World Bank, 45th Session Issues, www.munfw.org/archive/45th/ecosoc3.htm.
Muhammad Al-Ghazali, *Fiqh-Us-Seerah: Understanding the Life of the Prophet Mohammad* (2nd edn), Riyadh: International Islamic Publication House (1999).
Murphy, C., 'A Kingdom Divided', Global Post (15 July, 2010), http://islamdag.info/story/415.
Naqvi, S.N.H., *Ethics and Economics: An Islamic Synthesis*, London: The Islamic Foundation (1981).
Nielsen, N.J., and Christoffersen, L. (eds), *Legal Traditions and the Encounter with Europe*, Part of the *Cultural Diversity and Law* series, Farnham: Ashgate Publishing (2010).
Obligations and Benefits of IMF Membership, International Monetary Fund. https://www.imf.org/external/np/exr/center/mm/eng/mm_bnfts.htm
O'Connell, D., 'Why Intellectual Property Matters', *Intellectual Property Research Centre, Imperial College, London*, www3.imperial.ac.uk/intellectual-property-research/aboutus/why-ip.
Roger, O., *State, Power and Politics in the Making of the Modern Middle East* (3rd edn) London and New York: Routledge (2000).
Sahih Bukhari, Vol. 4, Hadith No.385.

Samad, A., and Hassan, M.K., 'Riba and Islamic Banking', *Journal of Islamic Economics, Banking and Finance*, http://ibtra.com/pdf/journal/v3_n1_article1.pdf at page 10 online.

Samir, M.K., *Riba and Paper Money- Riba in The Shari'ahh (the Islamic Law)*, Syria: Islamic Business Research Centre, www.kantakji.com/fiqh/Files/Riba/Y417.

Satoshi, I., *A New Approach to Human Economics: A Case Study of an Islamic Economy, The Institute of Middle Eastern Studies*, Niigata: International University of Japan (1985).

Saud, A. D., *Judicial Systemization in the Kingdom of Saudi Arabia, Riyadh*, Hanifah Press (1430H–1982).

Saudi Cleric Allows Visits to non-Muslim Place of Worship, social Media Use, Al-Arabiya News (9th October 2012), www.alarabiya.net/articles/2012/10/08/242630.html.

Sfeir, A., and Tirado, J., 'The International Comparative Legal Guide To: International Arbitration 2010', *Global Legal Group*, Vogel and Hayes, p. 87, "Saudi Arabian Law Overview", Hatem Abbas Ghazzawi & Co. "Law of the Board of Grievances".

Siddiqi, M.N., *Principles of International Economic Relations in Islam* (edited by Mannan, M.A. et al.) Jeddah: International Economic Relations from Islamic Perspectives, Islamic Development Bank, Islamic Research and Training Institute (1992).

The Kingdom of Saudi Arabia: An Overview, *Macro Insight*, Issue No. 14 of September, 2012, www.casuisse.com/c12575de004f6944/lkpresources/mi_14_ksa/$file/mi_14_ksa.pdf

The Library of Congress Country Studies; CIA World Factbook, *Saudi Arabia: Money and Banking*, www.photius.com/countries/saudi_arabia/economy/saudi_arabia_economy_money_and_banking.html.

The Open University – OpenLearn, 'Playing By the Rules? Developing Countries in the World Trade Regime', www.open.edu/openlearn/society/politics-policy-people/geography/developing-countries-the-world-trade-regime/content-section.

The WTO's Agreement on Trade-Related Aspects of Intellectual Property Rights (TRIPs).

Thomas, A. (ed.), *Interest in Islamic Economics: Understanding Riba*, Oxfordshire: Routledge, 2006.

Vogel, F.E., and Hayes, S.L., *Islamic Law and Finance Religion Risk and Return*, Leiden: Koninklijke Brill NV (2006).

Watt, W.M., *Muhammad at Makkah*, Oxford: Oxford University Press (1953).

Wilson, R., Al-Salamah, A., Malik, M., and Al-Rajhi, A., *Economic Development in Saudi Arabia*, London and New York: Routledge Curzon, Taylor & Francis Group (2004), p. 60.

Wilson, R., *Banking and Finance in the Middle East*, London: Financial Times Publication (1983), pp. 234–235.

WIPO-Administered Treaties, WIPO. https://www.wipo.int/treaties/en/

World Trade Organization, WTO | What is the WTO? - Who we are, www.wto.org/english/thewto_e/secre_e/budget_e.htm (accessed 17 January 2013).

World Trade Organization (WTO), The Agreements Intellectual Property: Protection and Enforcement; www.wto.org/english/thewto_e/whatis_e/tif_e/agrm7_e.htm.

World Trade Organization, *Report of the Working Party on the Accession of the Kingdom of Saudi Arabia to The World Trade Organization*, WT/ACC/SAU/61, 1 November, 2005.

Wright, J.W. (Jr), *Islamic Banking in Practice: Problems in Jordan and Saudi Arabia*, Washington College; Centre for Middle Eastern and Islamic Studies; Durham and Stockton-on-Tees: University of Durham (1995).

Journals

Abderrahman, D.B., 'A Contribution to the Study of the Koranic Sources of Saudi Arabia Law', *Arab Law Quarterly* (1988), pp. 132–150.

Al-Ghadyan, A.A., 'The Judiciary in Saudi Arabia', *Arab Law Quarterly*, Vol. 1, No. 3, BRILL (1998), pp. 235–251.

Anderson, J.N.D., 'Invalid and Void Marriages in Hanafi Law', *Bulletin of the School of Oriental and African Studies*, Vol. 13, No. 2 (1950), pp. 357–366.

Laluddin, H., et al., 'Property and Ownership Right from an Islamic Perspective', *Advances in Natural and Applied Sciences*, Vol. 6, No. 7 (2012), pp. 1125–1129.

Malkawi, B.H., 'The Alliance between Islamic Law and Intellectual Property: Structure and Practice', *University of St. Thomas Law Journal*, Vol. 10, No. 3 (2012–2013), pp. 618–649.

Nicholas, K.P., 'Influence of Islamic Law on Contemporary Middle Eastern Legal Systems: The Formation and Binding Force of Contracts', *Columbia Journal of Transnational Law*, Vol. 9 (1970), pp. 384–435.

Raysman, R., Piscareta, E.A., and Adler, K.A., 'Intellectual Property Licensing: Forms and Analysis', *Law Journal Press* (1998–2008), pp. 2–10.

Wolf, E. 'The Social Organization of Makkah and the Origins of Islam', *South-western Journal of Anthropology*, Vol. 7 (1951), pp. 329–356.

Websites

www.alifta.com/Search/MoftyDetails.aspx?Type=Mofty&section=tafseer&ID=9&languagename=en.

www.alifta.net/Fatawa/FatawaChapters.aspx?languagename=en&View=Page&-PageID=3695&PageNo=1&BookID=14.

www.ibrahimm.com/Islamic%20Banking/RIBA%20IN%20HADITH.htm.

www.imf.org/external/np/exr/center/mm/eng/mm_bnfts.htm.

www.imf.org/external/np/exr/facts/glance.htm (accessed 24 January 2013).

www.imf.org/external/np/exr/facts/sdr.htm (accessed 4 May 2014).

www.imf.org/external/pubs/ft/aa/#art20 (accessed 22 January 2013).

www.islamicawakening.com/viewarticle.php?articleID=1351 (accessed 11 January 2013).

www.law.berkeley.edu/library/dynamic/guide.php?id=60 (accessed 17 January 2013).

www.law.cornell.edu/wex/international_trade.

www.nur.org/en/nurcenter/nurlibrary/Sahih_Bukhari_Hadith_Collections_86958?pg=293.

www.sama.gov.sa/sites/samaen/RulesRegulation/BankingSystem/Pages/Banking-SystemFD08.aspx.

www.wipo.int/treaties/en/ShowResults.jsp?lang=en&treaty_id=15.

www.wto.org/english/thewto_e/acc_e/completeacc_e.htm#sau.

www.wto.org/english/docs_e/legal_e/27-trips_03_e.htm.

www.wto.org/english/thewto_e/secre_e/budget_e.htm (accessed 17 January 2013).

International Monetary Fund (IMF), www.imf.org/external/np/sec/memdir/memdate.htm.

www.wto.org/english/thewto_e/whatis_e/tif_e/agrm7_e.htm.

International Monetary Fund, Factsheet, *The IMF at a Glance*, August 22, 2010.

International Monetary Fund, *List of Members*, www.imf.org/external/np/sec/memdir/memdate.htm.

Islamic Development Bank, *Principles of Operations*, www.isdb.org/irj/portal/anonymous?NavigationTarget=navurl://91b765e29a0bbf4da579f0c9bbf5f83f.
www.un.org/en/members/index.shtml.
www.un.org/en/members/index.shtml.

Fatwa, statutes, regulations, and government resolutions

Basic Law of Governance (Royal Order No. (A/91), 27 Sha'ban 1412H – 1 March 1992, *Umm al-Qura* Gazette No. 3397, 2 *Ramadan* 1412H – 5 March 1992.
Charter of the Saudi Arabian Monetary Agency Royal Decree No. 23 dated 23-5-1377AH (15-12-1957).
Fatawa Islamiyyah, No. 2/404 of the Saudi Arabian Standing Committee for Scholarly Research and Fatwa.
Fatwa No. 13/369 of the Saudi Arabian Standing Committee for Scholarly Research and Fatwa.
Fatwa No.18453 signed by Sheikh Abdul-Azeez ibn Baaz (late), Abdul-Azeez Aali-Shaikh, and Saalih al-Fauzaan and Bakr Abu Zaid.
Ministerial Decision No. 1277 of 15.5.1425H (3 July 2004).
Royal Decree No. 23 (dated 23-5-1377H) and Council of Ministers' Resolution No. 103 (dated 20/05/1377H).
Royal Decree No. M/41 of 2.7.1424H (30 August 2003).
Royal Decree No. M/51, 17 Rajab 1402 [10 May 1982]; Information Office of the Royal Embassy of Saudi Arabia.
Saudi Arabia Monetary Agency Circular No. M/A/1/291 dated 19-9-1390 (12-8-1979).
Trademarks Law issued pursuant to Royal Decree M/21 of 29.5.1423H (7 August 2002).

7 International arbitration and Islamic law in Saudi Arabia

7.1 Introductory remarks

The globalized economy has led to a phenomenal rise in the number of commercial interactions cutting across national borders.[1] Consequently, there has been significant commercial interaction between Western companies and their Middle Eastern counterparts over the last few decades.[2] This has added a complex dimension to interpretation of commercial agreements and practices due to differences in custom, language, culture, and religion, leading to increased disputes and disagreements between commercial players.[3]

Consequently, international arbitration stands as outstanding modus for dispute resolution arising from international commercial contracts and other related international issues. It provides an efficient and effective means of resolving international commercial, investment and state-to-state disputes.[4] The practice of international arbitration has developed to allow parties from different legal cultures to consensually resolve their disputes generally without a strict adherence to the formalities of their respective legal and court systems.[5] Parties who accede to arbitration have essentially resolved to settle their disputes outside of any national judicial system.[6] The underlined philosophy of Article II (1) of the UN Convention on the Recognition and Enforcement of Foreign Arbitral Awards (1958)[7] and other international arbitration laws is to ensure an effective "pro-arbitration regime" that safeguards the enforceability of international

1 Behr, V., 'Enforcement of United States Monetary Judgement in Germany', *Journal of Law & Commerce*, Vol. 13 (1994), p. 211.

2 See e.g., Kutty, F., 'The Shari'a Factor in International Commercial Arbitration', *Loyola of Los Angeles International & Comparative Law Review*, Vol. 28 (2006), pp. 565–624.

3 Volz, J.L., and Haydock, R.S., 'Foreign Arbitral Awards: Enforcing the Award against the Recalcitrant Loser', *William Mitchel Law Review*, Vol. 21 (1996), pp. 867, 868.

4 Born, G.B., *International Commercial Arbitration: Law and Practice*, United Kingdom: Wolters Kluwer Law & Business (2012), p. 3.

5 Ibid.

6 Moses, M.L., *The Principles and Practice of International Commercial Arbitration*, Cambridge: Cambridge University Press (2008), p. 1.

7 Hereinafter "New York Convention". See Section 1.2.1 below.

arbitration agreements and awards.[8] In effect, "each Contracting State shall recognize an agreement in writing under which the parties undertake to submit to arbitration...".[9]

The huge revenues from oil exports crystallized into the Saudi Arabia economic boom of the 1970s and 1980s. This was the time that foreign ownership of business was allowed and by the mid-1990s, foreign ownership rules were eased as investment plans were focused on key areas including telecommunications, utilities, and financial services.[10] This led to the influx of many foreign business investments into the country. Most often, due to the zeal to do things quickly, terms of business and commercial agreements were not properly scrutinized, analyzed, and properly and mutually understood between parties before the endorsement of such expensive commercial transactions. This unhappy situation, Ahmed Audhali observes, has brought about commercial relationships between various parties that were not properly understood or thought of thoroughly, and as a result, commercial disputes among partners and business associates were steadily springing up in large numbers.[11] Due to involvement of foreign partners and corporate personalities in most of the commercial disputes, coupled with large volumes of cases awaiting settlement, arbitration or alternative dispute resolution (ADR) became more convenient and better option for both local and foreign parties in the country. Consequently, arbitration rules and regulations in both classical and modern forms have become part and parcel of the Saudi legal system.

Today, Saudi Arabia is one of the 151 of the 193 UN Member States that have adopted the New York Convention and is a party to the UN Commission on International Trade Law (UNCITRAL).[12] Parties to these international legal instruments have committed themselves to enforcing foreign arbitral awards with limited exceptions. To what extent these norms of international arbitration have impacted on the application of Islamic law and the totality of legal development in the commercial-arbitration regimes of Saudi Arabia forms the subject of analysis of this chapter.

This chapter is divided into three parts. Part I provides a general analysis of the modern concept of arbitration and international commercial arbitration followed by an examination of the concept, rules, and practice of arbitration under classical Islamic law and jurisprudence in Part II, while Part III examines the practice of international commercial arbitration in Saudi Arabia and its impact on the application of Islamic law and the arbitration rules in the country.

8 Born, G.B., supra note no. 4.

9 Article II (1), United Nations Convention on the Recognition and Enforcement of Foreign Arbitral Awards (1958).

10 Tripp, H., and Peter, N., *CultureShock! A Survival Guide to Customs and Etiquette – Saudi Arabia* (3rd edn) London: Marshall Cavendish (2009), p. 225; see also Britannica, Economy, www.britannica.com/place/Saudi-Arabia/Economy (accessed 21 September 2020).

11 Audhali, A.A., Settlement of Commercial Disputes in Saudi Arabia (Civil Procedure), Al Khobar: Al-Eman P. Press (n.d.), p. i.

12 *New York Convention Countries* – New York Arbitration Convention, www.newyorkconvention.org/contracting-states/list-of-contracting-states (accessed 18 November 2014).

Part I

7.2 The concept of arbitration and international commercial arbitration

Arbitration is simply a form of Alternative Dispute Resolution (ADR) – a method of resolving disputes outside the conventional court system.[13] In this case, the parties to a dispute refer a case to one or more persons technically known as "arbitrators", "arbiters", or "arbitral tribunal", by whose decision, mostly in form of an "award" they agree to be bound. It is a resolution technique in which a third-party reviews the evidence in the case and imposes a decision that is legally binding for both sides and enforceable.[14] ADR includes mediation which is a form of settlement negotiation facilitated by a neutral third party and non-binding resolutions by experts.[15] Arbitration system is usually adopted in resolving commercial disputes, particularly in the context of international commercial transactions.[16]

7.3 Basic elements of arbitration

There are four basic elements of arbitration, namely, agreement to arbitrate; the choice of arbitrators; the decision of the arbitral tribunal; and the enforcement of the award,[17] each of which is briefly summarized below.

7.3.1 Agreement to arbitrate

There must be a *consensus ad idem* of parties to submit to arbitration to settle any disputes or differences between them. Not only does this mean that they must have consented to arbitrate the dispute that has arisen between them, it also means that the authority of the arbitral tribunal is limited to that which the parties have agreed.[18] Consequently, the award rendered by the tribunal must settle the dispute that was submitted to it and must not pronounce on any issues or other disputes that may have arisen between the parties. This is reflected in Article V of the New York Convention.[19]

13 Osullivan, A., and Sheffrin, S.M., *Economics: Principles in Action*, New Jersey: Pearson Prentice Hall (2003), p. 324.

14 Ibid. See also, Barin, B., et al., *The Osler Guide to Commercial Arbitration in Canada: A Practical Introduction to Domestic and International Commercial Arbitration*, The Netherland: Kluwer Law International (2006), p. 3.

15 See Jones, G., *ADR Glossary: Alternative Dispute Resolution, Arbitration, Expert Determination & Mediation/Conciliation*, http://gmjones.org/adr_glossary.php (accessed 17 November 2014) and, www.law.cornell.edu/search/site/types%20of%20ADR (accessed 17 November 2014).

16 Osullivan, A., and Sheffrin, S.M., supra note no. 13.

17 Ibid at p. 6.

18 Bergsten, E.E., 'Dispute Settlement, International Commercial Arbitration', *United Nations Conference on Trade and Development*, New York and Geneva (2005), p. 36.

19 Article V of The New York Convention provides *inter alia* conditions under which recognition and enforcement of the award may be refused.

7.3.2 Choice of arbitrators

The parties to arbitration are free to choose their own tribunal and this is a significant element that distinguishes arbitration from litigation. In doing this, certain factors are taken into account and that is why it is noted that a skilled and experienced arbitrator is one of the key ingredients of a fair and effective arbitration.[20] It has been rightly observed that "[t]he choice of the persons who composed the arbitral tribunal is vital and often the most decisive step in arbitration [and] ... that arbitration is only as good as the arbitrators".[21]

7.3.3 Decision of the arbitral tribunal

Another defining characteristic of arbitration is that it produces a binding award that resolves the dispute between parties in a conclusive manner and is subject only to limited ground for challenge in national courts.[22] Decision of an Arbitration is not a non-binding, advisory recommendation, which gives the parties an option to accept or reject – because it is not merely a process of negotiation, during which the parties are free to agree (or not) to settle their disputes.[23] An arbitration tribunal produces a final and binding decision by a third-party decision-maker – the arbitrator – that can be coercively enforced against the unsuccessful party or its assets.[24]

7.3.4 Enforcement of the arbitral award

Enforcement of arbitration agreements and awards is central to the arbitral concept. One important reason parties include an arbitration clause in an international contract is the relatively certain enforceability of the award.[25] The chance of enforcing arbitral awards is high due to the fact that many countries have become parties to the international conventions that are pro-enforcement, which in effect provides only limited grounds for refusing to enforce.[26] Once an arbitral tribunal has concluded its proceedings and made its decisions and awards, it has thus accomplished its task and its existence comes to an end. Its awards, however, give rise to specific and lasting legal effects. The awards imply binding decision on the dispute between the parties. It follows that if it is not

20 Redfern, A., et al., *Law and Practice of International Commercial Arbitration*, London: Sweet & Maxwell (2004), p. 11.

21 Lalive, J.F., "*Melanges en l'honneur de Nicolas Valticos*" in Droit et Justice (Editions Pedone) (1989), p. 289 as quoted by Redfern, A., et al., ibid.

22 Born, G.B., supra note no. 4 at p. 5.

23 Ibid.

24 Le Parmentier v. La Societe Miss France, XXX Y.B. Comm Arb. (2004), pp. 119, 123–124 (Paris Cour d'appel); Walkinshaw v. Diniz (2000), 2 All E.R. (Comm.) 237 (Q.B.).

25 Moses, M.L., supra note no. 6 at p. 202.

26 Ibid.

implemented voluntarily, the awards may be enforced by legal mechanism – both locally and internationally.[27]

Similarly, Article III of New York Convention stipulates that countries are to recognize arbitral awards as binding, and to ensure their enforcement in accordance with national law, consistent with the provisions of the Convention.

7.4 International conventions on arbitration

Deriving from the general concept of arbitration, international commercial arbitration is guided by a number of international legal instruments which include (i) international arbitration conventions, notably the New York Convention, (ii) national arbitration legislation, especially local enactments of the United Nations Commission on International Trade Law (UNCITRAL) Model Law, (iii) institutional arbitration rules, incorporated by parties' arbitration agreements, and (iv) arbitration agreement given effect by international arbitration conventions and national arbitration legislation.[28] Each of these categories is briefly summarized below.

7.4.1 International arbitration conventions

The UN Convention on the Recognition and Enforcement of Foreign Arbitral Awards, also known as the New York Convention, was formally endorsed by a UN diplomatic conference on 10 June 1958 and entered into force on 7 June 1959.[29] The Convention obliges courts of contracting states to give effect to private agreements to arbitrate and to recognize and enforce arbitration awards made in other contracting states.[30] The Convention applies to arbitrations which are not considered as domestic awards in the state where recognition and enforcement is sought. Though other international conventions apply to the cross-border enforcement of arbitration awards, the New York Convention is by far the most important.[31]

Historically, the earliest of the modern international commercial arbitration conventions were the 1923 Geneva Protocol on Arbitration Clauses in Commercial Matters[32] and the 1937 Geneva Convention for the Execution of Foreign Arbitral Awards.[33] The Protocol laid down rules for the recognition

27 This is specified, for example, under Article II (1) of the NYC and Article 8 of UNCITRAL; see also Redfern, A., et al., supra note no. 20 at p. 13.

28 Born, G.B., supra note no. 4 at p. 18.

29 Ayoub, C., *Convention on the Recognition and Enforcement of Foreign Arbitral Awards*, www.charlesayoub.com/life-style/index.php/more/1/769 (accessed 19 November 2013).

30 Ayoub, C., ibid.

31 Ibid.

32 Geneva Protocol on Arbitration Clauses in Commercial Matters ("Geneva Protocol"), 27 L.N.T.S. 158 (1924).

33 Geneva Convention on the Execution of Foreign Arbitral Awards ("Geneva Convention"), 92 L.N.T.S. 302 (1929).

of international commercial arbitration agreements, requiring contracting states to refer parties to such agreements to arbitration.[34] The Convention, on the other hand, provided for the recognition of arbitral awards made in other contracting states (subject to a number of exceptions).[35] The Geneva Protocol and Convention were subsequently replaced by the 1958 UN Convention on the Recognition and Enforcement of Foreign Arbitral Awards, known as "New York Convention".[36]

The New York Convention spells out rules within the scope of its few pages, with the instrument's essential substance contained in five concise provisions (Articles I through V).[37] Notwithstanding the brevity of this Convention, it is extensively recognized as "the cornerstone of current international commercial arbitration".[38] In Judge Stephen Schwebel's words, aptly, "It [the Convention] works".[39] A cardinal goal of the Convention was to establish a uniform set of international legal standards for the enforcement of arbitration agreements and awards.[40] It prescribes uniform international criteria that: (i) require national courts to acknowledge and enforce foreign arbitral awards as contained in its Articles II and IV, subject however, to a limited number of specified exception listed in Article V; (ii) require national courts to acknowledge the validity and legitimacy of arbitration agreements, subject to specified exceptions as contained in Article II; and (iii) require national courts to refer parties to arbitration when they have entered into a valid agreement to arbitrate that is subject to the Article II(3) of the Convention. The only acceptable exceptions to the obligation to recognize foreign awards are limited to issues such as jurisdiction, procedural regularity and fairness, compliance with the parties' arbitration agreement, and public policy.[41] Presently, 151 nations have ratified the Convention, including all major trading states and many Latin American, African, Asia, Middle Eastern, and former Socialist states.[42] Saudi Arabia ratified the New York Convention on 19 April 1994.[43]

34 Born, G.B., supra note no. 4 at p. 19.

35 Ibid.

36 330 U.N.T.S. (United Nations – Treaty Series), No. 4739; www.uncitral.org.

37 Born, G.B., supra, at its note no. 4.

38 Jan Van Den Berg, A., *The New York Arbitration Convention of 1958, towards a Uniform Judicial Interpretation* (1st edn), Netherlands: Kluwer Law International (1981), p. 1; Born, G.B., *International Commercial Arbitration*, Kluwer Law International (2009), p. 95.

39 Schwbel, S., 'A Celebration of the United Nations New York Convention on the Recognition and Enforcement of Foreign Arbitral Awards', *Arbitration International*, Vol. 12, No. 1 (1996), pp. 83, 85.

40 Jan Van Den Berg, A., supra note no 38 at pp. 54–55, 168–169, 262–263, and, 357–358.

41 Born, G.B., supra note no. 4.

42 United Nations Commission on International Trade Law, www.uncitral.org/uncitral/about/origin_history.html (accessed 21 November 2013).

43 New York Arbitration CMC Legal, and also www.newyorkconvention.org/contracting-states/list-of-contracting-states (accessed 18 November 2014).

7.4.2 UNCITRAL Model Law

The extensive trade patronage of the 1960s, impelled national governments to think along the line of adopting a global set of standard and rules with a view to harmonize national and regional legal regimes, which hitherto governed international trade. That perhaps explains why the UN Commission on International Trade Law (UNCITRAL) was established by the UN General Assembly with a view "to promote the progressive harmonization and unification of international trade law".[44]

The UNCITRAL Model Law on International Commercial Arbitration was prepared and subsequently adopted by UNCITRAL on 21 June 1985. In 2006 the model law was amended and now includes more detailed provisions on interim measures.[45] The model law is not binding, but individual states may adopt the model law by incorporating it into their domestic law (as, for example, Australia did, in the International Arbitration Act 1974, as amended).[46] It is noted that there is a distinct difference between the UNCITRAL *Model Law* on International Commercial Arbitration (1985) and the UNCITRAL *Arbitration Rules*.[47] Details of this are contained in UNCITRAL report.[48] The Model Law was designed to be enforced within the framework of the national legislatures, with a view to harmonize the treatment of international commercial arbitration in different countries.[49] This law contains 36 articles making provisions on a wide range of arbitral issues especially its enforcement mechanism.

7.4.3 Institutional and ad hoc *arbitrations*

Institutional arbitration is distinguished from *ad hoc* type of arbitration.[50] The former is administered by a specialist arbitral institution under its own rules of arbitration.[51] An administered arbitration may be wholly administered or semi-administered. In the former, arbitration is that of International Centre for Settlement of Investment Disputes (ICSID)[52] which is essentially responsible for a full service to the arbitral tribunal. In the latter, the responsible institute

44 UN General Assembly Resolution 2205 (XXI) of 17 December 1966.

45 United Nations Commission on International Trade Law, www.uncitral.org/uncitral/en/uncitral_texts/arbitration.html (accessed 21 November 2013).

46 Commonwealth Consolidated Acts, www.austlii.edu.au/au/legis/cth/consol_act/iaa1974276/ (accessed 21 November 2013).

47 International Commercial Arbitration & Conciliation, www.uncitral.org/uncitral/en/uncitral_texts/arbitration.html (accessed 21 November 2013).

48 FAQ – UNCITRAL and Private Disputes / Litigation, www.uncitral.org/uncitral/en/uncitral_texts/arbitration.html (accessed 21 November 2013).

49 Born, G.B., supra note no. 4.

50 Moses, M.L., supra note no. 25 at p. 9.

51 Redfern, A., et al., supra note no. 20 at p. 55.

52 ICSID is an autonomous international institution established under the Convention on the Settlement of Investment Disputes between States and Nationals of Other States with over 140 member states.

collects the initial advance on costs from the parties, appoints the arbitral tribunal, and then leaves it to the arbitral tribunal to communicate with the parties, arrange meetings, and other procedural matters. Semi-administered is an example of arbitration conducted in England under the rules of the Chartered Institute of Arbitrators.[53] In case of the *ad hoc* arbitration, there is no administering institution. Thus, the parties are not under obligation to pay the fees and expenses of the administering institution.[54] *Ad hoc* arbitration gives the parties more opportunity to craft a procedure that is very carefully tailored to the particular kind of dispute – they are at liberty to draft their own rules, or they may choose to use the UNCIRAL Arbitration Rules.[55]

Institutional Arbitration is administered by many institutions including the International Centre for Dispute Resolution (ICDR) which is a division of the American Arbitration Association (AAA), Inter-American Commercial Arbitration Commission (IACAC), International Centre for Settlement of Investment Disputes (ICSID), International Chamber of Commerce (ICC), and London Court of International Arbitration (LCIA). There are also regional arbitral institutions such as those in Singapore and the Chambers of Commerce of Switzerland, Stockholm, Vienna, Dubai, and Abu Dhabi.

The arbitral institutions have laid down procedural rules that apply where parties have agreed to arbitration pursuant to such rules characteristically by incorporating such rules in their arbitration agreements.[56] These set of rules elaborate on the basic procedural framework within which the arbitral proceedings are to be carried out and normally to authorize the arbitral institution to assist in selecting arbitrators in particular disputes; to work out challenges to arbitrators, to designate the place of arbitration, to fix the fees payable to the arbitrators, and to review the arbitrators' awards to reduce the risk of unenforceability.[57] In principle, the arbitral institutions do not themselves arbitrate the merits of the parties' dispute; rather it is the individuals selected by the parties or institution as arbitrators. Under normal circumstances, arbitrators are private persons selected by the parties and never employees of the arbitral institution.[58]

7.4.4 Arbitration agreement

When there is *consensus ad idem* between two parties to arbitrate their disputes, it implies that they give up the right to have those disputes decided by a national court.[59] It follows that the arbitration agreement represents the forfeiture of an important right – to have the dispute settled judicially and creates other rights.

53 Redfern, A., et al., supra p. 55 at its footnote no. 95.
54 Moses, M.L., supra note no. 6 at p. 9.
55 Ibid.
56 Born, G.B., supra note no. 4.
57 Born, G.B., ibid.
58 Ibid.
59 Moses, M.L., supra note no. 6 at p. 17.

These include rights to establish the process for resolving the dispute and thus, in the agreement, the parties can select the rules that will govern the procedure, the location of the arbitration, the language of arbitration, the law governing the arbitration, and often, the decision-makers, who the parties may choose on account of their particular expertise in the subject matter of the parties' dispute.[60]

Article 7(1) of the UNDCITRAL Model Law provides that: "[a]n arbitration agreement may be in the form of an arbitration clause in a contract or in the form of a separate agreement". Thus, giving parties freedom to draft arbitration agreements that are either clauses within underlying commercial contracts or stand-alone "arbitration agreements", that are very short, very long, or mid-way.[61]

Due to the importance of agreement between parties, certain elements are critical to the formation of arbitral agreements. These elements include (i) agreement to arbitrate, (ii) scope of disputes submitted to arbitration, (iii) institutional arbitration rules, (iv) arbitral seat, (v) arbitrators' number, qualifications and selection, (vi) language of arbitration, and (vii) choice-of-law clause.[62] Other provisions of International Arbitration Agreement include (a) allocation of legal costs, (b) interest and currency of award, (c) disclosure, (d) fast-track or other procedures, (e) multi-tier dispute resolution, (f) state/sovereign immunity, (g) confidentiality, and (h) waiver of annulment.[63]

7.5 The New York Convention: an intrusion into modern-nations domestic legislations?

The US's attitude to the New York Convention exemplified the typical reaction of the modern nation-states to international arbitration law. As an important ally of Saudi Arabia, the US position and attitude to the New York Convention at the formative stage of the instrument is very instructive. At first, the US was not disposed to the New York Convention,[64] and thus, did not sign the Convention at its 1958 adoption, and, in fact, did not become a party until 30 September 1970.[65] Its rejection of the Convention was based on its belief that many of the Convention's provisions were in conflict with US law.[66]

60 Ibid.

61 Born, G.B., supra at p. 34.

62 Ibid at p. 35.

63 Ibid.

64 Strub Jr., M.H., 'Resisting Enforcement of Foreign Arbitral Awards under Article V (1)(E) and Article 1W of the New York Convention: A Proposal for Effective Guidelines', *Texas Law Review*, Vol. 68 (1990), p. 1039.

65 American Arbitration Association, *The International Arbitration Kit: A Compilation of Basic and Frequently Requested Documents* (4th edn) (1993), pp. 19–20; Roy, K.T., 'The New York Convention and Saudi Arabia: Can a Country Use the Public Policy Defence to Refuse Enforcement of Non-Domestic Arbitral Award?' *Fordham International Law Journal*, Vol. 18, No. 3 (1994), p. 930.

66 House Committee on Judiciary, Foreign Arbitral Awards H.R. Rep. No. 1181, 91st Cong., 2d Sess. 1 (1970). "(T]he American delegation felt that certain provisions were in conflict with our domestic laws." Strub Jr., M.H., at 1039 (stating that United States believed Convention's provisions deviated from U.S. law).

It thus decided to maintain its own independent jurisdiction over disputes submitted to arbitration.[67] Yet, as the use of the international arbitration process became a generally accepted method of international dispute resolution, the US realized that it would need a method of dispute resolution and enforcement that would permit it to resolve international disputes more efficiently and inexpensively.[68]

With its accession to the New York Convention in 1970,[69] the US embraced international arbitration as an effective means of dispute resolution.[70] When deciding on the validity of a non-US arbitral award, US courts subordinate the Federal Rules of Civil Procedure to the rules of the New York Convention.[71] Many arbitral cases decided in the US demonstrate the recognition of the non-domestic arbitral awards enforced within its jurisdiction. These cases include Scherk v. Alberto-Culver Company[72] in which the validity of international arbitration agreements was put to test by the US Supreme Court soon after it ratified the New York Convention. Other cases that illustrate the application of the New York Convention in American arbitral matters include Oriental Commercial and Shipping Company, Ltd. v. Rosseel, N.V.,[73] and Haardt v. Binzag.[74]

Part II

7.6 The concept of arbitration in Islamic law and jurisprudence

Arbitration, conceptually known in Islamic terminology as "*tahkim*", has a long history in the Middle East dating back to the pre-Islamic era.[75] There was a prevalence of a culture of preference for resolving disputes privately through a number of methods, namely, negotiation, mediation, and conciliation rather than through formal and public litigation, which was practically non-existent in those

67 Roy, K.T., supra note no. 65.

68 Matlin, R.S., 'Comment, The Federal Courts and the Enforcement of Foreign Arbitral Awards', *Pace Law Review*, Vol. 5 (1984), pp. 157–159 see also, Paulsson, J., 'The Role of Swedish Courts in Transnational Commercial Arbitration', *Virginia Journal of International Law*, Vol. 21 (1981), pp. 211, 212.

69 House Committee on Judiciary, foreign arbitral Awards, H.R. REP. No. 1181, 91st Cong., 2d Sess. 1 (1970), supra note no. 66.

70 Roy, K.T., supra note no. 65 at p. 931.

71 *Parsons & Whittemore Overseas Co., Inc.* v. *Societe Generale De L'Industrie Du Papier*, 508 F.2d 969,975 (2d Cir. 1974). "By agreeing to submit disputes to arbitration, a party relinquished his courtroom rights… in favour of arbitration 'with all of its well-known advantages and drawbacks.' "*Parsons & Whittemore*, 508 F.2d at 975 (quoting Washington-Baltimore Newspaper Guild, Local 55 v. The Washington Post Co., 442 F.2d 1234, 1238 (D.C. Cir. 1971); Roy, K.T., supra note no 65 at p. 931 and footnote no. 78.

72 (1974) 417 U.S. 506.

73 (1985), 609 F. Supp. 75 (S.D.N.Y. 1985).

74 (1986), No. CIV.AH-83-5846, 1986 WL 14836, at *1 (S.D. Tex. Dec. 19, 1986).

75 Abdul Hamid, E.A., *Arbitration with the Arab Countries* (2nd edn), Netherlands: Kluwer Law International (1999) p. 11.

times.[76] There was no formal legal system in place at that time, but there was a form of tribal justice administration under the authority of tribal chiefs who used arbitration extensively.[77]Abdul Hamid El-Ahdab confirms this historical fact.[78]

Prophet Muhammad (pbuh) re-enacted this old cultural spirit of arbitration which was prevalent in the pre-Islam era shortly before his Islamic mission. The story goes that after the reconstruction of *Ka'ba* around the year 605 AD, there was dispute among the Makkan tribes as to who would have the honour of putting the Black Stone in its place. Abu Umayyah who was the Makkan oldest man at the time proposed that the first man to enter the gate of the mosque the following morning would arbitrate over the matter. That man was Muhammad. People were unanimous in accepting him as arbitrator over the dispute. He proposed a solution that all agreed to place the Black Stone on a cloak; the elders of each of the parties to the dispute held on to one edge of the cloak and carried the stone to its place. Prophet Muhammad then picked up the stone and placed it on the wall of the *Ka'bah*, and that single arbitral proposal finally resolved the dispute.[79]

It is noted that some of the major characteristics of arbitration at this period are that arbitral agreements were simple and spontaneous; the agreements were not in writing; and arbitration was similar to conciliation as the ultimate goal was to reach an agreement and settle the dispute by any amiable solution, not to give a binding judgement.[80] Interestingly, the arbitration agreements of that period contained, *albeit* rudimentarily, all the essential elements of modern agreements.[81] The parties to the dispute agree to submit the dispute to arbitration; the parties identify the issue involved, agree on the time and the seat of the arbitration and nominate the arbitrators.[82]

Abdulrahman Yahya Baamir notes that the applicable rules of arbitration of the pre-Islamic era were the result of the accumulated experience and practice of the ancient Arabs, based on the common sense of elders that had continued to be followed by later generations and was partly adopted by Islam.[83]

7.6.1 Arbitration in early Islam

At the advent of Islam, the culture of arbitration was recognized and adopted. It has been argued that arbitration was approved of in the *Qur'an*, particularly

76 Baamir, A.R., *Shari'ah Law in Commercial and Banking Arbitration, Law and Practice in Saudi Arabia*, England: Ashgate (2010), p. 45.

77 Mahmassani, S., *The Legislative Situation in Arab Countries: Its Past and Present* (2nd edn), Beirut: Dar El-Elm Lil Malain, pp. 31–33.

78 Abdul Hamid, E.A., supra note no. 75 at p. 11.

79 Hisham, I., *Seerat Ibn Hisham* (Ministry of Islamic Affairs, Saudi Arabia), www.al-islam.com (accessed 21 May 2009); Baamir, A.R., supra note no. 76 at p. 82 and its footnote no. 7.

80 Baamir, A.R., supra note no. 76 at p. 47.

81 Ibid.

82 Albejad, N., *Arbitration in Saudi Arabia* (1st edn), Riyadh: Institute of Public Administration (1999), p. 23.

83 Baamir, A.R., supra, note 76 at p. 46.

in matters relating to matrimonial causes. For example, settlement of issues between spouses as contained in *Qur'an* 4:35.

In the same vein, Prophet Muhammad was reported not only to have accepted the decision of an arbitrator, but he also advised others to arbitrate and in fact, his closest companions used it to resolve disputes as well.[84] The treaty of Medinah was the first treaty entered into by the Muslims. In this treaty which was about the relationship between the Muslims, Non-Muslim Arab, and Jews of Medinah, it was expressly stipulated that disputes among the parties should be resolved through arbitration.[85] Reference has been made, in a modern arbitration case, to the fact that in resolving the dispute between the Muslims and Banu Qurayza tribe, the Prophet resorted to *tahkim*.[86] *Ijma'* or consensus (considered to be the first secondary source of Islamic law) has also confirmed the use of *tahkim* as a legal mechanism to resolving disputes between parties.[87]

Prophet Muhammad being an embodiment of both spiritual and secular authority, regulated the legal system and, through that, contributed to the development of the law itself.[88] J. N. D. Anderson notes that "Islam is a complete way of life; a religion, an ethic, and a legal system all in one".[89] While Islam brought radical changes to the legal culture of the Arabs, the hitherto arbitral justice method was also improved. Arbitration was thus a successful and flexible dispute settlement mechanism in the Prophet's time, which was modified and accommodated into Islamic law.[90] Muslim jurists have categorized arbitration into two types, namely, general arbitration and arbitration in political disputes.[91] The general arbitration maintained its pre-Islamic voluntary feature, and accordingly, the Prophet Muhammad gave preference to settling disputes by adopting a peaceful settlement known as *Sulh* rather than by decreeing or enforcing a judgment on unwilling disputants; even so, a decision can be imposed especially where the parties do not accept the proposed settlement.[92]

This was the case in a Hadith narrated by Al-Bukhari. The story goes that an Ansari man quarrelled with Azzubair in the presence of the Prophet about the Harrah Canals which were used for irrigating the date-palms. The Ansari man told Azzubair, "Let the water pass", but Azzubair refused to do so. The matter

84 Abdul Hamid, E.A., supra, note 75, at p. 12.

85 Ibid.

86 Libyan American Oil Company (LIAMCO) v. Libyan Arab Republic (1977), 20 I.L.M. (1981) p. 41.

87 Abdul Hamid, E.A., supra, note 75, at p. 13.

88 Sayen, G., 'Arbitration, Conciliation and the Islamic Legal Tradition in Saudi Arabia', *University of Pennsylvania Journal of International Business Law*, Vol. 9, No. 2 (1987), pp. 211–227.

89 Anderson, J.N.D., *Islamic Law in the Modern World* (1st edn), New York: New York University Press (1959), pp. 60–81; Liebesny, H.J., *The Law of Near Middle East State*, Al Bany: University of New York Press (1975), pp. 3–4.

90 Baamir, A.R., supra note 76, at p. 53.

91 Saleh, S., *Commercial Arbitration in the Arab Middle East: A Study in Shari'ah and Statute Law* (1st edn), London: Graham & Trotman (1984), p. 16.

92 Baamir, A.R., supra note 76, at p. 53.

was brought before the Prophet who told Azzubair, "O! Zubair! Irrigate your farmland and then let the water pass to your neighbour". The Ansari furiously objected saying: "Is it because he (i.e. Zubair) is your cousin?" On that the colour of the face of Prophet changed (because of anger) and he said: "O! Zubair! Irrigate your farmland and then withhold the water till it reaches the wall between the pits round the trees". Zubair said, By Allah, I think that the following verse was revealed on this incident: "But no, by your Lord they can have No faith until they make you judge in all dispute between them".[93]

The treaty of Medinah of 662 AD was a good example of arbitration at the dawn of Islam. It was a security pact among the three major groups in the city, namely, the Muslims, non-Muslim Arabs, and Jews. There was an arbitration clause in the treaty which provided that in case of a dispute between the inhabitants of the city in a political matter the dispute should be settled through arbitration. Such arbitration should be administered by Prophet Muhammad personally or, subject to the approval of the parties, by an arbitrator appointed by Prophet Muhammad.[94] In a dispute between the Muslim and Jewish tribe Banu Qurayza, Prophet Muhammad applied arbitration in resolving the issue involved.[95]

It should be noted that as a matter of principle the rule in arbitrating in family disputes was that the two appointed arbitrators must agree on the judgment.[96] This rule was applied in the historic incident of *tahkim* between Caliph Ali and Mu'awiyah the governor of Syria in the year 659 AD. Following the stalemate that arose from the assassination of Caliph Othman, civil war erupted and lasted for more than two years. To resolve the conflict, it was agreed in writing to submit to arbitration of two men, with terms of the time limit for making the award, the applicable law, the place of issuing the award, full power to determine the dispute and that the decision should be on the *Qur'an* and *Sunnah*.[97]

In a comparative sense, it could be argued that arbitrations at both the early period of Islam and in the contemporary time share some common attributes, namely, in defining the disputing parties precisely by name, place of residence, and occupation; identifying the precise issue of the dispute; including the choice of the arbitrator(s); taking the form of a written contract; determining a deadline for issuing the final award; determining the applicable law in the arbitration proceedings; determining the seat of the arbitration; defining the supervisory authority; determining the authority responsible for the execution of the final award; and determining the terms of reference of the arbitral tribunal.[98]

93 Sahih Bukhari, Chapter 40, No. 548.

94 Hisham, I., 'Seerat Ibn Hisham, 'The Treaty of Medina' (*Ministry of Islamic Affairs, Saudi Arabia*), www.al-islam.com (accessed 21 May 2009).

95 Brower, C., and Sharpe, J., 'International Commercial Arbitration and the Islamic World: The Third Phase', *American Journal of International Law*, Vol. 97, No. 3 (2003), pp. 643–656.

96 Baamir, A.R., supra note 76, at p. 54.

97 Alqurashi, Z., 'Arbitration under the Islamic Shari'ah,' *Oil, Gas and Energy Intelligence*, Vol. 1, No. 2 (arch 2002), pp. 30–44.

98 Baamir, A.R., supra note no. 76 at pp. 54–55.

7.6.2 *Adaptability of Shari'ah to modern international commercial arbitration*

Muslim jurists hold that *Qur'an* and the *Sunnah* potentially promote the culture of reconciliation and avoidance of rancour, disputes, and disagreements. Thus, if arbitration is found in Islamic jurisprudence to be a preferred method of settling disputes, it is argued that it reflects the Islamic philosophy of peace and brotherliness. Majority of the Islamic Schools of Jurisprudence including the Shi'a sects such as Al-Zaiydia and some of the 12 Imamia hold that arbitration is a justice mechanism that enjoys approval from the *Qur'an*, *Sunnah*, and, of course, from the *Ijma* (consensus) and *Qiyas* (analogy). They thus provide proof about its legality in those sources of Islamic law.[99]

7.6.3 *Concept of arbitration in* Qur'an

Though it is always argued that the statement of *Qur'an* 4:35 is about conciliation in matrimonial disputes, Muslim jurists hold that the verse is a clear proof of the legality of arbitration and, of course, by extension, a foundation to give arbitral philosophy a generally application in all spheres of life. If the verse in question allows arbitration between two couples with a view to preserving the familial relationship with the possibility of solving the problem with no recourses to judicial authority, it follows that arbitration is permitted to be used in resolving disputes in other spheres of life too.[100]

Some scholars argue that the two arbitrators mentioned in the above verse of the *Qur'an* are meant to carry out reconciliation rather than arbitration.[101] Another group of scholars hold contrary view, saying that though the verse, in letter, is directed towards the married couple which may be said to be reconciliation between them, but in spirit, it amounts to arbitration as defined by scholars. In other words, if the text is supposedly directed to the married couple, it is understood that the couple has the legal right to appoint two arbitrators to settle their dispute because the couple constitutes the core of the subject. It then follows that appointing two arbitrators mutually is a kind of arbitration in that case.[102]

Qur'an 5:97 is also quoted as proof of arbitration. Here an intentional killing game by a Muslim in a state of *ihram* (for the rites of *Hajj*) within the sacred Precincts is forbidden. Violation of this rule demands expiation of an offering as judged by two just men. It means that the person involved is given right to

99 Al-Jarba, M.A.H., *Commercial Arbitration in Islamic Jurisprudence: A Study of Its Role in the Saudi Arabia Context*, Thesis submitted for the Degree of Doctor of Philosophy in Law of the University of Wales, Aberystwyth (2001), p. 48.

100 Ibid.

101 Zinuddin Bin Najeem, *Al Bahr Al Raig Sharh Kanz Al Dagaig*, Vol. 7 (2nd edn), Beirut: Dar Al Maarifa (1333 H., 1912 AD), p. 25.

102 Al-Jarba, M.A.H., supra note no. 99, at pp. 49–50.

choose just arbitrators to determine the appropriateness of the offering. Some scholars take this to mean that this verse indicates permissibility of arbitration.[103] It is argued that although God's rights are not debatable, however, arbitration is allowed for people's right in this instance, as their rights can be disputable whether they are commercial, domestic, or of any other type.[104] Again, the *Qur'an* says: "In most of their secret talks there is no good, but if one exhorts to a deed of charity or goodness or conciliation between people [then secrecy is permissible]...".[105]

7.6.4 Concept of arbitration in the Sunnah

Prophet Muhammad as earlier stated had been a vanguard of arbitration even before the mission of Islam. This fact was confirmed when he and his followers migrated and settled in Medinah. In the first Charter of Medinah, arbitration was expressly provided for with a view to settling disputes among the confederating communities of this historical city. Prophet Muhammad was the author of this Charter.

In a Hadith narrated by Al-Nssai from Sharih Bin Hani and from his father who said that when he came to the Prophet (pbuh) along with his people, he (the Prophet) heard them saying: "Hani, father, Arbitrator". The Prophet called him and said: "God is the arbitrator, so why do they call you, father, and arbitrator?" Hani replied: "when my people disagree about something, they come to me to act as an arbitrator between them". The Prophet said: "then, that is good".[106] It is argued that the Prophet's acknowledgment of Hani's arbitral status recognized by his people is a clear evidence of the legality of the practice of arbitration.[107]

7.6.5 Arbitration among Islamic Schools of Jurisprudence

Majority of Muslim scholars agree on the legality of arbitration. Opinions differ only on the definition and scope of its application. A cross-section view arbitration as a type of non-compulsory conciliation while another section sees arbitration as similar to conventional judicial decision, fair and binding on the parties.

103 Ibid at p. 50.

104 Ibid.

105 *Qur'an* 4:114 (Emphasis added).

106 Narrated by Al Nissai in Judicial Authority Ethics, see Ibrahim Atta, I. (*Al Tahkim fi Alfgha), The Arbitration*, Riyadh: Imam bin Saud University (1990), p. 120 and Hadith narrated by Imam Mohamed Bin Ismail Al Bukhari, died 256 H, Arab Republic Library, Mohamed Sabih & Sons Printing Press, Egypt, Vol. 4 p. 212, narrated by Imam Muslim Al Nissaburi (died 261 H) Arab Republic Library, Mohamed Sabiha & Sons Printing Press, Egypt, vol. 5, p. 133.

107 Al-Jarba, M.A.H., supra note no. 99 at p. 51.

It follows that the validity of arbitration is unequivocal in Islam and the duty to reconcile the parties is imposed on anyone resolving disputes between disputing parties.

7.6.5.1 The Hanafi School

Jurists of the Hanafi School hold that arbitration is a valid process of attaining justice in the light of the primary and secondary sources of law in Islam. Arbitration is a legitimate dispute resolution process because it serves an important social need, and it simplifies dispute resolution. It is also less complex than the conventional court judicial processes.[108] They emphasize the contractual nature of arbitration and contend that it is binding like any contract. Thus, arbitrator has the same duties as a judge, but the former is closer to an agent or conciliator.[109]

On the scope of arbitration, the Hanafi School holds two views. One, arbitration is permitted in all subject matters except *Hudud* and *Qisas*. Second, arbitration is permitted in the case of murder by error.[110] In the former, *Hudud* is crimes against God with fixed punishments set by God Himself and well established in the *Qur'an* and *Sunnah*.[111] This is based on the contentions that since *Hudud* are crimes against God they could not be arbitrated upon. *Qisas*, on the other hand, are crimes committed against other human beings, the victims of such crimes or their heirs have the right to decide on the punishment, and on whether or not to execute it.[112] Jurists of this School emphasize the contractual nature of arbitration holding that it is binding like any other contract.[113] The School, however, stresses the close connection between arbitration and conciliation. Thus, to this School, an arbitral award more closely approximates conciliation than a court judgment, and, consequently, is of lesser force than a court judgment.[114]

7.6.5.2 The Shafi'i School

The Shafi'i School upholds the validity of arbitration but notes that an arbitrator is inferior to a judge as the arbitrator could be removed at any time

108 Al-Ramahi, A., *Sulh: A Crucial Part of Islamic Arbitration*, London School of Economics and Political Science, Law Department, http://ssrn.com/abstract=[1153659] (accessed 6 December 2013).

109 Ibid.

110 Baamir, A.R., supra note no. 76 at p. 75.

111 Ibid.

112 Ibid.

113 Al-Ramahi, A., *Sulh: A Crucial Part of Islamic Arbitration*, Islamic Law and Law of the Muslim World, Research Paper Series at New York Law School, No. 08-45 (2008), p. 15, http://eprints.lse.ac.uk/24598/1/WPS2008-12_Al-Ramahi.pdf (accessed 19 November 2014).

114 Gemmell, A.J., 'Commercial Arbitration in the Islamic Middle East', *Santa Clara Journal of International Law* Vol. 5, No. 1 (2006), p. 175 quoting Al-Qurashi, Z., 'Arbitration under the Islamic Sharia', *Oil, Gas and Energy Law Intelligence*, Vol. 1, No. 2 (2003), para. 4.1.

by the parties before an award is rendered.[115] Scholars of this School maintain that it is permitted for the parties involved in arbitration to choose an ordinary person that does not possess any of the judge's qualities to resolve the dispute, whether or not there is a judge available in the place where the dispute arose.[116]

A cross-section of Shafi'i jurists rejects the validity of arbitration especially when there is a court within the jurisdiction where a case requires judicial trail. It is reasoned that arbitration might diminish the authority of the court.[117] Another group of Shafi'i scholars put arbitration on the same pedestal as courts and thus the same scope and power as litigation. Another group allows arbitration to proceed in all subject matters except in criminal disputes.[118] Shafi'i School maintains that the binding force of an arbitral award finds its basis in the agreement of the parties, such that after the verdict and award of the arbitral tribunal, parties' consent is necessary for its enforcement.[119]

7.6.5.3 The Maliki School

This school places arbitration as one of the highest forms of dispute resolution. It contends that an arbitrator decides a case based on his conscience; therefore, it allows one of the disputing parties to be appointed as an arbitrator if he was chosen by the other party.[120] This School differs from others by contending that an arbitrator cannot be revoked after the commencement of arbitration proceedings. An arbitration award is binding on the parties except if a judge declares it to be flagrantly unjust.[121]

The Maliki School restricts the application of arbitration to commercial matters only, contending that cases involving any matter that are not monetary in nature must be decided by a judge.[122] This School does not however restrict the terms of reference of the arbitral panel. To that extent, if an arbitrator grants a valid award or judgment on a matter that is beyond his jurisdiction, the judgement would be valid subject to the ratification of a court judge; despite that, he would be cautioned not to do it again.[123]

115 Al Mawardi, *Adab Al Kadi*, T. II, Baghdad: *Ri`asah Diwan al-Awqaf*, University of Malaya (1971), p. 382.
116 Ibid.
117 Baamir, A.R., supra note no. 76 at p. 76.
118 Ibid.
119 Jalal El-Ahdab, A.H., *Arbitration with the Arab Countries*, Netherlands: Kluwer Law International (2011), p. 48.
120 Cunningham, R.B., and Sarayrah, Y.K., *Wasta: The Hidden Forces in Middle Eastern Society*, London: Praeger (1993), p. 19.
121 Al-Ramahi, A., supra note no. 110.
122 Baamir, A.R., supra note no. 76 at pp. 76.
123 Ibn Farhoun, B., *Tabsirat Alhokkam Fi Usul Alaqdiyah Wa Manahij Alahkam* (edited by Taha Abdulraouf Sa'd, 1st edn) Maktabat Alkolliyat Al-Azhariyah (1986), Vol. 1. p. 43.

7.6.5.4 The Hanbali School

The Hanbali School equates arbitration to the conventional court system. It holds that the decision of the arbitrator has the same binding force as a court judgment. An arbitrator must have the same qualification as a judge and must be chosen by the parties.[124] A cross-section of Hanbali jurists does not however, allow arbitration in criminal matters on the argument that the nature of criminal cases is different from that of commercial disputes. It is noted that Ibn Taymiyyah who is a notable model for this School did not restrict the scope of arbitration and he gave it the same scope as conventional litigation. He, however, contended that an arbitral award has no value without judicial review, which is the same concept followed by the Saudi legal system today.[125]

7.7 Basic rules of arbitration in Islamic jurisprudence

There are three important elements for an arbitration to be valid under Islamic jurisprudence. They are: (a) parties to arbitration (arbitratees and arbitrators); (b) offer and acceptance; and (c) subject matter of arbitration.[126] Details of these elements are adequately discussed in several texts and papers published by experts on the subject.[127] However, due to its critical connection to these elements, enforcement requires some details.

7.7.1 Enforcement of arbitration award under Islamic law

Under Islamic law, an award is enforceable and binding on the parties from the moment it becomes final and has the same effects and power as a court judgment.[128] It loses its objectives of resolving dispute if arbitral award lack enforceability.[129] Some jurists hold that the disputants are required to give approval to the award of the arbitration.[130] However, this is debatable. It is

124 Cunningham, R.B., and Sarayrah, Y.K., supra note no. 122 at p. 20.

125 Al-Kenain, A., *Al-Tahkim fi Al-Shari'a Al-Islamiyyah: Al-Tahkim Al-'Am, wa Al-Tahkim fi Al-Shiqaq Al-Zaouji* (1st edn) Riyadh: Dar Al-Asimah (2000), p. 49.

126 Al-Jarba, M.A.H., supra note no. 99 at p. 60.

127 See for example Fraje, A.R., *Sources of Obligation, Memoires for Students of Law*, Riyadh: College of Administrative Sciences, Department of Law, King Saud University (1404H – 1932 AD), p. 22. El Hadab, A.H., *Arbitration with Arab Countries* (1st edn), The Netherland: Kluwer Law and Taxation Publisher Deventer (1990), p. 35; Ramadan, S., *Islamic Law, Its Scope and Equity* (2nd edn), Malaysia: Muslim Youth Movement of Malaysia (1970), p. 152 Op. Cit. P. 152. Aboul-Enein, M.I M., 'Liberal Trends in Islamic Law (Shari'a) on the Peaceful Settlement of Disputes', Papers Presented to the Seminar of (The Practice of International Arbitration), *Oxford* (July 13th 1999), p. 22; Atta, I., supra note no. 108 at p. 113; Saleh, S., *Commercial Arbitration in the Middle East* (1st edn) London: Graham of Trotman Limited (1984), p. 36; Vogel, F.E., *Islamic Law and the Legal System*, Netherlands: Brill (2000), p. 31.

128 Baamir, A.R., supra note no. 76 at p. 91.

129 Al-Kenain, A., supra note no. 127 at pp. 141–145.

130 Ibid.

noted that arbitral award is enforceable if it is correct and free from questionable reasons after being revised by the concerned judicial authority.[131] Vincent Powell-Smith argues that the award has the binding effects as the judgment of the judge according to majority view.[132]

It is noted that in modern conventional arbitral rules, disputing parties are free to challenge the award within a specified period. Despite that, after a final award has been decided, it cannot be nullified even if it is proved not to be valid.[133] Under Islamic law, the judicial award is given the power of enforceability and an appeal against the award is not generally accepted unless there is adequate proof of fresh evidence which would then lead to a review.[134]

The substance of arbitral award is not different from any conventional court judgement. However, it is expected to sufficiently describe the merits and the dispute at issue, the findings of fact substantiated by principles of Islamic law of evidence, the juristic rational from *Usul al-Fiqh* with references to the basic sources of law and the final judgement arrived at. Any decision that lacks the composite elements described above will be unacceptable.[135] The arbitrators are free to carry out material correction in the award from the time of its issuance until it is referred to the court for an enforcement order.[136]

A judicial award that complies with the basic rules of law has several judicial implications, namely, that an award issued by a court of competent jurisdiction cannot be modified by another judge. This is the position of the Hanbali School, especially if the issuing judge is knowledgeable and just.[137] Thus, Ibn Qudamah remarks that "the arbitrator should not [merely] follow the decisions of his former judges or arbitrators because those decisions are true and correct".[138] Jurists of Shafi'i and Maliki Schools agree with this position. They argue that the judge is not allowed to consider the award of former judges basing their argument on the fact that a judge is not allowed to concern himself with past cases, rather, he should focus on the case at hand; an attempt to do that would amount to an affront to the judges who formally sat on the case and this should not occur within the judicial hierarchy.[139]

Judges are not capable of renouncing awards they have earlier decided simply because of the latest experience in the subject matter of disputes. It is argued that

131 Al-Jarba, M.A.H., supra note no. 99 at p. 307.

132 Powell-Smith, V., *Aspects of Arbitration Common Law Shari'a Compared*, Printed by Success Label Enterprise (1995), p. 60.

133 Al-Jarba, M.A.H., supra note no. 99 at p. 311.

134 Ibid at p. 310.

135 Baamir, A.R., supra note no. 76 at p. 91.

136 See generally Al-Kenain, A., *Tasbeeb Alahkam Al-Qadaiyah fi Al-Shari'a Al-Islamiyyah* (1st edn), Riyadh: Dar Ibn Farhoon (1999).

137 Baamir, A.R., supra note no. 76 at p. 312.

138 Ibn Qodamah, *Al-Mugni* (The Preacher), General Directorate of Scientific Research Administration, Saudi Arabia (n.d.), Vol. 9, p. 58.

139 Yassen, M., *Hajeyat Al-Hokem Al-Qadai* (Validity of Judicial Award in Islamic Jurisprudence) (1st edn), Jordan: Dr. Alfargan Press (1984), p. 15.

he could not do so even if he realizes a mistake has been made or it has deviated from the basic rules of Islamic jurisprudence.[140]

If a judicial award is in conformity with the *Qur'an*, or the *Sunnah* or *Ijma*, the award becomes enforceable and should not be revoked if the same case is brought before another judge afterwards. The award remains enforceable even if it is refused by the second judge on the argument that "matters of perseverance usually bring about divergent points of view, which should be avoided".[141]

Having said that however, parties to the dispute are at liberty either to accept the arbitral award and implement it, or they may request for further judicial review.[142] The chance of parties to challenge the arbitral award is viewed differently among schools of thoughts. For example, Maliki School considers arbitral awards to be unchallengeable – a judge cannot revoke an award so long it is not inconsistent with the main sources of the *Shari'ah*, except however, if it is seriously biased or partial.[143] The Hanbali School holds that an arbitral award has the same effect as a conventional court decision and can be revoked under the same condition applicable to a court judgment. Thus, the School recognizes the possibility of revoking an arbitral award in cases where the award is not in conformity with the appellant's *madhhab*, or School.[144] The Shafi'i School holds that the arbitral award has the same effect as a court judgment, in which case the judge must treat the arbitral award in the same way as any other judgment. Secondly, an arbitral award would only be enforceable if both parties agreed to it.[145] This position arguably renders arbitration status closer to a form of conciliation or mediation.[146]

Part III

7.8 International commercial arbitration in Saudi Arabia

Consequent to the emergence of oil booms, most parts of the Muslim world, particularly Saudi Arabia has become a focal point of many investors from various parts of the world. Thus, the culture of arbitration had started to take shape and assumed developmental dimension. Bahrain, for example, was an international commercial-arbitration centre long before Paris and London.[147]

140 Al-Jarba, M.A.H., supra note no. 99 at p. 312.

141 Ibid at p. 313.

142 Baamir, A.R., supra note no. 76 at p. 91.

143 Ibid.

144 Ibid.

145 Abdul Hamid El-Ahbad, 'The Moslem Arbitration Law', *in Proceedings of the International Bar Association First Arab Regional Conference*, Cairo, February 1987, Vol. 1, p. 341.

146 Moens, G., *International Trade & Business Annual*, University of Queensland, London: Cavendish Publishing USA (2003), p. 200.

147 Ali Radhi, H., 'State Courts and Arbitration in the Gulf Cooperation Council (GCC) Countries', *ICC International Committee on Arbitration Bulletin*, Vol. 57, No. 5 (May 1992), Spec. Supp., at p. 57.

Three developmental stages of arbitration justice in the Middle East region had been identified.[148] The first stage, from the end of World War II to the 1970s, was a time when Islamic domestic laws were undermined and negated and the "superior" Western laws were imposed in the arbitration of long-term oil concession disputes.[149] The second developmental stage was typified by combination of some factors which include, *inter alia*, post colonialism that was marked by the emergence of nationalism; rise against capitalism, and increasing oil fortunes.[150] The third and current stage is marked by flourishing participation in, and promotion of, the international arbitration movement by Muslim majority states.[151]

7.8.1 The dawn of international arbitral norms in Saudi Arabia

Before the era of oil boom, commercial arbitration had existed in the Saudi legal system as far back as the period of enacting the Code of Commercial Courts in 1931.[152] Despite that, international arbitration was simply, at that time, a "taboo". For example, in the classic case of *Wahat Al-Buraim* (Buraimi Oasis Case,)[153] Saudi Government was averse to using international arbitration. The proceedings of this international arbitration case took place in Jeddah and the British Government was acting on behalf of the ruler of Abu Dhabi and the Sultan of Oman. According to the terms of agreement between the parties, a tribunal consisting of five members was to be set up. The purpose was to determine and settle the dispute arising from the disagreement on the location of common border between Saudi Arabia and Abu Dhabi, and as to the sovereignty of the *Buraimi Oasis*. The tribunal was to take due cognizance of all relevant laws, fact, and equity, and particularly to the historical rights of the rulers in the area: the traditional loyalties, tribal organization, and way of life of the inhabitants of the area as well as the exercise of jurisdiction and other relevant issues.[154]

Much as this case could be a landmark in the history of international arbitration in Saudi Arabia, it is noted that it did not have a significant impact on the Kingdom's legal and judicial systems. It was later that the impact began to manifest in a staggering manner.[155] The hope of advancing the norms of international arbitration in the Kingdom of Saudi Arabia was dashed in 1958. It was in this year that the celebrated case of *ARAMCO v. Saudi Arabia*[156] came to the consideration of an international arbitration body. The arbitral decision and

148 See generally, Brower, C.N., and Sharper, J.K., supra note no. 95 at pp. 643–656; and Kutty, F., supra note no. 2.

149 Brower, C.N., and Sharper, J.K., ibid at p. 643.

150 Ibid at p. 645.

151 Ibid at p. 646.

152 Baamir, A.R., supra note no. 76 at p. 95.

153 (1954) HMSO Cmd 9272, cited in Kelly, J.B., 'The Buraimi Oasis Dispute', *International Affairs*, Vol. 32, No. 3 (July 1956), pp. 318–324; Baamir, A.R., ibid at p. 95.

154 Kelly, J.B., ibid.

155 Baamir, A.R., supra note no. 76 at p. 95.

156 (1963), 27 ILR, 117.

award in this case was considered by the Saudi Government as an affront to its much-cherished culture and legal system.

The *ARAMCO v. Saudi Arabia* was a celebrated arbitration case relating to the interpretation of a concession agreement made on 29 May 1933, between Saudi Arabia and the Standard Oil Company of California. The agreement was subsequently assigned to the California Arabian Standard Oil Company, which later changed its name to the Arabian American Oil Company (ARAMCO). On 20 January 1954 the Government of Saudi Arabia concluded an agreement with Mr. A. S. Onassis and his company, Saudi Arabian Maritime Tankers Ltd. (SATCO), by virtue of Articles 4 and 15 of which the Company was given a 30 years' "right of priority" for the transport of Saudi Arabia oil.[157] The point of contention in the present case was the conflict arising from the provisions of the Agreement with SATCO and the one with ARAMCO, which gave the latter the exclusive right to transport the oil which it had extracted from its concession area in Saudi Arabia.[158]

Under Article 5 of the agreement with SATCO, Saudi Arabia was obliged to enact a Maritime Law. But Articles 4 and 15 of the same agreement stipulated that the SATCO had the right of priority for the transport of oil for a period of 30 years from the date of signing the agreement, renewable for a further period by mutual agreement.[159] Disagreement arose when the Saudi Arabia Government ordered ARAMCO to apply Royal Decree No. 5737 of 9 April 1954, which ratified the Onassis agreement concluded on 20 January 1954. This Royal decree granted the Onassis Agreement a legal status like the ARAMCO concession agreement of 1933.

The focal point of the dispute for arbitration was to determine the rights that were conferred on SOCC (in the ARAMCO Concession Agreement), since the Government contends that the exclusive right of transportation by sea was not included within the expectations of the parties as no express stipulation to that effect is to be found in the Agreement. In its Final Memorial, the Government stated that this question was of the highest importance. The question was thus, in the first place, one of Interpretation of the Concession.[160]

ARAMCO contended that although the Concession Agreement related to the *Hanbali* School of Islamic jurisprudence applicable in Saudi Arabia and from which it derives its validity and effectiveness, the interpretation of this agreement should not be based on that law alone. It stated that:

> interpretation of contracts is not governed by rigid rules; it is rather an art, governed by principles of logic and common sense, which purports to lead to an adaptation, as reasonable as possible, of the provisions of a contract to the facts of a dispute.[161]

157 See TRANS-LEX, Saudi Arabia v. Arabian American Oil Company (ARAMCO), www.trans-lex.org/260800/_/aramco-award-ilr-1963-at-117-et-seq/ (accessed 01 December 2013).

158 Ibid.

159 (1963), 27 ILR, 117 at p. 128.

160 TRANS-LEX, Saudi Arabia v. Arabian American Oil Company (ARAMCO), ibid.

161 Ibid.

Saudi Arabia contended that in addition to the principles of Islamic and international law, the general principles of law recognized by civilized nations do not support the contention that the concession agreement of 1933 exempts ARAMCO from the regulatory power of Saudi Arabia Government. According to Article 4 of the agreement, the arbitral tribunal would have to decide on the dispute in accordance with Saudi Arabian law insofar as matters fell within the jurisdiction of Saudi Arabia. The tribunal would be free to decide the applicable law where matters were outside the jurisdiction of Saudi Arabia.[162] It is noted that the parties agreed to apply the principles of Islamic law according to the Hanbali School.

The Arbitral Panel decided *inter alia* that the regime of mining concessions, and, consequently, also of oil concessions, has remained embryonic in Muslim law and is not the same in the different schools. The principles of one School cannot be introduced into another unless this is done by the act of authority. Hanbali law contains no precise rule about mining concessions and [is] *a fortiori* about oil concessions.[163] The Arbitral Panel explained further that Saudi laws had to be "interpreted or supplemented by the general principles of law, by the custom and practice in the oil business and by notions of pure jurisprudence", because ARAMCO's rights could not be "secured in an unquestionable manner by the law in force in Saudi Arabia".[164] In other words, the arbitral tribunal's position implied that the applicable law (Saudi Law) was not sufficient and that it should be complemented by other sources of law. Thus, the arbitral award was granted in ARAMCO's favour.

Al-Jarba, Mohammad, a Saudi scholar, has observed that

> it does appear that the arbitral award mentioned in the case of ARAMCO was not valid since it discarded the Saudi law and did not include ways of solving the existing dispute. It was noted that the inability to infer awards of jurisprudence from their origins does not necessarily mean that they are non-existent.[165]

He further noted that the combined effects of the arbitral decision in ARAMCO case as well as other cases involving Arab and Gulf countries, the attitude of Saudi Arabia's government towards arbitration not only changed but also underwent "radical reform".[166]

Abdul Rahman Yahya Baamir, another Saudi scholar, remarks that the arbitral panel erred in holding that Saudi law has no rules governing oil concessions, saying that if the Hanbali School lacks legal rules capable of governing

162 Baamir, A.R., supra note no. 76 at p. 102.

163 (1963), 27 ILR, 117 at pp. 162–163.

164 Kutty, F., supra no. 2 at p. 592.

165 Al-Jarba, M., *Commercial Arbitration, A Study of Its Role in the Saudi Arabia within Islamic Jurisprudence*, Aberystwyth: The University of Wales (2001), p. 92.

166 Ibid at p. 93.

the concession agreement, the tribunal should have considered other Schools through the method of *Qiyas* [or *takhayyur*][167] and by so doing, the issue should have been resolved within the confine of Islamic law. He further argues that the applicable rules to the exploitation of hidden wealth such as gold and silver, which have been extensively regulated under Islamic law right from the early period of Islam, should have been applied to oil and gas by means of *Qiyas* (analogical deduction).[168]

7.8.2 Aftermath of ARAMCO on arbitration in Saudi Arabia

The ARAMCO case transfigured the hitherto Saudi authority's lukewarm attitude towards arbitration, and particularly international commercial arbitration. Thus, it came out with an official policy forbidding government entity from accepting arbitration as a method of resolving disputes with third parties. This policy was expressly stated in the Council of Ministers Resolution No. 58 of 1963.[169] This Resolution was supplemented by the Ministry of Commerce Circular of 1979 which put some restrictions on acceptance of arbitration clauses and agreements.

Another Ministry of Commerce supplementary circular[170] declared that a clause providing for arbitration (outside the Kingdom) as stipulated in the Articles of Association of Saudi companies would be considered null and void. Such Articles of Association would neither be approved nor registered.[171] It follows that reference can be made to domestic arbitration in the articles of association of a jointly formed company of foreign and local businessmen for the purpose of carrying out investment operations in Saudi Arabia.

Another impact of the ARAMCO case was the emergence of the Organization of Petroleum Exporting Countries (OPEC).[172] Fran Hendryx, former Venezuelan Oil Minister, was one of the authors of the OPEC concept. He was also a former ARAMCO legal adviser to the Saudi Arabian Directorate General of Petroleum and Mineral Affairs.[173] OPEC is an oil cartel whose mission is to coordinate the policies of the oil-producing countries. The goal is to secure a steady income to the member states and to secure supply of oil to the consumers.[174] OPEC was also established to enhance national sovereignty over natural resources and profit-sharing with the foreign concessionaires. It was proposed that all petroleum agreements should be periodically re-negotiated when they no

167 The practice of choosing which rules to follow from various schools of thought http://financial-dictionary.thefreedictionary.com/Takhayyur (accessed 25 November 2014).
168 Baamir, A.R., supra note no. 76 at p. 103.
169 Council of Ministers Resolution No. 58 dated 17/1/1383H (25/6/1963).
170 The Ministry of Commerce Circular No. 31/1/331/91 of 1979.
171 Ibid.
172 Baamir, A.R., supra note no. 76 at p. 108.
173 Ibid.
174 "*Our Mission*" www.opec.org/opec_web/en/about_us/23.htm (accessed 23 December 2013).

longer suit one of the parties, or when conditions change to such a degree that the agreement becomes out-dated.[175]

7.9 New phases of arbitration norms in Saudi Arabia

As part of efforts towards attracting foreign investors, Saudi Arabia introduced some legislative reforms as incentive to foreign investors and industrialists from abroad. It first joined the International Centre for Settlement of Investment Disputes (ICSID) in 1970/1980. It also promulgated the Arbitration Acts of 1983, ratified the New York Convention on the enforcement and recognition of foreign arbitral awards of 1958. It also played a significant role in the establishment of regional commercial and investment organizations, including, GCC Commercial Arbitration Centre, giving effect to some regional arbitration-related conventions and adopting several bilateral investment agreements.[176] Before examining Saudi Arabia membership of regional and international arbitral bodies, it is pertinent to discuss its Arbitration Act of 1983.

7.9.1 Saudi Arabia Arbitration Act of 1983

The Arbitration Act of 1983 was introduced essentially to repeal the related provisions in the Code of Commercial Courts of 1931.[177] It is a codification of the Hanbali rules of arbitration providing a framework for commercial arbitral disputes settlement in a flexible manner.[178] The relevant Hanbali rules were those elaborated by Ibn Taymiyyah in his collection of *Fatawas*,[179] and Ibn Qudamah in his comprehensive work *Almughni*.[180] The Act serves two important objectives, namely, to provide a comprehensive, uniform set of rules which are accessible to foreign business persons and their legal counsels with a view to allay their fears over the previous lack of judicial and legislative support for commercial arbitration.[181] It also established governmental control over arbitration procedures in general as well as over the actual arbitration proceedings by providing for supervision by governmental agencies, courts, or perhaps the Chambers of Commerce and Industry.[182]

175 Duguid, S., 'A Biographical Approach to the Study of Social Change in the Middle East: Abdullah Tariki as a New Man', *International Journal of Middle East Studies*, Vol. 1, No. 3 (1970), p. 195.

176 Ibid at pp. 109–110.

177 Ibid at p. 111.

178 Ibid.

179 Ibn Taymiyyah, M., *Majmoou' Alfatawa* (2nd edn), Riyadh: Ministry of Islamic Affairs of Saudi Arabia (1995), Vol. 29.

180 Ibn Qodamah, M., *Almoghni* (1st edn), United Kingdom: Hajar Publications (1992), Vol. 10.

181 Sayen, G., supra note no. 88 at p. 912; see also, Allam, *Saudi Arabia/Arbitration in the Kingdom: The New Implementation Rules*, Middle East Executive Rep. (August 1985) p. 9.

182 Saudi Arabia Regulation on Arbitration – Royal Decree M/46 of 7/12/1403H (April 25, 1983), reprinted in 9 Year Boom Commercial Arbitration 316-18 (1984) (Implementing Rules –

Three aspects of the procedure established by the Act have caused serious concern to experts in international arbitration. In the first instance, while the Regulation recognizes the validity of a contractual clause calling for arbitration of future disputes, it is not clear how such a clause is to be enforced if it happens that one party declines to cooperate when a dispute arises. Also, it cannot be clearly determined the extent to which Saudi law must be applied to the substance of the dispute; and, the Regulation does not specify the grounds on which the Authority may set aside or refuse to execute an award.[183] The Arbitration Act is silent on a number of procedural issues such as the rules pertaining to the delivery of arbitral awards, notifications as to the process and communication between the parties and the arbitral tribunal and between the arbitral tribunal and third parties, the seat of the arbitral tribunal and others.[184]

The Act contains 25 Articles making provisions for a wide range of issues relating to arbitral disputes. It provides for two types of arbitration agreements, namely, where parties may agree either "to arbitrate a specific existing dispute" or to make a "prior agreement to arbitrate...any dispute resulting from the performance of a specific contract".[185] It is also observed that the binding effect of an arbitration clause under Article 5 is ambiguous in view of the fact that parties to a dispute are required to file an arbitration "document" or "instrument" with the Authority for validation when a dispute arises. This is because this instrument is expected to contain the names of arbitrator(s) and their acquiescence to hear the dispute and its details which must be signed by both parties. The question arises as what happens if a party, having agreed in advance to arbitration of any disputes arising from a specific contract, refuses to cooperate in the preparation of an arbitration instrument when a dispute actually arises. Thus, experts interpret the provisions under this Article and reached different conclusions regarding the legal effects, by itself, or an agreement to arbitrate future disputes.[186]

Details of matters relating to arbitral awards and their enforceability are contained in the provision under Articles 15–21. Arbitration experts in the Western world contend that there are ambiguities in some of these provisions particularly Article 19.[187]

It will be recalled that following the decision in the ARAMCO case the Saudi authority outlawed any attempt to resort to arbitration by all government

Council of Ministers Resolution No. 7 of 8/9/1405H (May 27, 1985), Sayen, G., supra in its footnote no. 21.

183 Sayen, G., supra note no. 88 at p. 913.

184 Baamir, A.R., supra note no. 76 at p. 117.

185 Article 1 of the Arbitration Act (Royal Decree M/46).

186 Sayen, G., supra note no. 88 at p. 914.

187 Ibid at p. 917.

agencies without prior approval from the Council of Ministers.[188] This policy had remained in effect in spite of the fact that Saudi Arabia ratified, in 1980, the International Convention for Settlement of Investment Disputes between States and Citizens of another State (ICSID), which provides for arbitration under the auspices of the World Bank.[189] An ICSID arbitration clause has never been approved by the Council of Ministers.[190] Commercial arbitration was not governed by a comprehensive set of rules until the enactment of 1983 Arbitration Law.[191] As a result of this lack of clear procedures and judicial support, George Sayen notes that arbitration between private parties has been sporadic, explaining that the arbitration rules agreed on by the parties in advance were not enforced and it was unclear how awards were to be enforced, especially if they were rendered outside of Saudi Arabia.[192]

In what analysts describe as a turning point, Saudi Arabia began to ratify international and regional arbitration conventions and thus, began to enforce arbitral awards in observance of those conventions. These include the 1958 New York Convention on the Recognition and Enforcement of Foreign Arbitral Awards; The 1965 Washington Convention; Convention approved by the Council of the Arab League Countries on 14/9/1952; The 1983 Riyadh Convention for Judicial Cooperation; The 1987 Aman Convention for International Commercial Arbitration; and The 1993 International Commercial Arbitration System in Arbitration Centre for GCC.

7.9.2 The New York Convention – Saudi Arabia as a signatory

As earlier noted, the globalized economy has led to a phenomenal growth in commercial disputes cutting across national borders, adding to a complex dimension of interpreting commercial agreements and practices.[193] Consequently, the need to adopt a uniform international arbitration system that requires the systematic and effective enforcement of international arbitral awards became

188 Royal Government of Saudi Arabia Gazette, *reprinted in* Van den Berg, *supra* note 14, at 15 [hereinafter Resolution].

189 The Saudi government ratified the ICSID Convention on 7 June 7 1980. Convention of the Settlement of Investment Disputes Between States and Nationals of Other States, *opened for signature*, 18 March 1965, 17 U.S.T. 1270, T.I.A.S. No. 6690, 575 U.N.T.S. 160; *see* Van den Berg, *supra*, at 15; *see also* Chaudhri and Clodfelter, supra note no. 185 at p. 9.

190 Saudi ratification of ICSID "reserves the right of not submitting all questions pertaining to oil and pertaining to acts of sovereignty" for arbitration or conciliation under ICSID. *See* Alison, L., and Mian, A.J., *Saudi Business and Labour Law: Its Interpretation and Application*, London: Graham & Trotman (1982), pp. 181–182.

191 Rules of Saudi Arabia Commercial Court Regulation – Royal Decree M/32 of 1/15/1350 AH (1931 AD) – formally repealed in 1983.

192 Sayen, G., 'Arbitration, Conciliation, and The Islamic Legal Tradition in Saudi Arabia', *University of Pennsylvania Journal of International Economic Law*, Vol. 24, No. 4 (2003), p. 911, quoting with approval, Saba, *Saudi Arabia Investment Climate: Its Risks and Returns*, Middle East Executive Rep. (1986), at I, pp. 16–19.

193 Behr, V., supra note no. 1 at p. 211.

more pronounced.[194] The New York Convention came on board requiring all signatories to recognize and enforce foreign arbitral awards.[195] At the initial stage of promulgating this Convention, many countries viewed the development as yet another intrusion of international norms into their domestic affairs and thus hesitant to be signatories.[196]

Saudi Arabia was known for its reserved attitude to recognizing and enforcing non-domestic arbitral awards on the justification that these awards were contrary to its law (Islamic law) and public policy.[197] However, when it adopted the New York Convention, there was a wide-spread feeling that it has eventually come to relax its aged-long historical resistance to international commercial arbitration.[198] At the same time, it had the belief that Article 5(2)(b) of the Convention will serve as a safety-valve against any attempt of foreign arbitral awards violating its law and public policy.[199] Following this ratification, Saudi Arabia became the 94th party to the Convention, which requires all signatories to recognize the arbitration agreements and awards[200] issued by other member nations.[201]

7.9.3 Enforcement of foreign arbitral awards in Saudi Arabia

An arbitral award issued outside Saudi Arabian jurisdiction relating to a non-domestic dispute will be considered foreign. Furthermore, if the arbitral award relating to a domestic dispute is issued outside Saudi Arabia, it will be also considered foreign. It follows that in both cases, the provisions of the New York Convention will apply.[202] Saudi Arabia bases enforcement of foreign awards under its jurisdiction on three important principles, namely, (i) the principle of conformity with Islamic *Shari'ah*; (ii) the principle of reciprocity under international law; and (iii) the content of international conventions which Saudi Arabia has ratified.[203]

Regarding the conformity with the *Shari'ah*, it is perceived that since the applicable law in the Kingdom is the Islamic *Shari'ah* any arbitral award that

194 Strub, Jr., M. H., supra note no. 64 at pp. 1031–1032; Westin, D., 'Enforcing Foreign Commercial Judgment and Arbitral Awards in the United States, West Germany, and England', *Law and Policy in International Business*, Vol. 19 (1987), p. 325.

195 Convention on the Recognition and Enforcement of Foreign Arbitral Awards, 10 June 1958, 21 U.S.T. 2517, 330 U.N.T.S. 38 [hereinafter New York Convention]; *see International Legal Framework*, 1 World Arb. Rep. 1, 37 (1994) (listing accession dates for all New York Convention signatories).

196 Strub, Jr., M. H., supra note no. 64 at pp. 1038–1039.

197 *Saudis Accept New York Convention*, Dispute Resolution Journal (1994), p. 26 [hereinafter *Saudis Accept]*.

198 Ibid.

199 Roy, K.T., supra note no. 65.

200 Strub, Jr., M. H., 'Resisting Enforcement of Foreign Arbitral Awards under Article V (1)(E) and Article VI of the New York Convention: A Proposal for Effective Guidelines', *Texas Law Review*, Vol. 68 (1990), p. 1031.

201 Article III, New York Convention.

202 Baamir, A.R., supra note no. 76 at p. 141.

203 Al-Jarba, M., supra note no. 99.

violates any of its principles is null and void. The Saudi Board of Grievances is saddled with the responsibility of determining the conformity or otherwise of any award with the rules of the *Shari'ah*. Apparently, this is the intendment of Article 20 of the 1983 Saudi Law of Arbitration.[204]

This position was articulated in the decision of the Saudi Arabia Board of Grievances in two arbitration cases. The cases are: (1) No. 1903/1/9 of 1414 H (1994) and (2) No. 1851/1/9 of 1414 H (1994).[205] In the two cases, the awards contained some claims that were partly in conformity with the Islamic *Shari'ah* and partly in its violation. The parts that violated the Islamic rules were in respect of usury (interest). Interest has been widely argued to be unacceptable in Saudi Arabia as it is contrary to the Islamic *Shari'ah*. Those parts that conformed to the applicable *Shari'ah* rules in Saudi Arabia were duly enforced.[206]

The principle of reciprocity was articulated in a Royal Decree[207] following Saudi Arabia's ratification of the 1958 New York Convention.[208] The Kingdom declared, according to Article 1 (1) paragraph 3 of the convention that the basis of reciprocity will apply to what the convention regards as recognition and enforcement of arbitral awards in another contracting country.[209] This was inferred in a general declaration made by the President of the Saudi Board of Grievances when he stated that: "The party requesting enforcement of the foreign arbitral award must prove that the country to which he belongs abides by the principle of reciprocity as Saudi Arabia…".[210]

Under the principle of reciprocity, the Saudi Board of Grievances has implemented three judicial awards issued by the British High Court of Justice.[211] The Saudi Board of Grievances issued the enforcement order in favour of these

204 Royal Decree No. M/46, 12 Rajab 1403 (25 April 1983).

205 Efforts to get the reports of these and other related cases from the Saudi Arabia Board of Grievances in Riyadh proved abortive after official letters addressed to the President of the Board by the King Faisal Centre for Research and Islamic Studies in Riyadh (on behalf of this author) were neither acknowledged nor replied.

206 Al-Jarba, M., supra note no. 99.

207 Royal Decree N M/11 dated 16/7/1414H. (29 January 1993) based on Council of Ministers Resolution No. 78 of 1417/1414H (27th January 1993).

208 Saudi Arabia ratified the Convention on 19 April 1994.

209 Article I (1) Paragraph 3 states that:

> When signing, ratifying or acceding to this Convention, or notifying extension under article X hereof, any State may on the basis of reciprocity declare that it will apply the Convention to the recognition and enforcement of awards made only in the territory of another Contracting State. It may also declare that it will apply the Convention only to differences arising out of legal relationships, whether contractual or not, which are considered as commercial under the national law of the State making such declaration.

210 Decision of the President of the Saudi Broad of Grievances, issued on, 15/8/1405 H (5th May 1985). See Al Magsudi, M., and Alamer, A. *Conditions of Executing Arbitral Awards*, King Abdulaziz University, College of Economy and Administration Jeddah (1998), p. 7.

211 Al-Jarba, M., supra note no. 99.

awards based on the testimony of the English Lord Chancellor's Department which emphasized the possibility of executing, in the United Kingdom, awards issued by Saudi Arabia's Courts of Justice. The British Attorney General presented proof that a British Court, in 1985, implemented an award issued by Saudi Arabia.[212] It is noted that the principle of reciprocity must also conform to the principle of the *Shari'ah*.[213] This was stressed in the Procedural Rules before the Saudi Arabia Board of Grievances (*Diwan Al-Mazalim*).[214]

The New York Convention spells out general guideline on the procedure for enforcing foreign arbitral awards. Accordingly, the party applying for recognition and enforcement shall, at the time of the application, supply: (a) the duly authenticated original award or a duly certified copy thereof; (b) the original agreement referred to in article 2 or a duly certified copy thereof. If the said award or agreement is not made in an official language of the country in which the award is relied upon, the party applying for recognition and enforcement of the award shall produce a translation of these documents into such language. The translation shall be certified by an official or sworn translator or by a diplomatic or consular agent.[215] Also, the party applying for recognition and enforcement of arbitral award is bound by the internal procedure of the place of enforcement of the award.[216]

In line with the New York Convention, the Saudi Arabia Board of Grievances is saddled with the responsibility of recognition and enforcement of foreign arbitral awards. It is similarly responsible for the enforcement (in the Kingdom) of judgments issued from the jurisdictions of the Arab Leagues countries.[217] When the Decree establishing the Board of Grievances was repealed, this position was retained and further stipulated that the administrative department of the Board is the competent authority for the enforcement and recognition of foreign arbitral awards in the Kingdom.[218]

Article 13 of the law of Saudi Board of Grievances determines the procedure for filing an application for the enforcement of a foreign arbitral award in Saudi Arabia.[219] This Law requires the party applying for the enforcement of a foreign arbitral award in Saudi Arabia to submit a request for the enforcement of the award in the same way as bringing a new claim before the Board.

The Decree of the Board of Grievances is criticized for several reasons. For example, it has been argued that the idea of *de novo* trial is not only a waste of

212 Alsmaan, Y., *The Role of Arbitration in Settling Investment Disputes*, Ministry of External Affairs, Symposium on Foreign Investment, Conference Institute Diplomatic Studies, Riyadh, 24–25 November, 1997.

213 Al-Jarba, M., supra note no. 99.

214 Council of Ministers Resolution No. 190 dated 16.11.1409 H. (19 July 1989) published in Um Al Qura Newspaper (official state newspaper) issue N 3266 dated 4/12/1409 H (7th August 1989).

215 Article 4 of the New York Convention.

216 Baamir, A.R., supra note no. 76 at p. 141.

217 Royal Decree No. 51/M dated 17/02/1402H (1981).

218 Baamir, A.R., supra note no. 76 at p. 141.

219 Article 13 of the Diwan Al-Mazalim's Circular No. 7 dated 15/05/1405H (1985).

time and money, but also a critical challenge to the authenticity of Arbitration trial as a reliable dispute resolution mechanism.[220] Similarly, it is noted that the law provides remedies in cases where the award is challenged before the Board. However, when it comes to the foreign arbitral awards, those remedies are denied. The law is totally silent on this. Here, the law is criticized for being partial and discriminatory.[221]

As earlier noted, one of the bases upon which Saudi Arabia enforces arbitral awards is the principle of reciprocity.[222] It is noted, however, that the countries that have not ratified the New York Convention are treated differently.[223]

7.9.4 Saudi Arabia and public policy concept of the New York Convention

The New York Convention spells out its principle of public policy in its Article 5(2). Saudi Arabia legal and public policy positions stand out clear in this regard on two issues, namely, interest (*riba*) and speculation (*gharar*) in insurance contracts. The principle of commercial contract recognized under the Hanbali School applicable in Saudi Arabia is considerably different from the principle of contract well-known in the Western legal system.[224] It must be noted that the modern international commercial arbitration rules are greatly Euro-centric. One of the principles that usually conflicts with the Western notion of commercial contract is the issue of usurious interest ("*Riba*").[225] Generally, *riba* is forbidden under Islamic law on the notion that obtaining something for nothing is inherently immoral, oppressive, and wrong.[226] It follows that any contract that charges an unusually high interest rate amounts to *riba*.[227] In other words, building in an excessive profit margin will be void as unethical, repressive, and exploitative.[228] Consequently, a contract containing *riba* as an element will not be enforced by a Saudi Arabian court.[229]

220 Baamir, A.R., supra note no. 76 at p. 142.
221 Ibid.
222 Supra.
223 Baamir, A.R., supra note no. 76 at p. 142.
224 Turck, N.B., 'Dispute Resolution in Saudi Arabia', *22 The International Lawyer,* (1988), pp. 415–442 at 416.
225 Karl, D.J., 'Islamic Law in Saudi Arabia: What Foreign Attorneys Should Know', *25 George Washington Journal of International Law & Economics,* 131 (1992), pp. 131–170 at pp. 151-152; Sloane, P.D., 'The Status of Islamic Law in the Modern Commercial World,', *The International Lawyer,* Vol. 22, No. 3 (1988), pp. 748–749 at p. 745.
226 Coulson, N.J., *Commercial Law in the Gulf States: The Islamic Legal Tradition*, London: Springer (1984), p. 103; Karl, D.J., supra at pp. 152.
227 Sloane, P.D., 'The Status of Islamic Law in the Modern Commercial World,', *The International Lawyer,* Vol. 22, No. 3 (1988), p. 743, at pp. 748–749; Roy, K.T. supra note no. 228.
228 Weeramantry, C.G., *Islamic Jurisprudence: An International Perspective*, London: Macmillan (1988), p. 67.
229 Karl, D.J., supra at p. 152.

Similarly, the Islamic law perspective of risk ("*gharar*") is different from the Western perspective of the concept in relation to contracts of insurance.[230] In this regard, any contract containing speculation or contract clause that turns on the happening of a specified but unsure event is void under the principle of *gharar*.[231] Accordingly, any corporation that intends to have its contract enforceable under the rules and procedures of Saudi Arabia must be specific in all terms of the contract.[232]

Insurance contract, therefore, comes under the speculation practices prohibited by the concept of *Gharar* in Islamic law as it is considered speculative.[233] The rationale behind its prohibition is that the policy-holders do not benefit unless there is a loss, and a loss is not a guaranteed event, the contract is void as being ill-defined or speculative.[234] However, as the Saudi Arabian economy and commerce became amenable to Western investments, the authority began to realize that insurance companies play a major role in modern commerce and industry.[235] Thus, it has relaxed its restrictive policies regarding insurance.[236] Saudi Arabia now allows parties to utilize insurance as an investment tool, so long as the insurance companies invest all insurance profits within the Saudi Arabian territory.[237]

In another instance, the Saudi Arabian attitudinal policy to the remedies awarded for a breach of contract differs from that of the Western legal concept. Judges in the Saudi courts are not bound by the principle of *stare decisis* (precedence).[238] It is thus observed that award and remedies granted by the Saudi Courts are usually inconsistent[239] – a Saudi judge may award the remedy he considers appropriate to the situation, with little or no regard to prior judicial decisions.[240] As *Riba* is forbidden in Islamic law,[241] any arbitral award that grants *Riba* may not be enforceable in Saudi Arabia as this is considered a violation of its public policy. In such cases, Saudi courts may require the entire damages aspect of an arbitration to be reheard, especially where the payment

230 Sloane, P.D., supra note no. 230 at pp. 745–746.

231 Roy, K.T., supra note no. 65 at p. 947.

232 Ibid at p. 948.

233 Sloane, P.D., supra at pp. 749–750.

234 Ibid.

235 Roy, K.T., supra note no. 65 at p. 948.

236 Acker, C.E., 'The Insurance Business', *Middle East Executive Reports Journal* [Washington, D.C.]: Middle East Executive Reports, Ltd. (c1978). Vol. 1, No. 1 (Sept. 1978) - Vol. 25, No. 2 (Feb. 2002). Vol. 1, No. 1 (Sept. 1978) - Vol. 25, No. 2 (Feb. 2002) in (July 1982), p. 25.

237 Acker C.E. notes that the Saudi Arabian authority now requires private insurance companies to invest their profit in land development or business enterprises within the Kingdom of Saudi Arabia". See Roy, K.T., supra note no. 65 at p. 948 at its footnote no. 226.

238 Karl, D.J., supra at pp. 149–150; Home v. Moody (1940), 146 S.W.2d (Civ. Ct. App. Tex., pp. 509–510; Roy, K.T., ibid.

239 Sloane, P.D., supra at p. 747; Roy, K.T., supra.

240 Ibid.

241 Karl, D.J., supra at pp. 151–152.

of interest is not severable from the award.[242] However, Saudi Arabian courts generally restrict damages awarded to immediate, tangible, and measurable losses.[243] Consequently, awards granted for breaches of contract are significantly lower than what is obtained under the common law rules.[244]

As could be seen from the above, the Article 5 (2)(b) of the New York Convention provides a leverage for Saudi Arabia to reject any arbitral award that violates its legal and public policy rules. This was demonstrated in the case of *Jadawel Intl. v. Emaar Property.* Here Jadawel in 2006 instituted an arbitration before a three-member tribunal seated in Saudi Arabia. It claimed damages in the amount of US$1.2 billion based on the breach by Emaar of a joint venture agreement relating to a construction project. Jadawel argued that Emaar had formed a partnership with another party in breach of the joint venture agreement. Jadawel's claim was dismissed and was ordered to pay legal costs. As the award was submitted to the Board of Grievances for enforcement, the Board re-examined the decision to ensure compliance with the principles of the *Shari'ah.* In its ruling, the Board of Grievances reversed the award; the damages awarded to Emaar were annulled and Emaar was ordered to pay more than US$250 million of damages to Jadawel.[245] It has been noted, however, that the scenario in this case is unlikely to happen under the new applicable Enforcement Law in Saudi Arabia.[246]

Kristin Roy remarks that Article 5(2)(b) of the New York Convention allows Saudi Arabia clout to accomplish both of its current needs: (1) the need to modernize in the international community and (2) the need to maintain its history and religious beliefs.[247] He then notes that a problem arises for non-Saudi Arabian investors and contractors who choose to do business with Saudi Arabia. Saudi Arabia's adoption of the New York Convention is intended to give the international community security in commercial contracts with Saudi Arabia, and confirmation that disputes will be adjudicated fairly.[248] He further contends that Article 5(2)(b) appears to allow Saudi Arabia to reject all arbitral awards that are against its public policy. In essence, he says, Saudi Arabia may not be required to enforce any more non-domestic arbitral awards that it did prior to its

242 Cueto, S.A., 'Enforcement of International Arbitration Awards in Saudi Arabia Just Got Easier', *in Arbitration News (*2013), http://internationalarbitrators.com/enforcement-of-international-arbitration-awards-in-saudi-arabia-just-got-easier/ (accessed 22 November 2014).

243 Karl, D.J., supra at p. 162; Roy, K.T., supra note no. 65 at p. 949.

244 Sloane, P.D., supra at p. 746; Roy, K.T., ibid, at p. 949.

245 INSIGHT, 'The New Enforcement Law of Saudi Arabia: An Additional Step Toward a Harmonized Arbitration Regime' (2013), www.jonesday.com/en/insights/2013/09/the-new-enforcement-law-of-saudi-arabia-an-additional-step-toward-a-harmonized-arbitration-regime (accessed 28 September 2020); see also STA Law Firm, 'United Arab Emirates: Enforcement of Arbitral Awards in Saudi Arabia' (2020), www.mondaq.com/arbitration-dispute-resolution/891538/enforcement-of-arbitral-awards-in-saudi-arabia (accessed 28 September 2020).

246 Ibid.

247 Roy, K.T., supra note no. 65 at p. 954.

248 Ibid.

1994 accession to the New York Convention.[249] Roy then suggests a revision of Article 5(2)(b) of the New York Convention to limit its ability to circumvent the purpose of the Convention.[250]

Abdulrahman Yahya Baamir on the other hand argues that some Western arbitral legislation provides that the award requires ratification by the courts before enforcement proceedings can be undertaken.[251] He says that as with Western public policy dictated by reference to local laws and perhaps social customs, so it is with Saudi Arabia that *Shari'ah* is the benchmark in respect of public policy. Considering this, he explains, Saudi arbitration law does not seem to differ much from that of its Western contemporaries. He then asks, why is it deemed problematic?[252]

Wherever the arguments go, the fact remains that through international commercial arbitration rules, international law encroached on domestic legislation of Saudi Arabia.

7.9.5 Riyadh Convention for Judicial Cooperation of 1983

Following the Declaration of the First Arab Conference of Ministers of Justice held in Rabat in 1977, several Arab countries signed the Riyadh Arab Agreement on Judicial Cooperation, which was subsequently approved by the Council of Arab Ministers of Justice on 6 April 1983. It entered into force on 30 October 1985. The signatories to this Convention include Jordan, United Arab Emirates, Bahrain, Tunisia, Algeria, Djibouti, Saudi Arabia, Sudan, Syria, Somalia, Iraq, Oman, Palestine, Qatar, Kuwait, Lebanon, Libya, Morocco, Mauritania, and Yemen.[253]

One important principle enunciated in this convention was barring courts of ratifying countries from re-examining the merits of the dispute, this was expressly stated under Article 37 of this Convention.[254] Here, courts in the place of enforcement of arbitral awards are restricted from trying the cases of awards *de novo*.[255] However, there are provisos to this rule which make its application conditional. The provisos include the rules of Islamic Law, public order, or the general morals of the contracting party.

Comparatively, the Riyadh Convention for Judicial Co-operation could be said to be similar to the New York Convention in that it is also concerned with cases upon which reliance can be placed to refuse implementation of foreign arbitral awards.[256] The underlined difference between the two is that the Riyadh

249 Ibid.

250 Ibid at p. 955.

251 Baamir, A.R., supra note no. 76 at p. 147; Redfern, A., et al., supra at Chapters 9 and 10.

252 Baamir, A.R., ibid.

253 Shiyapova, D.I., 'The Riyadh Arab Agreement for Judicial Cooperation: Specificity of The Region', *Business in Law*, Vol. 4 (2014), pp. 101–103.

254 Ibid.

255 Saleh, S., *Commercial Arbitration in the Arab Middle East: Shari'a, Syria, Lebanon, and Egypt* (2nd edn) Wickford: Heart Publishing (2006), p. 151.

256 Al-Jarba, M., supra note no. 99.

Convention contends clearly that the award should not be contrary to Islamic Law as stipulated in paragraph (e) of the above text. It can be argued that the two are similar in that though, the New York Convention's public policy concept is general while the Riyadh Convention is specific not only on Islamic law but also on public order or the general morals of the contracting party in whose interest the enforcement is sought, they both stand to make such enforcement conditional.

7.10 Saudi Arbitration Law 2012: a local perspective of international law

On 8 June 2012, Saudi Arabia published its long-awaited arbitration reform law.[257] It replaces the Arbitration Regulation of 1983[258] and the Rules for the Implementation of the Arbitration Regulation[259] of 1985. The New Law which became effective on 7 July 2012 introduces several reforms. It is noted that though, this new law is within the framework of a broader and continuing reorganization of Saudi's judicial system, it is a clear and practical impact of international law on Saudi Arabia arbitral norms. This new law has been described as a forward thinking that embraces national and international arbitration proceedings.[260] It is largely based on the UNCITRAL Model Law. It addresses many *lacunae* found in the 1983 law as it increases party autonomy, grants arbitrators wider powers, and curbs court intervention in the arbitral process.[261]

The reforms introduced by the 2012 law serve as a perspective of Saudi Arabia domestication of arbitral legislation of UNCITRAL Model Law which cover a wide range of scopes. For example, Article 2 states that the law is applicable to all arbitrations – domestic and international – wherein the parties have agreed to subject their dispute to that law. Article 3 on the other hand, defines an international arbitration in line with the definition contained in Article 1(3) of the UNCITRAL Model Law.

On substantive and procedural rules, the 2012 introduced a variety of reforms. For example, under its Article 38(1)(a), parties are free to designate the substantive law applicable to their dispute and under the provisions of Article 38(1)(b), failing such designation, the tribunal is required to apply the law that is most intricately connected to the dispute. Also, under Article 28, parties are free to choose a foreign seat of arbitration, and in the absence of the parties'

257 Royal Decree No. M/34 Dated 24/5/1433H – 16/4/2012.

258 Royal Decree No. M/46 of 1983.

259 Ministerial Resolution No. 7/2021/M) (the "Old Law") of 1985.

260 Zadkovich, J.K., Saudi Arabia: Saudi Arabia's New Arbitration Law (2012), www.mondaq.com/x/197592/International+Courts+Tribunals/Saudi+Arabias+New+Arbitration+Law+2012 (accessed 27 December 2013).

261 Reform of the Saudi Arabia Arbitration Law – Insight: International Arbitration – White & Case, www.whitecase.com/ (accessed 24 November 2014).

agreement on the seat, the tribunal is required to select the seat considering the circumstances of the case and the convenience of the parties.[262]

On rules of procedure, Section 25(1) of this new law allows parties to select the rules applicable to the arbitral proceedings by, for example, incorporating institutional rules such as rules of International Chamber of Commerce (ICC), International Dispute Resolution Centre (IDRC), Dubai International Arbitration Centre (DIAC), or London Court of International Arbitration (LCIA). However, the provisions of these rules will prevail to the extent that they do not contravene the principles of *Shari'ah*. Similarly, if the parties fail to agree on the applicable rules of procedure, the default provisions of the 2012 Law will become applicable.[263] In another development, Article 14 of this new law gives guideline on the appointment of arbitrators. It says that the sole arbitrator (or the chairperson where the tribunal is a panel) hold a degree in law or *Shari'ah*. This contrasts the requirement under the provision of the 1983 Law which stipulated a "working knowledge of *Shari'ah* tenets, business regulations and of the customs and traditions of the Kingdom".[264]

Most importantly, this new law confers a significant power on the arbitrators to determine jurisdiction and competence of their arbitral tribunal. This is widely provided for under Article 20 of the law. It also gives the arbitrators power to rule on challenges to their arbitral authority as contained in the provision under Article 17(1). Consequent to the well-known practice of court intervention in arbitral processes in Saudi Arabia, wider range of powers are granted to the arbitrators under the new law with a view to curb this traditional intervention in the arbitral processes. Thus, Article 15 of this law restricts the participation of the competent Saudi court in the constitution of the tribunal only to the extent that it is called upon to make an appointment by the parties or where the appointed arbitrators are unable to jointly appoint a chairperson. After the tribunal is appointed, the court retains a subsidiary role in the conduct of the proceedings.[265]

Prior to 2012 law, parties had an unfettered right to challenge the arbitral award by applying for annulment before the competent Saudi court, including merits of such awards. The reform brought to this practice is to allow limited grounds for annulment in accordance with the NY Convention. The grounds here include the invalidity of the arbitration agreement, an irregularity in the constitution of the tribunal, and the tribunal's non-compliance with the mandate given to it by the parties. These are provided for under Article 50(1)(a)-(g)). Thus, under Article 51(1), a party may file a request for annulment within 60 days of receipt of the arbitral award. Under Article 50(2), a court can on its own motion annul an award if it is contrary to public policy or *Shari'ah*, if the parties' agreement was not respected, or if the subject matter of the dispute was not capable of being a subject of arbitration. However, under the provision of Article

262 Ibid.
263 Ibid.
264 Ibid.
265 Ibid.

50(4), the court, in deciding the application, must not re-examine the facts or merits of the case.[266]

On Recognition and Enforcement of the awards, Article 55(1) provides that parties can apply for the recognition and enforcement of an arbitral award after the expiry of the 60-day annulment period. Under Article 55(2)(a)-(c) the competent Saudi court can refuse enforcement where the award is contrary to an existing court decision or order, public policy or *Shari'ah*. Under Article 55(2)(b), to the extent that infringing portions can be separated from the remaining part of the award, an order shall be issued for the enforcement of the non-infringing part of the award. It follows that an award that directs a party to pay interest (*Riba* considered to be in violation of the *Shari'ah* applicable law in Saudi Arabia) on principal sums awarded would not necessarily be entirely void as is the case under the 1983 Law.[267]

Other reforms introduced by the 2012 law include guiding rule on duration of the arbitral proceedings. This law relaxes the timelines stipulated for arbitral proceedings under the 1983 law. Under Article 40(1), the arbitrators are required to render their award within 12 months of the start of the proceedings (this timeline can be extended by a further six months at the tribunal's discretion, or longer if the parties so agree).[268] Similarly, under the old law, an arbitral award was neither final nor binding until approved by the Saudi Board of Grievances – a process which could take several months. The reform introduced by 2012 law recognizes the final and binding effect of arbitral awards without requiring any further approval by the competent court. This is contained in its Article 52.[269] Experts suggest that Saudi concerned authority must initiate steps to provide enabling environment to explore the practicality of this new law.[270]

7.11 Conclusion

Several conclusions can be drawn from the above analysis. In the first instance, it has been established that international law has encroached on domestic legislation of modern Saudi Arabia particularly from the perspective of the New York Convention of 1958. Secondly, it has been established that contrary to the argument that Islamic law is not capable of interpretation and re-interpretation it has been proved that it can be interpreted to adapt to modern international norms generally and particularly modern international commercial arbitration law. The *Qur'an* and the *Sunnah* have been interpreted to justify arbitration as a justice mechanism by the methodologies of *Ijma* (consensus) and *Qiyas* (analogy).

266 Ibid.

267 Ibid.

268 Ibid.

269 Ibid.

270 This statement was made by Qaroub, M. in an interview. Qaroub was a member of the consultant arbitration committee of the Saudi Arabia Ministry of Justice, and Assistant Head of the Arab Chamber of Arbitration and Documentation.

Therefore, in Saudi Arabia mutual interaction between Islamic law and international legal norms enjoys acknowledgement, but, in marked position vouchsafed by New York Convention on "public policy" in this regard. This is further contextualized in the notion that the *Shari'ah* is influenced by international law and in its turn the predominately Western international order is enhanced by Islamic values. Saudi Arabia's ratification of the New York Convention represents a practical shift from the traditional position to the modern reality. The Saudi Arabia's 1983 Arbitration Law is a shift towards modernity in the sphere of arbitral rules. But 2012 Arbitration Law is a further shift that considered the rules under the New York Convention and the UNCITRAL Model Law which are clear manifestations of the impact of international law regime on its local legislations.

Bibliography

Books

Abdul Hamid, E.A., *Arbitration with the Arab Countries* (2nd edn), Netherlands: Kluwer Law International (1999).

Albejad, N., *Arbitration in Saudi Arabia* (1st edn), Riyadh: Institute of Public Administration (1999).

Alison, L., and Mian, A.J., *Saudi Business and Labour Law: Its Interpretation and Application*, London: Graham & Trotman (1982).

Al-Jarba, M., *Commercial Arbitration, A Study of Its Role in the Saudi Arabia within Islamic Jurisprudence*, Aberystwyth: The University of Wales (2001).

Al-Kenain, A., *Al-Tahkim fi Al-Shari'a Al-Islamiyyah: Al-Tahkim Al-'Am, wa Al-Tahkim fi Al-Shiqaq Al-Zaouji* (1st edn), Riyadh: Dar Al-Asimah (2000).

Al-Kenain, A., *Tasbeeb Alahkam Al-Qadaiyah fi Al-Shari'a Al-Islamiyyah* (1st edn), Madinah Al Munawara: Dar Ibn Farihun (1999).

Al Magsudi, M., and Alamer, A., *Conditions of Executing Arbitral Awards*, Jeddah: King Abdulaziz University, College of Economy and Administration Jeddah (1998).

Al Mawardi, *Adab Al Kadi, T. II, Baghdad: Ri`asah Diwan al-Awqaf*, Malaysia: University of Malaya, (1971).

Al-Ramahi, A., 'Sulh: A Crucial Part of Islamic Arbitration, London School of Economics and Political Science, Law Department', http://ssrn.com/abstract=[1153659].

Al Sharif, S.U., *Euro-Arab Arbitration System and Islamic Sharia Law* (Master of Philosophy Thesis), University of Salford, the International Studies Unit (1990).

American Arbitration Association, *The International Arbitration Kit: A Compilation of Basic and Frequently Requested Documents* (4th edn) (1993), pp. 19–20.

Anderson, J.N.D., *Islamic Law in the Modern World* (1st edn), New York: New York University Press (1959).

Atta, I., Al Tahkim fi Al-Fiqha (The Arbitration), Riyadh: Imam bin Saud University (1990).

Audhali, A.A., Settlement of Commercial Disputes in Saudi Arabia (Civil Procedure), Al Khobar: Al-Eman P. Press (n.d.).

Ayoub, C., *Convention on the Recognition and Enforcement of Foreign Arbitral Awards*, www.charlesayoub.com/life-style/index.php/more/1/769 (accessed 19 November 2013).

Baamir, A.R., *Shari'ah Law in Commercial and Banking Arbitration, Law and Practice in Saudi Arabia*, England: Ashgate (2010).

Barin, B. et al., *The Osler Guide to Commercial Arbitration in Canada: A Practical Introduction to Domestic and International Commercial Arbitration*, The Netherland: Kluwer Law International (2006).

Bergsten, E.E., *Dispute Settlement, International Commercial Arbitration, United Nations Conference on Trade and Development*, New York and Geneva (2005).

Born, G.B., *International Commercial Arbitration*, Netherlands: Kluwer Law International (2009).

Born, G.B., *International Commercial Arbitration: Law and Practice*, United Kingdom: Wolters Kluwer Law & Business (2012).

Britannica, *Economy*, www.britannica.com/place/Saudi-Arabia/Economy.

Coulson, N.J., *Commercial Law in the Gulf States: The Islamic Legal Tradition*, London: Springer (1984).

Cueto, S.A., 'Enforcement of International Arbitration Awards in Saudi Arabia Just Got Easier', *Arbitration News* (2013), http://internationalarbitrators.com/enforcement-of-international-arbitration-awards-in-saudi-arabia-just-got-easier/ (accessed 22 November 2014).

Cunningham, R.B., and Sarayrah, Y.K, *Wasta: The Hidden Forces in Middle Eastern Society*, London: Praeger (1993).

El Hadab, A.H., *Arbitration with Arab Countries* (1st edn), The Netherland: Kluwer Law and Taxation Publisher Deventer (1990).

Fraje, A.R., *Sources of Obligation, Memoires for Students of Law*, Riyadh: College of Administrative Sciences, Department of Law, King Saud University (1404H – 1932 AD).

Hisham, I., 'Seerat Ibn Hisham, 'The Treaty of Medina', Ministry of Islamic Affairs, Saudi Arabia), www.al-islam.com.

Ibn Farhoun, B., *Tabsirat Alhokkam Fi Usul Alaqdiyah Wa Manahij Alahkam* (edited by Taha Abdulraouf Sa'd, 1st edn), Maktabat Alkolliyat Al-Azhariyah, Vol. 1 (1986).

Ibn Qodamah, *Al-Mugni (The Preacher)*, General Directorate of Scientific Research Administration, Saudi Arabia, Vol. 9 (n.d.).

Ibn Qodamah, M., *Al-Mugni* (1st edn), Riyadh: Hajar Publications, Vol. 10 (1992).

Ibn Taymiyyah, M., *Majmoou' Alfatawa* (2nd edn), Riyadh: Ministry of Islamic Affairs of Saudi Arabia, Vol. 29 (1995).

Ibrahim Atta, I. *(Al Tahkim fi Alfgha), The Arbitration*, Imam bin Saud University (1990).

INSIGHT, 'The New Enforcement Law of Saudi Arabia: An Additional Step toward a Harmonized Arbitration Regime' (2013), www.jonesday.com/en/insights/2013/09/the-new-enforcement-law-of-saudi-arabia-an-additional-step-toward-a-harmonized-arbitration-regime.

Jalal El-Ahdab, A.H., *Arbitration with the Arab Countries*, Netherlands: Kluwer Law International (2011).

Jan Van Den Berg, A., *The New York Arbitration Convention of 1958, towards a Uniform Judicial Interpretation* (1st edn), Kluwer Law International (1981).

Liebesny, H.J., *The Law of Near Middle East State*, Al Bany: University of New York Press (1975).

Mahmassani, S., *The Legislative Situation in Arab Countries: Its Past and Present* (2nd edn), Beirut: Dar El-Elm Lil Malain (n.d.).

Moens, G., *International Trade & Business Annual*, University of Queensland, London: Cavendish Publishing USA (2003).

Moses, M.L., *The Principles and Practice of International Commercial Arbitration*, Cambridge: Cambridge University Press (2008).
Mustapha Zarqaa, *Explanation of Islamic Rules Jurisprudence*, a Review (2nd edn), Damascus: Dar Al Qalani (1989).
Osullivan, A., and Sheffrin, S.M., *Economics: Principles in Action*, New Jersey: Pearson Prentice Hall (2003).
Ramadan, S., *Islamic Law, Its Scope and Equity* (2nd edn), Malaysia: Muslim Youth Movement of Malaysia (1970).
Redfern, A. et al, *Law and Practice of International Commercial Arbitration*, London: Sweet & Maxwell (2004).
Saleh, S., *Commercial Arbitration in the Arab Middle East: A Study in Shari'ah and Statute Law* (1st edn), London: Graham & Trotman (1984).
Saleh, S., *Commercial Arbitration in the Arab Middle East: Shari'a, Syria, Lebanon, and Egypt* (2nd edn) Wickford Heart Publishing (2006).
Saleh, S., *Commercial Arbitration in the Middle East* (1st edn) London: Graham of Trotman Limited (1984).
Tripp, H., and Peter, N., *CultureShock! A Survival Guide to Customs and Etiquette – Saudi Arabia* (3rd edn) Marshall Cavendish (2009).
Vogel, F.E., *Islamic Law and the Legal System*, Netherlands: Brill (2000).
Weeramantry, C.G., *Islamic Jurisprudence: An International Perspective*, London: Macmillan (1988).
Yassen, M., *Hajeyat Al-Hokem Al-Qadai (Validity of Judicial Award in Islamic Jurisprudence)* (1st edn), Jordan: Dr. Alfargan Press (1984).
Zadkovich, J.K., *Saudi Arabia: Saudi Arabia's New Arbitration Law* (2012), MONDAQ, www.mondaq.com/saudiarabia/arbitration-dispute-resolution/197592/saudi-arabias-new-arbitration-law-2012
Zinuddin Bin Najeem, *Al Bahr Al Raig Sharh Kanz Al Dagaig* (2nd edn), Beirut: Dar Al Maarifa Vol. 7 (1333 H., 1912 AD).

Journals

Abdul Hamid El-Ahbad, 'The Moslem Arbitration Law', *Proceedings of the International Bar Association First Arab Regional Conference*, Cairo, February, Vol. 1 (1987).
Aboul-Enein, M.I M., 'Liberal Trends in Islamic Law (Shari'a) on the Peaceful Settlement of Disputes', *Papers Presented to the Seminar of (The Practice of International Arbitration)*, Oxford (July 13th 1999).
Acker, C.E., 'The Insurance Business', *Middle East Executive Reports Journal* [Washington, D.C.]: Middle East Executive Reports, Ltd., (c1978) - Vol. 1, No. 1 (Sept. 1978) - Vol. 25, No. 2 (Feb. 2002).Vol. 1, No. 1 (Sept. 1978) - Vol. 25, No. 2 (Feb. 2002) in (July 1982).
Ahmed Bin Taymiya, 'Legal Opinions', Enquiry of Abdurrahman Al Qassim, edited by *Scientific Researches and Preaching Administrations*, Riyadh, Vol. 3 (n.d.).
Ali Radhi, H., 'State Courts and Arbitration in the Gulf Cooperation Council (GCC) Countries', *ICC International Committee on Arbitration Bulletin*, Spec. Supp., Vol. 57, No. 5 (1992).
Allam, 'Saudi Arabia/Arbitration in the Kingdom: The New Implementation Rules', *Middle East Executive Rep.* (1985).
Alqurashi, Z., 'Arbitration under the Islamic Shari'ah,' *Oil, Gas and Energy Intelligence*, Vol. 1, No. 2 (2003).

Al-Ramahi, A., 'Sulh: A Crucial Part of Islamic Arbitration, Islamic Law and Law of the Muslim World', *Research Paper Series at New York Law School*, No. 08-45 (2008).

Alsmaan, Y., 'The Role of Arbitration in Settling Investment Disputes, Ministry of External Affairs', *Symposium on Foreign Investment, Conference Institute Diplomatic Studies*, Riyadh, 24–25 November (1997).

Behr, V. 'Enforcement of United States Money Judgments in Germany', *J.L., & Com*, Vol. 13 (1994), p. 211.

Brower, C.N., and Sharpe, J.K., 'International Arbitration and the Islamic World: The third Phase', *The American Journal of International Law*, Vol. 97, No. 3 (2003), pp. 643–656.

Duguid, S., 'A Biographical Approach to the Study of Social Change in the Middle East: Abdullah Tariki as a New Man', *International Journal of Middle East Studies*, Vol. 1, No. 3 (1970), pp. 195–220.

Gemmell, A.J., 'Commercial Arbitration in the Islamic Middle East', *Santa Clara Journal of International Law*, Vol. 5, No. 1 (2006), p. i.

Kelly, J.B., 'The Buraimi Oasis Dispute', *International Affairs*, Vol. 32, No. 3 (July 1956), pp. 318–326.

Kutty, F., 'The Shari'ah Factor in International Commercial Arbitration', *Loyola of Los Angeles International and Comparative Law Review*, Vol. 28, (2006), pp. 565–624.

Lalive, J.F., 'Melanges en l'honneur de Nicolas Valticos', *Droit et Justice* (Editions Pedone) (1989).

Matlin, R.S., 'Comment, The Federal Courts and the Enforcement of Foreign Arbitral Awards', *Pace Law Review*, Vol. 5 (1984), pp. 151–184.

Paulsson, J., 'The Role of Swedish Courts in Transnational Commercial Arbitration', *Virginia Journal of International Law*, Vol. 21 (1981), pp. 211–250.

Roy, K.T., 'The New York Convention and Saudi Arabia: Can a Country Use the Public Policy Defence to Refuse Enforcement of Non-Domestic Arbitral Award?' *Fordham International Law Journal*, Vol. 18, No. 3 (1994), pp. 920–958.

Saudi Arabia Investment Climate: Its Risks and Returns, *Middle East Executive Rep.* (1986), US Department of State, https://www.state.gov/reports/2020-investment-climate-statements/saudi-arabia/.

Saudis Accept New York Convention [hereinafter Saudis Accept], *Dispute Resolution Journal* (1994), pp. 920–958.

Sayen, G., 'Arbitration, Conciliation and the Islamic Legal Tradition in Saudi Arabia', *University of Pennsylvania Journal of International Business Law*, Vol. 9, No. 2 (1987), p. 211.

Sayen, G., 'Arbitration, Conciliation, and the Islamic Legal Tradition in Saudi Arabia', *University of Pennsylvania Journal of International Economic Law*, Vol. 24, No. 4 (2003), pp. 905–956.

Schwbel, S., 'A Celebration of the United Nations New York Convention on the Recognition and Enforcement of Foreign Arbitral Awards', *Arbitration International*, Vol. 12, No. 1 (1996), pp. 83–88.

Shiyapova, D.I., 'The Riyadh Arab Agreement for Judicial Cooperation: Specificity of the Region', *Business in Law*, Vol. 4 (2014), pp. 101–103.

Sloane, P.D., 'The Status of Islamic Law in the Modern Commercial World', *The International Lawyer*, Vol. 22, No. 3 (1988), pp. 743–766.

Strub, Jr., M. H., 'Resisting Enforcement of Foreign Arbitral Awards under Article V (1) (E) and Article VI of the New York Convention: A Proposal for Effective Guidelines', *Texas Law Review*, Vol. 68 (1990), p. 1031.

Volz, J.L., and Haydock, R.S., 'Foreign Arbitral Awards: Enforcing the Award against the Recalcitrant Loser', *William Mitchel Law Review*, Vol. 21 (1996), p. 867.

Westin, D., 'Enforcing Foreign Commercial Judgment and Arbitral Awards in the United States, West Germany, and England', *Law and Policy in International Business*, Vol. 19 (1987), p. 325.

Websites

http://eprints.lse.ac.uk/24598/1/WPS2008-12_Al-Ramahi.pdf.

http://financial-dictionary.thefreedictionary.com/Takhayyur.

"Our Mission" www.opec.org/opec_web/en/about_us/23.htm.

www.mondaq.com/x/197592/International+Courts+Tribunals/Saudi+Arabias+New+Arbitration+Law+2012.

www.mondaq.com/arbitration-dispute-resolution/891538/enforcement-of-arbitral-awards-in-saudi-arabia.

www.newyorkconvention.org/contracting-states/list-of-contracting-states.

www.uncitral.org/uncitral/about/origin_history.html.

www.uncitral.org/uncitral/en/uncitral_texts/arbitration.html.www.uncitral.org/uncitral/en/uncitral_texts/arbitration.html.

www.uncitral.org/uncitral/en/uncitral_texts/arbitration.html.

www.whitecase.com/.

Cases

Hecht v. United States (1985), 609 F. Supp. 75 (S.D.N.Y. 1985).

Le Parmentier v. La Societe Miss France, XXX Y.B. Comm Arb. (2004), pp. 119, 123–124 (Paris Cour d'appel); Walkinshaw v. Diniz (2000), 2 All E.R. (Comm.) 237 (Q.B.).

Libyan American Oil Company (LIAMCO) v. Libyan Arab Republic (1977), 20 I.L.M. (1981).

Parsons & Whittemore Overseas Co., Inc. v. Societe Generale De L'Industrie Du Papier, 508 F.2d 969,975 (2d Cir. 1974).

Powell-Smith, V., Aspects of Arbitration Common Law Shari'a Compared, Printed by Success Label Enterprise (1995).

Saudi Arabia v. Arabian American Oil Company, (1963), 27 ILR, 117.

Scherk v. Alberto-Culver Co., (1974) 417 U.S. 506.

Statutes, legislations, and resolutions

Arbitration Act (Royal Decree M/46).

Commonwealth Consolidated Acts.

Council of Ministers Resolution No. 58 dated 17/1/1383H (25/6/1963).

Council of Ministers Resolution No. 78 of 1417/1414H (27th January 1993).

Council of Ministers Resolution No. 190 dated 16.11.1409 H. (19 July 1989) published in Um Al Qura Newspaper (official state newspaper) issue N 3266 dated 4/12/1409 H (7th August 1989).

Decision of the President of the Saudi Board of Grievances of 15/8/1405 H (5th May 1985).

Diwan Al-Mazalim's Circular No. 7 dated 15/05/1405H (1985).

Geneva Convention on the Execution of Foreign Arbitral Awards ("Geneva Convention"), 92 L.N.T.S. 302 (1929).

Geneva Protocol on Arbitration Clauses in Commercial Matters ("Geneva Protocol"), 27 L.N.T.S. 158 (1924).
Implementing Rules – Council of Ministers Resolution No. 7 of 8/9/1405H (May 27, 1985).
Ministerial Resolution No. 7/2021/M) (the "Old Law") of 1985.
Royal Decree No. M/34 Dated 24/5/1433H – 16/4/2012
Royal Decree N M/11 dated 16/7/1414H. (29 January 1993).
Royal Decree No. M/46, 12 Rajab 1403 (25 April 1983).
Royal Decree No. 51/M dated 17/02/1402H (1981).
Rules of Saudi Arabia Commercial Court Regulation – Royal Decree M/32 of 1/15/1350 AH (1931 AD) – formally repealed in 1983.
Saudi Arabia Regulation on Arbitration – Royal Decree M/46 of 7/12/1403H (April 25, 1983).
The Ministry of Commerce Circular No. 31/1/331/91 of 1979.
The New York Convention.
UN General Assembly Resolution 2205 (XXI) of 17 December 1966.
United Nations Convention on the Recognition and Enforcement of Foreign Arbitral Awards (1958).

8 Conclusions and recommendations

8.1 Conclusions

This study was based on the hypothesis that modern international law, which is conceivably underpinned by western and specifically Eurocentric secular values, has, despite the traditional concept of sovereignty, steadily encroached upon the domestic legislation of modern nation-states generally, and in particular, Saudi Arabia, a Muslim majority state that strictly adheres to Islamic law as the basis of its domestic legislation. It asserted that while international pressure may be a factor, the derivable benefits from modern international law also play a significant role in influencing Saudi Arabia to maintain necessary equilibrium between its classical and conservative interpretation of Islamic law and relevant rules of modern international law.

In the preceding seven chapters and with particular reference to three important aspects of international law, namely, international human rights law, international economic law, and international arbitration law, the research has endeavoured to establish the impact of international law on the application of Islamic law in Saudi Arabia within the framework of the classical and modern notions of the concept of sovereignty. It has been argued that, in the ambitious spirit of the traditional notion of sovereignty, the independent states that form the basic structure of the international system were presumed to be truly sovereign in terms of their legislative independence. Contrary to this presumption, the growing impact of international law rules had significantly encroached on the legislative independence of modern nation-states thereby weakening their presumed legislative sovereignty. The development of domestic legislations of modern Saudi Arabia typifies this encroachment. Despite its presumed strict adherence to the traditional, conservative, and textualist interpretation of Islamic law, this Muslim majority state, has acceded to many rules and regulations of modern international law, which has consequently influenced its shifting to a more liberal interpretation of Islamic law to enable it enjoy the inherent benefits of international law in the three specific areas examined in this thesis.

Apparently, modern nation-states are prepared to accede to the norms of international law, not only on account of presumed international pressures, but also due to the potential benefits derivable therefrom. They are, for example, motivated by economic and political benefits, security interests as well as international prestige attached to the membership of international organizations such as the UN, WTO, IMF, and the EU, among others.

It has also been established in this study that the *Qur'an* and the *Sunnah,* the two primary sources of Islamic law, are divine and can be said to deal with every conceivable eventuality, but certainly not in explicit details. Thus, in the course of history, there had been conscious efforts in formulating rules from these basic sources so as to address ever-growing challenges of life. Practically, the rules derived from these two sources are flexible and adaptable to necessary changes from time to time. Similarly, it was in the course of this historical development that leagues of jurists and schools of jurisprudence had emerged. The institutions and Islamic schools of jurisprudence arose out of the need to respond to challenges and different circumstances of human existence through the utilization of *Ijtihad* by the jurists in interpreting the provisions of the fundamental sources of the law. From the analysis of this study, it is apparent that Islamic law, despite its foundation on divine sources that are considered to be immutable, can accommodate secular principles, such as those of international law. Thus, this research has engaged with and challenged the contention that there is no room for Islamic law to be interpreted and reinterpreted differently by different generations of Muslims, suggesting that international law, with its secular underpinnings should have nothing to do with it even in modern times.

This study has demonstrated that on one hand, Saudi Arabia's historical antecedent and status in the Muslim world does account for its adoption of a literalist conservative ideology and often hardline perspective of Islamic law. On the other hand, its economic and security interests coupled with its desire for international prestige have necessitated its cautious adoption of a moderate approach in relation to the norms of modern international law, thus swinging between conservative and moderate paradigms depending on the issues in question. In doing so its legislative and judicial developments have been influenced not only by views and doctrines formulated by other Islamic schools of jurisprudence apart from the Hanbali jurisprudence which is its officially adopted School, but also by other values, including that of international law.

From the perspective of relationship between international and domestic laws, this study has proposed that international and municipal legal systems as conceived by both the "dualists" and "monists" schools underscored the philosophy of Article 13 of the UN Draft Declaration on Rights and Duties of States 1949, which stipulates that every state has the duty to carry out in good faith its obligations arising from treaties and other sources of international law, and it may not invoke provisions in its constitution or its laws as an excuse for failure to perform this duty. In this regard, Saudi Arabia being a member of the UN and the "international community", has attempted to cope with a clash between its traditional Islamic norms and modern international law principles through creative accommodation, seeking modernization without secularization. It has been operating cautiously on the basis that the interaction between Islamic law and international law can be mutual – that is, the *Shari'ah* could be positively influenced by international law and in its turn the predominately Western secular international order could be enhanced by Islamic values.

The basic arguments of this research has been substantiated by reference to the Saudi Arabian foreign policy which is focused on a combined co-operation with the Gulf States, the unity of the Arab world, solidarity with Muslim countries, and support for the UN and other Eurocentric – international organizations. Similarly, Saudi Arabia has been a State party to a good number of international treaties. It is argued that its acquiescence to these international instruments is underscored by, among other things, pragmatism, economic interests, desire to consolidate its international status and to maintain good relations with the outside world. It, nevertheless, cautiously but constantly declares its acquiescence to international law as being subject to some fundamental norms of the Islamic *Shari'ah*. Consequently, the notion of the modern nation-state and the division of Muslim nations into separate political entities has not diminished Saudi Arabia's strong commitment to Islamic law and there appears a general agreement among contemporary Saudi Arabian jurists and scholars that the modern nation-state system is acceptable to Islam and compatible with Islamic law. It has affirmed their position which demonstrates that the spiritual unity of the Muslim *Ummah* persists with important beneficial effects that can be injected into modern international relations and international law.

In the move to maintain a balance between its classical and conservative interpretation of Islamic law and the relevant rules of international law Saudi Arabia has obviously extended its exercise of *Ijtihad* beyond the traditional limits of classical hardline Hanbali jurisprudence. Fortunately, the concepts of progress, rationality, and public welfare have all been accepted by contemporary Islamic jurists as being consistent with the overall objective of Islamic law (*maqasid al-Shari'ah*).

With specific reference to international human rights law, this study has shown that Saudi Arabia's notion of human rights is contextualized within the general proposition that Islamic law and international human rights could be either compatible or incompatible depending on the scope of definitions of some of the concepts. It has consistently and persistently reflected this contentious perspective at both international human rights forums and in its local legislative policy. Nevertheless, there is a subtle but firm acceptance of the need to respect and improve its human rights policy in one form or the other within the accommodating limits of its commitment to the Islamic *Shari'ah*. This has been demonstrated in many different ways such as: the adoption of the concept of constitutionalism through the enactment of the Saudi Basic Law of Governance, which includes a bill of rights (albeit with a proviso in Article 26 that the state will protect human rights in accordance with Islamic *Shari'ah*); relevant legislative reforms; creation of relevant institutional mechanisms; judicial reforms and endeavours to improve fair trial and due process; some positive response to human rights criticisms; and improvement in the scope of women's rights including bridging the wide gap that previously existed in women representation in government, education and labour rights.

With respect to the proviso in Article 26 of the Saudi Basic Law of Governance that the state will protect human rights in accordance with the Islamic *Shari'ah*, it has been submitted in this research that the proviso should not necessarily lead to indiscriminate violations of Saudi Arabia's international human rights obligations if it sustains the political will to adopt liberal interpretations of the Islamic *Shari'ah* based on justifiable Islamic legal principles such as ***darura*** (necessity), ***maslahah*** (benefit), and ***maqasid al-Shari'ah*** (overall objective of the *Shari'ah*) among many others.

With reference to international economic law, this study has also established that economic benefits and perhaps the need to protect its international prestige are the principal factors that motivated Saudi Arabia's membership of, and accession to IMF conventions. This has also demanded a cautious shift from its traditional hardline to a more liberal approach in its interpretation of Islamic law to facilitate its accommodation of modern transnational economic and trade policies and, particularly, in the areas of banking and finance. Here it faces the challenge of veering between mandatory prohibition of *riba* and some degree of permissibility allowed by liberal interpretation of some Islamic schools of jurisprudence. For Saudi Arabia, under the traditional Hanbali jurisprudence, *riba* is basically and expressly forbidden, but Saudi banks and financial institutions, it is averred, charge "commission" and "service charge" in the alternative. Whether this can be equated with "interest" in modern banking parlance remains a contentious issue left for further research especially in the areas of Islamic banking and finance. Saudi Arabia has however also utilized its special drawing rights under the IMF Agreement despite the fact that it is an interest based system as clearly specified in Article XX of the IMF Agreement. This study has proposed that while Saudi Arabia's membership of the IMF and utilization of its special drawing rights despite being based on interest could be justified under the Islamic legal principles of ***darura*** (necessity) or ***maslaha*** (benefit), it is nevertheless motivated by the inherent benefits of such membership to the country and its people.

The analysis in this study has also shown clearly that commercial and trade benefits provided by the concept of intellectual property rights are inherently beneficial for both nation-states and individuals. Although the concept of intellectual property rights is not directly rooted in the basic sources of Islamic law, leading Saudi scholars were able to validate it through the interpretational mechanism of *Ijtihad* and principle of *Maqasid al-Shari'ah*. As a signatory to the Paris Convention for the Protection of Industrial Property and also the Berne Convention for the Protection of Literary and Artistic Works, series of legislative enactments have been passed in Saudi Arabia to ensure implementation of the international obligations under those conventions. The justification of the concept of intellectual property law from within the Islamic sources and the consequent promulgation of domestic applicable rules in that regard in Saudi Arabia, expressly confirm not only the influence of international legal norms on local legislation of a Muslim majority state, but also the appreciation of the commercial and trade benefits therein by Saudi Arabia.

The study has similarly established that the New York Convention on International Commercial Arbitration also exemplifies the benefits accruable from amicable settlement of disputes arising from commercial relations of Saudi Arabia and commercial organizations outside its jurisdiction. Although the concept of arbitration is recognized under classical Islamic law, the rules of modern international arbitration take the concept much further in response to modern transnational commercial needs. For example, the New York Convention requires the 'recognition and enforcement of foreign arbitral awards' within the jurisdiction of the state parties to it, which may sometimes include foreign awards consisting of interests (*riba*). Therefore, as far as Saudi Arabia is concerned, mutual interaction between Islamic law and international legal norms enjoys acknowledgement in respect of this Convention, but subject to "public policy" as recognized under the New York Convention itself. Under the concept of "public policy" Saudi Arabia is able to proportionately subject its obligation under the New York Convention to its Islamic *Shari'ah,* particularly in relation to the enforcement of foreign arbitral awards that may include interests (*riba*).

In the light of the potential benefits inherent in international legal norms, this study has established that Islamic law certainly contains relevant jurisprudential principles that provide the necessary platform for Saudi Arabia to cautiously espouse and protect its national interests within the rules of international law while also sustaining its commitment to Islamic *Shari'ah.* This is demonstrated in its membership, participation, and maintenance of relations in and with Western oriented secular institutions such as the UN, IMF, WTO, and multinational organizations like ARAMCO and others. In all, Saudi Arabia is not resistant to a preponderating regime of the international system despite its commitment to the Islamic *Shari'ah.* Its position is influenced by the cautious interplay of interests and values.

From the findings of this research, it could be argued that there are three degrees of extent to which international law has encroached and impacted on the application of Islamic law in Saudi Arabia. These could be classified into high, medium, and low degrees. The impact is high where the basic sources of Islamic law (the *Qur'an* and the *Sunnah*) are silent on a particular subject, which then gives leverage to an extensive exercise of *Ijtihad* by the country. For example, in the cases of intellectual property rights and international commercial arbitration the degree of the impact of international law is very high. The impact is average where the two basic sources are capable of several interpretations, like in the case of *riba* in relation to its banking and financial transactions, for example, as a member of and signatory to the IMF Agreement. Finally, the degree of impact is low where the basic sources are considered to be specific on particular issues, such as in the area of international human rights pertaining to issues such as freedom of religion and rights of women in a number of matrimonial matters.

While this research has been able to establish the encroachment of international law on the domestic legislation of modern states like Saudi Arabia and its consequent impact on its application of Islamic law, it, nevertheless, also raises some doubt about the possible attainment of a full "universal legal order" without consideration for the recognized norms of other civilizations such as Islam. For example, it is observed that of the three aspects of international law examined in this study, the lowest degree of impact is in the area of international human rights law. It is submitted that for the norms of international human rights law regime to be universally accepted and globally enforced, relevant norms of relevant civilizations in the international community, such as Islam, should be taken into consideration and reasonably accommodated.

In this conclusion, it must be mentioned that there were a number of challenges encountered during this research. The principal challenge was in respect of collecting relevant information in a country like Saudi Arabia. In the course of the research, it has been discovered and confirmed that Saudi Arabia is very restrictive and always suspicious of scholars coming from the Western hemispheres for research work. Without prejudice, all efforts to get information from government departments particularly, the judiciary, including some leading Muslim jurists and scholars proved very difficult indeed. Also, some people in the private sector organizations such as law firms and industrial set-ups were not always ready to offer information. Those who volunteered to offer such information did it out of sheer interest and belief in the importance of subject of research.

8.2 Recommendations

Before putting forth recommendations thought to be necessary as a consequence of this research, it is necessary to first acknowledge that Saudi Arabia's demonstration of political will over time to enable it maintain some balance between the conflicting forces of tradition, Islamic legal values, modernism, and international development is commendable. It is an incontrovertible fact that due to its unique traditional religious pedigree in relation to the Muslim world and its recent evolving international economic and political status, Saudi Arabia appears to be caught, proverbially, between a rock and a hard place. Despite that, it has been weathering the storm successfully by trying to strike a cautious balance between the two. However, there is always room for further improvement. That possibility of improvement informs some of the recommendations hereunder.

In the light of the findings of this study, it is humbly recommended that a number of issues relating to international law and application of Islamic law in Saudi Arabia should be considered for reformulation.

8.2.1 Conceptual redefinition of "sovereignty"

The concept of sovereignty should be redefined in line with contemporary development and needs. A UN Report[1] had recommended in that regard in

1 A More Secure World: Our Shared Responsibility, *Report of the High-level Panel of Threats, Challenges and Change*, United Nations (2004) Report; see Anne-Marie, S., 'Security, Solidarity, and Sovereignty: The Grand Theme of UN Reform', *The American Journal of International Law*, Vol. 99, No. 3 (2005), pp. 619–631.

2004 that "In signing the Charter of the United Nations, States not only benefit from the privileges of sovereignty but also accept its responsibilities".[2] These responsibilities include both "the obligation of a State to protect the welfare of its own peoples" and its obligation to "meet its obligations to the wider international community". Power allocation model should be taken into consideration in this regard.[3] Proponents of this model explain that characteristics are both "vertical" and "horizontal". This is likened to the separation of powers within a government entity (e.g., legislative, executive, judicial) and division of powers among various international organizations (e.g., the WTO, the International Labour Organization, the IMF, and the World Bank).[4] For example, in relation to international human rights issues, which are closely related to policy matrix and thus, arguably, different human rights may call for different power allocations.[5] It means that those that are domestic in structure should be handled by the relevant nation-state power while other areas with international orientation should be handled by international organizations.[6] This model can help to address the accusations of "hypocrisy" and "double standards" often labelled against the implementation of international human rights law.[7]

8.2.2 Ijtihad *and challenges of modernity*

In view of the many challenges posed by modern international law to Islamic law today, the Saudi Arabian religious scholars should be proactive rather than reactive or defensive against change and modernity. The strict orthodox notion of Islamic law as divine and not capable of interpretation and re-interpretation is

2 UN Panel Report (2004), at parg. 203; Anne-Marie, S., ibid.

3 Jackson, J.H., 'Sovereignty –Modern: A New Approach to an Outdated Concept', *American Journal of International Law*, Vol. 97 (2003), p. 790.

4 Jackson, J.H., ibid at p. 791.

5 Jacobs, F., and White, R., *The European Convention on Human Rights* (3rd edn), USA: Oxford University Press (2010).

6 See generally, Irwin, D.A., *Free Trade Under Fire*, Princeton, NJ: Princeton University Press (2002) (and citing Grossman, Gene M., and Krueger Alan B., 'Economic Growth and the Environment', *The Quarterly Journal of Economics*, Vol. 110 (1995), p. 353; *see* UN Report of the World Summit on Sustainable Development – UN Doc. A/CONF.199/20 (2002), UN Sales No. E.03.II.A.1, *available at* <wwwJohanneshurgsummit.org/html/ documents/documents.htlll; see also Steve, G., 'A World cl/Vironlllent Organization', *Colombia Journal of Environmental Law*, Vol. 27 (2002), p. 323.

7 Jackson also articulates this point in his other publications. See, for example, Jackson, J.H., *The Jurisprudence of the GATT and the WTO: Insights on Trealy Law and Economic Relations*, Cambridge: Cambridge University Press (2000) [hereinafter Jackson, the GATT and the WTO; Jackson, J.H., *The World Trading System: Law and Policy of International Economic Relations* (2nd edn, 1997), Cambridge: MIT Press; Jackson, Davey, & Sykes, *Legal Problems of International Economic Relations: Cases, Materials and Text on The National and International Regulation of Transnational Economic Relations* (4th edn, 2002), St Paul, MN: West Group, Chapter 7; Jackson, J.H., 'Dispute Settlement and the WTO: Emerging Problems', *Journal of International Economic Law*, Vol. 1 (2003), at 251 (1998) [hereinafter Jackson, J.H., 'Dispute Settlement'].

not in tune with reality. Therefore, the lukewarm and apathetic attitude of some of the Saudi scholars to *Ijtihad* has to change proactively rather than reactively and defensively as is the case currently. Saudi scholars should be bold to accept that *Ijtihad* is an important mechanism for developing the law in response to necessary modern developments, particularly international developments that cannot be avoided. *Ijtihad* is not an invention of modern times, its relevance and application has historical origin right from the lifetime of the Prophet of Islam. Therefore, to prove that *Shari'ah* is potentially dynamic, *Ijtihad* must be allowed to play its evolutional role in the continued development of Islamic law to enable it make positive contributions to international affairs.

8.2.3 Rethinking human rights and cultural relativism

In analysing cultural relativism from a human rights perspective a number of guidelines have been suggested by different scholars. These include a close examination of relevant cultural practice focusing on the historical background leading to a cultural norm that conflicts with a particular human rights norm; and the apparent rationale or reasons that have created that cultural norm;[8] a critical appraisal of notable individuals who determine that cultural norm against the background of whether many voices have been involved in its metamorphosis or just only by a few segments of society;[9] a critical analysis of the cultural practice within a contemporary human rights standard with a view to determine whether there is possibility of a comparison and harmonization between the two. This is necessary because cultural norms that have been in existence for many years may apparently appear incompatible with present human rights standard but with positive engagement could be successfully harmonized. Such an approach will make it easy for determining the possible positive accommodation of relevant cultural norms within human rights discourse.[10] It is in that regard that Saudi Arabia has, presumably, been contending that the international community should take into consideration "the diverse and specific historical, religious, cultural and social connotations of these rights" positively.[11]

8.2.4 Human rights reform in Saudi Arabia

The human rights provisions in the Saudi Arabian Basic Law of Governance should be explicitly amplified and detailed so as to cover all areas of rights recognized under Islamic *Shari'ah*. While the different improvements in the human rights owing

8 Reichert, E., 'Human Rights: An Examination of Universalism and Cultural Relativism', *Journal of Comparative Social Welfare*, Vol. 22, No. 1 (2006), p. 31.

9 Ibid at p. 32.

10 Reichert, E., ibid.

11 An Address delivered in December 1996 at the United Nations General Assembly; see Embassy of Saudi Arabia, Washington, DC, News and Press (1996); see also, Jerichow, A., *The Saudi File, People, Power, Politics*, Richmond, VA: Curzon Press (1998), p. 155.

to the impact of international law in Saudi Arabia are commendable, the country should do more in terms of reform to its general human rights policy especially in the areas of women rights, criminal interrogation, and prosecution systems, which are always criticized for being, most often, subjecting criminal suspects to torture, *incommunicado* detention, unfair trial or pre-trial procedures.[12] It is necessary that steps should be taken to ensure that individuals are not arrested arbitrarily, imprisoned for non-violent opposition to the authority, or tortured for any reason as all these acts equally violate the principles of Islamic law and the overall objective of the *Shari'ah* (*maqasid al-Shari'ah*), which is to protect and ensure human welfare.

8.2.5 Codification of laws

A cross-section of Muslim jurists has expressed concern that codification could lead to alteration of originality of the *Shari'ah*. Other groups have equally argued that codification only amounts to regulating the law in strict compliance with the spirit and letter of the original sources. Codification of applicable Islamic laws should be given utmost priority with a view to attaining clarity and uniformity to judicial rulings as well as easy reference for stakeholders in the Kingdom's legal system. The on-going law and judicial reform in Saudi Arabia should give codification of law the adequate attention it deserves to ensure certainty.

8.2.6 Judicial protections in the implementation of intellectual property rights law

Saudi Arabia's accessions to the WTO and the G20 club of influential economies means that its legal system should meet international guidelines for commercial transactions. It has been argued that though Saudi judges do not discriminate against foreign businesses, they lack enforcement powers. As a result, even when foreigners obtain favourable rulings in commercial disputes, they often find it difficult if not impossible to enforce such rulings.[13] It has been noted that "It's easy to win your case, but the problem is enforcement".[14] Therefore, an effective enforcement mechanism should be put in place so as to protect the interest of parties in commercial and trade disputes.

Bibliography

Books

Jackson, J.H. et al., *Legal Problems of International Economic Relations: Cases, Materials and Text on the National and International Regulation of Transnational Economic Relations* (4th edn), St Paul, MN: West Group (2002).

12 Jerichow, A., ibid at p. 122.

13 Murphy, C., 'Saudi to Codify *Shari'ah* 'for Clarity', *The National* (July 21, 2010), www.thenational.ae/news/world/middle-east/saudi-to-codify-sharia-for-clarity (accessed 1 May 2013).

14 Ibid., quoting Ronald E. Pump, an American lawyer practising in Saudi Arabia in criminal and civil cases.

Jackson, J.H., *The Jurisprudence of the GATT and the WTO: Insights on Trealy Law and Economic Relations*, Cambridge: Cambridge University Press (2000).

Jackson, J.H., *The World Trading System: Law and Policy of International Economic Relations* (2nd edn), Cambridge: MIT Press (1997).

Jacobs, F., and White, R., *The European Convention on Human Rights* (3rd edn), "Margin of Appreciation" Is Close to a Concept of "Deference" to Another (Lower?) Level of Government. Sometimes This Operates as a "Standard of Review," Particularly in Court Proceedings. Illinois (2002).

Jerichow, A., *The Saudi File, People, Power, Politics*, London: Curzon Press (1998).

Murphy, C., 'Saudi to Codify *Shari'ah* 'for Clarity', *The National*, (July 21, 2010).

Journal

Anne-Marie, S., 'Security, Solidarity, and Sovereignty: The Grand Theme of UN Reform', *The American Journal of International Law*, Vol. 99, No. 3, (2005), pp. 619–631.

Jackson, J.H., 'Dispute Settlement and the WTO: Emerging Problems', *Journal of International Economic Law*, Vol. 1 (2003), at p. 251 (1998).

Jackson, J.H., 'Sovereignty –Modern: A New Approach to an Outdated Concept', *American Journal of International Law*, Vol. 97 (2003), p. 790.

Krueger, B., 'Economic Growth and the Environment', *The Quarterly Journal of Economics*, Vol. 110 (1995), p. 353.

Reichert, E., 'Human Rights: An Examination of Universalism and Cultural Relativism', *Journal of Comparative Social Welfare*, Vol. 22, No. 1 (2006), pp. 23–36.

Steve, G., 'A World cl/Vironlllent Organization', *Colombia Journal of Environmental Law*, Vol. 27 (2002), p. 323.

Online materials

Irwin, D.A., *Free Trade under Fire*, Princeton University Press, (2002), http://www.thenational.ae/news/world/middle-east/saudi-to-codify-sharia-for-clarity (accessed 1 May 2013).

Reports and resolutions

A More Secure World: Our Shared Responsibility, *Report of the High-level Panel of Threats, Challenges and Change*, United Nations Report (2004).

Saudi Arabia's Address delivered in December 1996 at the United Nations General Assembly – Embassy of Saudi Arabia, Washington, DC, News and Press (1996).

UN Report of the World Summit on Sustainable Development – UN Doc. A/CONF.199/20 (2002), UN Sales No. E.03.II.A.1, http://wwwJohanneshurgsummit.org/html/ documents/documents.htlll.

Index

Note: Page number followed by "n" refer to end notes.

For Product Safety Concerns and Information please contact our EU representative GPSR@taylorandfrancis.com
Taylor & Francis Verlag GmbH, Kaufingerstraße 24, 80331 München, Germany

www.ingramcontent.com/pod-product-compliance
Lightning Source LLC
LaVergne TN
LVHW011114300926
849160LV00008B/379
9780367679194